DEVELOP YOUR ENGLISH SKILLS

SECOND EDITION

DEVELOP YOUR ENGLISH SKILLS

SECOND EDITION

KAY VANSTONE
Seneca College of Applied Arts and Technology
Willowdale, Ontario

Editorial Development: Marion Elliott

Copp Clark Pitman Ltd.
A Longman Company
Toronto

ISBN 0-7730-5220-8

Editing/Sheila Fletcher
Cover and text design/Kyle Gell
Typesetting/Heidy Lawrance Associates
Printing & Binding/John Deyell Company

Copp Clark Pitman Ltd.
2775 Matheson Blvd. East
Mississauga, Ontario
L4W 4P7

Printed and bound in Canada
1 2 3 4 5 5220-8 97 96 95 94 93

Preface

Purpose

Designed for either self-study or teacher-directed classroom use, *Develop Your English Skills, 2nd Edition* can be used in a variety of ways; however, it is primarily designed for self-paced study.

Units 1 to 4 present the basic points of grammar, punctuation, and the mechanics of style. Unit 5 alerts the students to common difficulties in written expression. Units 6 and 7 provide an organized approach to the production of acceptable business correspondence.

Organization

The text is organized so that each unit is divided into sub-units, containing:

- theory instruction with examples,
- mini-tests for each point of theory, with answer keys that provide the student with immediate feedback, and
- a summary of important points.

There are two sets of exercises for each sub-unit at the end of each unit. The exercises could be used to establish which sub-units need to be studied and which students could be exempted from further study on that particular sub-unit. The exercises could also be used to evaluate the students' learning and to identify areas where further study may be needed. In Unit 7, supplementary letters for each sub-unit are provided for extra practice.

An effort has been made to express theory in simple terms, and alternative explanations have been offered to help the student fully understand the points presented.

How To Use the Text

Method of Study

- Do the pretest at the end of the unit that you are studying. Compare your answers carefully with the key, following the directions given for scoring. Your score will indicate the areas in which you need to concentrate as you work through the unit.
- Study the rules and examples for each point of theory.
- Find similar examples illustrating that point in your own reading.
- When you understand the theory, do the mini-test, keeping the key hidden by a piece of paper. It is important to follow this procedure as it is your confirmation that you are ready to move on to the next point.
- If you have made more than one error in any mini-test, go back and reread the examples and rules, making sure you understand the parts with which you had difficulty.
- If you are in any doubt, ask for help *before* moving on.
- Do the exercise at the end of the sub-unit using a coloured pen or pencil for ease in checking. Compare your answers carefully with the key, following the directions given for scoring.

Diagnostic Testing

A pretest and a posttest is included at the end of every unit. These tests cover the main points in each sub-unit and are keyed to the sub-unit for easy reference. The pretest could be used to establish which sub-units need to be studied; the posttest could then be used for testing after the lesson has been completed. This is one suggested method for using these tests; there are many alternatives.

Use of Reference Books

The use of a dictionary or reference manual is expected for all work, including exercises and pretests and posttests, with the possible exception of the exercises for the vocabulary units. Instructors may prefer to limit the use of reference books to study time only and to restrict the use of reference material during tests, in which case testing time should be adjusted accordingly. Because the student is expected to use a dictionary regularly, references to plurals and word division have been omitted.

The reference books used as the standard in this text are the *Gage Canadian Dictionary*, published by Gage Educational Publishing Company, for spelling, and *The Gregg Reference Manual, Third Canadian Edition*, by Sabin and O'Neill, published by McGraw-Hill Ryerson Limited, for style.

Answer Key

An answer key is available for exercises and pretests and posttests. No sample letters are provided for Unit 7 pretests and posttests or for the exercises for that unit, however, since the standards for an acceptable letter will vary considerably. If letters are conscientiously proofread and checked with the evaluation chart to ensure that they follow the principles of good letter writing, there should be no difficulty in assessing the work.

Contents

Unit **One**

GRAMMAR

All of us communicate in order to understand and be understood. To do so, we use words—the basis of our language. Grammar is the study of words and how they are combined and organized into sentences. Studying grammar will help you to understand how words work and how you can best use them to convey your thoughts and ideas clearly.

PARTS OF SPEECH

❍ 1.1 Nouns, Pronouns, and Adjectives

Words are grouped into eight classes called parts of speech:

noun	verb
adjective	preposition
pronoun	adverb
conjunction	interjection

How a word is classified depends on its use; therefore, one word may serve as several parts of speech. For example, *light* can have three different classifications as follows:

Be careful when you *light* the fire. (*Verb*)

A *light* lunch was served at the reception. (*Adjective*)

The *light* over the front entrance needs replacing. (*Noun*)

Nouns

A noun is a word or a group of words that names a person, place, thing, or quality.

The *president* wrote to Mr. Johnston. (*Persons*)

We visited *Toronto*, *Montreal*, and *Halifax*. (*Places*)

Leave the *book* on the *table*, please. (*Things*)

Her *courage* and *heroism* were rewarded. (*Qualities*)

The following questions will help you to test whether a word is a noun:

Does it answer the question *Who?* or *What?*

Can it be replaced by a pronoun such as *he*, *she*, *it*, *they*, *him*, *her*, or *them*?

Can it be preceded by *a*, *an*, or *the*?

Can it be modified by an adjective?

In the following sentences, which test questions do the italicized nouns answer?

Susan sent *samples* to *Marcel Morney*.

The *Skydome* is the *home* of the *Toronto Blue Jays*.

The interesting *history* was written by an *Italian*.

Nouns can perform the following different functions in a sentence:

- as subject of the sentence (doer of the action)
- as object of the verb (person or thing that is acted upon)
- as object of a preposition

This information will be useful during the discussion of pronouns, words that represent nouns, since pronouns change form depending on their function. In the first sample sentence, the functions of the nouns are as follows:

Susan	subject—doer of the action
samples	object of verb *sent*
Marcel Morney	object of preposition *to*

Mini Test

Underline all the nouns in the following sentences. Check your answers with the key.

1. The quality of the crystal is shown in the photograph.
2. Charlottetown is the capital of Prince Edward Island.
3. Dr. Norman Bethune was greatly respected by the Chinese for his dedication.
4. The plumber repaired the leaking tap.

5. The high price of gasoline has caused the cost of transportation to rise greatly.

KEY

1. quality, crystal, photograph 2. Charlottetown, capital, Prince Edward Island 3. Dr. Norman Bethune, Chinese, dedication 4. plumber, tap 5. price, gasoline, cost

Pronouns

A pronoun is a word that is used in place of a noun.

Mary's supervisor read the report and asked *her* to have someone photocopy *it*.

Pronouns are grouped as personal, compound personal, demonstrative, indefinite, or relative according to their use.

Personal Pronouns

Nouns do not change whether they are the subject of a sentence or the object of a verb or preposition. Pronouns, on the other hand, take different forms.

Mini-Test

Underline the correct pronouns in the following paragraph.

Alina asked her father for the car. "I/They need it/him to get to school on time," she/her told he/him. "The teacher is working on a special project with I/me. She/Her wants me/it to be there early."

KEY

Alina asked her father for the car. "I need it to get to school on time," she told him. "The teacher is working on a special project with me. She wants me to be there early."

You have just proved that you already know something about the forms of personal pronouns. These forms are defined as follows:

gender masculine (*he, him, his*); feminine (*she, her, hers*); or neuter (*it, its*)

number singular (one) or plural (more than one)

person person speaking (1st) – *I, we*
person spoken to (2nd) – *you*
person or thing spoken about (3rd) – *he, she, it, they*. All nouns are also 3rd person

case subjective – if the pronoun is the subject of a verb
objective – if the pronoun is the object of a verb or preposition
possessive – if the pronoun shows ownership

The following chart shows all the forms of personal pronouns.

Case	Person					
	First		Second		Third	
	Sing.	Pl.	Sing.	Pl.	Sing.	Pl.
Subjective	I	we	you	you	he she it	they
Objective	me	us	you	you	him her it	them
Possessive	my mine	your ours	your yours	your yours	his her his hers its	their theirs

Tom said *he* gave the shirts to *her* so that *she* could show *them* to *me*.

he masc., sing., 3rd person, subject of *gave*

her fem., sing., 3rd person, object of *to*

she fem., sing., 3rd person, subject of *could show*

them neuter, plural, 3rd person, object of *could show*

me masc. or fem., sing., 1st person, object of *to*

Note: A possessive pronoun followed by a noun is an adjective.

Was the decision *yours*? No, the decision was *his*. (pronouns—no nouns following)

Has Don put *his* name on *his* application? (adjectives followed by nouns *name* and *application*)

Mini-Test

Complete the following chart by referring to the previous mini-test on personal pronouns. The first line has been filled in for you.

Pronoun	Gender	Number	Case
I	fem.	sing.	subj.
it			
she			
him			
me			
She			
me			

KEY

Pronoun	Gender	Number	Case
I	fem.	sing.	subj.
it	fem.	sing.	subj.
she	fem.	sing.	subj.
him	masc.	sing.	obj.
me	fem	sing.	obj.
She	fem.	sing.	subj.
me	fem.	sing.	obj.

Note: The first *her* is an adjective because it is followed by the noun, *father.*

Compound Personal Pronouns

There are only eight compound personal pronouns which are used to refer back to the subject or for emphasis.

myself yourself himself herself
itself ourselves yourselves themselves

Marie gave *herself* credit for a job well done. (refers back to *Marie*)

We *ourselves* are responsible for control of household waste. (refers back to *we* for emphasis)

Demonstrative Pronouns

Demonstrative pronouns draw attention to particular persons or things.

this that these those

What is *this*? Who is *that*? Are *these* ready for shipment? No, but *those* over there are.

Note: The following demonstratives are adjectives because they are followed by nouns:

This recipe calls for wheat flour.

We believe that *these* exercises will improve *our* health.

Indefinite Pronouns

Indefinite pronouns indicate persons or things in an unspecific way. Here are some of the indefinite pronouns.

Singular			Plural	
each	any	everybody	both	several
either	one	everyone	some	few
neither	none	somebody	all	many
another	nobody	someone		
each other	anyone			

Everyone has questions; *few* have answers.

Note: An indefinite coming before a noun is an adjective, not a pronoun.

Each question was relevant; *many* answers were evasive.

Relative Pronouns

Relative pronouns act both as pronouns and as subordinate conjunctions to introduce dependent clauses. (See Unit 1.8)

who whom that
whoever whichever whatever
whose which what
whomever

I am the official *who* is responsible for the clean-up.

Give the award to *whoever* has earned the highest points.

The damage from the floods *that* occurred yesterday will take weeks to repair.

Sometimes these pronouns are used to ask questions. They are then called interrogative pronouns.

What is the date for the launching? *Who* won the gold medal?

Note: A relative or interrogative followed by a noun is an adjective, not a pronoun.

Whichever course appeals to you most will be acceptable.

What time should I arrive? *Which* route should I take?

Mini-Test

Underline the pronouns in the following sentences. Remember, a word used to modify or describe a noun is an adjective, not a pronoun.

1. She has been so ill I cleaned the garage myself.
2. All of the staff went to the lecture, and many of them asked questions.
3. We hope to have your order ready for delivery to you by noon.
4. Who found the error in the statement? The cashier found it.
5. This case is mine. Where is yours?

KEY.

1. She, I, myself 2. All, many, them 3. We, you (*not* your) 4. Who, it 5. mine, yours (*not this*)

Adjectives

An adjective is a word used to modify or describe a noun or pronoun. An adjective will answer *What kind? How many? Whose?* or *Which?* about the noun or pronoun it modifies.

What kind? The job calls for an *industrious* worker.

How many? Make *three* copies of each photograph, please.

Whose? The *actor's* scream terrified the audience.

Which? *These* children have reacted well to the vaccine.

The articles *a, an,* and *the* are counted as adjectives.

The annual meeting will take place on *a* date to be announced later.

Mini-Test

Underline the adjectives in the following sentences. Remember, some words that look like pronouns may be adjectives. Do not underline the articles *a, an,* and *the.*

1. Where are the latest samples of cotton material?
2. The training program has produced excellent results.
3. My printer needs a new ribbon.
4. Whose papers are those on the filing cabinet?
5. Sixteen people have applied for the vacant position.

Are the words in italics in the following pairs of sentences adjectives or pronouns?

6. *Everyone* should read *this.*
   Every member should read *this* notice.
7. *You* have been promoted.
   Your brother has been promoted.
8. *Several* of the books are *mine.*
   Several books were left on *my* desk.
9. At least, he said it was *his.*
   The reporter phoned in *his* copy.

KEY

1. latest, cotton 2. training, excellent 3. My, new 4. Whose, filing 5. Sixteen, vacant 6-9 In each pair of sentences the italicized words in the first sentence are all pronouns; in the second, they are all adjectives.

SUMMARY FOR UNIT 1.1

Words are classified according to their use in a particular sentence.

- A **noun** names a person, place, thing, or quality and can be identified by four tests, two of which are:
  - Can you put *a, an,* or *the* in front of it?
  - Can you substitute *it, he, she,* or *they* for it?
- A **pronoun** takes the place of a noun. Personal pronouns vary according to gender, number, person, and case.
- If a pronoun is followed by a noun, it is acting as an adjective and should be classified as an adjective, not as a pronoun.
- Personal pronouns in the possessive case are adjectives unless they stand alone.
- An **adjective** tells something about a noun or pronoun.

Confirm Your Knowledge

Complete Exercise for Unit 1.1 on page 34.

1.2 Verbs and Adverbs

Verbs

A verb is a word or group of words that expresses action or state of being. A verb made up of two or more words is called a verb phrase.

The electrician *connected* the loose wires. (Action)

Ms. Lapierre *is* a politician. (State of being)

The mechanic *has installed* new spark plugs. (Verb phrase)

Most verbs are active verbs because they describe the action of the subject.

Abdul *visits* his mother regularly.

The heavy rains *caused* severe flooding.

Composters *create* excellent fertilizer.

I *will complete* my assignment on time.

Mini-Test

Underline the verbs and verb phrases in the following sentences. Indicate whether they are active or state of being by writing *A* for active and *S* for state of being above the verb or verb phrase.

1. The supervisor gave clear instructions to the workers.
2. You have answered all the questions correctly.
3. Apples are the main crop in the Okanagan Valley.
4. The storm broke all the windows in the house.
5. I shall read the manuscript tomorrow.

KEY

1. gave—A 2. have answered—A 3. are—S 4. broke—A 5. shall read—A

Linking Verbs

State of being verbs are known as linking verbs because they link the words that follow to the subject telling what that subject is or seems to be.

The custodian *is* a coach for the baseball team.

Valerie *appears* happy in her new position.

Linking verbs include all forms of the verb *be*, the verb *seem*, and several other verbs.

am	is	was	were	be	being
been	seem	become	smell	feel	prove
grow	keep	appear	look	taste	sound

Some verbs may be either linking or active depending on their meaning in the sentence.

Linking	The advice *proved* helpful. After a shower I *feel* clean.
Active	The scientist *proved* his theories were correct. Can you *feel* the roughness of the sandpaper?

If you can substitute some form of *be* or *seem* for the verb, then that verb is a linking verb. If you cannot, then it is an active verb.

The new fabric *looks* much brighter. The new fabric *is* (or *seems*) much brighter.

Hilda *appears* worried. Hilda *is* worried.

The leaves *turned* yellow. The leaves *were* yellow.

He *turned* the key in the lock. He *was* the key in the lock. (No, this does not make sense; therefore, *turned* is an active verb in this sentence.)

Mini-Test

Underline all the linking verbs in the following paragraph.

I am happy to state that Dr. Heinke has succeeded in his experiment. He appears satisfied with the results. The doctor is eager to let the world know about his achievements. He will appear on television on Saturday evening to discuss his findings with other famous scientists. It seems that everyone is very interested.

KEY

Sentence 1—am Sentence 2—appears Sentence 3—is Sentence 5—seems, is

Adverbs

An adverb modifies an active verb and answers one of the following questions about the verb.

How?	She writes *neatly* (*precisely*, *carelessly*).

When? He *seldom* takes a holiday (*never, often*).

Where? Put the package *down* (*outside, upstairs*).

An adverb also modifies an adjective or another adverb and answers the question *How?*

Sales this month are *unusually* high. (How high? *unusually*)

Surgeons must work *extremely* cautiously. (How cautiously? *extremely*)

She wrote a *very* good report. (How good? *very*)

Some words are used as both adverbs and adjectives.

Turn *right*. (Adverb)

You gave the *right* answer. (Adjective)

The following words are also adverbs.

Where? Why? How? When? (when asking questions)

yes no not (when making statements)

here there

Where is the meeting? *How* can we join the society?

When will Eileen hire an assistant? *Why* do you ask?

Yes, you may leave. *No*, they have not arrived.

Here are the specifications. *There* is no paper in the drawer.

Note: In a question, the verb phrase is split by the subject.

Mini-Test

Underline the adverbs in the following sentences.

1. Here is my order for raincoats. When shall I receive them?
2. Mr. Lebrun arrived yesterday and quickly took command.
3. Drive very carefully and always watch for children.
4. We often work late, and occasionally the office manager takes us for dinner.
5. She wrote an exceptionally clear description of the problem.

KEY

1. Here, When 2. yesterday, quickly 3. very carefully, always 4. often, occasionally 5. exceptionally

SUMMARY FOR UNIT 1.2

- A **verb** expresses action or state of being.
- An **active** verb tells what someone or something does.
- A **linking** verb links the words following it to the someone or something before it by describing or renaming that someone or something.
- Some verbs may be either active or linking.
- Test for a linking verb by substituting *is* or *seems*.
- An **adverb** modifies or describes:
  - a verb (answers *How? When? Where?*)
  - an adjective (answers *How?*)
  - another adverb (answers *How?*)

Confirm Your Knowledge

Complete Exercise for Unit 1.2 on page 35.

❍ 1.3 Conjunctions, Prepositions, and Interjections

A conjunction is a word that joins words or groups of words.

Moncton *and* Edmundston are cities in New Brunswick.

Write to the mayor *if* you support this proposal or *if* you have any other suggestions.

Co-ordinate Conjunctions

Co-ordinate conjunctions join parts of equal value (noun to noun, phrase to phrase, clause to another clause of the same type). The most common co-ordinate conjunctions are:

and but or nor yet for (when meaning "because")

Laptop computers *and* printers are on sale.

Louise wanted to go to a dance *or* to see a movie.

He just missed winning the award, *but* he wasn't discouraged.

The following words also act as co-ordinate conjunctions when they begin a clause that could stand alone as a sentence.

accordingly	consequently
indeed	still
afterward	furthermore
also	then
besides	meanwhile
otherwise	thus
nevertheless	therefore

The construction is ahead of schedule; *consequently*, we will be able to finish the project by April.

Mini-Test

Underline all the co-ordinate conjunctions in the following sentences.

1. Concentration and determination produce results.
2. The weather forecast predicted snow; therefore, I dressed warmly.
3. We had to wait, for the doctor was late.
4. Suzanne is an enthusiastic worker, but she talks too much.
5. Send your cheque today, or call us for further information.

KEY

1. and 2. therefore 3. for 4. but 5. or

Correlative Conjunctions

Correlative conjunctions are used in pairs to join sentence parts of equal value.

both...and	not only...but also
neither...nor	either...or

Care should be taken to make sure that these conjunctions are used only to join parts of equal value, for example, noun to noun, phrase to phrase, or clause to clause.

Recycling of *both* bottles *and* newspapers has been implemented. (joining nouns)

Jonas is trying *not only* to be successful *but also* to be healthy. (joining phrases)

Either you can call me from your car *or* you can call me from a pay phone. (joining clauses)

Mini-Test

Underline the pairs of conjunctions in the following sentences and tell what they are joining (for example, nouns).

1. Our fashions are not only very chic but also very economical.
2. Neither the pilot nor the navigator was aware of the danger.
3. Both the politician and her aide came to the meeting.
4. We shall either fly to Victoria or take the ferry from Vancouver.
5. Not only did he offer me the job, but he also offered me transportation.

KEY

1. not only, but also (adjectives) 2. neither, nor (nouns) 3. Both, and (nouns) 4. either, or (phrases) 5. Not only, but also (clauses)

Subordinate Conjunctions

Subordinate conjunctions always begin dependent clauses and join the dependent clause to an independent clause to form a sentence. (See Unit 1.8.) The following are the most common subordinate conjunctions.

if	when	after
while	during	though
before	since	as
because	where	whenever
unless	although	until
so that	in order to	

Hint: A clause beginning with "if" is *always* a dependent clause. Try to remember all the words in the above list as "if" words; then you will have no difficulty recognizing subordinate conjunctions. If the "if" word begins the sentence, note the comma at the end of the "if" clause. There is no comma if the "if" clause comes in the middle of a sentence after the main clause.

If you have finished your work, you can go home.

You can go home *if* you have finished your work.

When you have finished your work, you can go home.

After you have finished your work, you can go home.

You cannot go home *until* you have finished your work.

I shall read a book *while* you are finishing your work.

The relative pronouns (see Unit 1.1) are also subordinate conjunctions because they too always begin dependent clauses.

Ms. Shorney, *who* joined us recently, has just returned from Italy.

People need friends *whom* they can trust.

The statistics *that* we have show an increase in population.

We shall be pleased to accept *whatever* you can donate.

Mini-Test

Underline all the subordinate conjunctions in the following paragraph.

When the order for 23 aircraft was received, the factory went on overtime. Every employee who could worked an extra shift. The effort that was made by all of the workers enabled the company to complete the order on time. Because they had worked so well as a team, the manager said that while the weather was good the employees could take an afternoon off. If you had seen the surprised look on their faces when they heard this news, you would have laughed!

KEY

Sentence 1—When Sentence 2—who Sentence 3—that Sentence 4—Because, that, while Sentence 5—If, when

Prepositions

A preposition is a word that usually begins a phrase, a short group of words with no subject or verb, that adds more information to the sentence. A preposition is always followed by a noun or pronoun. The most common prepositions are:

to	at	in	on
by	for	from	with

The following phrases and sentences show the use of prepositions.

by laser	*with* care
around the edges	*after* Thanksgiving
like this	*off* the map
to them	*up* the creek
down the tube	*over* the limit
along the border	*across* the city
during the crisis	*for* him
in the video	*as* a favour
at the end	*above* reproach
beyond belief	*under* the desk
except me	*without* permission
of the country	*through* the centre
into the goal	*against* all odds
on the roof	

The announcement came *from* the president.

The designs will be delivered *by* courier.

Spring comes *before* summer.

The price is *within* our budget.

The work is to be divided *between* you and me.

Sometimes a group of words makes up a single preposition.

according to our records

because of your decision

by way of Sault Ste. Marie

in spite of the cost

in accordance with your request

in case of emergency

in front of the truck

on account of the weather

Many other words are also used as prepositions. If you are in doubt, substitute a word that you are sure is a preposition.

Nobody helped *but* John. (*except* John)

I have received your letter *concerning* the explosion. (*about* the explosion)

In the following examples, the words that look like prepositions are in fact adverbs as they have no noun or pronoun immediately following them.

The presses have been shut *down*. The cost of living is going *up*.

Mini-test

Go back to the mini-test on page 8 in which you underlined subordinate conjunctions. This time look for all the prepositions and mark them with a *P*.

KEY

Sentence 1—for, on Sentence 3—by, of, to, on Sentence 4—as Sentence 5—on

Interjections

An interjection is a word or phrase used to express emotion or to capture the reader's attention. It is usually followed by an exclamation mark. Interjections are commonly used in sales promotional material and should be used sparingly in all other styles of writing. The following are some common interjections:

Fantastic!	Congratulations!
Free!	Special!
At last!	Oh!
Great news!	Help!
Ouch!	Ah, spring at last!

You want to negotiate a new contract? Great!

Mini-Test

Underline the interjections in the following sentences.

1. Free! We shall send you Volume 1 as a gift.
2. Reaction to the drop in the bank rate was "At last!"
3. Amazing! The team won again on Saturday.

KEY

1. Free! 2. At last! 3. Amazing!

SUMMARY FOR UNIT 1.3

- A **conjunction** joins words or groups of words.
- A **co-ordinate conjunction** joins words or groups of words that have the **same** value.
  - The most common co-ordinate conjunctions are *and, but, or, nor, for, yet.*
  - Words like *however, therefore, accordingly* act as conjunctions when they join independent clauses; that is, there must be a complete sentence coming after the however.
- **Correlative** conjunctions are used in pairs such as *both...and.*
  - The parts joined by correlative conjunctions must have the same form.
- A **subordinate** conjunction begins a dependent clause; that is, the clause cannot stand alone as a sentence.

Hint: Remember subordinate conjunctions as "if" words.

  - Relative pronouns are also subordinate conjunctions (*who, when, which, whichever*).
- A **preposition** begins a short phrase adding information.
  - The most common prepositions are *to, at, in, on, for, by, with, from.*
  - Sometimes two or more words form a preposition.
  - Test if a word is a preposition by substituting a word you are sure is a preposition.
- An **interjection** is a word or group of words used alone to create a strong impression.

Confirm Your Knowledge

Complete Exercise for Unit 1.3 on page 36.

VERB FORMS AND PHRASES

Verbs are very important words because sentences are built around them. You already know that a verb may consist of one or more words. Sometimes, though, words that look like verbs are used as other parts of speech. The next two units will help you understand more about verb phrases and other forms of verbs and phrases.

❍ 1.4 Verb Phrases, Voice, and Gerunds

Verb Phrases

A verb may require help from another verb to make the correct verb form for that sentence. The simple or principal verb and the helping verb make up a verb phrase. (See also Unit 1.2)

The chairperson *changed* the order of the agenda. (Simple)

The chairperson *has changed* the order many times. (Verb phrase)

Sally *will* not *be arriving* until 08:30 tomorrow. (Verb phrase)

Dr. Kulek *arrives* today. (Simple)

Note: The word *not* as well as its contracted form *n't* is an adverb, not part of a verb or verb phrase.

Dave *has* not *sold* his stereo yet, but he *has*n't *stopped trying.*

Auxiliary Verbs

The words used with the simple or principal verb to make a verb phrase are called auxiliary or helping verbs. All parts of the verbs *be* and *have* may be used as auxiliary verbs as well as the following words.

should	do	can	could	may
shall	must	might	should	did

In the following examples, the principal verbs are underlined twice and the auxiliary verbs are underlined once.

We have sent your order by express.

The bank will not extend any more credit to him

Marcel is learning to drive.

He might have come earlier if he had known that the meeting would start on time.

These letters must be mailed before 4:30 p.m.

Mini-Test

In the following sentences, underline the auxiliary verbs once and the principal verbs twice.

1. Our new tape deck has been designed with you in mind.
2. How can you prevent rust on your car?
3. If you are considering a move, do call us for an estimate.
4. The new arrangement may mean better working conditions.
5. The doctor did not say whether the patient would recover.

KEY

1. has been designed 2. can prevent 3. are considering, do call 4. may mean 5. did say, would recover

Voice

As stated in Unit 1.2, most verbs are active, that is to say they are "doing" words, such as *run, answer, mix, read, think, give*. If the subject of the sentence is doing the action, then the verb is in the active voice.

Steve *entered* the data.

The radio announcer *interrupted* the music.

Our store *will give* a discount for prompt payment.

Many farmers in Saskatchewan *grow* wheat.

If the subject receives the action of the verb, then the verb is in the passive voice. Note that passive voice verbs are always verb phrases.

The data *was entered* by Steve.

The music *was interrupted* by the radio announcer.

A discount *will be given* for prompt payment.

Wheat *is grown* in Saskatchewan.

Hint: Sentences written in the passive voice usually contain a phrase beginning with "by." If the "by" phrase is not included, check to see if one could be added without changing the meaning.

A discount *will be given* (by our store) for prompt payment.

Wheat *is grown* (by farmers) in Saskatchewan.

Mini-Test

Are the verbs or verb phrases in the following sentences in the active voice or the passive voice? Underline all verbs and verb phrases and write above them *A* for active or *P* for passive.

P

Example: An assistant was hired by my father.

1. The merchandise will be shipped from our Brandon plant.
2. Has Rene accepted the new position?
3. Our end-of-season sale will begin next Friday.
4. The exhibition was opened by the Lieutenant-Governor.
5. The faulty cars must be recalled immediately.

KEY

1. will be shipped—P 2. Has accepted—A 3. will begin—A 4. was opened—P 5. must be recalled—P

Gerunds

Some words ending in *-ing* look like verbs but are in fact nouns. These are called gerunds. Compare the notices below.

Dogs Prohibited

Smoking Prohibited

No Dogs

No Smoking

Dogs can be fun

Smoking is dangerous

The words *dogs* and *smoking* are nouns in these signs. Use the noun tests (see Unit 1.1) to check whether an *-ing* word is working as part of a verb phrase or as a noun (gerund).

Digging is hard work. (What is hard work? *Digging*—gerund)

Do you enjoy *digging*? (Enjoy what? Enjoy *digging*—gerund)

Harold is *digging* a swimming pool. (Harold *is digging* something—verb phrase)

As it is a noun, a gerund may be modified by an adjective; however, as it is also part verb, a gerund may also be modified by an adverb.

Clear thinking helps you to arrive at practical decisions. (*Clear*—adjective modifying *thinking*)

By speaking *clearly*, you will keep the attention of your audience. (*clearly*—adverb modifying *speaking*—answers "How?")

Mini-Test

Underline only the gerunds in the following sentences. Remember that gerunds are nouns.

1. We are arranging for the signing of the agreement today.
2. Careful breeding and training are the key factors in the success of a racehorse.
3. Please confirm the booking you made yesterday by telephone.
4. Trafficking illegally in drugs is a major offence; the police are doing everything they can to stop this heinous crime.
5. David's writing has improved greatly, and he is now thinking of a career in journalism.

KEY

1. signing 2. breeding, training 3. booking 4. trafficking 5. writing

SUMMARY FOR UNIT 1.4

- **Verb phrases** are composed of the simple verb plus one or more **auxiliary** or helping verbs.
- The most common auxiliary verbs are all parts of the verbs *be* and *have* as well as *should, would, could, may, might, must, can, do,* and *did.*
- A verb is in the **active voice** if the subject is doing the action of the verb.
- A verb is in the **passive voice** if the subject is receiving the action of the verb.
- Usually, in a passive voice sentence there is a phrase beginning with *by* or such a phrase could be added easily.
- A **gerund** is an *-ing* word that looks like a verb but is in fact a noun.

  Gerunds can be tested by using the tests for nouns.

Confirm Your Knowledge

Complete Exercise for Unit 1.4 on page 38.

❍ 1.5 Prepositional Phrases and Infinitives

Prepositional Phrases

A prepositional phrase always starts with a preposition (see Unit 1.3 for a list of the most common prepositions) and consists of that preposition and the noun or pronoun following it.

Please see me *about your trip to Vancouver in January.*

The role *of Canadian Forces in peacekeeping* is sometimes dangerous *for them.*

When will the new technology *for refrigeration* be ready?

Mini-Test

Underline the prepositional phrases in the following sentences.

1. I hope that the meeting of technical advisers scheduled for the fall in Regina will be well attended.
2. After careful consideration, I have referred your suggestions to Mme. Benoit for her decision.
3. Personal telephone calls should be made during your coffee break.
4. Without a doubt, our Nusome soap is the best on the market.
5. A copy of the document complete with signatures will be kept in the safe in the manager's office.

KEY

1. of technical advisers, for the fall, in Regina 2. After careful consideration, to Mme. Benoit, for her decision 3. during your coffee break 4. Without a doubt, on the market 5. of the document, with signatures, in the safe, in the manager's office

Infinitives

The infinitive of a verb is the preposition *to* followed by the principal form of the verb.

to write to read to sell to speak

Infinitives may include auxiliary verbs and be in the passive voice.

to have gone to be sold
to have been written to have spoken

The infinitive sign *to* is not always used. Test if *to* can be inserted before the verb; if so, then that verb is an infinitive.

Will you please help Grant (*to*) *arrange* transportation.

Be careful not to confuse infinitive phrases with prepositional phrases starting with *to.*

to + verb = an infinitive

to + noun or pronoun = a prepositional phrase

You should go *to the ball game* by subway. (*to* + noun = prepositional phrase)

You should try *to arrive* before the game starts. (*to* + verb = infinitive)

Mini-Test

Underline all the infinitives in the following sentences.

1. The insurers are eager to settle the claim.
2. They want to submit the papers for signature immediately.
3. We hope to come to a decision tomorrow.
4. The personnel officer will be delighted to help you complete the questionnaire.
5. We have the tools to manufacture the precision instruments you need to operate efficiently.

KEY

1. to settle 2. to submit 3. to come 4. to help 5. to manufacture, to operate

---

SUMMARY FOR UNIT 1.5

- **A prepositional phrase** begins with a preposition.
- The **infinitive** is *to* plus simple verb form, e.g., *To pay, to read, to see, to manufacture.*
- The infinitive may also include auxiliary verbs, e.g., *to have paid, to be advertised.*

Confirm Your Knowledge

Complete Exercise for Unit 1.5 on page 40.

GRAMMATICAL FUNCTIONS

Each word in a sentence carries out one of five grammatical functions: subject, predicate, complement, modifier, or connective. The next two units will help you understand the functions of subjects, predicates, and complements. Modifiers are adjectives and adverbs, and connectives are conjunctions and prepositions, all of which are covered in other units.

❍ 1.6 Subjects and Predicates

Subjects

In Unit 1.1, you learned something about subjects when nouns and pronouns were discussed. This unit goes into more detail.

The subject of a sentence or clause names the person, place, or thing that does the action of the verb or is the main topic of the sentence.

The *lawyer* signed the affidavit.

Winnipeg offers many opportunities to engineers.

The *storeroom* was very hot.

Sometimes the subjects consist of more than one word.

Winnipeg, Regina, and Edmonton offer many opportunities to engineers.

Sometimes the subject may be a phrase or a clause.

Talking too long on the telephone can waste a lot of time.

Whoever comes to the meeting may vote.

Sometimes the subject is not stated, as in commands.

Report tomorrow, please. (*You* report tomorrow, please)

In sentences beginning with *here* and *there*, the subject comes after the verb.

Here are *the orders* for Saks Drug Company.

There is a *great improvement* in her work.

In questions, the subject may be before or after the verb.

Who is the receptionist?

Is the *new receptionist* a good keyboard operator?

Clues to Finding the Subject

The fastest way to find the subject in a sentence is to find the verb or verb phrase first; then ask who or what is doing the action of the verb.

Several files are missing.	Verb phrase—*are missing.* Who or what are missing? *Several files*—subject

In a longer sentence, this may not be so easy, but if you first identify the verbs, then each verb must have a subject. Look at the sentence you have just read. How many verbs or verb phrases are there?

may not be identify must have

What are the subjects of these verbs?

this may not be *you* first identify

each verb must have

This method of finding the subject is extremely helpful in sentences written in an unusual or inverted way.

Gone are the days when gas was cheap	Verbs—*Gone are* (are gone), *was* What are gone? What was? *Days* are gone. *Gas* was. Subjects—*days, gas*
How many calls have you made today?	Verb—*have made* Who have made? *You* have made Subject—*you*

The subject of the last example is *you*, not *calls*, because *you* is the word doing the action of the verb.

Mini-test

Underline the verbs or verb phrases in the sentences on the following page; then put a circle around the subjects for those verbs.

Examples: A new postal guide has been ordered for the mailing room. Here is the fax that you requested.

1. This collator is in need of repair.
2. Many people believe that good diet and exercise are necessary for good health.
3. There are four answers given for each question; choose whichever one you think is the correct answer.
4. When can you let me have your suggestions
5. Are there many applicants for the job?

KEY

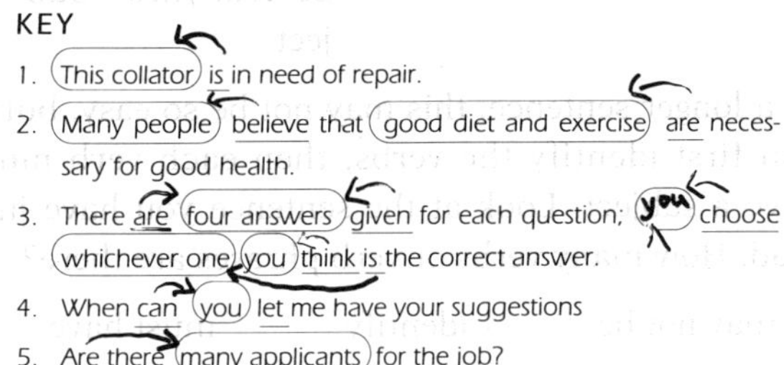

1. This collator is in need of repair.
2. Many people believe that good diet and exercise are necessary for good health.
3. There are four answers given for each question; you choose whichever one you think is the correct answer.
4. When can you let me have your suggestions
5. Are there many applicants for the job?

Predicates

A predicate is another name for a verb or verb phrase. The predicate states what the subject is or does and must agree with the subject in form, so it is very important to be able to identify subjects and predicates. In the following examples, the subjects have been underlined once, and the predicates (verbs and verb phrases) have been underlined twice.

1. Simple subject
   Michael has won first prize.
   The girls have won the relay race.
2. Compound subject
   The players and their coach are leaving.
   Vidal and Milan have been nominated.
3. Words coming between the simple subject and the predicate
   A stack of money was piled on the counter.
   Many of the returning students are eligible for a scholarship.
4. Inverted or unusual order
   Right to the bottom of the pile went my submission.
   After all our work came the decision to cancel the project.

Mini-Test

Underline the subject once and the predicate (verb or verb phrase) twice in the following sentences.

Example: The example explains the procedure.

1. Having asthma can be exhausting.
2. A survey of the smoking habits of teenagers has just been completed.
3. Several children and their teacher joined in the singing.
4. Each one of us is entitled to a raise.
5. Out of the blue came the decision to leave.

KEY

Underline once	Underline twice
1. Having asthma	can be
2. A survey	has just been completed
3. Several children and their teacher	joined
4. Each one	is
5. the decision	came

SUMMARY FOR UNIT 1.6

- The **subject** of a sentence or clause names who or what is doing the action of the verb or is the main topic of the sentence.
- The subject may consist of more than one word, be a clause or phrase, or be clearly understood rather than stated.
- The subject always comes after the verb in sentences beginning with *Here* or *There*.
- In a question, the subject may be before or after the verb.

Hint for finding the subject
- Find the **verb first**; then ask **who** or what goes before the verb.

This method works even though the sentence may be in an unusual order.

- The **predicate** of the sentence or clause is the **verb** or **verb phrase** that says what the subject does.
- Special care in identifying subjects and predicates is necessary with:
  - compound subjects
  - words coming between the simple subject and the predicate
  - sentences in unusual order (inverted or questions)

Confirm Your Knowledge

Complete Exercise for Unit 1.6 on page 42.

❍ 1.7 Complements

Complements in a sentence are the words necessary to complete the meaning of the sentence after the subject and verb have been identified. There are several different types of complements.

Direct Objects

The direct object of a verb receives the action of the verb. It answers the question *Who?* or *What?* receives the action of the verb.

The team captain chose *Mark.* (answers *chose who*?)

The storm blew down *many hydro poles.* (answers *blew down what*?)

Mrs. Fieldberg reported on *the conditions in the Prince Rupert plant.* (answers *reported what*?)

Mini-Test

Underline the direct objects in the following sentences.

1. The company changed its working hours.
2. Many visitors to Canada visit Ottawa.
3. The secretary of the Student Council recorded the minutes of the meeting.
4. Joanne mailed the package at lunchtime.
5. Send out all the brochures for the Flower Show.

KEY

1. its working hours 2. Ottawa 3. the minutes of the meeting 4. the package 5. all the brochures for the Flower Show

Indirect Objects

An indirect object names the person or thing for whom or to which the action of the verb was done.

Francis wrote a letter to Joseph. (*Joseph*—to whom the letter was written—is the indirect object.)

Warren gave the door a coat of paint. (*The door*—to which the coat of paint was given—is the indirect object.)

Quite often the indirect object appears immediately after the verb.

Francis wrote *Joseph* a letter.

Save *me* a good seat.

To test for an indirect object, put *to* or *for* before the word.

Francis wrote a letter *to* Joseph.

Save a good seat *for* me.

Mini-Test

Underline the indirect objects in the following sentences. Use the *to* and *for* test.

1. The sales department has sent the customer our latest catalogue.
2. The referee awarded the player a penalty shot.
3. Please write me a memo explaining your absence.
4. The ticket agent will give you your tickets at the airport.
5. We shipped Mr. Osborn the goods he had ordered.

KEY

1. the customer 2. the player 3. me 4. you 5. Mr. Osborn

Predicate Nouns and Predicate Adjectives

In Unit 1.2, linking verbs are discussed. The word or words following a linking verb are called predicate nouns (or pronouns) or predicate adjectives. These words are linked to the subject and tell more about the subject.

Joyce is *the principal.* (Predicate Noun)

The assignment seems *complete.* (Predicate Adjective)

It was *I* who telephoned. (Predicate Pronoun)

Note: If a pronoun is used to complete the subject after a linking verb, that pronoun is in the subjective case—it tells more about the subject.

Note carefully the use of certain verbs that may be linking or active. If in doubt, substitute a form of *be* or *seem* for the verb. (See Unit 1.2.)

The pie filling *tasted bitter.* (Linking Verb—Predicate Adjective)

Midori *tasted the pie filling.* (Active verb—Direct Object)

Rotten eggs *smell awful*! (Linking Verb—Predicate Adjective)

The police dog *smelled the blood stains.* (Active Verb—Direct Object)

Mini-Test

Underline the predicate nouns or pronouns and predicate adjectives in the following sentences. Indicate what they are by writing above them *PN* for predicate noun, *PP* for predicate pronoun, or *PA* for predicate adjective.

1. The young woman whom you met at the luncheon is my sister.
2. When athletes become tired, a cool drink of Get-Up-and-Go will quickly refresh them.
3. Michelle will be a first-class navigator.
4. Tom delivered the speech; in fact it was he who wrote it.
5. When milk turns sour, it can sometimes be used to make cheese.

KEY

1. my sister—PN 2. tired—PA 3. navigator—PN 4. he—PP 5. sour—PA

SUMMARY FOR UNIT 1.7

- A **complement** is the word or group of words which tells more about the subject.
- A **direct object** is the word or words acted upon by the verb. It tells who or what received the action of the verb.
- An **indirect object** tells to whom or for whom the verb acted.
  - To find an indirect object, use the *to* or *for* test.
- A **predicate noun,** pronoun, or adjective is the word or group of words following a linking verb that completes the meaning of the subject
- Predicate pronouns are always in the subjective case.

Confirm Your Knowledge

Complete Exercise for Unit 1.7 on page 43.

SENTENCES AND CLAUSES; SENTENCE FRAGMENTS

A sentence is a group of words containing at least one subject and verb and giving the reader a complete thought or meaning. It may contain one or more clauses.

A clause is a group of words also containing a subject and verb which may or may not be a complete sentence. This unit will help you identify different types of clauses and complete sentences.

❍ 1.8 Dependent and Independent Clauses

Dependent Clauses

A dependent clause contains a subject and a verb and always begins with a subordinate conjunction. (See Unit 1.3 for a list of subordinate conjunctions.) In other words. a dependent clause always begins with an "if" word.

He will write *if* he needs advice.

He will write *when* he needs advice.

Because he needs advice, he wrote a long letter.

A dependent clause cannot stand alone as a sentence.

If the funds are received on time...

Whenever you feel a desire for fine music...

That he has succeeded in his career goals...

None of these clauses makes sense on its own. All of them require more information to make them meaningful to the reader. They are therefore dependent clauses.

Hint: To help you identify dependent clauses, remember two things.

1. The clause must begin with a subordinate conjunction. Think of these as "if" words. (See list in Unit 1.3, page 7.)
2. The clause does not make sense on its own; it needs more information to make it into a complete thought or sentence.

Mini-Test

Underline the dependent clauses in the following sentences.

1. Whenever Richard is late, he has an original excuse.
2. Here is a copy of the fax that I received yesterday.
3. Children who are followed home by strangers should tell their parents.
4. We shall buy a cellular phone if it is not too expensive.
5. After the players left, the groundspeople rolled the field.

KEY

1. Whenever Richard is late 2. that I received yesterday 3. who are followed home by strangers 4. if it is not too expensive 5. After the players left

Independent Clauses

An independent clause has a subject and a verb and can stand alone as a sentence. An independent clause makes sense to the reader without any further information. Every sentence must have at least one independent clause.

John Clemens used the laser.

Lewis Yapp finalized the project.

An independent clause may have two subjects and one verb, two subjects and two verbs, one subject and two verbs, or any combination of subjects and verbs! The tests for an independent clause are as follows:

1. Does it contain at least one subject and verb?
2. Can it stand alone as a sentence?

All hardcover books and paperbacks are being reduced and are on sale at 40 percent discount. (two subjects—*books* and *paperbacks*; two verbs—*are being reduced* and *are*)

Miss Henschel arrived yesterday and will open the new theatre tomorrow. (one subject—*Miss Henschel*; two verbs—*arrived* and *will open*)

Independent clauses are sometimes difficult to identify because of other groups of words in the sentence. In the following examples, the independent clauses are in italics.

1. After an introductory word, phrase, or clause

   Yes, *the building will be completed on time.*

   The building having been completed on time, *the company moved away.*

   When the building is finished, *the company will move into its new offices.*

2. Two or more independent clauses

   A sentence may contain two or more independent clauses joined by a co-ordinate conjunction. (See Unit 1.3)

   John Clemens used the laser, and *Lewis Yapp finalized the project.*

   John Clemens used the laser, but *Lewis Yapp finalized the project.*

   John Clemens used the laser; however, *Lewis Yapp finalized the project.*

3. Independent clause and dependent clause

   An independent clause may be followed by a dependent clause, have a dependent clause as an interruption, or be preceded by a dependent clause.

   John Clemens used the laser before *Lewis Yapp finalized the project.*

   John Clemens, who is the head of the laboratory, *used the laser.*

   After John Clemens used the laser, *Lewis Yapp finalized the project.*

Mini-Test

Underline the independent clauses in the following sentences.

1. During this period of inflation, we shall have to change our policy.
2. I plan to leave on Friday if the strike is settled.
3. The conference is scheduled for 3 p.m.; therefore, all files must be ready and on the table by 2:30 p.m.
4. Both Aeroflot and Aer Lingus airlines applied for and received permission to refuel at Gander Airport.
5. Mr. Fletcher, to whom you wrote yesterday, called this afternoon.

KEY

1. we shall have to change our policy 2. I plan to leave on Friday 3. The conference is scheduled for 3 p.m.; all files must be ready and on the table by 2:30 p.m. 4. (The whole sentence should be underlined as it consists of only one independent clause.) 5. Mr. Fletcher...called this afternoon. (Do not underline to *whom you wrote yesterday* as this is a dependent clause.)

Elliptical Clauses

In elliptical clauses, some words are missing because they are obvious and can easily be supplied by the reader. A subject, a verb, or a conjunction may be omitted.

Restock the shelves, please. (subject omitted—*You* restock...)

She is stronger than he. (verb omitted—She is stronger than he *is*)

While in Vancouver, Mr. Monk visited the aquarium. (subject and verb omitted—While *he was* in Vancouver,...)

I understand the new wallpaper designs are beautiful. (conjunction omitted—I understand *that* the new wallpaper designs...)

It is important to be able to identify elliptical clauses so that you know the correct form of the pronoun to use. (See Unit 2.5.)

Mini-Test

Supply the missing words in the following elliptical sentences. Use the proofreaders' mark for insert (∧) and write the words to be inserted above the sentence.

Example: When ∧*she was* returning from Thunder Bay, Mrs. Post had a mild heart attack.

1. I know Mr. Schwartz can reply to your question as he is more qualified than I.
2. Begin work as soon as possible, and report to me each day.
3. "To err is human, to forgive divine."
4. Give the statistics to Herman rather than Frank.
5. While waiting for a replacement part, we lost valuable time.

KEY

1. I know ∧*that* Mr. Schwartz; ...than I ∧*am*. 2. ∧*You* Begin work...
3. "...to forgive ∧*is* divine" 4. ∧*You* Give the...than ∧*to* Frank
5. While ∧*we were* waiting for...

Sentence Fragments

Every sentence must have a subject and a verb and contain all the information for a complete thought. Groups of words that do not have a subject and a verb, or which do not make complete sense on their own, are called sentence fragments. Sentence fragments may be used in conversation and occasionally in advertising, but should not be used in written material.

Test for sentence fragments by asking: Does the group of words make sense without more information?

If there are sufficient entries.

The satellite dish on the house next door.

In answer to your question.

These groups of words do not make sense; however, by adding something more to these examples of sentence fragments, we can make complete sentences.

If there are sufficient entries, consolation rounds will be arranged.

The satellite dish on the house next door is noisy when it rotates.

In answer to your question, child care is available at no charge.

Be careful with long, involved sentences. Check first for verbs and clauses; then make sure that there is at least one independent clause.

With reference to your request for information on hotel prices in New York City. (no verb, no clause—sentence fragment)

Your request for information on hotel prices in New York City has come at a most appropriate time. Prices have just been reduced. (two independent clauses—two sentences)

The samples in the top drawer of the filing cabinet in Miss MacIntosh's office, which is on the fifth floor. (verb is in a dependent clause; no independent clause—sentence fragment)

The samples are in the top drawer of the filing cabinet in Miss MacIntosh's office, which is on the fifth floor. (subject—*samples*; verb—*are*; one independent clause and one dependent clause—a complete sentence)

Mini-Test

Are the following groups of words sentence fragments or complete sentences? Write beside them *Frag.* for fragment or *Sent.* for complete sentence.

1. If I remember all the details correctly.
2. Your efforts to raise money for the food bank by holding a garage sale.
3. After checking to see whether the plans were ready.
4. In order to be sure you have made the right choice.
5. Most people who want to own their own home arrange for financing through a bank or trust company.

KEY

1. Frag. 2. Frag. 3. Frag. 4. Frag. 5. Sent.

Summary for Unit 1.8

- A **sentence** contains a subject and a verb and gives the reader a complete thought.
- A **clause** contains a subject and a verb and may or may not be a sentence.
- A **dependent clause**:
  - always begins with a subordinate conjunction
  - does not make sense on its own
- An **independent clause:**
  - can stand alone as a sentence; it makes sense on its own
  - may have one or more subjects and one or more verbs
  - may follow an introductory word, phrase, or clause
  - may be joined to another independent clause with a co-ordinating conjunction
  - may be followed, interrupted or preceded by a dependent clause
- Tests for dependent and independent clauses are:
  - Does the clause make sense without more information? (independent)
  - Does it begin with a subordinate con junction (an "if" word)? (dependent)
  - Does it contain at least one subject and verb? (either dependent or independent)
- An **elliptical** clause has words omitted because they are obvious to the reader.
- A **sentence fragment** is a group of words that does not make sense without more information.
- Sentence fragments are not generally acceptable.

Confirm Your Knowledge

Complete Exercise for Unit 1.8 on page 45.

DEVELOPING YOUR LANGUAGE SKILLS

❍ 1.9 Vocabulary

The vocabulary units are divided into three sections:

1. **Definitions**—introducing words which may be new to you but which are commonly used
2. **Usage**—Helping you make decisions about choice of confusing words
3. **Spelling**—making sure you can spell some of the common problem words

Definitions

All writing should use vocabulary that is easily understood by the reader; however, too simple writing sometimes sounds childlike and insincere. Occasionally a more unusual word will spark the reader's interest. This section of the vocabulary units will cover words which you should try out in your own writing—but use them sparingly!

Check your dictionary for the definitions of the following words; then match them up with the definitions given. Write the letter of the definition you choose from Column 2 in the space provided in Column 1.

Column 1	Column 2
_____ absorb	a) a list of things to be done
_____ acquiesce	b) unfavourable, unfriendly
_____ acquire	c) the receipt or obtaining of something
_____ acquisition	d) soak up, take in
_____ adjacent	e) next to, beside, neighbouring
_____ advantageous	f) receive, get, obtain
_____ adverse	g) part of a poem
_____ agenda	h) give in quietly
_____ appreciable	i) helpful, favourable
_____ arbitrary	j) according to one's own thinking
	k) measurable, enough to be felt

Mini-Test

Complete the following sentences by choosing the most appropriate word from Column 1 under "Definitions."

1. It will be __________ to Alberta's economy if the price of oil is raised.
2. The other provinces had __________ criticism of the new price.
3. The __________ of items for the museum's collections depends on donations from the general public.
4. The items on the __________ for the meeting will take at least four hours to cover.
5. Invest wisely if you want to __________ wealth.
6. We are not moving far, just into the __________ building.
7. Sponges __________ liquids easily.
8. He reluctantly had to __________ to our proposals.
9. There has been no __________ drop in unemployment over the last twelve months.
10. His __________ ruling did not agree with how others thought the matter should be handled.

KEY

1. advantageous 2. adverse 3. acquisition 4. agenda 5. acquire 6. adjacent 7. absorb 8. acquiesce 9. appreciable 10. arbitrary

Be sure you checked your spelling of these words!

Usage

There are quite often no rules to help you know what preposition to use, which of two words with a similar meaning to use, or which of two words to use that sound alike. This part of the vocabulary units will help you clarify some of the common problems.

---

accept/except

accept—take, receive	We accept your apology.
except—leave out, omit	All employees, emergency staff excepted, must leave the building.

adapt/adopt/adept

adapt—change, adjust	Adapt the design for your use.
adopt—take on	We want to adopt your ideas.
adept—clever, skilled	Jay is adept at finding errors.

advice/advise

advice (noun)—opinion, counsel	Our consultant's advice is usually good.
advise (verb)—inform, give counsel	A parent will often advise a child on health problems.

Hint: Remember the difference between these two by listening to the sound of the words.

The noun *advice* ends in *-ice*. We often don't like advice because it sounds cold!

The verb adv*ise* has a *z* sound in it. I advise you to be sure of these two words.

affect/effect

affect (verb)—influence, change (something)	High interest rates have affected housing starts.
effect (verb)—bring about	How can we effect better relations with the union?
effect (noun)—result	The effects of micro surgery have been amazing.

Hint: An easy way to remember which is the noun is to remember *the effect* is the noun with the two *e*'s coming together.

all right

—always two words	Your answers are all right. It is all right to cry.

all ready/already

all ready—all is ready	The goods are all ready for shipping.
already—before now	They have already been checked.

all together/altogether

all together—in one group	The boxes are all together by the door.
altogether—completely	Your claim is altogether unfair.

Hint: To test for one or two words, if *all* could be omitted and the meaning remain the same, then *two* words are necessary.

Mini-Test

Complete the following sentences by choosing the correct word from those shown at the beginning of the sentences.

1. *accept/except*

   Mr. Sawyer said he will _________ all offers _________ those that have conditions attached to them.

2. *adapt/adopt/adept*

   We hope to ________ the suggestions you have made, but may we have your permission to _________ them slightly? We feel our staff may not be sufficiently _________ at one or two of the skills required.

3. *advice/advise*

   My _________ to you is to _________ your client to accept the terms already set out.

4. *affect/effect*

   What _________ will inflation have on your wages? Will it _________ the agreement now being arranged? Will you _________ any changes in your salary policies?

5. *all right/alright*

   The idea for the commercial is _________

6. *all ready/already*

   The notices have _________ been sent out and the members are _________ to vote.

7. *all together/altogether*

   There is ___________ no basis for the claim that the workers were ___________ on the rig when it collapsed.

KEY

1. accept, except 2. adopt, adapt, adept 3. advice, advise 4. effect, affect, effect 5. all right 6. already, all ready 7. altogether, all together

Spelling

Correct spelling, like correct grammar and punctuation, is vital in communications to ensure there is nothing to distract the reader from the meaning of the messsage. This section of the vocabulary units lists some of the most commonly misspelled words with the troublesome letters underlined to help you remember the correct spelling. Study these words letter by letter, write them out at least *ten* times each, and be sure you know the meaning of each!

Double Letters

accommodate	exaggerate	marriage
committee	embarrass	processor
possession	accompany	professor
occurrence	communicate	succeed
occurred	innovation	questionnaire

Mini-Test

Circle any misspelled word and write the correct spelling beside the word.

professor	accomodate
succeed	comittee
accompany	innovation
communicate	exagerate
processor	questionaire
possession	occurrence
marriage	embarrass
occured	

KEY

Circle	accomodate	should be spelled	accommodate
	comittee	should be spelled	committee
	exagerate	should be spelled	exaggerate
	questionaire	should be spelled	questionnaire
	occured	should be spelled	occurred

SUMMARY FOR UNIT 1.9

- Study words and be sure of their meanings (**definitions**).
- Study words and be sure of their correct **usage**.
  - Effect is a noun meaning "result" or a verb meaning "bring about."
  - In a choice-between "all together and "altogether," if *all* can be omitted, then write as two words.
  - the noun *advice* sounds like *ice*.
  - *Affect* by itself means "change."
- Study words to be sure of their **spelling.** Note each letter in them. Know their meanings as well.

Confirm Your Knowledge

Complete Exercise for Unit 1.9 on page 47.

1.10 Introduction to Proofreading

The importance of proofreading can never be overstated. Proofreading is the last line of defence to make sure any written communication is accurate in all details. Proofreading demands concentration and requires a good knowledge of spelling, grammar, and punctuation. Proofreading also requires the use of common sense as sometimes a sentence may be correct grammatically but contain vocabulary errors. It is the proofreader's job to catch and correct such errors.

Proofreaders' Marks

Certain symbols or marks have become standard for marking errors. A table of these marks is included on the inside back cover of this book. A few of them will be introduced in each proofreading section and will be included in subsequent sections. Practise using these marks.

Sometimes you may find it easier to use your own marks for making corrections. Whichever method you use, make sure all proofreading corrections are clear and easy to follow for the person producing the final document.

Insert ^

This mark is used for any insertion, be it a single letter, one or more words, or most punctuation marks.

accomodate (m inserted) insert word (this inserted) insert words (quite a few inserted)

In the final document, these examples would appear as:

accommodate insert this word
insert quite a few words

Delete

This mark is used to take out any letter, word, or material that is not required in the final document.

accross delete this word delete quite a few words

In the final document, these examples would appear as:

across delete word delete words

How to Proofread

Because the proofreader's job is so important, the way in which you proofread is also important. The proofreader must pay particular attention to:

1. Meaning and grammar
2. Spelling and punctuation
3. Set-up and general appearance

In order to proofread effectively, follow these three steps:

1. Read through the material for meaning and obvious errors.
2. Read through a second time, letter by letter, checking thoroughly for errors in spelling, punctuation, usage, and grammar.
3. Check again for overall appearance—margins even, corrections neatly made, no smudges or fingermarks, etc.

Methods of Proofreading

1. Proofread a document by using a pencil or pen to follow each word as you check it. A ruler will help you check each line.
2. Mark any error as soon as you find it. Use the appropriate proofreaders' mark or circle the error. Make sure the error is clearly marked using a contrasting colour to attract attention.
3. Proofread computer screens using your finger or the eraser end of a pencil. Check very carefully word by word, line by line. As proofreading a screen is very difficult, the printout must also be proofread.

Note: When completing the mini-tests and exercises in the proofreading units, practise using the proofreaders' marks that are being presented. In other mini-tests and exercises, mark errors and corrections in whichever way you find most suitable for you, always remembering that someone else may have to interpret your corrections.

Mini-Test

Proofread the following sentences carefully using the proofreaders' marks for *insert* ^ and *delete* where necessary. The errors you are looking for may relate to any point of grammar or vocabulary covered in Unit 1 or any other item your own knowledge tells you is wrong.

1. When preparing to profread a piece of writing, make sure you you have a good pen or pencil ready.
2. Did you find it advantagous to arrive at the at the airport early?
3. A sentence must not contain at least independent clause.
4. A dependent claus cannot stand alone a sentence.
5. Please complete all parts of questionaire and return it to us as soon possible.

KEY

1. profread, you 2. advantagous, at the 3. not, at least independent 4. claus, alone a 5. of questionaire, as soon possible

From this mini-test it will be obvious how easy it is to miss errors. It is essential that you learn now how important it is to proofread accurately and carefully. In the long run this skill will save you hours of rekeying or rewriting and in some instances may even save you embarrassment!

Transpose ∿ or ∽

The symbol for transpose can be written ∿ or ∽ whichever is the easier in the particular application. This sign is used around letters, words, or phrases that have been written or keyed the wrong way round.

hte Out order of

on the table, under the desk, or in the drawer

The final printing would read:

the Out of order

under the desk, on the table, or in the drawer

Change Word or Words ——

Write a line through the word to be changed and write clearly above it the word to be put in its place. If there is not enough room, write the correction in the margin on the same line and put a circle around it.

This is a ~~rough~~ *draft* copy.

How many ~~applications~~ *entry forms* have you received so far?

Mini-Test

Proofread the following material for transpositions, necessary word changes, and spelling errors. Use appropriate proofreaders' marks.

Dear Ms. Latif

Conrgatulations on your appointment as supervisor of our Word Processng Centre in Montrael. The company has made a wide choice in trasnferring you their. Your absence into this office will effect us greatly, however, as sunny your smil and always cheerful greeting started the day fir us in a happy way. Our lose is without doubt Montreal's gain.

Sincerely

KEY

Conrgatulations, Processng, Montrael, wide, trasnferring, their, into, effect, as sunny your smil, fir, lose

SUMMARY FOR UNIT 1.10

- Proofreading is the vital last step to take before sending out any written communication.
  - Read for meaning and grammar.
  - Read letter by letter for spelling and punctuation.

    Check finally for set-up and appearance.
- Proofreaders' marks:
  - ∧ Insert—letter, word, phrase, sentence.
  - Delete—anything!
  - ∿ Transpose—letters or words.
  - — Change words.

Confirm Your Knowledge

Complete Exercise for Unit 1.10 on page 49.

PRETEST FOR UNIT 1

Complete all the parts of this test according to the directions for each part. The figures in parentheses are the unit numbers for reference, if necessary, when you have completed the test.

Your Goal: To score a total of at least 80 points.

A. General Rules

Are the following statements true or false? If true, circle *T*; if false, circle *F*. Score 1 point for each correct answer.

			Score
1.	An adjective answers "What kind of?" (1.1)	**T F**	_____
2.	An adverb answers "*How? When? Where? Why?*" (1.2)	**T F**	_____
3.	An adverb may describe only a verb or an adjective. (1.2)	**T F**	_____
4.	A subordinate conjunction always begins an independent clause.(1.3)	**T F**	_____
5.	*And, but,* and *or* join items of different or unequal strength. (1.3)	**T F**	_____
6.	The "*-ing*" part of a verb can be used as a noun called a gerund. (1.4)	**T F**	_____
7.	An auxiliary or helping verb plus another verb form a verb phrase. (1.4)	**T F**	_____
8.	A prepositional phrase always begins with a pronoun. (1.3)	**T F**	_____
9.	A dependent clause (an "if" clause) can stand alone as a sentence. (1.8)	**T F**	_____
10.	A sentence must have at least one independent clause; if it does not, the group of words is known as a sentence fragment. (1.8)	**T F**	_____
		Score for Part A	_____

B. Parts of Speech (1.1, 1.2, 1.3)

In the following sentences what parts of speech are the words in italics? Write above them:

N for noun	*P* for Pronoun
Aj for Adjective	*Prep* for preposition
Av for Adverb	*V* for Verb (or *VP* for verb phrase)
C for Conjunction	*I* for Interjection

Score 1 point for each correct answer.

Example: *Ramona* [N] said she *was* [V] grateful *for* [Prep] the gift. 3

		Score
1.	*Congratulations!* You and Raoul *are* the *lucky* winners.	_____
2.	Drive *slowly* over a rough road *and* save your *tires.*	_____
3.	Have you heard *about* Jim's accident *at* his garage?	_____
4.	Yes, *he* told me all about *it.*	_____
5.	*When* Marie seemed *unhappy* with the *decision,* she *spoke* sharply *to* the referee.	_____
6.	*Who* signed the contract? No one *can read* the signature.	_____
7.	*If* the purchase order is mailed *today,* you *may receive* the nails by the end of next week.	_____
	Score for Part B	_____

C. Verbs (1.2)

Are the verbs in italics in the following sentences action or linking? Write above them *A* for action or *L* for linking. Score 1 point for each correct answer.

A

Example: At the concert Marjorie Ling *turned* the pages for the pianist. 1

Score

1. Management *seemed* unaffected by the workers' threat to strike. ______
2. *Write* a checkmark beside those values that *are* important to you. ______
3. Peter *felt* very disappointed when he *heard* the election results. ______
4. You *should listen* carefully to instructions so that you *can do* the job well. ______
5. Ms. Rowe *was* very angry when Irene *looked* at the answers. ______
6. Martin *looked* very pleased with the award he received. ______

Score for Part C ______

D. More Verbs (1.4)

Are the verbs in italics in the following sentences active or passive? Write above them *A* for active or *P* for Passive. Score 1 point for each correct answer.

Score

1. Some sales representatives *were encouraged* by the large turnout at the presentation. ______
2. The results of the referendum *will be recorded* later. ______
3. Dr. Firth's remarks *were* well *received* by the audience. ______
4. She *spoke* on the subject of acid rain. ______
5. Statistics *prove* that our decision was a wise one. ______

Score for Part D ______

E. Subject and Verb (1.6)

Underline the simple subject and the simple verb or verb phrase in the following sentences. Some sentences may have two subjects and verbs. Write *S* above the subject and *V* or *VP* above the verb or verb phrase. Score 1 point for each correct pair.

S V S V

Example: We hope that you are happy with your course. 2

Score

1. John Rinaldi was one of our best managers. ______
2. Mark has one of the oldest computers in the building. ______
3. The president disclosed a new project to the staff. ______
4. The new publicity campaign has raised over $35 000 already. ______
5. The first letter in the postal code represents a geographic area of population. ______
6. The latest electronic games are sure to give you much pleasure and entertainment. ______
7. On the news last night an important ruling about exhaust fumes from trucks was announced. ______
8. There are only two months left in which to take advantage of our offer. ______
9. Our aim is to serve you quickly and efficiently. ______

10. Parents and guardians are all invited to support their children's teams. ______
11. Sheet music, as well as compact discs and tapes, is stocked at our new Main Street store. ______
12. Few people today understand the difficulties that the pioneer families had to face. ______
13. Keep your photographs safe and clean in our special family album. ______
14. Here are the figures for the month-end report. ______
15. With today's rising prices, the homemaker finds it difficult to keep within a budget. ______
16. Try to complete the analysis by Friday so that the final report can be presented to the shareholders on Monday. ______
17. Gone are the days of the five-cent cup of coffee. ______
18. When will the samples be sent to North Bay? ______

Score for Part E ______

F. Prepositional Phrases (1.5)

Underline ten prepositional phrases in the following sentences. Score 1 point for each correct sentence.

Example: The role of the co-ordinator should be clearly defined. 1

Score

1. The need for skilled welders and fitters is great. ______
2. The tremendous number of career opportunities available today has increased night school enrolment. ______
3. Many local papers are associated with large national newspapers for international coverage. ______
4. The growth of the telecommunications industry over the last few years has been phenomenal. ______
5. We are concerned about the effect of radiation on the animals in the park. ______

Score for Part F ______

G. Dependent Clauses (1.8)

Underline ten dependent clauses in the following sentences. Score 1 point for each correctly underlined dependent clause.

Example: The poster which is above the water cooler is very appropriate. 1

Score

1. If you have time, will you please visit us on your next trip to Nelson. ______
2. Be sure to finish one piece of work before you start another one. ______
3. Ms. Sittler, who has been trained on very complex control panels, seems to be the most appropriate candidate for the job. ______
4. I believe that there is no need for panic at this stage. ______
5. Give the assignment to whoever you think can do the best job. ______
6. Until we have more information, it is difficult for us to make an accurate evaluation. ______
7. Mr. Roschman plans to visit Alabama after he has completed his work in New York City. ______
8. Although Gerry does not have time just now, he would very much like to work on that project later. ______
9. The new machine is much faster than the old one, which was constantly breaking down. ______
10. Because Louise needs more money, she has been forced to take a job in the evenings. ______

Score for Part G ______

H. Sentence Fragments (1.8)

Are any of the following groups of words sentence fragments? If so, write *Frag.* on the line provided. If the group of words is a complete sentence, write *Sent.* on the line. Score 1 point for each correct answer.

Example: Considering all the options. Frag. 1

I believe he will come. Sent. 1

Score

1. Although we have written three times. ______ ______
2. Referring to your letter of October 17. ______ ______
3. Your car is in very good shape considering the number of kilometres on it. ______ ______
4. May we suggest that you install insulation in your attic. ______ ______
5. If the parts are received this week. ______ ______
6. In answer to your query. ______ ______
7. If you prefer, you need not make any payment until January. ______ ______
8. The further you go on vacation, if you enjoy travelling, the more you will feel you have had a good holiday. ______ ______
9. The laundry and drycleaning service we offer will keep your clothes in tiptop condition. ______ ______
10. In investigating the complaint you made about the damage to the furniture we shipped to you by rail last week. ______ ______

Score for Part H ______

I. Proofreading and Vocabulary (1.9, 1.10)

Using proofreaders' marks, make any necessary corrections in vocabulary or spelling in the following sentences. Score 1 point for using the correct proofreaders' marks and making the correction.

Example: What is the ~~a~~^e^ffect of heat on vinyl? 1

Score

1. We need a larger room to accomodate the meeting. ______
2. What is the prupose of this questionnaire? ______
3. Please let us have your comments by by July 27. ______
4. The results of the survey will be complete no Friday. ______
5. The project is complete accept for the final tests. ______

Score for Part I ______

Total Score ______

If you achieved your goal of at least 80 points, proceed to Unit 2. If you did not score 80, check with your instructor what parts you need to study. Proceed through Unit 1 doing all the necessary work; then do the posttest for Unit 1.

POSTTEST FOR UNIT 1

Complete all the parts of this test according to the directions for each part. The figures in parentheses are the unit numbers for reference, if necessary, when you have completed the test.

Your Goal: To score a total of at least 80 points.

A. General Rules

Are the following statements true or false? If true, circle *T*; if false, circle *F*. Score 1 point for each correct answer.

			Score
1.	An adjective tells more about a noun.(1.1)	**T F**	_____
2.	An adverb may tell more about an adjective.(1.2)	**T F**	_____
3.	An adverb usually answers the question "What kind of?" (1.2)	**T F**	_____
4.	A dependent clause always begins with a subordinate conjunction. (1.3)	**T F**	_____
5.	*And, but,* and *or* join items of equal strength. (1.3)	**T F**	_____
6.	*Has, have, could, might be* are examples of linking verbs. (1.4)	**T F**	_____
7.	A dependent clause (an "if" clause) cannot stand alone as a sentence. (1.8)	**T F**	_____
8.	A pronoun such as *he* or *she* takes the place of a verb. (1.1)	**T F**	_____
9.	The words *at, of, about, with* are examples of adjectives. (1.3)	**T F**	_____
10.	A group of words without at least one subject and verb is known as a dependent clause. (1.8)	**T F**	_____

Score for Part A _____

B. Parts of Speech (1.1, 1.2, 1.3)

In the following sentences what parts of speech are the words in italics? Write above them:

N for noun	*P* for Pronoun
Aj for Adjective	*Prep* for preposition
Av for Adverb	*V* for Verb (or *VP* for verb phrase)
C for Conjunction	*I* for Interjection

Score 1 point for each correct answer.

Example: Ramona [N] said she *was* [V] grateful *for* [Prep] the gift. 3

Score

1. *At last*! Next year's *sports* cars *have arrived.* _____
2. The two of us *pulled* the oars *together* and reached the *shore.* _____
3. Did *you* read *about* the strike *in* the newspaper? _____
4. *We* are pleased to accommodate *you* in our *newest* suite. _____
5. *Although* the weather is improving *slightly*, the farmers are anxiously waiting for *sunshine*. _____
6. He *can play* tennis well *because* he practises *at* the club. _____
7. John Renaldi *and* Donna Underhill *are joining* the Rotary Club this year. _____

Score for Part B _____

C. Verbs (1.2)

Are the verbs in italics in the following sentences action or linking? Write above them *A* for action or *L* for linking. Score 1 point for each correct answer.

A

Example: At the concert Marjorie Ling *turned* the pages for the pianist. 1

Score

1. The carpenter *seemed* pleased with the lower lumber prices. ______
2. *Mark* those papers that you feel *are* exceptional with an asterisk. ______
3. Karl *looked* upset when he *saw* that someone had spilled coffee on his drawings. ______
4. You *should read* directions carefully so that you *can build* the bookshelves easily. ______
5. The woman *was* surprised when she *opened* her purse and found her lost wallet. ______
6. Donald *appeared* very happy with the cheque he received. ______

Score for Part C ______

D. More Verbs (1.4)

Are the verbs in italics in the following sentences active or passive? Write above them *A* for active or *P* for Passive. Score 1 point for each correct answer.

Score

1. Some representatives *were delighted* by the new product line. ______
2. The results of the interviews *will be discussed* tomorrow. ______
3. He *posted* the notices on the lunchroom wall. ______
4. Announcements from Ottawa *may influence* the stock market. ______
5. Ms. Ecob's suggestions *have been approved.* ______

Score for Part D ______

E. Subject and Verb (1.6)

Underline the simple subject and the simple verb or verb phrase in the following sentences. Some sentences may have two subjects and verbs. Write *S* above the subject and *V* or *VP* above the verb or verb phrase. Score 1 point for each correct pair.

Example: We hope that you are happy with your course. (S V S V) 2

Score

1. Frank Zigglestein was an excellent data processor. ______
2. Jolanne has one of the most expensive pens on the market. ______
3. The article exposed the corruption of the local government ______
4. This year's census has revealed some interesting facts. ______
5. The increase in the first quarter sales this year demonstrates the success of our new marketing strategy. ______
6. The multicultural television stations are helpful to those wishing to learn about other lifestyles. ______
7. At this month's meeting, a new method of recording the minutes on tape was employed. ______
8. There are two exciting new cars in our showrooms this year. ______
9. Our goal is to satisfy your gardening needs efficiently. ______
10. Mechanics and metal workers are skilled trades people. ______
11. Carpeting, together with sound-absorbent ceiling panels, is an effective way to cut down on family room noise. ______
12. Many people are hoping to establish world peace. ______
13. Guard your home or office with our complete line of locks and alarms so that your valuables are always safe. ______
14. Here is my latest report on the energy savings being made at the airport. ______
15. With the new technology available today, operating room nurses are finding their role changing. ______
16. Please complete your submission by Monday so that the tenders can be judged by the committee. ______
17. Long past are the days of the ten-cent comic book. ______
18. When can we expect the books from Britain? ______

Score for Part E ______

F. Prepositional Phrases (1.5)

Underline ten prepositional phrases in the following sentences. Score 1 point for each correct sentence.

Example: The role of the co-ordinator should be clearly defined. 1

Score

1. The demand for more fire marshalls is obvious. ____
2. The enormous volume of traffic has resulted in more highway construction across the city. ____
3. Unions with large memberships often provide better wages for their workers. ____
4. The expansion of the subway system and bus service over the last ten years has been extraordinary. ____
5. The sale continues until noon on Saturday. ____

Score for Part F ____

G. Dependent Clauses (1.8)

Underline ten dependent clauses in the following sentences. Score 1 point for each correctly underlined dependent clause.

Example: The poster which is above the water cooler is very appropriate. 1

Score

1. If you think it advisable, will you please arrange for us to visit your new research facility. ____
2. Be ready to answer all questions courteously when you are at the reception desk. ____
3. Martha Swan, whom I spoke to you about on Friday, has called again regarding the opening. ____
4. He reported that the supply of leather was getting low. ____
5. Send the circulars to whoever is on our mailing list. ____
6. When we have more information, we shall be happy to give you more details. ____
7. Mr. Miles intends to wait until his brother has signed the contract. ____
8. Although Jenny has not made any plans yet, she would very much like to visit Japan on her vacation this year. ____
9. We had an interesting demonstration of laser and ink jet printing which are extremely fast ways to produce documents. ____
10. Since the company is expanding rapidly, it hopes to hire seven students for summer jobs. ____

Score for Part G ____

H. Sentence Fragments (1.8)

Are any of the following groups of words sentence fragments? If so, write *Frag.* on the line provided. If the group of words is a complete sentence, write *Sent.* on the line. Score 1 point for each correct answer.

Example: Considering all the options. Frag. 1

I believe he will come. Sent. 1

Score

1. When the menus are ready. ______ ______
2. Since the interest rates have gone up. ______ ______
3. Your last medical check-up was on March 15 of last year. ______ ______
4. The government's plan to give a grant to homeowners who insulate their homes. ______ ______
5. Unless your signature is on the agreement. ______ ______
6. Seventy cartons of electrical components arrived today. ______ ______
7. If your cheque bounces, your bank should be informed. ______ ______
8. Today, with the high rate of inflation, it is difficult to maintain a satisfactory standard of living. ______ ______
9. The interior decorating service we are offering to help you furnish your new home. ______ ______
10. In response to your recommendation for merging our operations with those of your holding company. ______ ______

Score for Part H ______

I. Proofreading and Vocabulary (1.9, 1.10)

Using proofreaders' marks, make any necessary corrections in vocabulary or spelling in the following sentences. Score 1 point for using the correct proofreaders' marks and making the correction.

Example: What is the affect of heat on vinyl? (a struck out, e written above) 1

Score

1. We shall be be pleased to accommodate you. ______
2. Dull, wet weather affects all fo us. ______
3. Put the different shirt styles altogether on one rack. ______
4. Why has the register not ben signed? ______
5. We are happy to except your invitation. ______

Score for Part I ______

Total Score ______

EXERCISE 1.1 NOUNS, PRONOUNS, AND ADJECTIVES

Identify the nouns, pronouns, and adjectives in the following sentences by writing *N* for noun, *Pro* for pronoun, and *Aj* for adjective above the word. Do not identify *a*, *an*, or *the*. Score 1 point for each correct answer.

Your Goal: To score at least 25 points.

Example: The secretary (N) has given him (Pro) the large (Aj) package (N). 4

Score

1. John decided to go himself. _____
2. Shall we write down our suggestions? _____
3. She remembered her key. _____
4. All the keyboarding assignments have been completed. _____
5. Somebody should reply to your question. _____
6. Security is a child's right. _____
7. Whose drawings are those? _____
8. These are the latest printouts. _____
9. Both of us have read five books. _____
10. Who is going to attend the conference with Miss Wong? _____

Total Score _____

If you achieved your goal of at least 25 points, proceed to Unit 1.2. If you did not score 25, go back and review Unit 1.1 thoroughly; then do Exercise 2 and try to achieve your goal this time.

EXERCISE 1.1A NOUNS, PRONOUNS, AND ADJECTIVES

Use the same directions as for Exercise 1.

Your Goal: To score at least 25 points.

Score

1. His car is a red Toyota. _____
2. Everyone agrees, but only some understand. _____
3. This is my first choice. _____
4. We ourselves always shop at Markham Meat Company. _____
5. Karl is the pride of the team. _____
6. Someone closed the cabinet. _____
7. Her counsellor is Mrs. Green. _____
8. Whoever said those were yours? _____
9. Your future depends on yourself. _____
10. Conor's equipment was left in the school bus. _____

Total Score _____

If you achieved your goal of at least 25 points, proceed to Unit 1.2. If you did not score 25, ask your instructor for direction before moving on.

EXERCISE 1.2 VERBS AND ADVERBS

Identify the adverbs in the following sentences by writing *Av* above each one. Underline the verbs and verb phrases, and write *L* above each linking verb. Score 1 point for each correct answer.

Your Goal: To score at least 25 points.

L Av
Example: I am very happy you have sold your house. 3

Score

1. Shake vigorously and pour carefully. ______
2. I shall take this up to the mail room now. ______
3. The doctor was too late to save the injured man. ______
4. See our fully lined skirts at remarkably low prices. ______
5. We never borrow money needlessly. ______
6. The shop steward quickly replaced the dangerously loose wiring. ______
7. Noel writes rapidly but legibly. ______
8. There are several reasons for this approach to the problem. ______
9. When will the revised drawings arrive? ______
10 I will always respect your strictly personal opinions. ______

Total Score ______

If you achieved your goal of at least 25 points, proceed to Unit 1.3. If you did not score 25, go back and review Unit 1.2 thoroughly; then do Exercise 1.2A and try to achieve your goal this time.

EXERCISE 1.2A VERBS AND ADVERBS

Use the same directions as for Exercise 3.

Your Goal: To score at least 25 points.

Score

1. Unfortunately, my sister has lost her umbrella. ______
2. A restful vacation usually restores health very efficiently. ______
3. Where are you going so quickly? ______
4. Gasoline prices seem to be increasing daily. ______
5. Here are the magazines you requested. ______
6. Why did you come in? ______
7. If we begin soon, we shall finish early. ______
8. Mr. Goldberg leaves for Halifax tomorrow. ______
9. Do every job conscientiously, and you will succeed. ______
10. Our pears taste sweeter this year. ______

Total Score ______

If you achieved your goal of at least 25 points, proceed to Unit 1.3. If you did not score 25, ask your instructor for direction before moving on.

EXERCISE 1.3 CONJUNCTIONS, PREPOSITIONS, AND INTERJECTIONS

Underline the conjunctions, prepositions, and interjections in the following sentences. Identify them by writing *C* above conjunctions, *P* above prepositions, and *I* above interjections. Score 1 point for each correct answer.

Your Goal: To score at least 25 points.

I C P
Example: Hooray! You and your wife are going on a trip. 3

Score

1. You may work with Rachel or Naomi on this assignment. ____
2. Divide the profit between us so that we can plan for the future. ____
3. At last! Spring is here, and so is our new line of lawnmowers. ____
4. Proofread very carefully; otherwise, errors may pass uncorrected. ____
5. During the debate, the contestants became so angry that the moderator asked for a ten-minute break. ____
6. These parts have been imported for several years; however, they are not entirely satisfactory. ____
7. The market for portable telephones with good reception will reach billions of dollars as they become more readily available. ____
8. Although union dues are required from every employee, these dues are deducted at source from gross earnings. ____
9. If the drawings are ready by Monday, we can start construction on Tuesday of the following week. ____
10. The inventory must be completed before the plant closes on December 23 for the holidays. ____

Total Score ____

If you achieved your goal of at least 25 points, proceed to Unit 1.4. If you did not score 25, go back and review Unit 1.3 thoroughly; then do Exercise 1.3A and try to achieve your goal this time.

EXERCISE 1.3A CONJUNCTIONS, PREPOSITIONS, AND INTERJECTIONS

Use the same directions as for Exercise 5.

Your Goal: To score at least 25 points.

	Score
1. If you continue as you are doing, you will without a doubt be successful.	______
2. Dan and I were thrilled when we heard about your appointment.	______
3. The price of honey has risen because the bees have been affected by the weather.	______
4. Help! We need your assistance in testing our new product before we put it on the market.	______
5. I told Mr. Johnston that we could send the merchandise whenever he requires it.	______
6. Sorry! Your payment must be received within 30 days; otherwise, you are not eligible for the discount.	______
7. At the convention, which I attended last week, I was introduced to Mr. Shaw, who showed me some very interesting samples.	______
8. Please let me know by June 8 when you will be arriving so that I can make reservations for you.	______
9. While you are in Vernon, would you please ask Ms. Pawlowski to proceed with the convention arrangements.	______
10. The new laptop computers are very powerful; consequently, many people are becoming very interested in them.	______
Total Score	______

If you achieved your goal of at least 25 points, proceed to Unit 1.4. If you did not score 25, ask your instructor for direction before moving on.

EXERCISE 1.4 VERBS, VERB PHRASES, VOICE, AND GERUNDS

Underline the verbs, verb phrases, and gerunds in the following sentences. Write *Act* above each verb or verb phrase in the active voice; write *Pass* above each verb phrase in the passive voice. Write *G* above each gerund. Score 1 point for each correct answer.

Your Goal: To score at least 20 points.

Example: Trying (G) every possible way takes (Act) time. — Score: 2

		Score
1.	Clarity in speaking takes practice.	____
2.	Jumping to conclusions often causes misunderstanding.	____
3.	The engine was brought to the shop so that our mechanic could repair it.	____
4.	Procrastinating consumes more energy than completing the task.	____
5.	Pat is studying hard so that she can become a lawyer as her goal is a career in law.	____
6.	The directions should be clarified by your underlining the important points.	____
7.	Knitting is a useful hobby.	____
8.	A career in plumbing should also be considered.	____
9.	As the accounts must be finished today, I will work late.	____
10.	You should subscribe to our magazine; if you do, we can guarantee you will have many hours of enjoyment.	____
	Total Score	____

If you achieved your goal of at least 20 points, proceed to Unit 1.5. If you did not score 20, go back and review Unit 1.4 thoroughly; then do Exercise 1.4A and try to achieve your goal this time.

EXERCISE 1.4A VERBS, VERB PHRASES, VOICE, AND GERUNDS

Use the same directions as for Exercise 7.

Your Goal: To score at least 20 points.

Score

1. Helping a family move takes organization and patience. ______
2. Roberto visited him and helped him set out a budget. ______
3. The points we must discuss have been listed in the agenda ______
4. An understanding of tax law would help in completing tax returns. ______
5. Painting and sculpting provide relaxation. ______
6. Preparing for and writing an examination can be very stressful. ______
7. We will assist you in bringing your payments up to date and clearing your account. ______
8. I was asked what I thought about the hiring of an investigator. ______
9. The proposal submitted by Ms. Jennings must be prepared carefully. ______
10. The packaging which should have been delivered last week has not been received yet. ______

Total Score ______

If you achieved your goal of at least 20 points, proceed to Unit 1.5. If you did not score 20, ask your instructor for direction before moving on.

EXERCISE 1.5 PREPOSITIONAL PHRASES AND INFINITIVES

Indicate whether the words in italics are prepositional phrases or infinitives. Write *Prep* above each prepositional phrase and *Inf* above each infinitive. Score 1 point for each correct answer.

Your Goal: To score at least 12 points.

Example: During the hot weather, we like *to swim.* (Prep above "During the hot weather"; Inf above "to swim") 2

Score

1. Ms. Hardie flew *to Prince Albert* last week *to attend* a conference. _____
2. As our first choice has been sold, we are again looking *for a new building.* _____
3. The delegates were *in the meeting* all day. _____
4. Once he achieved his quota, the sales representative asked *for a cash advance.* _____
5. If you need *to cash* a personal cheque, we shall be happy *to help* you. _____
6. *During the baseball season,* buses run *to the park* every half hour. _____
7. Because all *of the students* completed their assignments *on time,* the teacher allowed them *to leave* early. _____
8. Gail asked *about the package* she was expecting. _____
9. Taking calculated risks is the accepted way *of becoming a millionaire.* _____
10. The experiments *under consideration* will be reviewed next week. _____

Total Score _____

If you achieved your goal of at least 12 points, proceed to Unit 1.6. If you did not score 12, go back and review Unit 1.5 thoroughly; then do Exercise 1.5A and try to achieve your goal this time.

EXERCISE 1.5A PREPOSITIONAL PHRASES AND INFINITIVES

Use the same directions as for Exercise 9.

Your Goal: To score at least 12 points.

Score

1. When you have opened the carton carefully, read the assembling instructions *on the inside package.* _____
2. The aircraft was flying *above its approved ceiling.* _____
3. The man *on my left* is Mr. Abbott. _____
4. You are fortunate that you were able *to sell* your stocks *without a heavy loss.* _____
5. Living in an age *of advanced electronic technology,* we are still impressed *by individual achievements.* _____
6. The weather has been so good that the tomato crop is excellent *in this region.* _____
7. Having urgent orders still *to fill,* they worked *until 2 a.m.* _____
8. Providing a child *with more toys* does not ensure its happiness. _____
9. *To design* high fashion clothes requires a very special talent. _____
10. People who decide *to invest* in real estate *in this neighborhood* are putting their money *to good use.* _____

Total Score _____

If you achieved your goal of at least 12 points, proceed to Unit 1.6. If you did not score 12, ask your instructor for direction before moving on.

EXERCISE 1.6 SUBJECTS AND PREDICATES

Underline all the simple subjects once and simple predicates twice in the following sentences. Score 1 point for each set of subject and predicate you have correct.

Your Goal: To score at least 10 points.

Example: Honesty on your part is essential. 1

Score

1. An assortment of discarded clothes will soon be donated to your sale. ______
2. Did you buy a new car? ______
3. I saw a large crowd of people waiting to be picked up. ______
4. Proofread for all kinds of errors. ______
5. All of the relatives were anxious to receive news about the crash. ______
6. Jack was one of the participants who came to the contest, and he performed enthusiastically. ______
7. On the car seat were the money clip and the missing keys. ______
8. Reading books can be one way of acquiring knowledge. ______
9. The equipment, along with all the instructions for its use, was shipped to the fitness centre. ______
10. During the wedding party, congratulations were offered to the bride and groom. ______

Total Score ______

If you achieved your goal of at least 10 points, proceed to Unit 1.7. If you did not score 10, go back and review Unit 1.6 thoroughly; then do Exercise 1.6A and try to achieve your goal this time.

EXERCISE 1.6A SUBJECTS AND PREDICATES

Use the same directions as for Exercise 11.

Your Goal: To score at least 10 points.

Score

1. Her singing was a joy to everyone. ______
2. Which of the six contracts is ready for signing? ______
3. Why have you refused to return my phone calls? ______
4. To sell at least four houses a month is her goal. ______
5. Waving a printed sign, the young political activist leaped up onto the wall. ______
6. If you decide to join our organization, your promotion will be assured. ______
7. To receive the best, you have to give your best. ______
8. In this building are housed the archives of all the departments. ______
9. Each of us will be at the exhibition on a different day. ______
10. Wherever you go, be prepared to report daily. ______

Total Score ______

If you achieved your goal of at least 10 points, proceed to Unit 1.7. If you did not score 10, ask your instructor for direction before moving on.

EXERCISE 1.7 COMPLEMENTS

Underline all complements and place the correct abbreviation above each.

DO for Direct Object	*PA* for Predicate Adjective
IDO for Indirect Object	*PN* for Predicate Noun
	PP for Predicate Pronoun

Score 1 point for each correct answer.

Your Goal: To score at least 12 points.

Pn ... IDO DO

Example: It was the forecast that persuaded me to bring you your boots. 3

Score

1. Parenting as we experience it today is made challenging by the demands of modern life. ______
2. I gave the agent six samples of purchasers' offers. ______
3. It was she who felt the disagreement between us was unnecessary and resolvable. ______
4. None of the students wrote the mid-term exam. ______
5. One of the hardest-working athletes at this school is Schmidt. ______
6. Mr. Peet will send your group full details of the various tours we offer. ______
7. Thailand, as well as India, is a country worth visiting. ______
8. My sources indicate that he is still the leading local political candidate. ______
9. The producer hoped that the film would attract an audience in Europe. ______
10. Maral insisted that it was she who had sought permission to attend the performance. ______

Total Score ______

If you achieved your goal of at least 12 points, proceed to Unit 1.8. If you did not score 12, go back and review Unit 1.7 thoroughly; then do Exercise 1.7A and try to achieve your goal this time.

EXERCISE 1.7A COMPLEMENTS

Use the same directions as for Exercise 13.

Your Goal: To score at least 12 points.

Score

1. You will find our store and local business community convenient and helpful. ______
2. These spring bulbs will be beautiful in your garden. ______
3. When his mother came for a visit, she gave Joel some housewares for his apartment. ______
4. Use our company coupons as cash. ______
5. The decision of the judges to award the prize to Yuri gave him a thrill. ______
6. Dorothy seemed eager and willing although the job was repetitive. ______
7. It felt comfortable to stay in a familiar hotel. ______
8. Both actor and director are well respected in theatrical circles. ______
9. As soon as they reached their destination, the team leader arranged to start the training program. ______
10. Facing her first classroom of students, Linda felt nervous but excited. ______

Total Score ______

If you achieved your goal of at least 12 points, proceed to Unit 1.8. If you did not score 12, ask your instructor for direction before moving on.

EXERCISE 1.8 DEPENDENT AND INDEPENDENT CLAUSES; SENTENCE FRAGMENTS

Underline independent clauses once; underline dependent clauses twice; insert omitted words from elliptical clauses; write *Frag* at the end of any sentence fragment. Score 1 point for each correctly underlined clause, 1 point for words inserted correctly, and 1 point for each sentence fragment correctly identified.

Your Goal: To score at least 18 points.

Example: If it is convenient, ^you come to our showroom. 3

After reading all the instructions in the brochure. Frag 1

Score

1. While you wait, we work quickly on your shoes. ____
2. From the date of your promotion to the position of senior assistant to the manager. ____
3. We advertise specials in cat and dog grooming, and this approach seems to attract customers in January. ____
4. Is it possible that Ms. D'Alfonso left the computer on the train? ____
5. Stroke victims who are badly disabled are taken to the centre for rehabilitation. ____
6. Let us know what time you will arrive at the airport; we will glady meet your plane. ____
7. Although we reached every subscriber possible, the circulation manager was not satisfied. ____
8. To help you become financially secure, after you have paid off your debts, make out a budget and stick to it! ____
9. The total, including all meats, vegetables, dairy products and canned goods currently in stock. ____
10. What might have caused such a huge decrease in the quality of the printing? ____

Total Score ____

If you achieved your goal of at least 18 points, proceed to Unit 1.9. If you did not score 18, go back and review Unit 1.8 thoroughly; then do Exercise 1.8A and try to achieve your goal this time.

EXERCISE 1.8A DEPENDENT AND INDEPENDENT CLAUSES; SENTENCE FRAGMENTS

Use the same directions as for Exercise 15.

Your Goal: To score at least 18 points.

Score

1. The hospital staff, wanting to be absolutely sure about emergency procedures. _____
2. Without being prejudiced, I believe the new spring styles are by far the best we have ever presented. _____
3. Animals that graze on vegetation in the lowlands are causing environmental problems. _____
4. How did they hope to establish a precedent before they had studied all the facts? _____
5. The prototype was expected to be supplied by Mills and Company, but we have not yet received it. _____
6. A few of those who helped during the move hoped to be given some expenses for lunch. _____
7. Please deliver the engines before June 30. _____
8. During our extensive research, we learned a lot about our background; nevertheless, we discovered far less information than we had expected. _____
9. Referring to the credit card receipt covering the disputed entry on your statement. _____
10. Check all the products in our latest catalogue and place your order early for fast delivery. _____

Total Score _____

If you achieved your goal of at least 18 points, proceed to Unit 1.9. If you did not score 18, ask your instructor for direction before moving on.

EXERCISE 1.9 VOCABULARY

Complete the three parts of this exercise according to the directions for each part.

Your Goal: To score at least 16 points.

A. Definitions

Complete the following sentences by choosing the most appropriate words from those given. Score 1 point for each correct answer.

absorb	acquire	acquisition	acquiesce
advantageous	adjacent	agenda	arbitrary
appreciate	adverse		

Score

1. When did the art gallery _______________ a genuine Paul Kane painting? _____
2. I hope we don't receive any _______________ comments about the changes in responsibility. _____
3. Having the service department in the _______________ building ensures speedy repairs. _____
4. Let me know when it would be _______________ to reopen this project so that it will succeed. _____
5. If you have any items for the _______________ , please give them to Pauline before May 10 so that she can prepare for the meeting. _____

Score for Part A _____

B. Usage

Use the same directions as for Part A.

accept	advice	except	adept
all right	affect	advise	adopt
altogether	already	all together	all ready
effect	adapt		

1. If you _______________ our offer immediately, we can have everything _______________ the final costing ready by May 1. _____
2. Hot water will not _______________ the finish, but alcohol has the _______________ of leaving a white mark; you can, however, _______________ an improvement in the appearance by rubbing the mark with Nufinish. _____
3. My _______________ is that we stand _______________ as a team on this point if we want to achieve our objective. _____
4. Is it _______________ to inspect the packages now, or have they _______________ been inspected? _____
5. Can you _______________ me which schedule we should _______________ to cover as many cities as possible? _____

Score for Part B _____

C. Spelling

Circle all of the following words that are misspelled and write the correct spelling above the word. Score 1 point for each correctly changed word; deduct 1 point for each word changed that was correct as written.

				Score
1.	embarass ______	marriage ______	innovations	_____
2.	occurence ______	suceed ______	professor	_____
3.	comittee ______	accompany ______	exaggerate	_____
4.	processor ______	possession ______	accommodate	_____
5.	questionaire ______	occurred ______	communicate	_____

Score for Part C _____

Total Score _____

If you achieved your goal of at least 16 points, proceed to Unit 1.10. If you did not score 16, go back and review Unit 1.9 thoroughly before moving on.

EXERCISE 1.10 INTRODUCTION TO PROOFREADING

Complete each part of this exercise according to the directions given.

Your Goal: To score at least 9 points.

Part A

Are the following statements true or false? If true, circle *T*; if false, circle *F*. Score 1 point for each correct answer.

		Score
1. Proofreading is not a very important function.	**T F**	_____
2. You need to proofread for meaning only.	**T F**	_____
3. The symbol ℓ means "delete."	**T F**	_____
4. When proofreading, you should read very carefully letter by letter.	**T F**	_____
5. The symbol ∿ means "transpose."	**T F**	_____
	Score for Part A	_____

Part B

Proofread the following letter very carefully using proofreaders' marks to make corrections where necessary. Score 1 point for each error found and marked correctly; deduct 1 point for each error missed! Do not make any changes to punctuation.

Example: Thank you for you letter of Feb‸uary 10. (Score 1 for correct marking of *Febuary*; deduct 1 for missing *your* before "letter.") 0

Dear Mr. Livingstone

Thank you for you letter telling us how delighted you are with the aquisition of your new Rosewood coffee table.

Your copy of our booklet about how to care for Rosewood fine furniture is enclosed. On page 3 you will find details on the on the types of cleaning fluids that should be used and the types that should be avoided. Although Rosewood is studry and well finished, there are certain precautions that should be taken if you want to have your coffee table looking like new for many years to come.

Rosewood representatives are located in cities right accross Canada and are always ready to you help. They are able to make minor repairs if necessary and can advise you on other pieces of Rosewood available to complete your collection.

May we have the opportunity to serve you again soon?

Yours very truly

Number of errors found and correctly marked	_____
Deduct for errors missed	_____
Score for Part B	_____
Total Score	_____

If you achieved your goal of at least 9 points, proceed to the Posttest for Unit 1. If you did not score 9, You will appreciate the need for accurate proofreading! Review Unit 1.10 thoroughly before moving on.

USAGE

In the working world, attention to detail is vital. As you prepare to enter that world, you must become aware of certain common difficulties in using English. Develop the habit of always checking in your dictionary or a good reference manual for unusual usage or unfamiliar items. For example, you know how to form the plurals of most words, but you may need to check for the correct plurals of certain words such as *crisis* or of certain abbreviations such as *CGA*. Always make sure when in doubt by checking an authoritative reference.

AGREEMENT OF SUBJECT AND VERB

❍ 2.1 Person and Number; Compound Subjects

Person and Number

In Unit 1.1, the terms *person* and *number* are defined. The verb must agree with its subject in person and number.

Person	Singular	Plural
1st	I am	We are
2nd	You are	You are
3rd	He, She, It is The driver is	They are The drivers are

Interrupting phrases—for example, those starting with *such as*, *as well as*, *of*, *together with*—are ignored when checking the agreement of the verb with its subject.

> *I*, as well as Bonnie, AM WILLING to work overtime.
>
> *The consignment* of digital clocks HAS BEEN CHECKED.
>
> *Your rear fender*, as well as the tail lights, NEEDS replacing.
>
> *A good teacher* PREVIEWS and REVIEWS every test she gives.(3rd person singular)
>
> *Good teachers* PREVIEW and REVIEW every test they give. (3rd person plural)

Note: The number of the verb always depends on the subject, not the predicate.

> *His students* WERE his only concern. (3rd person plural)
>
> The *X-ray* of the bones SHOWS breaks in three places. (3rd person singular)

Mini-Test

Underline the subjects once and the verbs or verb phrases twice in the following sentences. Write beside the sentence whether the subjects are 1st, 2nd, or 3rd person and singular or plural.

1. You, as well as the shop steward, are responsible for safety.
2. The cars coming off the assembly line now are the best ever.
3. We service and inspect all equipment before installation.
4. The manager wants answers to his questions.
5. The price of spare parts is rising rapidly.

KEY

1. You...are (2nd sing. or plur.) 2. cars...are (3rd plur.) 3. We service and inspect (1st plur.) 4. manager wants (3rd sing.) 5. price...is rising (3rd sing.)

Compound Subjects

Compound subjects—two or more subjects joined by *and*—usually take a plural verb. Sometimes a compound subject really refers to one thing, and a single verb is used. Test for plural or singular meaning by substituting *they*, *he*, *she*, or *it* for the compound subject. Take special care with long, involved sentences.

> The *negative* and the *print* WERE both destroyed. (*They* were...)

The scented *markers* that you bought and the neon paper that you suggested as perfect for the kindergarten children ARE very inspiring. (*They* are...)

Fish and chips WAS a staple in my diet as a child. (It was...)

The owner and manager of the store on the corner next to the private garages WORKS long hours. (*He* or *She* works...)

Note: To make a plural subject clear, use *the, an,* or *a* before the second noun.

The owner and manager works long hours. (one person)

The owner and *the manager* work long hours. (two people)

Subjects joined by *or* or *nor, not only...but also*

Or and *nor* really act as separators; therefore, with subjects joined *by or* or *nor*, the verb agrees with the part of the subject nearest to it.

John or *Joan* IS GOING to make the announcement.

John or *his parents* ARE GOING to make the announcement.

John, his parents,or Joan's *parents* ARE GOING to make the announcement.

This rule also applies to *either...or, neither...nor, not only...but also*

Neither the actor nor the *stage hands* WERE aware of the danger.

Either the actor or *his dresser* HAS the costume.

Not only the workers but also the *administration* WAS in favour of the plan.

Not only the administration but also the *workers* WERE in favour of the plan.

Mini-Test

Underline the subjects in the following sentences; then write the correct form of the verb (*is* or *are*) to complete the sentence. Explain why you made that choice.

1. The block and tackle for the pulley __________________ being repaired.
   ____
2. The message you left yesterday and the comment you wrote on my report __________________ proving very useful.
   ____
3. Either Ms. Kucharski or two of the operators __________________ being asked to attend the lecture. __________________
4. Not only the doctors but also the hospital __________________ receiving a great deal of criticism. __________________
5. Mr. Brendel or Mrs. Laskie __________________ currently training the staff on the new telephone system.
   ____

KEY

1. block and tackle...is (one unit) 2. message...comment...are (compound subject) 3. Ms. Kucharski or two...are (agrees with two—nearest subject) 4. doctors...hospital...is (agrees with nearest subject) 5. Mr. Brendel or Mrs. Laskie is (agrees with nearest subject)

SUMMARY FOR UNIT 2.1

- A verb must agree with its subject in person and number.
- Regular verbs after *it, he, she,* or a singular noun have an *s* at the end.
- Expressions such as *along with* or *as well as* are not part of the simple subject and do not affect verb agreement.
- Compound subjects joined by *and* are plural unless they refer to a single unit.
- If *the, an,* or *a* is repeated before the second noun in the compound subject, the subject is plural; if not, it may be singular.
- When parts of the subject are joined by *or* or *nor, not only...but also,* the verb must agree with the part closest to it.

Confirm Your Knowledge

Complete Exercise for Unit 2.1 on page 84.

❍ 2.2 Collective Nouns

A collective noun represents a group of people or things, such as *crowd, company, herd, group, collection, majority*. These nouns take a singular verb when the group is considered a single unit.

The *crowd* WAS in an angry mood. (It was...—one unit)

The *herd* of prize cattle IS being auctioned on Friday. (It is...—one unit)

The *jury* IS STUDYING the evidence.(It is...)

If the members of the group are considered as acting separately, use a plural verb.

The *crowd* WERE already going their separate ways. (They were...—the separate people in the crowd)

The *herd* of prize cattle ARE BEING TESTED for tuberculosis. (They are..each separate cow)

The *jury* ARE UNABLE to agree on a verdict. (They are...)

Sometimes it is better to rewrite such constructions:

All the people in the crowd WERE ready to go home.

All the cows in the herd ARE BEING TESTED for tuberculosis.

The *members* of the jury ARE UNABLE to agree on a verdict.

Hint: Use *it* or *much* to test for a singular meaning; use *they*, *several*, or *many* to test for a plural meaning.

The *number* of faulty vehicles IS confidential. (*It* is confidential.)

A *number* of faulty vehicles HAVE BEEN RETURNED. (*Several* have been returned.)

The *majority* of the wool IS from Scotland. (*Much* of the wool is from Scotland.)

The *majority* of the class HAVE PASSED. (*Many* have passed.)

One-third of the report IS finished. (*It* is finished.)

One third of the cellular phones ARE black. (They are black.)

Mini-Test

Circle the correct verb in the following sentences. Write on the line provided the word you used to help you choose.

1. The company is/are expanding its operation into the Maritimes. ____________________
2. A number of prominent people agree/agrees with the proposal. ____________________
3. Two-thirds of the material has/have been used. ____________________
4. The committee was/were asked for their individual opinions. ____________________
5. The number of faxes we have received is/are encouraging. ____________________

KEY

1. is (it) 2. agree (several) 3. has (it) 4. were (they) 5. is (it)

Company Names

Company names are treated as singular collective nouns even when they contain the names of many individuals.

Bisbee, Busby, Boothby, & Basil prepares our advertising copy. (*It*, the firm, prepares our copy.)

Karman and Woods is a high quality clothing outlet.

But: *Bisbee* and *Basil* are our copy writers. (*They*, two people, are our copy writers.)

Mini-Test

Use the delete mark (⁄) or otherwise indicate the correct verb in the following sentences.

1. Paulsson, Dilcher, & Linden is/are opening another branch soon.
2. Mitchell and Kopek is/are the two designers.
3. Nader and Green is/are a large accounting firm.
4. Dun & Bradstreet collect/collects credit information for its clients.
5. McDougall, Hammil and Change is/are the doctors involved with the case.

KEY

1. is 2. are 3. is 4. collects 5. are

Plural Forms

Some nouns look like plurals but in fact have singular meanings and therefore take singular verbs. The following list includes some of these nouns.

aerobics	measles	news
summons	robotics	civics

computer studies (and all such nouns relating to subjects of study or special courses, for example, mathematics, physics, economics)

The news of the disaster is terrifying.

Aerobics is an energetic form of exercise.

The summons was delivered by courier.

Some nouns look like plurals and always take a plural verb although they may refer to a single thing.

belongings	premises	headquarters
earnings	thanks	pliers
scissors	pants	glasses
proceeds	savings	winnings

His prescription sunglasses *were* very expensive.

The headquarters of the company *have* been moved to Regina.

The premises *have* passed the fire marshall's inspection.

Some nouns, depending on their meaning, may be singular or plural. *Data* is actually plural, but a singular verb is commonly used in general writing.

A series of fund-raising events *has* been planned for the fall.

Four series of lectures on fund-raising *have* been planned.

The data received from various sources *are* (or *is* in common usage) very important. (many items of information)

Ceramics *is* taught on Monday evenings only. (one course)

Ceramics *are* reduced by thirty percent. (ceramic items)

General Guidelines

If the word refers to a science, an illness, a subject of study, a game, or a sport, use a singular verb.

Economics *is* a very exacting science.

Dominoes *is* played by all ages.

If the word refers to the individual parts making up the science, subject of study, game, or sport, use a plural verb.

A teenager's economics sometimes *leave* a lot to luck!

The dominoes *are* made of wood.

Mini-Test

Use the delete mark (𝛾) or otherwise indicate the correct verb in the following sentences.

1. The premises is/are not open after 6 p.m.
2. Physics is/are a subject which all electronics students must study.
3. The data from the survey has/have been sorted. (common usage)
4. The series is/are finishing on June 30.
5. Proceeds from the lottery is/are being donated to the hospital.

KEY

1. are 2. is 3. has 4. is 5. are

Indefinite Pronouns

The singular indefinite pronouns (see list in Unit 1.1) take singular verbs. For most of them, the word *one*, which is singular, could be used.

Every man, *every* woman, and *every* child *has* been vaccinated.

Nobody is excused from attending class.

Neither of the animals *was* rabid. (Neither one...)

Nothing but some kitchen utensils *was* left after the fire. (Not one thing...)

Each of the children *was* given a glass of orange juice.

Mini-Test

Are the verbs correct in the following sentences? If so, write C in the space provided; if not, write X and make the correction.

1. Each is responsible for being on time. _____
2. Nobody has to work late this month. _____
3. Neither of the surveys have been completed. _____
4. Every book, every magazine, and every bulletin have to be catalogued. _____
5. Anything is acceptable for the rummage sale. _____

KEY

1. C 2. C 3. X—has 4. X—has 5. C

SUMMARY FOR UNIT 2.2

- Use a singular verb with a collective noun if the group is acting as one unit.
- Use a plural verb if the parts of the group are acting individually.
- *The number* is singular; *a number* is plural.
- Company names are singular.
- Use a singular verb with the names of sciences, subjects, sports, games, or illnesses.
- Use a plural verb if the subject refers to parts of sciences. subjects, sports, or games.
- Use a singular verb with most indefinite pronouns.
- If you can substitute or insert *one*, then it must be singular.

Confirm Your Knowledge

Complete Exercise for Unit 2.2 on page 85.

❍ 2.3 Inverted Order and Other Special Cases

Inverted Order

In sentences in an unusual or inverted order, take care in identifying the subject. (See also Unit 1.6.) Rearranging the sentence to its more normal order will help you find the subject so that the correct verb is used.

On stage at the opening curtain WERE *Sophie Jones and Miles Hardwick.*

Rearranged: *Sophie Jones and Miles Hardwick* WERE on stage at the opening curtain.

HAVE *the youngest child and the three oldest children* been told about their parts?

Rearranged: *The youngest child and the three oldest children* HAVE been told about their parts.

The words *here* and *there* are never subjects.

Here IS the *answer* to your question.

Here ARE the *airline tickets* for your flight to Amsterdam.

There HAS been a *flood* of enquiries about the train crash.

There HAVE been many *victims* in the accident.

Again, changing the sentence by rearranging it or omitting the *here* or *there* will help you to identify the subject.

The *answer* to your question IS here.

A *flood* of enquiries about the train crash HAS been received.

Many *victims* HAVE been in the accident.

Mini-Test

Underline the subjects of the following sentences.

1. There was bound to be at least one protester present.
2. Have the necessary supplies for the Science Department been ordered yet?
3. In only four weeks' time will your new home be ready for you to move in.
4. Here are the sample menus for your approval.
5. Did you make the bookings for the concert in Medicine Hat?

KEY

1. protestor 2. supplies 3. home 4. menus 5. you

Special Cases

None, Some, Any, *and* All

None, *some*, *any*, and *all* may be singular or plural in meaning. The *of* phrase coming after them usually indicates which is meant.

Some of the gasoline HAS spilled onto the floor.

Some of the nails HAVE fallen onto the floor.

Where is the wood? Is there any left?

Where are the logs? ARE there any left?

All (of) the flight attendants ARE fully trained.

All that matters IS to save the seals. (The only thing)

None of the material IS ready.

None of the samples ARE suitable.

Mini-Test

Use the delete mark (℘) or otherwise indicate the correct verb in the following sentences.

1. None of the pears is/are ripe.
2. All the participants is/are highly competitive.
3. Some of the correspondence has/have been answered.
4. Does/Do any one of you know the way to fillet a fish?
5. None of the milk has/have turned sour.

KEY

1. are 2. are 3. has 4. Does 5. has

Only one of, One of

Use a singular verb after *the only one of*. (If there is "only one," it must be singular!)

He is the only one of the servers who IS always on time. (No one else is on time.)

This is the only one of the stereo systems that HAS been advertised. (No other stereo system has been advertised.)

Use a plural verb after *one of...who* or *one of...that*. (The verb agrees with the antecedent of "who" or "that.")

He is one of the servers who ARE always on time. (*who* refers to servers)

This is one of the stereo systems that HAVE been advertised. (*that* refers to stereo systems)

Each...and, Every...and

Combinations of *each...and* and *every...and* take a singular verb.

Each cat and dog IS given a thorough examination.

Every cat, dog, and pet monkey HAS to have rabies shots.

Numbers and Money

Numbers that represent a single unit, for example, *dozen*, take a singular verb; numbers that represent more than one item considered separately take a plural verb.

Fifty cents IS the price of the ticket.

Fifty loonies WERE distributed to the children.

Forty kilometres IS a long way to run.

A baker's dozen IS made up of thirteen items.

Do you think $500 IS too much to pay for rent?

There WERE five $100 bills lying on the counter!

Titles

Use a singular verb with the title of a book, play, magazine, film, video, or other literary or artistic work.

Literary Lapses WAS written by Stephen Leacock.

Anne of Green Gables IS a popular musical.

Mini-Test

Use the delete mark (℘) or otherwise indicate the correct verb in the following sentences.

1. Each nut, bolt, and screw has/have been carefully adjusted.
2. Don't you think that $90 000 is/are too high a price for that painting?
3. *Les Sylphides* has/have been a popular ballet for many years.
4. Marco is one of those who insists/insist on paying their share in full.
5. Herman is the only one who insists/insist on paying the whole bill himself!

KEY

1. has 2. is 3. has 4. insist 5. insists

SUMMARY FOR UNIT 2.3

- Rearrange inverted sentences to find the subject.
- **Here** and **there** are never subjects.
- With **none**, **some**, **any**, and **all**:
  - Check the noun after "of."
    - Use singular verbs if only one or one part is meant.
    - Use plural verbs if more than one is meant.
- Use singular verbs after **the only one of**.
- Use plural verbs after **one of those who**, **one of the things that**.
- Use singular verbs with **each**...**and**, **every**...**and**
- With numbers and money:
  - Use singular verbs if acting as one unit.
  - Use plural verbs if individual items are meant.
- Use a singular verb with titles.

Confirm Your Knowledge

Complete Exercise for Unit 2.3 on page 86.

PROBLEMS WITH PRONOUNS

The English language contains such a variety of pronouns that many people have difficulty choosing the correct one. Units 2.4 to 2.6 will help you to use pronouns correctly in your writing.

❍ 2.4 Antecedents; Clear Reference

Antecedents

An antecedent is the word or words for which a pronoun is used. The pronoun chosen must agree with its antecedent in person, number, and gender. (See Unit 1.1.)

Mr. Ridicki insisted that *he* be allowed to write *his* own speech.

He and *his* refer to *Mr. Ridicki*, the antecedent, and agree with the antecedent—3rd person, singular number, masculine.

Pronouns whose antecedents are indefinite pronouns such as *every*, *each*, *either*, *nobody*, must be singular.

Is *either* of the women willing to give up *her* rights?

Everybody is responsible for *his* or *her* own luggage.

To avoid the awkward *his or her* construction, rearrange the sentence if possible.

Awkward: Everyone has been asked to submit his or her choice of colour for the walls of his or her office.

Improved: The staff have been asked to submit their choice of colours for their office walls.

Awkward: If anyone wants a copy, he or she should write to Mr. Adams.

Wrong: If anyone wants a copy, you should write to Mr. Adams.

Improved: Anyone wanting a copy should write to Mr. Adams.

A pronoun whose antecedent is a collective noun is either singular or plural depending on the meaning of that noun. (See Unit 2.2.)

The class had *its* photograph taken for the yearbook. (One picture)

The class brought *their* photographs for the yearbook. (The students in the class)

Better: Each student in the class brought a photograph for the yearbook.

Mini-Test

Make any necessary corrections in the following sentences by using proofreaders' marks and writing the corrections above the sentences. If a sentence is correct as written, write C beside it.

1. All the men agreed that everyone should bring their own sandwiches.
2. The committee had to report its findings to the president.
3. I have asked Ms. Saso and Mr. Walenski to let me have his recommendations by April 2.
4. Everybody must sign his or her time dockets before they send it to the payroll department.
5. The staff have been asked to hang its coats in the cupboard.

KEY

1. ~~their~~ his (meaning *each man*) 2. C 3. ~~his~~ their 4. Rewrite: All time dockets must be signed before they are sent to the payroll department. 5. ~~its~~ their

Clear Reference to Antecedents

Each pronoun must have a clear and precise antecedent so that the reader is not confused.

Confusing: When she graduated from high school, her mother was thrilled. (Who graduated?)

Clear: When Amanda graduated from high school, her mother was thrilled.

Confusing: Smith & Jones are the suppliers of sophisticated home security systems, but we don't need them as we have no valuables.

Clear: Smith & Jones are the suppliers of sophisticated home security systems, but we don't need such a system as we have no valuables.

An antecedent may be in a previous sentence provided the reference is clear.

Last week, Mr. Yamamoto flew to Japan to try to arrange for the building of a hotel in Tokyo. *He* found everyone very co-operative to *his* suggestions.

They *and* It

Do not use *they* or *it* without a clear antecedent.

Confusing: They sometimes have earthquakes in California. (Who?)

Clear: Earthquakes sometimes occur in California.

Confusing: They forecast rain for tomorrow. (Who?)

Clear: The weather people forecast rain for tomorrow.

Clear: Rain is forecast for tomorrow.

Confusing: In the instructions it says to attach the handle last. (What does *it* refer to?)

Clear: The instructions say to attach the handle last.

Note: In expressions of weather, time, and distance, *it* may be properly used.

It's raining. It is much colder this year.

It's a long time since the meter was read.

It was over a hundred kilometres to the nearest hospital.

Which, That, *and* This

Which, that, and *this* must always have a clear single word as an antecedent, never a clause or statement.

Wrong: The radio station did not have a sponsor for the overseas vacation being offered as a prize, which proved to be embarrassing. (What was embarrassing?)

Clear: The radio station was embarrassed because it did not have a sponsor for the overseas vacation being offered as a prize.

Wrong: The train was on time. That meant the taxi did not have to wait.

Clear: As the train was on time, the taxi did not have to wait.

Wrong: Some employees have been leaving early on Fridays. This must be stopped. (What must be stopped—the employees?)

Clear: Some employees have been leaving early on Fridays. This practice must be stopped.

Mini-Test

Make any necessary corrections in the following sentences by using proofreaders' marks and writing the corrections above the sentences. If a sentence is correct as written, write *C* beside it.

1. On the news, it mentioned that the cost of living had risen again.
2. Your shipment of china was not received until today, which means it was too late for our promotional sale.
3. They say that our facilities are the best of any tourist lodge in the area.
4. Mark would like to meet with Sacha to discuss his proposal.
5. I suggest we plan to leave early because it is 400 km to Regina and they say driving conditions are bad.

KEY

Your answers may be quite different from those given here. If yours follow the rules in this unit, accept them as correct. If you would like reassurance that you are making appropriate corrections, ask your instructor to go over your work.

1. The news reporter mentioned... 2. Delete *which means it was*. 3. Delete *They say that,* or change to *Our guests say that...* 4. Mark would like to discuss his proposal with Sacha. Or: Mark would like to discuss Sacha's proposal with him. (We don't know who had the proposal!) 5. Delete *they say,* or change to *the police report that...*

Special Situations

One *and* You

In general writing, the use of *one* instead of *you* should be avoided as it sounds unnatural and stilted.

Awkward: When installing complicated electronic equipment, one must be very careful.

Better: When installing complicated electronic equipment, you must be very careful.

Awkward: During a recession, one has difficulty meeting all one's expenses.

Better: During a recession, people have difficulty meeting all their expenses.

Possessives as Antecedents

The antecedent of a pronoun cannot be an adjective. Nouns in the possessive case are acting as adjectives and therefore cannot be used as antecedents.

Wrong: In Shakespeare's plays, he often uses historical references.

Correct: In his plays, Shakespeare often uses historical references.

Same

Do not use *same* as a pronoun.

Wrong: Your contribution of $100 is very welcome. A receipt for same will be issued shortly.

Correct: Your contribution of $100 is very welcome. A receipt for that amount will be issued shortly.

Compound Personal Pronouns

Use a compound personal pronoun only for emphasis where the person to whom it refers has already been mentioned.

He himself broke the news to his boss.

You will have to complete the questionnaire *yourself.*

Do not use compound personal pronouns when the simple personal pronoun should be used.

Yvette and *I* (not *myself*) designed the wall hangings.

The design has already been approved by Ted and *you*. (not *yourself*)

Mini-Test

Make any necessary corrections in the following sentences by using proofreaders' marks and writing the corrections above the sentences. If a sentence is correct as written, write *C* beside it.

1. One must take care when repairing electrical circuits.
2. The new office hours are set out in Mr. Stoddart's memo. A copy of same has been posted on the bulletin board.
3. After Rose's promotion, she requested an additional telephone for her department.
4. Peter and myself will go to Kamloops.
5. Please return the minutes to myself as soon as possible.

KEY

Your answers may be different. They are most likely correct, but if you are in any doubt, check with your instructor.

1. Care must be taken when... 2. ...memo, a copy of which has been... 3. After her promotion, Rose requested... 4. Peter and I... 5. ...to me...

Summary for Unit 2.4

- An **antecedent** is the word that a pronoun replaces or represents.
- A pronoun must agree with its antecedent in person, number, and gender.
  - After *each, any, every*, and similar pronouns, use a singular pronoun; if the gender is not clear, use *his or her*.
  - To avoid using an awkward sentence, rewrite!
- A pronoun must have a clear antecedent.
- Don't use *they* or *it* without a clear reference. (*It* may be used for time, distance, and weather.)
- Don't use *which, that*, or *this* to refer to long phrases or sentences. Rewrite with a clear word for reference.
- Use *you* instead of *one* where there is a clear antecedent; rearrange the sentence if it is awkward.
- Make sure a pronoun does not refer to a possessive antecedent as such a possessive is, in fact, an adjective.
- Don't use *same* as a pronoun.
- Don't use compound personal pronouns except for emphasis where the noun or pronoun has already been used.

Confirm Your Knowledge

Complete Exercise for Unit 2.4 on page 87.

❍ 2.5 Pronoun Cases; Who *and* Whom

The different cases for personal pronouns are summarized in the following table. (Review also the table in Unit 1.1)

	Personal Pronouns	Interrogative pronouns
Subjective Case 1. Subject of a verb	She read a book.	Who read a book? Send it to whoever reads the book.
2. Predicate noun	It is I.	Does he know who it is?
Objective Case 1. Direct object of a verb	We heard them.	Whom did you hear?
2. Indirect object of a verb (Preposition *to* understood)	We sent them a letter.	You sent whom a letter? (not often used)
3. Object of a preopostion	We sent it to them.	To whom did you send it?
4. Object of an infinitive	They hoped to hire him.	Whom did they hope to hire.
Possessive Case 1. To indicate possession	Here is his book.	Whose book is this?
2. To modify a gerund	He likes my baking.	Whose baking does he like?

Basic Rules

Appositives

An appositive is an extension of the subject or object giving more details about that subject or object. Any pronouns involved must therefore be in the same case as the subject or object they explain.

> We two, Cathy and *I*, write for the school paper. (*Cathy and I* is appositive to the subject *We two*; therefore the pronoun must be *I* — subjective case.)
>
> They sent it to us, Cathy and *me*. (*Cathy and me* is appositive to *us*, the object of the preposition *to*; therefore the pronoun must be *me* — objective case.)

To find the correct case, take out the noun or pronoun in apposition and leave the sentence with only the part that is causing concern.

> We two, Cathy and I, write for the school paper. (Omit *We two*, and you are left with *Cathy and I* write for the school paper.)

Taking this one step further, leave the pronoun alone in the sentence to be absolutely sure.

> *I* write for the school paper.

Some further examples are:

> The company told *us* welders about the new safety regulations. (The company told *us* about...)
>
> *We* welders were told about the new safety regulations. (We were told...)

Elliptical (Incomplete) Expressions

The most helpful way to find the case of a pronoun in expressions of contrast or comparison when the sentence ends with a pronoun is to complete the sentence.

> Mr. Boudreau sent the contract to the supplier rather than *him*. (rather than *to him*)
>
> Mr. Boudreau likes the new accountant better than *me*. (than he *likes me*)
>
> Mr. Boudreau likes the new accountant better than *I*. (than *I like the new accountant*)

Compound Constructions

Be careful with compound constructions.

> The personnel officer had advice for all of *us* — Tom, Dick, and *me*.
>
> The successful candidates were Tom, Dick, and *I*.
>
> The personnel officer asked the new employees and *me* to attend the meeting.

As a check, leave the pronoun alone in the sentence.

> The personnel officer had advice for *me*.
>
> The successful candidate was *I*.
>
> The personnel officer asked *me*...

Mini-Test

By using the delete mark (𝒥) or otherwise, indicate the correct pronoun in the following sentences.

1 Seth enters data much faster than I/me.
2. Give the instructions to we/us operators.
3. Aunt Elizabeth believes she/her to be the only heir.
4. Mrs. Dumas has enrolled her three sons — Athos, Porthos, and he/him.
5. The two in the machine shop, Jerry and I/me, were not informed of the change.

KEY

1. I 2. us 3. her 4. him 5. I

Who *and* Whom

To be sure with *who* and *whom*, isolate the part containing the *who* or *whom* and substitute *he* or *him*. (Don't worry about whether a singular or plural, masculine or feminine is required.) In this test, *he* equals *who* and *him* equals *whom*—the *m*s go together!

May I introduce Mr. Backhaus, whom you may recognize.

1. Isolate the *whom* part—whom you may recognize.
2. Substitute *he* or *him* to make a sentence: You may recognize *him*.
3. *Him* equals *whom*; therefore *whom* is correct.

May I introduce Mr. Backhaus, who is well known to all of you.

1. Isolate the *who* part—who is well known to you.
2. Substitute *he* or *him* to make a sentence: *he* is well known to you.
3. *He* equals *who*; therefore *who* is correct.

Don't be confused by reference to female gender or plurals; still substitute *he* or *they* (for *who*) and *him* or *them* (for *whom*) to check the correct use.

The women *who* have replied will all be interviewed. (*They* have replied; *who* is correct.)

The woman to *whom* you wrote telephoned today. (You wrote to *him* (*her*); *whom* is correct.)

Interrupting expressions such as *do you think* should be ignored.

Who do you think will win? (*Who* will win?)

Whom do you think they rewarded for his honesty? (They rewarded him.)

Don't be confused by clauses that are the objects of prepositions. Again, isolate the clause and substitute *he* or *him*.

Send copies of the photos to whoever has asked for them.

1. Isolate the clause *whoever has asked for them.*
2. Substitute *he* or *him*: *He* has asked for them.
3. *He* equals *who*; therefore *whoever* is correct.

Send the copies to whomever you choose.

1. Isolate the clause *whomever you choose.*
2. Substitute *he* or *him*: You choose *him*.
3. *Him* equals *whom*; therefore *whomever* is correct.

Mini-Test

By using the delete mark (𝒥) or otherwise, indicate the correct pronoun in the following sentences.

1. Mr. McNamara is the man who/whom we appointed.
2. Who/Whom do you feel is best suited for the position?
3. I will approve whoever/whomever you think is best.
4. I have written to the lawyer who/whom you recommended.
5. Who/Whom did Ms. Robinson write about?

KEY

1. whom 2. Who 3. whoever 4. whom 5. whom

SUMMARY FOR UNIT 2.5

- Personal pronouns have three cases used in the following ways:

Subjective	– as the subject of a verb – as a predicate noun
Objective	– as the direct object of a verb – as the indirect object of a verb – as the object of a preposition – as the object of an infinitive
Possessive	– as an adjective before a noun to show possession – before a gerund

- Mentally take out extra words to make sure of agreement.
- Complete elliptical phrases (after *than*) to find the correct pronoun.
- To check for *who* and *whom*:
  - Isolate part of sentence (clause).
  - Substitute *he* or *him*.
  - Use *who* for *he* and *whom* for *him*.

Confirm Your Knowledge

Complete Exercise for Unit 2.5 on page 88.

❍ 2.6 Pronouns with Infinitives and Gerunds

With Infinitives

A noun or a pronoun immediately followed by an infinitive is *always* in the objective case.

Sam asked the *men* to move. (*men*—object of verb *asked* and before infinitive *to move*)

Sam *asked* them to move.

They believed *him* to be in Australia.

Whom have you invited to attend?

With the infinitive *to be*, remember that *be* is a linking verb and therefore takes the same case after it as before.

I heard that the intruder was *he*. (subject—agrees with *intruder*)

If it have been *she* who stole the cookies, her parents would have been informed. (subject—agrees with *it*)

The thief was thought to be *I*. (*I* agrees with subject *thief*)

The police thought the thief to be *me*. (me agrees with *thief*, the object of the verb *thought*)

Mini-Test

Are the pronouns correct in the following sentences? If so, write *C* in the space provided; if not, write *X* and make the correction.

1. I am sure it was her who filed the papers. _____
2. Ms. Nicholson knows the auditors to be Chen and I. _____
3. The woman at the reception desk was thought to be me. _____
4. Whom do you expect to be elected? _____
5. Francis does not want we stitchers to do that. _____

KEY

1. X—she 2. X—me 3. X—I 4. C. 5. X—us

With Gerunds

Before a gerund, a noun or pronoun must be in the possessive case. The noun or pronoun is acting as an adjective describing the action of the gerund. Ask "Whose action?" to find the right form.

The *athlete's* training is particularly strenuous. (The training is strenuous. Whose training?—the athlete's)

The children were upset by *our* moving to France. (Whose moving?—our moving)

Whose writing is this?

If you are tempted to use *him, her,* or *us* in this type of sentence, check to see whether the sentence could end immediately after the pronoun. If it could not, then the possessive must be used.

The children were upset by us moving to France. (Can the sentence end at *us*? No, because the sense of the sentence is not complete.) *The children were upset by our moving to France* is therefore correct.

Mini-Test

Are the following sentences correct? If so, write *C* in the space provided; if not, write *X* and make the correction.

1. Would you object to us working on the holiday? _____
2. Him moving the truck from the scene of the accident prevented a traffic jam. _____
3. We are trying to arrange his being promoted to assistant manager. _____
4. I approve of you cycling to work. _____
5. Have you made plans for your son going to college? _____

KEY

1. X—our 2. X—his 3. C 4. X—your 5. X—son's

SUMMARY FOR UNIT 2.6

- Pronouns before an infinitive are always in the objective case.
- *Be* is a linking verb; therefore it takes the same case after it as before it. This rule also applies to the infinitive *to be*.
- Pronouns and nouns coming before a gerund are always in the possessive case.

Confirm Your Knowledge

Complete Exercise for Unit 2.6 on page 89.

PROBLEMS WITH MODIFIERS AND VERBS

❍ 2.7 Adjective or Adverb; Comparisons

Adjectives modify nouns or pronouns; adverbs modify verbs, adjectives, or other adverbs.

1. Use an adverb, not an adjective, to modify a verb.

   He spoke loudly (*not* loud) to the old man.
2. Use an adverb, not an adjective, to modify an adjective or another adverb.

   The snow is really (*not* real) good for skiing this year.
3. Use an adjective after a linking verb. If in doubt, substitute *is* for the verb; if the sentence still makes sense, then you have a linking verb and an adjective, not an adverb, should be used after it.

   The proposal sounds good to me. (The proposal is good.)

   The child looks happy. (The child is happy.)

   The figures appear accurate. (The figures are accurate.)

These adjectives describe the subject of the sentence. They answer the question "What kind of?" subject.

An adverb describes the manner of the action. It answers the questions How? When? Where? or Why?

The child looks happy. (describes the child)

The child looks happily at the new toy. (describes how the child looked)

Some verbs are sometimes linking verbs and sometimes action verbs. (See Unit 1.2.) Care must be taken in using an adjective or an adverb with such verbs.

The doctor looked calm. (describes the appearance of the subject—adjective)

The doctor looked calmly at the wreckage. (describes how the doctor acted—adverb)

1. In general, use *well* and *ill* to describe health; use *good* and *bad* to describe state of mind or spirit.

   I feel well. (in good health)

   I feel good. (happy—in good spirits)

   I feel ill. (in had health)

   I feel bad. (upset, sorry—*never* badly)

Mini-Test

By using the delete mark (ℊ) or otherwise, indicate the correct words in the following sentences.

1. This is a real/really good report you have written.
2. The customer appeared impatient/impatiently at the delay.
3. Having won the sales contest, I feel good/well.
4. Charlie pulled strong/strongly on the wire and fastened it to the post.
5. Mr. Wilson drives too slow/slowly for safety.

KEY

1. really 2. impatient 3. good 4. strongly 5. slowly

Comparisons

Adjectives

When two persons or things are compared, use the comparative form. This is made by adding *-er* to the adjective.

He is the *smarter of* the two boys.

This rope is *stronger* than hemp rope.

When three or more persons or things are compared, use the superlative form. This is made by adding *-est* to the adjective.

He is the *smartest* of the three boys.

This rope is the *strongest* we have in stock.

If the adjective is long and if adding *-er* or *-est* makes it difficult to say, use *more, most, less,* or *least* instead.

This year's dresses are *more beautiful* than ever.

They are the *most beautiful* dresses we have ever had.

This schedule is *less demanding* than last week's.

This is the *least demanding* schedule of them all

Some adjectives are irregular in comparison.

good	better	best
bad	worse	worst
little	less	least
some	more	most

Adverbs

Adverbs are compared in exactly the same way as adjectives. An irregular adverb to remember is:

well	better	best

He works well.

Gordon works well, Kay works better, and Richard works best.

Mini-Test

Are the adjectives and adverbs correct in the following sentences? If so, write *C in* the space provided; if not, write *X* and correct the adjective or adverb only.

1. He came early than we expected. _______
2. She is the most accurate target shooter of the two. _______
3. This material is the most crease-resistant on the market. _______
4. Of the three plans, which is the better? _______
5. I have only a little work to do, but Ken has even less.

KEY

1. X—earlier 2. X—more 3. C 4. X—best 5. C

Absolute Adjectives

If a glass is full, then no more can be put in it—it cannot be "fuller" than it is! If it is empty, then it cannot be "emptier"! Adjectives such as *full, empty, complete, perfect, free,* are called absolutes and cannot be compared.

The carton was empty.

The accounts are correct.

This vase is unique.

If however, you want to compare things that are not quite full, complete, correct or any other of these adjectives, then use *nearly* to emphasize that the adjective is not absolute.

The first carton is nearly full.

The second carton is more nearly full

Of all the drawings, Roxanne's is the most nearly square

Sometimes this becomes a very awkward construction. If another suitable word or expression can be used, rewrite the sentence.

Other, Any, *and* All

To use these correctly in comparison, you must consider the meaning.

Correct: Prince Edward Island is a small province.

Wrong: Prince Edward Island is smaller than any province. (This implies that Prince Edward Island is not a province since it cannot be smaller than itself.)

Correct: Prince Edward Island is smaller than any other province. (By putting in the word *other*, you tell the reader that Prince Edward Island is also a province.)

Prince Edward Island is the smallest of all provinces. (not *any*, because it cannot be the smallest of itself)

Mini-Test

Are the adjectives and adverbs correct in the following sentences? If so, write *C* in the space provided; if not, write *X* and correct the adjective or adverb only.

1. This design is more complete than that design. _______
2. Hannah drives more carefully than any driver I know. _______
3. Your estimate is more correct than Roger's. _______
4. His opinion is the most valuable of all the criticisms received. _______
5. Our antiques are unique and more nearly perfect than any others available. _______

KEY

1. X—more nearly complete 2. X—any other 3. X—more nearly correct 4. C 5. C

Common Problems with Modifiers.

1. Do not use double negatives.

   Not: They didn't have hardly any food left.

   But: They had hardly any food left.

   Not: He didn't do nothing.

   But: He didn't do anything. *Or:* He did nothing.
2. Use *this* or *that* with *kind*; *these* or *those* with *kinds.*

   These kinds of cars, compact and mid-size, are economical.

   This kind of video appeals to teenagers.
3. Always use the possessive case of a pronoun as an adjective, not the objective.

   Those (not *them)* runners have already left.
4. Do not use the expressions *this here, these here, that there* and *them there.*

   These (not *These here*) dishes are clean.

   This (not *This here*) dish is not clean.
5. Do not use the article *a* with *kind of.*

   That kind of (not *kind of an*) answer is not acceptable.
6. Use *most* and *almost* carefully. *Almost* means "nearly."

   Most players practise daily.

   The season is almost over. (nearly over)

   Use *almost,* not *most,* with *all*, *everybody*, and *everyone.*

   Almost (not *Most)* all of the players practise daily.

   Almost (not *Most*) everybody likes to play.
7. Do not use *quicker* as an adverb; use *more quickly* or *faster.*

   Louise runs more quickly than Marie.

   Quicker is correctly used as an adjective.

   We are looking for a quicker way to make deliveries.

Mini-Test

By using the delete mark ( ) or otherwise, indicate the correct words in the following sentences.

1. Almost/Most all of us have reccived a raise.

2. He completed the course quicker/more quickly than his brother.
3. This kind of a/kind of wine is very popular.
4. These here/These supplies are not to be removed by no one/anyone.
5. I strongly believe that most/almost everyone is honest.

KEY

1. Almost 2. more quickly 3. kind of 4. these, anyone 5. almost

SUMMARY FOR UNIT 2.7

- Use an **adjective:**
  - after a linking verb to describe the subject
- Use an **adverb:**
  - to modify a verb, to describe the manner of the action
  - to modify an adjective or another adverb
- Compare **two** things, persons, or situations by using the *–er* form of an adjective or adverb.
- Compare **three or more** things, persons, or situations by using the *–est* form of the adjective or adverb.
- Use *more, most, less, least,* rather then *–er* or *–est* with long words.
- Absolute adjectives such as *full, complete, correct* cannot be compared; however, *nearly full, nearly complete,* and *nearly correct* can be compared by using *more* or *most.*
- Take care with *any, other,* and *all* in comparisons.
- Special points:
  - Do not use double negatives.
  - Do not use *this here, that there.*
  - *Do* not use *kind of a.*
  - Do not use *quicker* for *more quickly.*
  - Use *almost* (not *most*) when meaning "nearly."
  - Use *really* (not *real*) when meaning "very."
  - Use *bad* for upset or sorry—never *badly*!

Confirm Your Knowledge

Complete Exercise (for Unit 2.7) on page 90.

❍ 2.8 Tenses and Moods

Tenses

Tenses are different verb forms that are used to describe the time of the action of the sentence. Choosing the correct tense form of an irregular verb or keeping the tenses uniform within the same sentence is not always easy. This section will help you overcome problems with tenses.

Present Tense

The present tense describes current action or continuous action happening now.

The cat *wants* food.

Harold *likes* to swim.

I *am studying* French.

Facts that are always true are written in the present tense.

Laslo told us that Paris *is* the capital of France.

He informed us that Georgio *is* the correct spelling of his name.

Past Tense

The past tense describes action that happened before the current time.

I *wrote* to her yesterday. (a one-time action I did in the past)

At that time I *was* ready to make a statement. (a particular point of time in the past)

To indicate action completed at some indefinite time in the past or continuing in the past, use the auxiliary verbs *has* or *have* with the past participle.

We *have collected* all the facts now.

He *has sent* applications to many agencies.

I *have agreed* to join the group.

Note: When *already* and *yet* are used for emphasis, use *has* or *have* plus past participle.

He *has* already *sent* applications to many agencies. (not *He already sent*...)

Have you *memorized* your part yet? (not *Did you memorize*...)

To describe action that was *completed* before a definite time in the past, use the auxiliary verb *had* with the past participle.

We *had collected* all the facts before the witness arrived.

Had you *memorized* your part before you learned that the play was cancelled?

Some Points About Participles

1. The past participle usually adds *d* or *ed* to the simple form of the verb.

   They *have lived* in Toronto for ten years.

   Alex *has joined* a jazz band.

   He *had entered* all the data by noon.

2. Many past tenses and participles are irregular. The following table shows the correct forms for some of the more common irregular verbs.

Irregular Verb Forms

Present	Past	Past Participle
begin	began	begun
blow	blew	blown
break	broke	broken
burst	burst	burst
choose	chose	chosen
come	came	come
dive	dived	dived
drink	drank	drunk
eat	ate	eaten
fall	fell	fallen
forget	forgot	forgotten
freeze	froze	frozen
get	got	got
go	went	gone
hide	hid	hidden
lay	laid	laid
lead	led	led
lie	lay	lain
lose	lost	lost
pay	paid	paid
prove	proved	proved or proven
ride	rode	ridden
rise	rose	risen
run	ran	run
say	said	said
set	set	set
shine	shone	shone
show	showed	shown
shrink	shrank	shrunk
sink	sank	sunk
sit	sat	sat
speak	spoke	spoken
swim	swam	swum
take	took	taken
tear	tore	torn
wear	wore	worn
write	wrote	written

3. Always use *has, have,* or *had* with the past participle.

   I *have eaten* (not *ate*) all my lunch.

   He *has* often *spoken* (not *spoke*) on this subject.

4. Always use the past participle when an adjective is needed.

   The *fallen* pole was *hidden* behind the wall.

Future Tense

The future tense describes action that is going to happen at some time yet to come.

Your lawnmower *will be* ready on Tuesday.

I *will go* to Victoria on August 19.

Sometimes the present tense and the *-ing* form of the verb also describe action about to happen.

We *are starting* production tomorrow.

Mr. Wang *is bringing* his brother with him next week.

Mini-Test

Are the verbs in italics correct in the following sentences? If so, write *C* in the space provided; if not, write *X* and make the correction.

1. I have read the letter before I talked to you. _____
2. Has Max spoke to Avril about the exchange? _____
3. The accountant already reported the deficit. _____
4. On July 24, 1991, we opened a branch in Thunder Bay. _____
5. These jeans have shrank so much I want to return them. _____

KEY

1. X—had read 2. X—spoken 3. X—has already reported 4. C 5. X—have shrunk

Mood

The mood of a verb indicates the way the verb is used. There are three moods in the English language.

1. **Indicative**

   The indicative mood states a fact or asks a question.

   The cellular phone is a useful invention.

   Who invented the cellular phone?

2. **Imperative**

   The imperative mood gives a command or makes a request.

   Send your suggestions to Ms. Heinrich immediately.

   Please let me have a copy of your itinerary in Mexico.

   (The subject *you* is understood, not stated, in the imperative mood.)

3. **Subjunctive**

   There are three main uses of the subjunctive mood.

   a) In certain traditional phrases, indirect commands, and legal resolutions.

      So *be* it. (not *is)*

      He insists that we *be* included. (not *are*)

      I move that Ranjan *complete* the presentation. (not *completes*)

   Note that the verb takes the simple infinitive form.

   b) In statements that cannot be facts:

      If she *were* James, she would understand. (She can't be James.)

      If I *were* not riding with you, I would stay at home. (but I am riding with you)

   Note the use of *were* in all cases.

   c) After *as if* and *as though* when the condition is unreal or improbable.

      She looked as if she *were* going to deny it. (but she didn't)

      They cared for the lost boy as though he *were* their own. (but he wasn't)

   Note the use of *were* in all cases.

   But: It looks as if the estimates *are* closed. (They are closed—no unreal or improbable condition.)

Transitive and Intransitive Verbs

Transitive verbs, indicated by *v.t.* in most dictionaries, take objects; intransitive verbs (*v.i.*) do not take objects.

We made spaghetti for supper. (*Spaghetti* is the object of *made*—transitive verb.)

We *hope* that the weather will improve. (no object—intransitive verb)

Hint: The prefix *trans* means "across"; for transitive verbs, the action moves "across" to an object.

Mini-Test

In the following sentences some verbs are in italics. What mood are these verbs in, and are they transitive or intransitive? In the spaces provided, write *IND* for indicative, *IMP* for imperative, or *SUB* for subjunctive; write *v.t.* for transitive or *v.i.* for intransitive.

Example: Who *was driving* the car? IND v.t.

1. The travel agent *made* the reservations for us. _____ _____
2. *Wrap* the package carefully. _____ _____
3. If he *were* prepared, he would not take so long. _____ _____
4. Ms. Velez demands that all mail *be* ready by 4 p.m. _____ _____
5. Please *reply* before October 9. _____ _____

KEY

1. IND v.t. 2. IMP v.t. 3. SUB v.i. 4. SUB v.i. 5. IMP v.i.

SUMMARY FOR UNIT 2.8

- **Tenses** of verbs indicate the time of the action.
- There are three major groups of tenses.
  - present—now, today, not changing, continuous; also just about to happen
  - past—before now, yesterday, a particular action or time in the past
  - *has* or *have* + past participle for action completed sometime in the past or continuous in the past
  - *had* + past participle for action completed at a particular time in the past before another action in the past
  - future—tomorrow, next year, or some time yet to come
- Use *have* or *has* with *already* and *yet.*
- The **past participle** is always used with *has, have,* or *had.*
- The past participle is also used as an adjective.
- Take care with irregular past participles.
- The **mood** of a verb indicates the way in which it is used.
  - indicative—statement or question
  - imperative—command or request
  - subjunctive—indirect command, impossible situation, or after *as if* or *as though*
- Verbs in the subjunctive mood:
  - Use *be* (not *is, are*) for indirect commands and in legal resolutions
  - Use the simple infinitive form of other verbs for all persons. (*Note*: there is no *s* on the 3rd person singular.)
  - Use *were* for all statements that are not true.
- Transitive verbs take objects; intransitive verbs do not.

Confirm Your Knowledge

Complete Exercise for Unit 2.8 on page 92.

2.9 Troublesome Verbs

Some verbs are particularly confusing. Study this unit very carefully to be absolutely sure of their use.

Lie–Sit

Remember that *lie* and *sit* (each has an *i* in it) are *i*ntransitive verbs; therefore, they do not take an object.

If you are tired, *lie* down for a while.

Garbage *is lying* all over the yard.

He *lay* under the sun lamp for so long that he got a bad burn. (past tense)

Please *sit* in the reception area while you are waiting.

The children *are sitting* on the floor.

The dog *sat* quite patiently looking at its master.

Lay–Set

Lay and *set* are transitive verbs; therefore, they have objects.

Please *lay* the documents on the desk.

The builders are *laying* the foundation.

They *laid* most of it yesterday.

She *set* the displays around the room.

We *are setting* the stage for the show.

Yesterday, he *set* the posts in concrete.

Lain–Laid

Remember *lain* is *in*transitive and must always have *has*, *have*, or *had* with it.

I *have lain* in the sun too long.

The old stock *has lain* on the shelves for months.

Laid is transitive and must have an object.

I *have laid* the dishes on the table.

Tom *laid* the old stock on the floor.

Mini-Test

Complete the following short sentences with the correct form of *lie* or *lay*.

1. He has decided to _____ down.
2. _____ the samples on the counter.
3. The samples are _____ on the counter.
4. They have _____ there all week.
5. She has _____ the tiles on the bathroom floor.
6. Yesterday, he _____ in his bed till noon.
7. Calgary _____ south of Edmonton in Alberta.
8. David is _____ out the plans for the garden.
9. He _____ the grass beside the driveway last week.
10. Are my keys _____ on my desk?

KEY

1. lie 2. Lay 3. lying 4. lain 5. laid 6. lay 7. lies 8. laying 9. laid 10. lying

Other Verbs to Watch

Should–Would

Use *should* to express obligation.

She should telephone home. (*Ought to* may be used in place of *should.*)

Use *would* to express a wish or request.

Would you like to go to the theatre with me on September 29?

Can–May

Do not confuse *can* and *may*. *Can* means "to be able to."

Matthew can run really fast.

Can you pay your bill in full by the end of the month?

May means "to be allowed to."

May we visit you in hospital? (Are we allowed to?)

You may answer the mail in my absence. (You are allowed to.)

May we send you samples of our new line? (Will you allow us to?)

May also expresses possibility.

He may be late if the roads are bad.

Might

Might is the past tense of *may*. In expressing possibility, *might* suggests more doubt than *may*.

She may leave. We told her that she might leave early. (permission)

We might be able to complete the project sooner than scheduled. (possibility)

Mini-Test

By using the delete mark ( ) or otherwise, indicate the correct word in the following sentences.

1. Can/May you divide the work fairly among the whole crew?
2. He said he may/might be able to come, but I doubt it.
3. They should/would like to go to Hawaii this year.
4. If you require a rental car, you should/would give us at least one day's notice.
5. Can/May we use your name as a satisfied customer so that we can/may promote our products in your region?

KEY

1. Can 2. might 3. would 4. should 5. May, can

SUMMARY FOR UNIT 2.9

- **Lie** and **sit** are intransitive verbs and take no object.
  - *Lain* is intransitive—no object.
  - *Lay* is the past tense of *lie.* Yesterday I lay in the sun.
- **Lay** and **set** need objects.
  - *Laid* needs an object. I laid the dishes on the table.
- Use *should* for obligation and condition.
- Use *would* for a wish or request.
- *Can* means "able to;" *may* means "allowed to."
- *Might* implies a possibility.

Confirm Your Knowledge

Complete Exercise for Unit 2.9 on page 93.

DEVELOPING YOUR LANGUAGE SKILLS

❍ 2.10 Vocabulary

Definitions

Check your dictionary for the meanings of the following words; then match them up with the definitions given. Write the letter of the definition you choose from Column 2 in the space provided in Column 1.

Column 1	Column 2
_____ ascertain	a) amount owing, not paid
_____ appraise	b) find out, determine
_____ arrears	c) having more than one meaning, not clear
_____ ambiguous	d) clearly said, detailed
_____ accrue	e) estimate the value of
_____ apportion	f) without action for the time being
_____ abeyance	g) shortage between amounts of money
_____ solicit	h) divide fairly
_____ explicit	i) make an appeal for
_____ deficit	j) add up
	k) give a compliment

Mini-Test

Complete the following sentences by choosing the most appropriate word from Column 1 under "Definitions."

1. Please __________________ from the comptroller the amount of interest that will __________________ in five years.
2. The lawyer will __________________ the balance of the estate among the heirs.
3. Because of a temporary shortage of funds, the decision regarding the new building is being held in __________________
4. Be sure your instructions are __________________ so that there is no chance of their being __________________
5. After allowing for the __________________ between the amount actually owing and the amount showing on the bill, the customer is still $27.50 in __________________
6. Have your jeweller __________________ your ring and necklace so that we can insure them.
7. May we __________________ your help in arranging transportation for the delegates?

KEY

1. ascertain, accrue 2. apportion 3. abeyance 4. explicit, ambiguous 5. deficit, arrears 6. appraise 7. solicit
Be sure you checked your spelling of these words!

Usage

Study the following groups of words carefully so that you are sure which one to use.

amount/number

amount—quantity by mass (how much?—cannot be counted)	The amount of gas used was considerable.
number—quantity by count (how many?—can be counted)	A number of cats were fighting.

bring/take

bring—carry toward the speaker	Please bring me the latest figures.
take—carry away from the speaker	Take the garbage to the dump.

cannot/can not

cannot—most common way	I am sorry I cannot attend.
can not—emphatic	I can not support your decision.

canvas/canvass

canvas—rough cloth	Canvas is a strong, rough material.
canvass—to solicit	He agreed to canvass for the Red Cross.
—to examine carefully	We have canvassed the neighbourhood for the opinions of the residents.

cite/site/sight

cite—to quote or summon	The lawyer cited the precedent.
—to mark for special notice	He was cited for his brave action.
site—place or location	Have you chosen the site for the new ice rink?
sight—vision, view	His sight is good. Keep your goals in sight.

Mini-Test

Complete the following sentences by choosing the correct word from those shown at the beginning of the sentences.

1. *amount/number*
   What is the __________________ of concrete needed? Please let me know the __________________ of kilograms required.

2. *bring/take*

   ________________ last month's sales figures with you when you go to New York.

   ________________ last month's sales figures with you when you come on Wednesday.

3. *cannot/can not*

   Gene said the installation ________________ be finished by Friday.

   I have repeatedly said that we ________________ wait any longer.

4. *canvas/canvass*

   The sturdy ________________ in our backpacks ensures that they will withstand rough handling.

   Do you want to ________________ the area for votes?

5. *cite/site/sight*

   Please ________________ the documents from which your reference was taken.

   The ________________ for the new church has been approved.

   Keep in ________________ the final dates for submission of ________________ plans for the new houses.

KEY

1. amount, number 2. Take, Bring 3. cannot, can not 4. canvas, canvass 5. cite, site, sight, site

Spelling

Study the following words very carefully paying particular attention to the letters underlined. Write out the words at least ten times each, and be sure you know their meanings!

One Single and One Pair

omitted	satellite	cellular
omission	necessary	across
disappoint	*proceed	accumulate
disapprove	recommend	occasion
parallel	dilemma	commit

*Note the spelling of *procedure* (one *e* is dropped).

Mini-Test

By using the delete mark (ℊ) or otherwise, correct any errors in spelling in the following words. There may be more than one error in a line.

1. commit	dilemma	dissapprove
2. paralell	cellular	satellite
3. across	ommission	disappoint
4. omited	acummulate	reccommend
5. procede	neccessary	occasion

KEY

1. dissaprove 2. paralell 3. ommission 4. omited, acummulate, reccommend 5. procede neccessary

SUMMARY FOR UNIT 2.10

- Use your dictionary to check meanings.
- Usage
  - Number you can count; amount you cannot.
  - Bring to me; take from me.
  - Only use *can not* as two words for extreme emphasis.
  - A building location is a site.
- Spelling
  - Remember words with one single letter and one pair of letters.

Confirm Your Knowledge

Complete Exercise for Unit 2.10 on page 94.

2.11 Proofreading

As everyone makes mistakes, it is important to be able to correct them easily. Editors and proofreaders have agreed on certain symbols to represent certain corrections or changes, some of which are included in Unit 1.10. This unit and subsequent proofreading units will introduce you to some more symbols.

Don't forget the importance of the method and technique you use for proofreading: concentrate on the meaning and details of grammar and punctuation, checking every detail thoroughly.

Space # Close-up Marks ⊂

To indicate that a space is required, use the insert mark (^) and the symbol for a space #

Insert aspace here.

Separate these twowords.

Occasionally too much space is left between words or letters. To indicate this, use close-up marks.

Delete the space between the se letters.

Delete too much space between these   words.

In the final printed copy, these examples would appear as follows:

Insert a space here.

Separate these two words.

Delete the space between these letters.

Delete too much space between these words.

Move [ ] ⌐ ⊔

Depending on the position of these symbols, the revised text will be moved to the left, to the right, up, or down. If the distance of the move is not obvious, the number of spaces the material should be moved is written inside the bracket.

Line up the second line

 with the first line.

  Move this line over to the left margin.

5 Indent this line five spaces.

This   was out of line.
word

These examples would appear in the final material as follows:

Line up the second line

with the first line.

Move this line over to the left margin.

     Indent this line five spaces.

This word was out of line.

Mini-Test

Use the space, close up, and move symbols to proofread the following paragraphs, which should all have an indention of five spaces.

A legal document requires very careful proofreading. The figures and words must becarefully checked for accuracy, and the wor ding of the document must be absolutely clear so that there is no chance of misinterpretation by anyone reading it.

It is very difficult to proofread your own work. I therefore suggest that you always have someone else check   your work with you, particularly ifthe document is very important or contains alot of figures.

With practice you will become a proficient proofreader. One thing you must always check is that nospaces between words have been omitted.

KEY

Line 2—becarefully Line 3—wor ding Line 5—chance Line 6—5 It
Line 8—check your, —ifthe Line 9—alot Line 13—nospaces

Reinstate or "Stet" (.....)

Occasionally a proofreader or an editor will delete or change a word unnecessarily. To correct the proofreader's marks, draw a dotted line underneath, and write the word *stet* (Latin for "let it stand") in the margin.

Do not remove this word.

Your application has been very carefully considered.

These examples will appear in the final text as follows:

Do not remove this word.

Your application has been very carefully considered.

Mini-Test

In the following sentences some words have been deleted or changed. In some cases the change is correct; in others, the original writing is correct. By using the reinstate marks and writing *stet* in the margin beside the sentence, show which sentences should be left as they were originally written. Write *C* beside those sentences where the proofreader's changes are correct.

1. The ~~procedure~~ proceedure for reporting injuries is posted on the wall by the door.
2. The manager has ~~has~~ announced the date for the sales contest.
3. Leave the brochures ~~laying~~ lying on the counter beside the display.

KEY

1. stet procedure 2. C 3. C

SUMMARY FOR UNIT 2.11

- Proofreading is very important as everyone makes mistakes.
- Pay attention to detail and content when proofreading.
- Symbols for changes to spacing:
  - # ^ insert space
  - delete ⁀ space (close-up)
- Symbols for moving material:
  - ⊓ move up
  - ⊔ move down
  - ⊏ move to left
  - ⊐ move to right
  - 10] move to right ten spaces
- Reinstate (stet) (.....)
  - A dotted line underneath a proofreader's mark means the material is to be left as it was before it was changed.
  - *Stet* means "let it stand" and is written in the margin.

Confirm Your Knowledge

Complete Exercise for Unit 2.11 on page 95.

PRETEST FOR UNIT 2

Complete all the parts of this test according to the directions for each part. The figures in parentheses are the unit numbers for reference, if necessary, when you have completed the test.

Your Goal: To score a total of at least 64 points.

A. General Rules

Are the following statements true or false? If true, circle *T*; if false, circle *F*. Score 1 point for each correct answer.

			Score
1.	Words coming between the subject and the verb are ignored when checking whether the verb is correct. (2.1)	**T F**	_____
2.	It is not important to know the subject of a sentence before you choose a singular or plural verb. (2.1)	**T F**	_____
3.	Inserting "one" after "each" will help you remember to use a singular verb. (2.2)	**T F**	_____
4.	The use of *his or her* depends on whether you are referring to one or more people. (2.4)	**T F**	_____
5.	The words *here* and *there* are never subjects. (2.3)	**T F**	_____
6.	Facts that are always true are written in the present tense. (2.8)	**T F**	_____
7.	Expressions such as "this here" or "that there" are good ones to use. (2.7)	**T F**	_____
8.	Collective or group nouns such as *jury* and *committee* are always singular in meaning.(2.2)	**T F**	_____
9.	The "self" prounouns such as *himself* are used only for emphasis and cannot be used alone. (2.5)	**T F**	_____
10.	There are very few irregular verbs in English.(2.8)	**T F**	_____
		Score for Part A	_____

B. Agreement of Subject and Verb (2.1, 2.2, 2.3)

Complete the sentences by choosing the correct word from the following list and writing it in the space provided.

is are has have

Score 1 point for each correct answer.

		Score
Example:	Maria, as well as Thomas, has received a raise.	1
1	The results of the survey _____ been summarized.	_____
2.	Neither the cold weather nor the bad road conditions ____ responsible for the delay.	_____
3.	Half of the work _____ been completed.	_____
4.	The acoustics of the hall _____ being tested.	_____
5.	I think that $50 _____ too much to pay for one hour's work.	_____
6.	The head custodian or one of his helpers _____ repaired the broken window.	_____
7.	The company _____ opening a new branch in New Glasgow.	_____
8.	The only really important item on the agenda for Friday's meeting ______ production schedules.	_____
9.	Mumps _____ a childhood disease that causes a great deal of discomfort.	_____
10.	Everybody _____ invited to the opening ceremonies.	_____

11. Natchez, Holmes, & Rodriguez _____ sending an estimate for the electrical work. _____
12. This is one of the jobs that _____ waiting for spare parts. _____
13. There _____ been only six replies to our questionnaire. _____
14. One of you _____ sure to get the answer if you keep at it. _____
15. Neither of the supervisors _____ ready to submit a design. _____
16. The proceeds from the campaign _____ to be used for cancer research. _____
17. On the counter beside the water cooler _____ the sheets for signing in and out. _____
18. Some of the wire _____ not the right size. _____
19. Smith and Robertson _____ the two partners in the firm. _____
20. _____ the premiums for the insurance policy and the bill for the telephone been paid yet? _____

Score for Part B _____

C. Agreement of Pronouns (2.4)

Make any necessary corrections in pronouns in the following sentences. If a sentence is correct as written, write *C* beside it. Score 1 point for each correct answer.

Score

1. The committee has decided to allow Sunday shopping in their community. _____
2. All the women agreed that everyone should arrange their own transportation. _____
3. Peter and myself have investigated the claim. _____
4. Miss Marlowe was a much better performer than her. _____
5. The rule applies to the superintendent as well as to we tenants. _____
6. Everyone had to vacate his chair when the alarm rang. _____
7. Between you and me, I am greatly relieved at the drop in interest rates. _____
8. Roger is more confident than me. _____
9. I have not yet heard if Franco and me are both going. _____
10. Mr. Barbeau objected to him speaking so rudely. _____

Score for Part C _____

D. Unclear Reference of Pronouns (2.4)

Correct the following sentences to make sure all pronoun references are quite clear. Use your imagination to add any necessary information. Score 1 point for each correct sentence.

Score

1. They say the company was founded in 1911.

   ____ _____

2. In the manual it says to assemble the wiring carefully.

   ____ _____

3. The assembly line has been stopping for an afternoon break. This must not continue.

   ____ _____

4. Herbert & Sons allows its customers to leave bills unpaid for more than six months, which is not good business practice.

   ____

   ____ _____

5. Miriam said she would speak to Claire about her suggestion.

   ____ _____

Score for Part D _____

E. Who or Whom? (2.5)

Delete the incorrect word in italics in the following sentences. Score 1 point for each correct answer.

Score

1. *Who/Whom* did you ask about smoking regulations? _____
2. The mechanic *who/whom* works well will be promoted. _____
3. Many people *who/whom* I tried to interview would not make any comment. _____
4. Give the contract to *whoever/whomever* will complete the job earliest. _____
5. The adjuster, *who/whom* I understand from witnesses to the accident arrived within ten minutes, has sent you an estimate for the damage to my client's property. _____

Score for Part E _____

F. Problems with Modifiers (2.7)

Make any necessary changes to correct the following sentences. Write *C* beside any sentence that is correct as written. Score 1 point for each correct sentence.

Score

1. Newfoundland is larger than any of the Atlantic provinces. _____
2. The preparation work will be completed much quicker if you can let us have exact details of what is required. _____
3. These containers are more nearly full than the ones we received last week. _____
4. Of the two methods, the first one listed seems best. _____
5. Miss Hampton was real happy to be of assistance. _____
6. Almost everyone has agreed to the proposal. _____
7. I don't know of no other store which carries such a large assortment of fabrics. _____
8. Pack the fragile crystal very careful so that it will not be broken. _____
9. Your fruit trees should be pruned and sprayed regular to ensure good quality, healthy fruit. _____
10. We feel very badly about the death of your president. _____

Score for Part F _____

G. Problems with Verbs (2.8, 2.9)

Are the words in italics correct in the following sentences? If so, write *C* at the end of the sentence. If not, write *X* and make the necessary correction. Score 1 point for each correct answer. If the correction is not made, no marks will be allowed for that sentence.

Score

1. I discovered yesterday that oil *is* a fossil fuel. _____ _____
2. Ms. Rochester *has read* the article before she left last Wednesday. _____ _____
3. *Has* Mavis *wrote* to Mr. Kinsella yet? _____ _____
4. If I *were* the premier, I would be sure to have competent, well-informed advisers. _____ _____
5. You already *spoke* to Mr. Sampson about the faulty switch. _____ _____
6. Who left the photographic paper *laying* in the sun? _____ _____
7. *Can* you be sure to have the documents signed, sealed, and delivered by May 17? _____ _____
8. You *should* wear warm clothes in cold weather. _____ _____
9. The auditor told me that his name *was* Apa. _____ _____
10. Roberta *laid* the swatches of material on the table. _____ _____
11. Now that we have the necessary money, we *may* go ahead with the building of the new wing. _____ _____
12. Ian *was* staying here since Thursday. _____ _____
13. *Having completed* the survey, the doctors proceeded to compile statistics of the results. _____ _____
14. Those boxes have *laid* in the corner for six months now. _____ _____
15. *Have* you *went* through the records yet? _____ _____

Score for Part G _____

H. Proofreading and Vocabulary (2.10, 2.11)

Using proofreaders' marks, make any necessary corrections in the following sentences. Score one point for using the correct proofreaders' marks and making the correction; no marks are allowed for wrong symbols.

Example: What is the affect of heat on vinyl? (a marked out, e written above) 1

Score

1. The amount of coats on the rack makes it difficult to see them. _____
2. Doyou know the dates for the winter carnival? _____
3. You will not be disapointed with the materials we have substituted. _____
4. The Board of Directors agreed on the sight for the out-of-town branch. _____
5. It is neccessary to proofread carefully. _____

Score for Part H _____

Total Score _____

If you achieved your goal of at least 64 points, proceed to Unit 3. If you did not score 64, check with your instructor what parts you need to study. Proceed through Unit 2 doing all the necessary work; then do the posttest for Unit 2.

POSTTEST FOR UNIT 2

Complete all the parts of this test according to the directions for each part. The figures in parentheses are the unit numbers for reference, if necessary, when you have completed the test.

Your Goal: To score a total of at least 64 points.

A. General Rules

Are the following statements true or false? If true, circle *T*; if false, circle *F*. Score 1 point for each correct answer.

			Score
1.	The form of a verb in a sentence depends on whether the subject is singular or plural. (2.1)	**T F**	_____
2.	Two words separated by "or" take a verb that agrees with the first word. (2.1)	**T F**	_____
3.	A company or firm is usally considered as one unit taking a singular verb. (2.2)	**T F**	_____
4.	The "of" phrase coming after "some" will help you choose the correct verb form. (2.3)	**T F**	_____
5.	The words *who* and *whom* are interchangeable. (2.5)	**T F**	_____
6.	A pronoun must have a clear antecedent (one word to which it refers. (2.4)	**T F**	_____
7.	In comparing two things, use the "-est" form of an adjective, such as "strongest." (2.7)	**T F**	_____
8.	With group words such as "crowd" or "class" the verb may be singular or plural depending on the meaning. (2.2)	**T F**	_____
9.	"Which" and "this" should be used to refer to complete statements. (2.4)	**T F**	_____
10.	Verbs don't change to show differences in when the action takes place. (2.8)	**T F**	_____
		Score for Part A	_____

B. Agreement of Subject and Verb (2.1, 2.2, 2.3)

Complete the sentences by choosing the correct word from the following list and writing it in the space provided.

is   are   has   have

Score 1 point for each correct answer.

		Score
Example:	Maria, as well as Thomas, has received a raise.	1
1.	The marks from the exam _____ been entered in the computer.	_____
2.	Neither eggs nor chocolate _____ the cause of my allergic reaction.	_____
3.	A quarter of the assignment _____ been entered already.	_____
4.	The costs of renting the hall _____ been double checked.	_____
5.	I think that $120 _____ too much to pay for one hotel room in the city.	_____
6.	The manager or one of his salespersons _____ dealt with the customer's complaint.	_____
7.	The restaurant _____ closing because of the fire damage.	_____
8.	The only really important item on this month's office supply order _____ printer ribbons.	_____
9.	Measles _____ a very contagious childhood disease, which can be very severe in adults.	_____
10.	Everybody _____ requested to attend the monthly meeting.	_____
11.	Zannella and Bardwell Carpeting _____ sending an estimate for the carpeting in the reception area.	_____

12. This is one of the desks that _____ waiting to be repaired. _____
13. There _____ been only two requests for computer time today. _____
14. One of you _____ sure to win the office lottery. _____
15. Neither of the counsellors _____ available just now. _____
16. The proceeds from the bike-a-thon _____ to be used for leukemia research. _____
17. On the desk beside the switchboard _____ the forms for the president to sign. _____
18. Some of the paper _____ not the correct colour. _____
19. Farnell and Jonathon _____ the two coaches of the team. _____
20. _____ the car rental fees and the bill for the hotel conference room been paid yet? _____

Score for Part B _____

C. Agreement of Pronouns (2.4)

Make any necessary corrections in pronouns in the following sentences. If a sentence is correct as written, write *C* beside it. Score 1 point for each correct answer.

Score

1. The group has decided to publish their report in May, instead of September. _____
2. All the actors agreed that everyone should buy their own costumes and props. _____
3. George and myself have researched the new drug. _____
4. Madame Marlonzie was a much better magician than her. _____
5. The regulation applies to the parking attendants as well as to we supervisors. _____
6. Everyone rose to his feet when the anthem was played. _____
7. Between you and me, I am very excited about the new laser printer. _____
8. Emmanuel is a faster driver than me. _____
9. I have discovered that Lynn and me both speak French fluently. _____
10. Miss Jonti appreciated him finishing the sanding for her. _____

Score for Part C _____

D. Unclear Reference of Pronouns (2.4)

Correct the following sentences to make sure all pronoun references are quite clear. Use your imagination to add any necessary information. Score 1 point for each correct sentence.

Score

1. They say that smoking contributes to pollution.

   ______________________________ _____

2. In the article it says to prune fruit trees in the fall.

   ______________________________ _____

3. The truck has been breaking down. This must not continue.

   ______________________________ _____

4. Turner Isaacson department store gives unlimited credit, which is not good business practice.

   ____

   ______________________________ _____

5. Carl said he would write to Trevor about his idea

   ______________________________ _____

Score for Part D _____

E. Who or Whom? (2.5)

Delete the incorrect word in italics in the following sentences. Score 1 point for each correct answer.

Score

1. *Who/Whom* did you speak to about repairing the screens? _____
2. The writer *who/whom* works consistently will become published. _____
3. Many farmers *who/whom* I asked to try our new fertilizer were hesitant about it. _____
4. Give the music to *whoever/whomever* will be able to perform it best. _____
5. The vice-president, *who/whom* I understand from the board of directors has extensive advertising experience, was very helpful in the planning of the campaign. _____

Score for Part E _____

F. Problems with Modifiers (2.7)

Make any necessary changes to correct the following sentences. Write *C* beside any sentence that is correct as written. Score 1 point for each correct sentence.

Score

1. Prince Edward Island is the smallest of any Canadian province. _____
2. The final report will be completed much sooner if you answer the questionnaire promptly. _____
3. These boxes are more nearly full of paper clips than the ones I opened last month. _____
4. Of the two letters, the second one seems clearest. _____
5. Miss Frederick was real pleased to receive a raise. _____
6. Most everyone has agreed to repaint the dressing rooms. _____
7. I don't know of no other sport that is half as exciting as football. _____
8. Pack the microwave oven very careful so that it will not be damaged. _____
9. Your oil should be checked and changed regular to ensure fuel efficiency in your car. _____
10. We will send you the latest phone book when it is ready. _____

Score for Part F _____

G. Problems with Verbs (2.8, 2.9)

Are the verbs in italics correct in the following sentences? If so, write *C* at the end of the sentence. If not, write *X* and make the necessary correction. Score 1 point for each correct answer. If the correction is not made, no marks will be allowed for that sentence.

Score

1. I read in the paper yesterday that sand *is* simply eroded quartz rock. _____ _____
2. Ms. McDonlan *has found* that the fax machine broke down before she needed to use it._____ _____
3. Has Kate *spoke* to the mail clerk yet?_____ _____
4. If I *were* the floor supervisor, I would make sure that all the merchandise was clearly displayed. _____ _____
5. He already *wrote* to Mr. Wells concerning the city map. _____ _____
6. Who left the compact discs *laying* in the sun? _____ _____
7. *Can* you please make sure that the reports are proofread, corrected, and on my desk in the morning? _____ _____
8. Your credit has been approved so you *would* have no more problems. _____ _____
9. The secretary told me that today's date *was* May 5. _____ _____
10. Evelyn *laid* the memos on the desk. _____ _____
11. Now that we have government funding, we *may* proceed to update our communications system. _____ _____
12. Ivan *was staying* in the shop late today. _____ _____
13. Having finished examining the application forms, the personnel manager *decided* which applicants to interview. _____ _____
14. Those forms *have set* in that drawer for days now. _____ _____
15. Has he *went* to Calgary for the conference yet? _____ _____

Score for Part G _____

H. Proofreading and Vocabulary (2.10, 2.11)

Using proofreaders' marks, make any necessary corrections in the following sentences. Score one point for using the correct proofreaders' marks and making the correction; no marks are allowed for wrong symbols.

Score

Example: What is the affect of heat on vinyl? (a struck through, *e* written above) 1

1. The number of carton in the warehouse is growing rapidly, as new shipments are constantly arriving. _____
2. Is it possible for youto attend our seminar? _____
3. The election commitee has only two weeks left to buy radio time for advertising. _____
4. Which sight has been chosen for the company picnic? _____
5. No correction should be ommitted in this test. _____

Score for Part H _____

Total Score _____

If you achieved your goal of at least 64 points, proceed to Unit 3.If you did not score 64, check with your instructor what parts you need to review before moving on.

EXERCISE 2.1 PERSON AND NUMBER; COMPOUND SUBJECTS

By using the proofreaders' marks to delete wrong words, indicate the correct words in the following sentences. Score 1 point for each correct answer.

Your Goal: To score at least 8 points.

Example: Neither Brian nor the Attwoods was/were to be found 1

Score

1. Mr. Pelez, as well as his assistant, is/are expected to come. _____
2. His goal was/were to produce three different models each week. _____
3. The chest of toys was/were sitting on the kitchen floor. _____
4. Neither Eric nor I am/are experienced in drilling. _____
5. A banquet and dance is/are being planned in honour of Mrs. Lee. _____
6. Not only the electricians but also the designer need/ needs the wire immediately. _____
7. The result of the investigation was/were increases in the number of arrests. _____
8. The secretary and treasurer has/have heavy responsibilities. _____
9. The special assignment you gave Roberto and the time limit you placed on completing the work is/are totally impracticable. _____
10. Either the accountant or one of her assistants has/have made an error. _____

Total Score _____

If you achieved your goal of at least 8 points, proceed to Unit 2.2. If you did not score 8, go back and review Unit 2.1 thoroughly; then do Exercise 2.1A and try to achieve your goal this time.

EXERCISE 2.1A PERSON AND NUMBER; COMPOUND SUBJECTS

Use the same directions as for Exercise 2.1.

Your Goal: To score at least 8 points.

Score

1. A needle and thread is/are included in each package. _____
2. The vice president and general manager has/have to sign all cheques. _____
3. Mme. Benoit, together with M. Goulet and M. Henri, has/have accepted our invitation _____
4. Your suggestions has/have made a great improvement in our operations. _____
5. Either Nancy or one of the trainees is/are needed at the store next week. _____
6. A truckload of freezers was/were dispatched on November 25 to your Saskatoon warehouse. _____
7. Neither petitions nor a walkout was/were effective in preventing the shutdown. _____
8. Not only the mechanics but also the civil engineer request/requests a longer lunch break. _____
9. The aftermath of the storm was/were broken windows, damaged roofs, and downed hydro poles _____
10. The manual, which will run to several hundred pages and which will not be ready for two months, has/have already been started. _____

Total Score _____

If you achieved your goal of at least 8 points, proceed to Unit 2.2. If you did not score 8, ask your instructor for direction before moving on.

EXERCISE 2.2 COLLECTIVE NOUNS

By using the proofreaders' marks to delete wrong words, indicate the correct verbs in the following sentences. Score 1 point for each correct answer.

Your Goal: To score at least 8 points.

Example: Mathematics is/~~are~~ her favourite subject. 1

Score

1. One of the cars has/have been marked down by $500. ______
2. Politics is/are a time-honoured career. ______
3. Each one of these printers need/needs servicing. ______
4. Much of the theft by employees has/have been stopped. ______
5. One-quarter of the books has/have been damaged in transit ______
6. Many a successful entrepreneur has/have worked seven days a week without any vacation. ______
7. A number of customers was/were in the store at the time of the robbery. ______
8. Black, Greene, & Grey has/have the largest selection of hiking boots and backpacks. ______
9. The hockey team was/were asked to donate their old sticks to their community teams. ______
10. The savings during our pre-school sale is/are fantastic. ______

Total Score ______

If you achieved your goal of at least 8 points, proceed to Unit 2.3. If you did not score 8, go back and review Unit 2.2 thoroughly; then do Exercise 2.2A and try to achieve your goal this time.

EXERCISE 2.2A COLLECTIVE NOUNS

Use the same directions as for Exercise 2.2

Your Goal: To score at least 8 points.

Score

1. Many a person has/have regretted dropping out of school. ______
2. Only five percent of the population has/have voted. ______
3. No one was/were available for comment after the debate. ______
4. Mathematics is/are essential for an engineer. ______
5. Anybody is/are eligible to try for the vacant position. ______
6. The number of accounts outstanding has/have risen. ______
7. Secrett and Foster is/are a large advertising agency. ______
8. The co-operative is/are being asked to renew its lease. ______
9. Each of the items was/were checked thoroughly. ______
10. Every one of the carpenters was/were working overtime. ______

Total Score ______

If you achieved your goal of at least 8 points, proceed to Unit 2.3. If you did not score 8, ask your instructor for direction before moving on.

EXERCISE 2.3 INVERTED ORDER AND OTHER SPECIAL CASES

By using the delete mark, indicate the correct verbs in the following sentences. Score 1 point for each correct answer.

Your Goal: To score at least 8 points.

Example: Do you think that thirteen is/~~are~~ an unlucky number? 1

Score

1. A hundred kilometres is/are too far to drive after the game. ______
2. Is/Are any of the flower arrangements ready for dispatch? ______
3. He claimed that $240 was/were the price he paid. ______
4. Theirs is one of the automobiles that is/are being recalled. ______
5. All the pieces of the puzzle is/are falling into place. ______
6. Some of the customers has/have complained about the delay in deliveries. ______
7. Every hammer, every screwdriver, and every wrench is/are owned by the company. ______
8. Rossi is the only one of the accountants who is/are familiar with fax machine maintenance. ______
9. *Meatballs* was/were a film that started a Hollywood career for a Canadian actor. ______
10. There is/are only 27 shopping days to Christmas. ______

Total Score ______

If you achieved your goal of at least 8 points, proceed to Unit 2.4. If you did not score 8, go back and review Unit 2.3 thoroughly; then do Exercise 2.3A and try to achieve your goal this time.

EXERCISE 2.3A INVERTED ORDER AND OTHER SPECIAL CASES

Use the same directions as for Exercise 2.3

Your Goal: To score at least 8 points.

Score

1. Ten hours is/are a long time between flights. ______
2. Mr. Pike is the only one of the data processors who is/are able to program the machine. ______
3. Is/Are there any of the samples left over? ______
4. The $100 is/are a bonus for exceptional work. ______
5. Some of the pipeline is/are being laid today. ______
6. Leah is one of the models who wants/want to be considered. ______
7. None of them is/are responsible for the accident. ______
8. Each brush and mop has/have to be requisitioned from supplies. ______
9. There is/are among the papers a letter from James Brothers. ______
10. I understand The Pirates of Penzance is/are still being performed by professional and amateur groups. ______

Total Score ______

If you achieved your goal of at least 8 points, proceed to Unit 2.4. If you did not score 8, ask your instructor for direction before moving on.

Exercise 2.4 Antecedents and Clear Reference

Where necessary, correct or rewrite the following sentences. Write the corrections or revisions above the errors. If a sentence is correct as written, write *C* beside it. Score 1 point for each correct answer or rewritten sentence. Your answers may vary slightly from the key. Check with your instructor if you are not sure how to score your answers.

Your Goal: To score at least 8 points.

has received

Example: ~~They have given~~ this play ^ excellent reviews. 1

Score

1. Valerie's teacher is proud of what she writes. ______
2. Every one of the astronauts did their part in promoting the project. ______
3. The committee was relieved at their success. ______
4. They say that Mary is often late for work. ______
5. I am glad Suzanne and yourself have entered the contest. ______
6. First the items must be assembled, which has to be done in the receiving room. ______
7. Costs have risen greatly this month, and it is difficult for poor families to manage. ______
8. Wingfield and Law have hired two new sales representatives, but we haven't used their services yet. ______
9. One should complete one's income tax return immediately one receives all one's T4 slips. ______
10. Your request for our latest catalogue has just been received. Same is being mailed to you today. ______

Total Score ______

If you achieved your goal of at least 8 points, proceed to Unit 2.5. If you did not score 8, go back and review Unit 2.4 thoroughly; then do Exercise 2.4A and try to achieve your goal this time.

Exercise 2.4A Antecedents and Clear Reference

Use the same directions as for Exercise 2.4

Your Goal: To score at least 8 points.

Score

1. He said that he had agreed to the suggestion. ______
2. If parents would only make time to talk with their teenagers, it would save a lot of heartache. ______
3. In Mustafa's essay he tells about life in India. ______
4. Asparagus is difficult to grow; that is why I have none in the garden. ______
5. Everyone has to wash his or her own dishes. ______
6. Do not put electric appliances in water. This is very dangerous. ______
7. The executive has agreed to their meeting again in two weeks. ______
8. Miles and myself have just opened a new store in your neighbourhood. ______
9. Milk turns sour very easily, which makes it difficult to take on a long trip. ______
10. Planning for one's retirement may call for the advice of a financial expert. ______

Total Score ______

If you achieved your goal of at least 8 points, proceed to Unit 2.5. If you did not score 8, ask your instructor for direction before moving on.

EXERCISE 2.5 CASE OF PRONOUNS; WHO AND WHOM

By using the delete mark, indicate the correct pronouns in the following sentences. Score 1 point for each correct answer.

Your Goal: To score at least 8 points.

Example: Who/~~whom~~ is your supervisor? 1

Score

1. Jacinthe can calculate interest more quickly than he/him. _____
2. Send out a brochure to whoever/whomever wants one. _____
3. With who/whom have you discussed this? _____
4. Everybody has reported except Mr. Crowther and he/him. _____
5. Your invitation to my wife and I/me is very much appreciated. _____
6. The mailing clerks know who/whom is responsible for packaging the samples. _____
7. Our customers have asked we/us sales representatives to call early in the day. _____
8. Have we received a reply yet from whoever/whomever asked for the applications? _____
9. Ms. Vail, who/whom I am sure you will remember, has agreed to speak at the luncheon. _____
10. We are all to blame for the mistake—Miss Cory, Mr. Simpson, and I/me. _____

Total Score _____

If you achieved your goal of at least 8 points, proceed to Unit 2.6. If you did not score 8, go back and review Unit 2.5 thoroughly; then do Exercise 2.5A and try to achieve your goal this time.

EXERCISE 2.5A CASE OF PRONOUNS; WHO AND WHOM

Use the same directions as for Exercise 2.5

Your Goal: To score at least 8 points.

Score

1. Give the vouchers to whoever/whomever needs them most. _____
2. The document has to be signed by all of us—Fred, Arlene, and I/me. _____
3. From who/whom are we awaiting confirmation? _____
4. We/Us sportsminded people like good equipment. _____
5. The decision rests with you and he/him. _____
6. She is the only one on who/whom we can really depend. _____
7. The thank-you letter should be addressed to whoever/whomever sent the donation. _____
8. Marguerite, who/whom I am honoured to report has won another trophy, will be the guest speaker at the banquet. _____
9. Sarah Goldstein told us that Michael and she/her would represent the company at the fair. _____
10. Ed has been asked to work overtime more often than they/them. _____

Total Score _____

If you achieved your goal of at least 8 points, proceed to Unit 2.6. If you did not score 8, ask your instructor for direction before moving on.

EXERCISE 2.6 PRONOUNS WITH INFINITIVES AND GERUNDS

Are the pronouns in the following sentences correct? If so, write *C* beside the sentence; if not, make the correction. Score 1 point for each correct answer.

Your Goal: To score at least 8 points.

Example: ~~Who~~ Whom do you want to complete this task? 1

Score

1. Have you agreed to him taking his vacation now? ______
2. Tell him to leave the car at the airport. ______
3. The dancers seemed to be them. ______
4. Who do you want to have the new desk? ______
5. Do you know whose writing was on the memo? ______
6. Your progress depends on you taking some night school courses during the winter. ______
7. Mikhail has requested our assessing the damage caused by the hurricane. ______
8. I believed the intruders to be them. ______
9. You scoring the test yourself would save time. ______
10. We do not want to influence him thinking. ______

Total Score ______

If you achieved your goal of at least 8 points, proceed to Unit 2.7. If you did not score 8, go back and review Unit 2.6 thoroughly; then do Exercise 2.6A and try to achieve your goal this time.

EXERCISE 2.6A PRONOUNS WITH INFINITIVES AND GERUNDS

Use the same directions as for Exercise 2.6

Your Goal: To score at least 8 points.

Score

1. We appreciate you allowing us to leave early. ______
2. I am confident that Brian studying so hard will ensure his success. ______
3. Are you ready for us expanding our services? ______
4. Please ask her to be waiting in the reception area. ______
5. You reported that the witness was her. ______
6. Who do you want to complete the job? ______
7. Whose advertising shall we use this year? ______
8. Him recording the results as soon as possible would be appreciated. ______
9. Good audio-visual equipment will help their learning in difficult subjects. ______
10. The visitor was believed to have been me. ______

Total Score ______

If you achieved your goal of at least 8 points, proceed to Unit 2.7. If you did not score 8, ask your instructor for direction before moving on.

EXERCISE 2.7 ADJECTIVE OR ADVERB; COMPARISONS

Use the directions given for each part. Score 1 point for each correct answer.

Your Goal: To score at least 12 points in total.

Part A

Are the following sentences correct? If so, write C beside them; if not, make the correction.

Example: Quebec is larger than any ^other province. 1

Score

1. Do you know what sort of a job you would like? ______
2. He had to ask the child to speak louder. ______
3. Of all the dancers, he worked harder. ______
4. These answers are more correct than the first ones. ______
5. Your most recent art work is better than any you have previously submitted. ______

Score for Part A ______

Part B

By using the delete mark or otherwise, indicate the correct word in the following sentences.

Example: Of the two lamps, this one sheds the softer/~~softest~~ light. 1

Score

1. Cedric didn't do too bad/badly in the exam. ______
2. It was real/really good of you to volunteer. ______
3. The new layout for the garden looks good/well to me. ______
4. She brought the flowers special/specially for June. ______
5. The jockey was real/really sorry to have lost the race. ______
6. I didn't see none/any of the intruders. ______
7. Pamela showed me her very unique/most unusual collection. ______
8. Of that group of performers, Bruce seemed the more/most talented. ______
9. Martina buys most/almost all her racquets at this store. ______
10. The class remained quiet/quietly while the inspector was there. ______

Score for Part B ______

Total Score ______

If you achieved your goal of at least 12 points, proceed to Unit 2.8. If you did not score 12, go back and review Unit 2.7 thoroughly; then do Exercise 2.7A and try to achieve your goal this time.

EXERCISE 2.7A ADJECTIVE OR ADVERB; COMPARISONS

Use the directions given for each part. Score 1 point for each correct answer.

Your Goal: To score at least 12 points in total.

Part A

Are the following sentences correct? If so, write C beside them; if not, make the correction. ______

Example: Quebec is larger than any ^other^ province. 1 Score

1. That there fruit has been badly damaged. ______
2. These fabrics are more perfect than those. ______
3. I have the same kind of a computer as you. ______
4. Victor is a more capable project leader than all the other leaders I have ever had. ______
5. Of all the hotels I have stayed in, the Pines Country Inn is the most luxurious. ______

Score for Part A ______

Part B

By using the delete mark or otherwise, indicate the correct word in the following sentences.

Example: Of the two lamps, this one sheds the softer/~~softest~~ light. 1 Score

1. You look good/well in that style of coat. ______
2. The drawings you submitted were real/really detailed. ______
3. Nicholas didn't listen close/closely enough to the instructions. ______
4. Ma Brown's is the tastier/tastiest of the two cakes. ______
5. Try to change gears smoother/more smoothly when you are driving. ______
6. Mr. Barrie said it would sure/surely be inconvenient if payment of the mortgage did not arrive soon. ______
7. He was so angry he could/couldn't hardly speak. ______
8. The panelist responded quick/quickly to the criticism. ______
9. She distributed the questionnaire to most/almost everyone in the building. ______
10. Meredith seemed real/really nervous before the presentation. ______

Score for Part B ______

Total Score ______

If you achieved your goal of at least 12 points, proceed to Unit 2.8. If you did not score 12, ask your instructor for direction before moving on.

EXERCISE 2.8 TENSES AND MOODS

Are the verbs in italics in the following sentences correct? If so, write *C* beside them; if not, make the correction. Score 1 point for each correct answer.

Your Goal: To score at least 8 points.

Example: I have already ~~*wrote*~~ written my thank-you letters. 1

Score

1. *Did* Mr. Saunderson telephone yet? ______
2. The latest studies *proved* that the rainforests in South America *were* responsible for the quality of our atmosphere. ______
3. It seems as if our estimate *was* correct after all. ______
4. I *was reading* this novel since I last saw you. ______
5. He called to make sure that she *had arrived.* ______
6. Because customer demand *has increased*, we had to enlarge our inventory. ______
7. I suggested that he *see* a doctor about his complaints. ______
8. If I *was* you, I would accept that offer. ______
9. Reminiscing about him like this makes me feel as though he *was* here. ______
10. We *have placed* an order with them last year. ______

Total Score ______

If you achieved your goal of at least 8 points, proceed to Unit 2.9. If you did not score 8, go back and review Unit 2.8 thoroughly; then do Exercise 2.8A and try to achieve your goal this time.

EXERCISE 2.8A TENSES AND MOODS

Use the same directions as for Exercise 2.8

Your Goal: To score at least 8 points.

Score

1. Alida already *completed* her section of the decorations. ______
2. The federal government announced that health care *was* a vital issue. ______
3. The VCR *was taping* since nine o'clock last night. ______
4. If she *was* here, she wouldn't know what to do either. ______
5. I informed the directors that I *had prepared* the statistics prior to the meeting. ______
6. Mr. Reinders insists that these photographs *are* enlarged. ______
7. Hans looked after that rented house as though it *were* his own. ______
8. I told Eleanor last week that this week *was* the final sale period for that item. ______
9. If he *was* more co-operative, you might have included him in the assessment committee. ______
10. Sheila *has* rode in so many bicycle races she is well prepared for this one. ______

Total Score ______

If you achieved your goal of at least 8 points, proceed to Unit 2.9. If you did not score 8, ask your instructor for direction before moving on.

EXERCISE 2.9 TROUBLESOME VERBS

By using the delete mark, indicate the correct verb in the following sentences. Score 1 point for each correct answer.

Your Goal: To score at least 12 points.

Example: His clothes were lying/~~laying~~ all around the room. 1

Score

1. I can/may finish the surveys today if you need them. _____
2. If you had the opportunity, should/would you attend? _____
3. The exhausted players were laying/lying on the gym floor. _____
4. It may/might be easier if we were to lie/lay some groundwork before trying to sell this package to them. _____
5. Thanks to your assistance, we can/may have this job completed by lunchtime. _____
6. Our small leather goods department can/may meet its monthly quota if you agree to continue the sale. _____
7. Should/Would the weather permit, you can/may expect us for the picnic lunch. _____
8. The chef asked him to sit/set the recipes on the table, but he lay/laid them on the counter. _____
9. If you would/should come in the side entrance, watch for the dog laying/lying by the door. _____
10. You have lain/laid in the sun so many times you may/might be at risk for skin cancer. _____

Total Score _____

If you achieved your goal of at least 12 points, proceed to Unit 2.10. If you did not score 12, go back and review Unit 2.9 thoroughly; then do Exercise 2.9A and try to achieve your goal this time.

EXERCISE 2.9A TROUBLESOME VERBS

Use the same directions as for Exercise 2.9

Your Goal: To score at least 10 points.

Score

1. Adam would/should think about continuing his studies. _____
2. The hostess would/should like to have the table lain/laid before the guests arrive. _____
3. In order to truly relax, you should/would remain sitting/setting in this recliner for thirty minutes. _____
4. Because of the leak, the plant should/would be shut down so that we can/may test all the containers. _____
5. I'm going to lie/lay down for a while before I go home. _____
6. Can/May we send you a copy of our new seed catalogue? _____
7. The bricklayers lay/laid all the bricks in one morning. _____
8. The threat of a bad snowstorm may/might mean that rush hour traffic will start earlier. _____
9. You will be lying/laying a solid foundation for your child's education by registering her in our preschool classes. _____
10. Can/May I help you to pick up your groceries at the store? _____

Total Score _____

If you achieved your goal of at least 10 points, proceed to Unit 2.10. If you did not score 10, ask your instructor for direction before moving on.

EXERCISE 2.10 VOCABULARY

Complete the three parts of this exercise according to the directions for each part.
Your Goal: To score at least 16 points.

A. Definitions

Complete the following sentences by choosing the most appropriate words from those given. Score 1 point for each correct answer.

ascertain	appraise	arrears	ambiguous	accrue
abcyance	solicit	explicit	deficit	apportion

Score

1. We have been asked to ______________ your advice on how to make up the ______________ in our budget. ______
2. I cannot understand your requirements as some of your statements are ______________. Please let me have a more ______________ request. ______
3. Mrs. Eddy has asked us to ______________ her furniture as she is thinking of selling some of it. ______

Score for Part A ______

B. Usage

Use the same directions as for Part A.

amount	number	cite	site	bring	take
sight	cannot	can not	canvas	canvass	

Score

1. The ______________ for the 1992 Olympic Games was Barcelona. ______
2. I have been asked to ______________ samples with me when I come in November. ______
3. The ______________ of rain this year has damaged the tomato crop, and we ______________ hope to make a profit. ______
4. Be sure to ______________ your hand luggage with you on the plane when you leave for Europe. ______
5. At the moment we ______________ hope to sell all the damaged chairs, so put them out of ______________ at the back of the store. ______
6. We have harvested a record ______________ of tonnes this fall. ______
7. Your help with our program to ______________ your employees for donations was very much appreciated. ______
8. Until recently, most tents and kitbags were made of ______________. ______

Score for Part B ______

C. Spelling

By using proofreaders' marks or otherwise, correct any spelling errors in the following words. Write the correct spelling above the word if necessary. Score 1 point for each correctly changed word; deduct 1 point for each word changed that was correct as written.

					Score
1. parallel	reccommend	omission	dissappoint	accumulate	______
2. across	ommitted	proceed	committed	cellular	______
3. occasion	disaprove	sattelite	dilemma	necessary	______

Score for Part C ______

Total Score ______

If you achieved your goal of at least 16 points, proceed to Unit 2.11. If you did not score 16, go back and review Unit 2.10 thoroughly before moving on.

EXERCISE 2.11 PROOFREADING

Complete each part of this exercise according to the directions given.

Your Goal: To score at least 8 points in total.

Part A

Are the following statements true or false? If true, circle *T*; if false, circle *F*. Score 1 point for each correct answer.

		Score
1. A swift glance is all that is necessary to proofread.	**T F**	_____
2. The symbol is used for a space.	**T F**	_____
3. The symbol means the material should be moved to the left	**T F**	_____
4. If the material is to be moved more than one space, the number of spaces is written inside the bracket.	**T F**	_____
5. The word *stet* and a dotted line under a deleted or changed word means that the original word is correct and should be reinstated.	**T F**	_____
Score for Part A		_____

Part B

Proofread the following letter very carefully using proofreaders' marks to make corrections where necessary. Score 1 point for each error found and marked correctly; deduct 1 point for each error missed! Do not make any changes to punctuation.

Example: Thank you for you letter of Febuary 10. (Score 1 for correct marking of Febuary; deduct 1 for missing *your* before "letter.") 0

Dear Mr. Joseph

The comments you made on December 18 concerning investment in oil and gas stocks greatly interest me. However, Iam not very well-informed on the stock market and would like some further guidance.

I have some bonds coming due next month, and I am interested in getting the best return possible when I reinvest them.

May I have your advice on howto apportion my funds among the various oil and gas stocks that you reccommend? I would appreciate meeting with you to discuss this matter at your office
some time before December 31. Will you please phone me at 753-6222 to set a convenient time.

Yours very truly

Number of errors found and correctly marked	_____
Deduct for errors missed	_____
Score for Part B	_____
Total Score	_____

If you achieved your goal of at least 8 points, proceed to the Posttest for Unit 2. If you did not score 8, you will appreciate the need for accurate proofreading! Review Unit 2.11 thoroughly before moving on.

PUNCTUATION

Imagine the chaos on the roads if there were no traffic signs or traffic lights! It would be almost impossible to get from one place to another. Similarly, if there were no punctuation, it would be almost impossible for the reader to understand any written communication; the reader might even act on a wrong message. Thank goodness for traffic signs and lights on the roads; thank goodness, too, for the help that punctuation gives us in understanding the written word. This, then, is the reason for punctuation—to make your message absolutely clear to your reader.

END PUNCTUATION

❍ 3.1 Period, Question Mark, and Exclamation Mark

A period indicates a complete stop and is used at the end of a statement, an indirect question, or a polite request.

Baseball is Stuart's favourite game. (*Statement*)

He asked when the train was due. (*Indirect Question*)

Will you please send us your cheque today. (*Polite Request*)

A period is also used with many abbreviations (see Unit 4) including titles.

Dr., Mr., Mrs., Ms.

a.m. or p.m. to indicate morning or afternoon (only used when time is expressed in figures, as 4:15 p.m.)

p. for page; pp. for pages

e.g. meaning "for example"

Note: Periods are usually omitted in names of companies, organizations, and the call letters of broadcasting stations.

IBM YWCA CNIB CBC NDP CHEX

A period is also used as the decimal point in writing numbers.

0.23 17.8 $42.50

Mini-Test

Insert periods where necessary in the following sentences.

1. The manager asked if I would take charge of the mailing room
2. The cost of $253 67 to repair the car seemed exorbitant
3. Will you please let me know if the flight departing at 6:30 p m is convenient
4. Ms Woods asked the volunteers at the C N I B to work evening shifts, e g from 5 p m to 7 p m , to help with suppers
5. The N H L ice hockey games on home ice are televised by C B C and are copyright

KEY

1. room. 2. $253.67, exorbitant. 3. 6:30 p.m., convenient. 4. Ms., e.g., 5 p.m. to 7 p.m., suppers. (No periods in CNIB) 5. copyright. (No periods in NHL or CBC)

Question Mark

A question mark is used at the end of a direct question, a question that requires an answer.

What are the current prices of oranges from Florida?

When do you want your new dishwasher installed?

Will you be able to replace the broken vase?

Why has the government refused to reduce income taxes?

You will let us know the date of your opening, won't you?

Has the blueprint been sent to the contractor yet?

Note: A question mark is not used at the end of an indirect or reported question. A period is used instead.

He asked me if I knew the current prices of oranges.

We are still wondering why the government refuses to reduce taxes.

The supervisor requested that the blueprints be sent to the contractor immediately.

Mini-Test

Insert the correct end punctuation marks in the following sentences.

1. Do you know the date when the season opens
2. Mr. Watson signed the deed before he left, did he not
3. Suzanne asked whether she could change her vacation dates
4. Where are the policies covering third party liability
5. You will be informed where to pick up your prize

KEY

1. opens? 2. not? 3. dates 4 liability? 5. prize.

Other Uses of the Question Mark

Quoted material is the recording of the exact words someone said. If the quoted material is a question, then the question mark goes inside the quotation marks.

Raoul asked, "When will the meeting end?"

"What are the advantages for the members?" asked the union representative.

"Are you sure," he asked, "that you understand the instructions?"

If the material quoted is not a question, but the whole sentence is, then the question mark goes outside the quotation marks.

Did the clerk say to the customer, "You're welcome"?

How many times have you said, "I know that"?

Do you believe in the expression, "Honesty is the best policy"?

Only one question mark is necessary at the end of a sentence if both the quoted material and the whole sentence are questions.

Are you sure the electrician said,"Where is the master control box?"

Did you specifically ask, "Who will bring the first aid kit?"

A question mark enclosed in parentheses is used to express doubt.

The first store was opened in the Yukon in 1874 (?) by my great uncle.

Mini-Test

Insert the correct end punctuation marks in the following sentences.

1. The interviewer asked, "How long have you worked for your present employer
2. Did you know that Richard said, "Mr. Lada is responsible for tennis lessons
3. "Are you prepared," the lawyer asked, "for the cross examination
4. Have you answered the employee who wrote on the suggestion form, "The company should provide better lunchroom facilities
5. The doctor asked, "Have you had these symptoms before

KEY

1. employer?" 2. lessons"? 3. examination?" 4. facilities"? 5. before?"

Exclamation Mark

While the exclamation mark adds emphasis in advertising and sales promotion, it should be avoided in general correspondence. Use it only to express strong feeling or surprise. The positioning of the exclamation mark is the same as for the question mark. Note that interjections (Unit 1.3) are always followed by an exclamation mark.

Congratulations on your new daughter!

You are top sales representative for the tenth consecutive month!

Try our blueberries from St. Andrews-by-the Sea. They are absolutely delicious!

At last! Our shipment of original Michael Jackson videos has arrived.

How dare you state,"All big business is corrupt"!

The customer demanded, "I must have a Kleenrite dishwasher!"

Mini-Test

Insert the correct end punctuation in the following sentences.

1. The politician cried out, "These allegations are absolutely false
2. I just can't believe it
3. A favourite expression to denote urgency is "I want this yesterday
4. Absolutely free We will give you a travel bag if you buy a complete set of our luggage
5. Don't ever say, "I told you so

KEY

1. false!" 2. it! 3. yesterday!" 4. free! ...luggage. 5. so"!

Reminder: Use only one end punctuation mark at the end of a sentence.

The flight leaves at 4:30 p.m. (*not* p.m..)

If you are not sure about involved punctuation at the end of a sentence, consult a reference manual or a style guide. Such situations arise so seldom it is best to check each time.

SUMMARY FOR UNIT 3.1

- A **period** signals the end of a statement, an indirect question, or a polite request.
- A period is also used with abbreviations.
- Periods are usually omitted in names of companies, organizations, and call letters.
- A period is used as the decimal point in numbers.
- A **question mark** is used at the end of a direct question.
- In quoted material, if the quoted material is a question, the question mark goes *inside* the quotation marks.
- If the whole sentence is a question, then the question mark goes *outside* the quotation marks.
- A question mark may be used to express doubt.
- An **exclamation mark** expresses surprise or strong feeling and should be used sparingly.
- Use only one end punctuation point at the end of a sentence.

Confirm Your Knowledge

Complete Exercise for Unit 3.1 on page 127.

SEMICOLON AND COLON

❍ 3.2 Semicolon and Colon

Two punctuation marks that are also used at the end of statements are the semicolon (;) and the colon (:). They have other functions as well, which are explained in this unit.

Semicolon

Two or more independent clauses that are very closely related in thought may be joined by a semicolon. In other words, each clause on each side of the semicolon could stand alone as a complete sentence and could be separated by a period; however, the writer feels that they are more effective combined by a semicolon.

The president agrees with the goal of reducing costs; he does not agree with the suggested ways of doing so.

Mr. Pooran takes his vacation in July; Ms. Khan prefers hers in January.

Always check to see that you have a complete sentence on each side of the semicolon.

If the second of the two independent clauses begins with a conjunction such as *however*, *nevertheless*, *therefore*, or *consequently* (see Unit 1.3 for a longer list), a semicolon is usually used at the end of the first independent clause.

Jane is a newcomer to animal husbandry; nevertheless, her enthusiasm has been evident from the beginning.

The price of sugar has risen; consequently, the price of candy has also rise.

Note: A comma is used after the conjunction in the second sentence.

A semicolon is also used in a long, involved sentence to separate independent clauses joind by a coordinate conjunction where the use of a comma would cause confusion. In other words, if commas have already been used in a sentence, use a semicolon to separate independent clauses instead of a comma.

If the meeting is delayed until the arrival of the samples, we shall have difficulty in having our price list ready in time for printing; and I feel very strongly that the price list should be prepared immediately.

Our order was for staples, paper clips, and thumb tacks; but we received a stapler, pads of paper, and carpet tacks!

A semicolon is used to separate items in a series or list where commas are already used within the items.

On my trip to the west coast, I visited Selkirk, Red Deer, and Penticton. (no confusion)

On my trip to the west coast, I visited Selkirk, Manitoba, Red Deer, Alberta, and Penticton, British Columbia. (confusing—unless you know your geography well.)

On my trip to the west coast, I visited Selkirk, Manitoba; Red Deer, Alberta; and Penticton, British Columbia.

Note: If the sentence continues, a comma is used after the last item, not a semicolon.

On my trip to the west coast, I visited Selkirk, Manitoba; Red Deer, Alberta; and Penticton, British Columbia, before I reached Vancouver.

A semicolon is usually used before *for example*, *namely*, and *that is* when these words begin a clause.

Some of our employees have been with us for many years; for example, Mr. Stewart has worked here for 28 years.

Her qualifications are excellent; that is, she meets our prerequisities for the course.

Mini-Test

Insert semicolons where necessary in the following sentences. Also put in any commas that are necessary.

Example: Our special sale begins on May 18; therefore, we must receive your order before that date.

1. Our Moncton office will be closing June 30 for renovations it will reopen for business on July 15.
2. The materials are of excellent quality however the designs are not very attractive.
3. When writing instructions, try not to be ambiguous instead be as clear and specific as you can.
4. The union representatives are John Cassidy supervisor Phyllis Weinberg lathe operator and Ralph Meyers stock control clerk.
5. The faulty transmission has cost us millions of dollars for example we have had to retool all our machines to correct the error.
6. Our new offices will not be ready for occupancy until November meanwhile we shall serve you as best we can from our current, cramped quarters.

KEY

1. renovations; 2. quality; however, 3. ambiguous; instead, 4. John Cassidy, supervisor; Phyllis Weinberg, lathe operator; and Ralph Meyers, stock control clerk. 5. dollars; for example 6. November; meanwhile,

Colon

A colon is used to begin a list or series if an introductory expression such as *the following, as follows*, or *these* is used in the first part of the sentence.

The following players have been chosen for the chess tournament: Elsa Hansen, Ahmad Ahsan, Jack Livesey, and Josephine Blink.

These items are required immediately: 10 boxes pencils, HB; 20 pads of paper, narrow ruled; 12 felt markers, broad tipped, assorted colours.

A colon may be used to introduce a quotation that is very important.

> The Premier stated: "The environment must be saved, and we are committed to clean up our act immediately."

A colon is also used to indicate a formal notice or announcement.

> The bulletin read: The company is pleased to announce the appointment of Mr. James Sampson as Chair of the Board of Governors.
>
> The report stated: All entertainment of overseas visitors should be approved by Ottawa.

The colon is used to separate the hour and the minutes in expressions of time and numerical ratios.

> 9:15 a.m. to 4:30 p.m. The time is 07:30
>
> a ratio of 2:1

Mini-Test

Insert colons where necessary in the following sentences.

Example: Your flight leaves at 10:30 p.m.

1. Please ship the following as soon as possible 1 Toastmaster Oven, Model 428; 3 Pyrex casseroles, Model 577; and 2 Spatterproof trays, Model 325.
2. Your hours are from 1600 to midnight.
3. The announcement read The principal expects every teacher to cooperate during this emergency.
4. These are the advantages you will receive by replying early you will receive your first copy sooner, you will be eligible for our lucky draw, and you will receive a wall map of Canada absolutely free.

KEY

1. possible: 2. 16:00 3. read: 4. early:

Complicated Sentences

In long, complicated sentences, consult a reference manual or style guide for the correct punctuation.

SUMMARY FOR UNIT 3.2

- A **semicolon** is used:
  - to join two or more closely related sentences
  - before adverbs used as conjunctions, e.g., *however, therefore, otherwise,* when they begin a complete sentence
  - before a co-ordinate conjunction (*and, but, or, yet*) in long complicated sentences that already contain commas
  - to separate items in a list or series that already has commas
  - before *for example, namely, that is,* when these words begin a clause
- A **colon** is used:
  - to begin a list or series if a "collecting" word or phrase, such as *as follows, the following, these,* is used in the first part of the sentence.
  - to introduce a very important quotation
  - to indicate a formal notice or announcement
  - to separate hours and minutes
  - in numerical ratios
- If in doubt about any punctuation, consult a reference manual or style guide.

Confirm Your Knowledge

Complete Exercise for Unit 3.2 on page 129.

Comma

The only reason a comma is used in writing is to make the meaning of the sentence clear to the reader. It may be used between two words that might mistakenly be read together, or it may be used to indicate that certain words are not essential to the main thought of the sentence. Too many commas, however, may interrupt the flow of the sentence and may even be a distraction to the reader. In other words, before using a comma, make sure you really need it. The following units will help you use commas correctly and not overuse them.

3.3 Comma

Between Independent Clauses

A comma is necessary between two independent clauses joined by a co-ordinate conjunction (*and*, *but*, *or*, *nor*, *for*, and *yet*).

> Marion is a competent flute player, but she has difficulty with the trombone.
>
> I am sure the blueprints are ready, for I saw them on Mr. Brown's desk yesterday.
>
> We do not have a branch in Yellowknife, yet I feel we should open one there soon.
>
> Our shipmment of broccoli has not arrived, nor has our shipment of avocados and lettuce.
>
> Either the property rates must come down, or homeowners will be faced with very high property taxes.

If the second part of the sentence is *not* an independent clause, no comma is necessary.

> He passed his final exam in May, and he started his summer job in June.
>
> He passed his final exam in May and started his summer job in June. (no subject for the verb after the conjunction *and*; therefore no comma)

Mini-Test

Insert commas where necessary in the following sentences.

1. The gardener was negligent yet the plants somehow survived.
2. Continuing education offers an opportunity for skill improvement and many people are taking advantage of the many courses available.
3. Instructions regarding overtime payment will be issued tomorrow but overtime work will not commence until next week.
4. Print the menus on both sides but print the wine list on a separate sheet.
5. Nutritionists agree that hamburgers do have some food value and can contribute to a balanced diet.

KEY

1. negligent, 2. improvement, 3. tomorrow, 4. sides, 5. no comma as no subject for the verb *can* after the conjunction *and*

In a Series

A comma is necessary to separate items in a list or series. The items should be parallel in structure, that is, in the same form. Note that there is no comma after the last item in the list. There must be at least three items in the list before commas are used.

> Our representative will visit Campbelltown, Fredericton, and Saint John on his trip to New Brunswick in March. (all towns)
>
> He will demonstrate stripping, sanding, and finishing with our fine materials. (all nouns)
>
> He will give his demonstration in school halls, at shopping centres, and in church halls. (all prepositional phrases)

But: Mr. Wehrle will not visit Bathurst or Edmunston on his trip. (only two places listed—no comma)

Etc.

Use a comma before and after the abbreviation *etc.* when it is used as the last item in a list.

> Our hardware stock of nails, screws, bolts, nuts, etc., is the largest in the city.
>
> Canada's export of wheat, fish, uranium, etc., contributed to a strong economy in the 1980s.

Mini-Test

Insert commas where necessary in the following sentences.

1. Derek Allison and Walter have all three been asked to attend the conference.
2. Be sure to include instructions on how to assemble the model how to wire the engine and how to install the starter motor.
3. When planning a picnic, be sure to include salt and pepper rolls and butter paper plates and serviettes and cutlery for everyone.
4. The advent of word processing equipment has made office assistants' jobs more challenging more varied and more interesting.
5. Our sale of summer suits jackets coats blouses etc. will begin on July 1.

KEY

1. Derek, Allison, and... 2. model, how...engine, and 3. pepper, rolls and butter, paper...serviettes, and... 4. challenging, more varied, and... 5. suits, jackets, coats, blouses, etc....

SUMMARY FOR UNIT 3.3

- Use a comma only if you really need one.
- Always use a comma between independent clauses joined by *and*, *but*, *or*, *nor*, *for*, or *yet*.
- Do not use a comma if there is no subject for the verb in the second part of the sentence.
- Use a comma to separate items in a list or series where there are more than two items.
- Always use a comma before the last item but not after it.
- Use a comma before and after the abbreviation *etc.* in the middle of a sentence.

Confirm Your Knowledge

Complete Exercise for Unit 3.3 on page131.

3.4 More About the Comma

Introductory Words, Phrases, and Clauses

Use a comma after any word, phrase, or clause coming at the beginning of a sentence before the main or independent clause.

Yes, the setting of the thermostat has been checked.

Mr. Thompson, may I call on you some time next month?

In other words, the gear connecting the rod to the drive shaft needs replacing.

During the hot summer months, your furs will be cool and comfortable in our controlled temperature storage rooms.

As soon as we have a reply from the designer, we shall let you know our decision.

Whenever the initial survey has been completed, the government will subsidize all in-depth studies.

Be careful that these introductory words are, in fact, that and not part of the main clause.

To become really proficient in electronics, you will need to study electrical engineering at a university. (introductory phrase)

To become really proficient in electronics is Les's main goal. (subject of verb *is*—not an introductory phrase; therefore no comma)

Do not use a comma when a dependent clause comes in its normal order after the independent or main clause.

Whenever we receive your instructions, we shall proceed with the plans. (introductory clause—comma)

We shall proceed with the plans whenever we receive your instructions. (independent clause followed by dependent clause—no comma)

Hint: Think of introductory clauses as *if* clauses as in the following sentences.

If the *if* has a capital letter, you need a comma.

You do not need a comma if the *if* has a small letter.

Mini-Test

Insert commas after the introductory elements in the following sentences.

1. Having examined all the evidence the jury came to a decision.
2. No we do not need a further supply of flower vases.
3. Although your references are excellent we regret we do not have a suitable opening just now.
4. Sally has the order from Saks arrived yet?
5. After he left the meeting continued for another hour.
6. The nutritionist wrote out the diet because the patient was afraid that he would forget it.
7. If you agree with our suggestion please call us this week.

KEY

1. evidence, 2. No, 3. excellent, 4. Sally, 5. left, 6. no comma 7. suggestion,

Interruptions

When a word, phrase, or clause interrupts the flow of the sentence and is not essential to the main thought, a comma comes before and after the interruption unless a period is required for the end of the sentence.

You are aware, of course, that our guarantee covers parts only.

The jury, after discussing the case for six hours, could not come to an agreement.

Mr. Roberts, who has been hired to replace Mr. Baetz, will start work on September 15.

The young defendant wanted to speak with his mother, who is a prominent criminal lawyer. (end of sentence)

Mini-Test

Insert commas where necessary in the following sentences.

1. My supervisor Ms. Balbanian is out of town this week.
2. The pianist concluded the concert with I think a medley by Andrew Lloyd Weber.
3. The high cost of salaries however prohibits us from hiring more staff.
4. Les Haversham who designed the new mall on King Street will give you rough plans for your new office complex.
5. The carton you returned which was badly damaged has been inspected by our insurance adjusters.

KEY

1. supervisor, Ms. Balbanian, 2. with, I think, 3. salaries, however, 4. Haversham, who...Street, 5. returned, which...damaged,

Restrictive or Nonrestrictive

Restrictive means that the word, phrase, or clause in question is essential to the meaning of the sentence. No commas are used in such sentences.

The writer who develops the best slogan will receive an award.

The design that was accepted was also the cheapest to produce.

The letter we received from you today was postmarked ten days ago.

Nonrestrictive means that the essential meaning of the sentence is clear without the word, phrase, or clause in question.

Cam Ritchie, the writer who developed the best slogan, will receive an award.

The design from Foster Designs, which we had already accepted, was the cheapest to produce.

Your letter dated April 14, which took ten days to reach us, has been sent to the editor for inclusion in our next newsletter.

In sentences with clauses which could be restrictive or nonrestrictive, appropriate punctuation is often the only way to make the meaning clear to the reader.

Restrictive: The interviewer called for the next applicant who had completed the written test. (Some applicants had not completed the written test—the interviewer wanted the next one who had.)

Nonrestrictive: The interviewer called for the next applicant, who had completed the written test. (The interviewer took whoever was next in line whether or not the written test had been completed.)

That

The word *that* always begins a restrictive (essential) clause; consequently, no commas are ever used before a *that* clause. Note that in many cases *that* is omitted but is clearly understood.

We are sure that you will be entirely happy with your new sewing machine.

I think this is the most difficult problem we have ever faced. (I think that...)

You are aware, of course, that our guarantee covers parts only. (commas around the interruption *of course*—nothing to do with the word *that*)

Mini-Test

Insert commas only where necessary in the following sentences.

1. Are you aware that the air-conditioning unit has not been installed yet?
2. The woman who is in charge of maintenance has asked for an assistant.
3. I understand you are the person who has bought the house which is located on the southeast corner of Elm and Maple.
4. The insurance policies Nos. 401768 and 401769 which were prepared yesterday should be sent to the clients today.
5. I telephoned Hans Jensen who said he would be pleased to give a demonstration.

KEY

1. no commas—a "that" clause 2. no commas—"who" clause necessary to identify the woman 3. no comma after *understand*—"that" could be inserted; no comma after *person*—"who" clause necessary to identify which person; no comma after *house*—"which" clause necessary to identify *house* 4. 401769, which...yesterday, —not necessary to meaning 5. Jensen, who—name has already identified "who"; no comma after *said*—"that" could be inserted

SUMMARY FOR UNIT 3.4

Always use a comma:

- after a word, phrase, or clause that comes before the main or independent clause
- after an *If* clause that begins a sentence
- around (on both sides of) an interruption to the main thought
- around nonrestrictive clauses or clauses not essential to the meaning of the main independent clause

Do not use a comma:

- if a dependent clause comes after an independent clause in regular order (if the *if* has a small letter)
- if the phrase or clause at the beginning of a sentence is the subject of the sentence
- if a word, phrase, or clause is necessary to the meaning of the main or independent clause or is necessary to identify a person or thing
- with *that* clauses

Confirm Your Knowledge

Complete Exercise for Unit 3.4 on page 133.

❍ 3.5 Still More About the Comma

With Adjectives

When two or more adjectives come before a noun, separate the adjectives with a comma if the word *and* could be inserted. Test to see if *and* could be used by rewording the group of words including the adjectives.

a fast, economical car	a car that is fast and economical
a magical, enthralling story	a story that is magical and enthralling
a patient, cheerful person	a person who is patient and cheerful

Note: The comma takes the place of the word *and*, and there is no comma after the last adjective.

Some common nouns already include an adjective as part of the noun.

income tax	letter carrier
stone building	life insurance
licence plates	financial report
filing cabinet	real estate
fax machine	old jewelry
high school	legal assistant

An adjective coming before these nouns would not need a comma

overdue income tax	quarterly financial report
valuable real estate	efficient legal assis-= tant
grey stone building	local high school

The adjectives of colour are usually considered part of the noun.

pale green wallpaper	light blue material

Again the *and* test applies; if the rearranged words do not make sense with *and* in them, then no comma is used.

large bath towels	towels that are large and bath? (no—therefore no comma)
an ambitious, intelligent young man	a man who is ambitious and (yes) intelligent (no) and young?
A large steel filing cabinet	a cabinet that is large and steel and filing? (no—no commas)

Mini-Test

Insert commas where necessary in the following word groups.

1. colourful alluring brochures
2. well-strung graphite tennis racket
3. a shiny golden flute
4. dented rusty licence plates
5. powerful electron microscope
6. tangy hot spices
7. loud telephones
8. pocket-sized notebooks
9. efficient cheap gaskets
10. dirty wet newspapers

KEY

1. colourful, 2. well-strung, 3. no comma 4. dented, 5. no comma 6. tangy, 7. no comma 8. no comma 9. efficent, 10. dirty,

Commas with Addresses; Dates in Sentences

A comma separates the street, city, and province or state in an address. The postal code or American ZIP code is considered part of the province or state and is not set off by commas.

> Please send your catalogue to me at 56 Claywood Road, Willowdale, Ontario M2N 2R2.
>
> The Watsons' postal address is 325 Fayette Avenue, Mamaroneck, New York 10543, where they have lived since moving to the States.
>
> Oshawa, Ontario, has a large General Motors plant.

Note the comma after the last part of the address if the sentence continues.

A comma separates the day of the week from the month and the date from the year.

> Thursday, March 12, 1992, was the date of my citizenship hearing.

Your appointment is for 10:30 a.m. on Tuesday, May 2.

Note: there is no comma if only one part of the date is used or if only the month and year are used.

If this is not convenient, perhaps you could come on the following Thursday at the same time.

Your salary will be reviewed on June 1 of each year.

One campsite opened in Kamloops in July 1991 and another in Kelowna in September 1992.

Mini-Test

Insert commas only where necessary in the following sentences.

1. The contract was signed on Monday September 8 1980 at the Seagram Tower Calgary Alberta.
2. The contestants will arrive on Saturday May 8 by train and will be taken by bus to the competition site at 52 Sherbrooke Street West in Montreal.
3. The Hudson's Bay Company was founded in May 1670.
4. Madame Thibodeau left for Whitehorse in the Yukon on November 15 1990.
5. Our west coast studio is at 1010 Granville Street Vancouver British Columbia V6Z 1L5 on the fifth floor.

KEY

1. Monday, September 8, 1980,...Tower, Calgary, 2. Saturday, May 8, 3. no commas 4. November 15, 5. Street, Vancouver,...V6Z 1L5,

Other Comma Uses

1. Direct Speech

   Commas are used after or around words such as *he said* or *Mr. Filletti commented* when the actual words spoken are written.

   She answered, "I'll be happy to assist you."

   "That," Mr. Filletti commented, "has still to be decided."

   "Commas and periods," the teacher stressed, "always go inside closing quotation marks."

Remember that no quotation marks or commas are used for recorded speech when the actual words spoken are not used.

The teacher stressed that commas and periods always go inside closing quotation marks.

2. Direct Address

   When a name is used as though speaking to that person, the name is enclosed in commas.

   Should I ask for another opinion, Dr. James?

   I am pleased to announce that you, Sean, have been elected class president.

   Ms. Prokipchuk, these styles have been designed with you in mind.

3. When two words might mistakenly be read together, use a comma to separate them.

   As Rita said, nothing has been left to chance. (*Not* As Rita said nothing...)

   By the way, he answered all questions satisfactorily. (*Not* By the way he answered...)

4. A comma is used to separate repeated words.

   There are many, many occasions when you will enjoy your barbecue.

   The pollution of our lakes is a very, very serious concern.

5. Do not use commas with large figures; leave space instead to divide the figure into groups of three digits starting to count from the right.

   75 389 6 498 661

But: 1000 (no space necessary with a four-digit number unless it is appearing in a column of figures with larger numbers)

Mini-Test

Insert commas where necessary in the following sentences. Use the insert mark with the space symbol #^ to show where a space is needed.

1. On your trip to the Maritimes Miss Bell be sure to visit Fundy National Park.
2. Theresa asked "Why do we use heavy bond paper paper that is very expensive?"
3. The odometer of the used car showed it had been driven 23330 km.

4. Many people do not know there is a dry dry desert in British Columbia.
5. Until he answers the question is still open for debate.

KEY

1. Maritimes, Miss Bell, 2. asked,...paper, paper 3. 23330 4. dry, dry 5. answers,

SUMMARY FOR UNIT 3.5

- **Always use a comma:**
  - between adjectives if the word *and* could be inserted
  - to separate parts of an address or a date in sentences
  - to separate words such as "he said" in recording the actual words spoken
  - around a name when writing as though speaking to a person
  - to separate words that might otherwise be read together
  - to separate repeated words
- **Do not use a comma:**
  - if only the month and year are used in a date
  - with large numbers; leave a space instead
  - when reporting what someone said but not using the actual words spoken

Confirm Your Knowledge

Complete Exercise for Unit 3.5 on page 135.

APOSTROPHE

❍ 3.6 Contractions and Possessives

There are two main uses of the apostrophe: to show where letters have been omitted in forming contractions and to form adjectives indicating possession.

Contractions

In a contraction, the apostrophe shows where certain letters have been omitted. Contractions are often used in conversation and advertising but should not be overused in writing.

can't (cannot)
haven't (have not)
don't (do not); doesn't (does not)
I'm (I am)
they'd (they would or they had)
won't (will not)
we've (we have)
it's (it is)
they're (they are)
he's (he is or he has)
who's (who is or who has)
she'll (she will)
o'clock (of the clock)

Mini-Test

Use the inverted insert symbol with an apostrophe to indicate where apostrophes are necessary in the following sentences.

1. You cant do without the latest edition of our new dictionary, which were offering right now for only $20.
2. Hes due to arrive on the ten oclock train tonight.
3. Well sign the contract as soon as its confirmed.
4. At an auction, dont let anyone distract you while youre bidding.
5. Whos the person youve transferred to New Zealand?

KEY

1. can't 2. He's, o'clock 3. We'll, it's 4. don't, you're 5. Who's, you've

Possessives

An apostrophe is added at the end of a noun to make it into an adjective of possession. Usually an *s* is required after the apostrophe.

Tom has a coat.	Tom's coat is on the chair.
Many women have successful businesses	Many women's businesses are successful.
Ms. Lewis has a cat.	Ms. Lewis's cat is fat.
Anybody can have a guess.	It is anybody's guess when the strike will end.
Alberta has oil.	Alberta's oil industry is booming.
Her mother-in-law made a will.	Her mother-in-law's will was read yesterday.

Mini-Test

In the following sentences add an apostrophe and an *s* to all nouns used as adjectives of possession.

1. Children shoes come in many styles.
2. Mrs. Daly driveway is the next to be repaved.
3. Mr. Velez has written a letter to the boy parents.
4. The report from the machine shop supervisor is very informative.
5. It is nobody concern how much you earn.

KEY

1. Children's 2. Mrs. Daly's 3. boy's 4. no apostrophe—no adjective of possession 5. nobody's

An *s* is not required after an apostrophe in the following instances.

1. When the noun to be made into an adjective of possession is plural and ends with an *s*. A helpful way to find where the apostrophe goes is to turn the phrase into an *of* phrase or a similar type of phrase.

   boys' roller blades (roller blades of the boys)

   students' records (records of students)

   the Adamses' garden (the garden of the Adamses)

   a girls' self-defence course (a self-defence course for girls)

2. When the noun to be made into an adjective of possession already has two sounds of *s* or is otherwise awkward to pronounce.

   Cassius' win Mr. Hedges' car

Note: Remember that proper nouns form plurals in the same way as other nouns.

Mr. Adams	The Adamses have moved to Moose Jaw.

Mini-Test

Add an apostrophe where necessary in the following sentences. Do not add an *s* after the apostrophe.

1. Babies clothing is on the third floor.
2. The plumbers union has called off the threatened strike.
3. The personnel department keeps all employees files.
4. All the drivers uniforms need to be cleaned.
5. The Rosses TV set has been repaired.

KEY

1. Babies' clothing 2. plumbers' union 3. employees' files 4. drivers' uniforms 5. Rosses' TV set

Special Uses of the Apostrophe for Possession

1. Joint or Individual Possession

   If two or more people own one thing, the apostrophe comes after the last name.

   Have you tried Otto and Karl's new salon?

   Mr. Wong and Miss Hue's design won the award.

   If two or more people each own a similar thing, an apostrophe is used after each name.

   It is seldom a buyer's and a seller's market at the same time.

   Mozart's and Beethoven's music is magnificent.

2. Expressions of Time and Measurement

a week's vacation	today's special
two months' supply	a moment's notice
fifty dollars' worth	six hours' delay
this morning's paper	

3. Before a Gerund

   In Unit 1.4, you learned that a gerund is always a noun. If a gerund follows a noun or pronoun, then an apostrophe or the possessive case of the pronoun must be used to turn the noun or pronoun into an adjective of possession.

   The fireman's reporting the damage was very helpful.

   Your revising the advertising copy saved me time.

4. Possessives Standing Alone

   Sometimes the noun following the adjective of possession is not written because it is clearly understood.

   The heavy equipment will be at the Browns' by March 15. (the Browns' house, yard, site)

   This year's productivity is much better than last year's. (productivity)

Mini-Test

Insert an apostrophe and an *s* where necessary in the following sentences.

1. Tony and Luigi workbench is being moved to a better position.
2. We need two weeks notice of any change in the schedule.
3. Rosa resigning has put a heavy workload on the rest of the staff.
4. An inspection of Hilda and Greta work habits showed that they both need help.
5. Make an appointment at the doctors for a thorough examination.

KEY

1. Tony and Luigi's workbench 2. two weeks' notice 3. Rosa's resigning 4. Hilda's and Greta's work habits 5. doctor's (office)

Summary for Unit 3.6

- The **apostrophe** is used for **contractions** in the place where letters have been omitted.
- The apostrophe is used to indicate possession by making nouns into adjectives of possession.
  - Usually an apostrophe and an *s* are added to the end of the noun to make it into an adjective of possession.
  - Only an apostrophe is needed if the noun is plural and ends in an *s*, if the noun already has two sounds of *s*, or if adding another *s* would make the word difficult to pronounce.
- When an apostrophe indicates **joint possession,** add the apostrophe at the end of the last name.
- When an apostrophe indicates **individual possession,** add the apostrophe at the end of each name.
- An apostrophe is used in expressions of **time and measurement** (one week's leave, a stone's throw, three days' absence).
- An apostrophe is used before a gerund to indicate possession.
  - The clerk's entering of the data...
  - Joni's handling of the situation...
- Possessives stand alone when the noun is not written but is clearly understood.
  - The meeting was held at the lawyers'.
  - Marjorie's understanding is better than Sue's.

Note: Remember that a word containing an apostrophe for possession must have a noun immediately following it or one that is clearly understood.

Confirm Your Knowledge

Complete Exercise for Unit 3.6 on page 137.

OTHER PUNCTUATION

3.7 Parentheses, Brackets, Ellipsis Marks, and Dashes

Parentheses ( )

A parenthetical expression is an interruption to the main flow of the sentence. If the word or group of words causes only a small break or a minor interruption, the parenthetical expression is set off by a pair of commas. (See Unit 3.4.)

> The environment, you will agree, has to be protected.
>
> They have, actually, already reduced emissions by ten percent.

However, if the interruption is stronger or provides an explanation, the interrupting words should be enclosed in parentheses ().

> I am (actually, I always have been) very eager to go.
>
> Only a very few items (six) remained unsold at the end of the garage sale.
>
> Stephen Leacock (1869-1944) was best known as a humorist.

With References

Parentheses are also used to enclose references or directions.

> The illustration on page 4 (Fig. VI) clearly shows the composition of the thorax.
>
> A glossary of medical terms (see Appendix A on page 117) is included for quick reference.
>
> Come visit our new clinic on Queen Street (opposite the City Hall), and you will be amazed at our wonderful facilities.

Brackets [ ]

Brackets are sometimes referred to as square brackets because of their appearance, which distinguishes them from parentheses. Brackets are used to show that the interruption has been provided from a source other than the writer or speaker. They are also used around the word *sic* meaning "thus" to indicate that a specific error did in fact appear in the original material.

> The Prime Minister reported: "Our gross national product has increased by 0.5 percent this month [cheers], but the unemployment figure has also risen by 0.5 percent [boos]."
>
> "Electricity could soon replace oil in home hearing [sic]," according to the Minister of Energy's bulletin.

Mini-Test

Insert parentheses or brackets where necessary in the following sentences.

1. Our company policy on hiring drivers see page 6 of the hiring manual is currently being revised.
2. The electrical circuit Diagram 17 is quite easy to understand.
3. The tolerances required for that tool see specifications in Appendix 5 on page 357 must be approved by a government inspector.
4. The report stated: "Our head office in Tronto sic will be moved to Thunder Bay some time next year."
5. The witness continued, "I know the driver was drunk, and I demand that he be locked up!" Subdued applause from the gallery.

KEY

1. (see page 6...manual) 2. (Diagram 17) 3. (see...page 357) 4. [sic] 5. [Subdued...gallery.]

Ellipsis Marks

Ellipsis is the omission of words from quoted material that are not really necessary for the meaning. The fact that something has been omitted from a quoted passage is shown by three periods.

> "The fact that something has been omitted...is shown by three spaced periods."

The keys for the mini-tests often use ellipsis marks to avoid repeating the whole sentence. Check the key immediately preceding this section for examples.

Dashes

Sometimes neither commas nor parentheses are suitable to enclose an interruption. If the interruption is very emphatic, changes the reader's direction completely, or already includes commas, use dashes.

> Fernandez & Company has only one concern—its clients.
>
> The star of the new show—have you met her yet?—will be here for a press interview at 10:30 a.m. on Thursday.
>
> Canada's chief exports—wheat,fish, and paper—have all increased over the last twelve months.

A dash is also used after a list is summarized by one word at the beginning of the following main clause.

> Wheat, fish, and paper—these are Canada's chief exports.
>
> Riveters, welders, and steelworkers—all are needed for our new plant.
>
> Farmers, transporters, wholesalers, retailers—everyone interested is invited to the forum on the price of food.

Mini-Test

Insert dashes where necessary in the following sentences.

1. Our guarantee provides for only one thing your complete satisfaction.
2. Nuts, bolts, and screws of every size these are essential items for every hardware store.
3. The orange carpet I'm absolutely certain of the colour was the one the customer returned.
4. All main dishes on the menu steak, lamb chops, roast beef, and pork sausages have been approved by the chef.
5. Most employees would you believe 87 percent? voted in favour of the five-day work week.

KEY

1. thing—your 2. size—these 3. carpet—I'm...colour—was 4. menu—steak...sausages—have 5. employees—would...percent?—voted

---

SUMMARY FOR UNIT 3.7

- Interruptions can be punctuated in three ways:
  - use commas for mild interruptions
  - use parentheses for stronger interruptions
  - use dashes for emphatic interruptions
- **Parentheses** are also used:
  - to enclose references or directions that interrupt
  - to enclose explanations
- **Brackets** (also known as square brackets) are used:
  - when an interruption comes from another source
  - around "sic"
- **Ellipsis** marks are three spaced dots used to show that something has been omitted from quoted material.
- **Dashes** are used:
  - for emphatic interruptions
  - for a complete change of direction, for emphasis, or when commas have already been used
  - after a list at the beginning of a sentence which is summarized by one word at the beginning of the main clause.

Confirm Your Knowledge

Complete Exercise for Unit 3.7 on page 138.

❍ 3.8 Quotation Marks and Underlining

Quotation Marks

Quotation marks have four functions: to enclose the actual words that were spoken, to enclose material that is excerpted from a longer passage, to draw attention to a particular word or phrase, and to display titles of parts of literary material.

Direct Speech

Quotation marks are used to enclose the actual words of a speaker.

> "Yes," she said, "there has been a great improvement in my health."
>
> "Canada's resort areas are among the best in the world," claimed the presenter of the travelogue.

The quoted sentence begins with a capital letter even when it does not start the complete sentence. An interrupted quotation resumes with a lower case letter.

> The moderator asked, "Do you have a pertinent question?"
>
> Armando told us, "We are going abroad again this summer."
>
> "Our next step," the controller said, "is to bring down costs."

A quotation of more than one sentence needs quotation marks only at the beginning and end of the complete quotation.

> The moderator asked, "Do you have a pertinent question? If not, would you please hand the microphone to the next candidate."

A quotation of more than one paragraph needs quotation marks at the beginning of every paragraph but only once at the end of the last paragraph.
With long quotations, however, many writers prefer to display the quotation by indenting the material, in which case no quotation marks are used.

Indirect Speech

Indirect speech does not use the actual words spoken and is not set off by quotation marks.

Hint: If the word *that* could be inserted into the material, then no punctuation is used.

> Mr. Santilli replied he had never before received such a warm welcome.
>
> (Mr. Santilli replied that... His actual words were "I've never before received such a warm welcome.")

Commas and Periods

Commas and periods are always written inside the closing quotation marks. Look at the position of periods and commas in the examples given in this unit.

Mini-Test

Insert quotation marks where necessary in the following sentences. Remember that closing quotation marks always come after a period or comma.

1. The engineer asked, When will we receive the parts we need?
2. These bricks, the shop steward reported, are of inferior quality.
3. Garbage collection will be reduced to one day a week, the mayor declared.
4. He went on to say this would help reduce his expenses considerably.
5. Mr. Roland stated, I shall always do my best to serve you. I shall even try to improve upon my best!

KEY

1. "When...need?" 2. "These bricks,"..."are...quality." 3. "Garbage...week," 4. no quotation marks—reported speech 5. "I shall...best!"

Excerpted Material

When only part of the material is being quoted exactly as was said, then only those words are put in quotation marks.

> We need only hear the words "Never in the field of human conflict" to be reminded of how Sir Winston Churchill inspired the people.
>
> The government considers 65 a "good age to retire," but I feel a healthy person has years of productivity left after that age.

For Attention

Certain words requiring special attention should be placed in quotation marks. The use of quotation marks for this purpose, however, should be kept to a minimum.

An "I don't care" attitude will not help you to succeed.

The word "widow" has a special meaning when used in printing.

Mini-Test

Insert quotation marks where necessary in the following sentences.

1. Mr. Reid went on to say he needed specific details, not general information.
2. The package should be marked Fragile and wrapped securely.
3. Try for your Chance of a Lifetime by buying a lottery ticket today.
4. The paragraph beginning When we have considered your recommendations should be deleted.
5. The expression What's new? is particularly appropriate today with new technology being developed daily.

KEY

1. "specific" (for emphasis) 2. "Fragile" 3. "Chance of a Lifetime" 4. "When...recommendations" 5. "What's new?"

Titles

The titles of complete published books, magazines, and newspapers are underlined. They appear in italics in printed material.

Margaret Laurence's The Stone Angel has been made into a film.

The stock market reports in The Vancouver Sun are always right up to date.

The titles of parts of these works, such as chapters, articles, editorials, etc., or smaller items, such as poems, reports, lectures, etc., are enclosed in quotation marks.

Have you read the article "Tennis is for Everyone" in this month's issue of Sports Illustrated?

The song "O Canada" became our official national anthem on July 1. 1980.

Note: Commas are used around a title if the title is unnecessary to the meaning of the sentence.

Our national anthem, "O Canada," has a very invigorating melody.

His latest article, "Tennis is for Everyone," will be printed next month.

Mini-Test

Insert quotation marks and commas where necessary to identify the titles in the following sentences.

1. The editorial What's Happening in Ottawa was very provocative.
2. Read the chapter The Advantages of Plastic Pipes before buying any materials.
3. The section on make-up Make-up and Its Application is especially useful.
4. The American national anthem The Star Spangled Banner is sung at all hockey games when American teams are playing.
5. The report entitled Management by Objective—How It Works has been circulated to all department heads.

KEY

1. "What's...Ottawa" 2. "The...Pipes" 3. make-up, "Make-up...Application," 4. anthem, "The ...Banner," 5. "Management...Works"

Single Quotation Marks

Single quotation marks are used to enclose a quotation within a quotation.

Ms. Stanford replied, "Put the cheques in envelopes marked 'Personal' and mail them today, please."

Other Punctuation with Quotation Marks

As already mentioned, periods and commas always go inside closing quotation marks. Question marks and exclamation marks may go inside or outside depending on the meaning of the sentence. Semicolons and colons are always placed outside quotation marks.

In your letter last week you wrote, "I'll let you know by Friday"; however, we are still waiting to hear from you again.

The following leading actors have been selected for "Romeo and Juliet": Brent Carver, Martha Henry, H. R. Thompson, and Pat Galloway.

For more involved punctuation, consult a style guide or reference manual.

Underlining

In handwritten and typewritten work, underlining has many special uses. In printing, these special uses are indicated by italic type.

1. Underline titles of major literary works, magazines, newspapers, government bulletins, and pamphlets.

   The National Dream by Pierre Berton is one of his most interesting books.

Note: Only capitalize or underline *a, an,* or *the* before book, newspaper, or magazine titles when it is the first word of the title.

the Winnipeg Free Press

The Lethbridge Herald

2. The titles of musical productions, plays, motion pictures, and television programs are underlined.

   Miss Saigon suffered many casting problems.

3. The names of specific ships, trains, aircraft, and space ships are underlined.

   To travel on the Orient Express is a wonderful experience.

   Howard Hughes's Spruce Goose is on display in Los Angeles beside the Queen Mary.

   The explosion of the Challenger set back the space program by several years.

4. Underline unusual foreign words and phrases that are likely to be unfamiliar to the reader.

   His plane arrived late, and ipso facto he missed his connection.

Note: Do not underline common foreign words or phrases such as:

au revoir   status quo   vice versa

Mini-Test

Underline where necessary in the following sentences.

1. Has this month's copy of Reader's Digest come yet?
2. The Queen Elizabeth and La Normandie were troop ships during World War II.
3. Richard Rohmer's Exxoneration is a fascinating book.
4. The government's bulletin Registered Retirement Savings Plans explains the best way to ensure adequate retirement income.
5. Ex libris is often used in book plates to show who is the owner of the book.

KEY

1. Reader's Digest 2. Queen Elizabeth, La Normandie
3. Exxoneration 4. Registered Retirement Savings Plans
5. Ex Libris

SUMMARY FOR UNIT 3.8

- **Quotation marks** have four functions:
  - to enclose the actual words someone spoke
  - to enclose material taken from another source
  - to draw attention to a particular word or phrase
  - to display titles
- Use quotation marks only at the beginning and end of the actual words spoken.
- Use quotation marks at the beginning of each paragraph of a long quotation and at the end of the last paragraph only. (Long quotations may be displayed by indenting without using quotation marks.)
- Do *not* use quotation marks with indirect speech (not the actual words spoken).
- With material from another source, use quotation marks around that material only.
- Use quotation marks sparingly around words for emphasis.
- Use quotation marks around titles of chapters, articles, editorials, or the titles of small units of writing such as poems, lectures, reports.
- Use single quotation marks for a quotation within a quotation.
- Other punctuation with quotation marks:
  - periods and commas are always inside
  - question marks and exclamation marks may be inside or outside depending on the meaning
  - semicolons and colons are always outside
- **Underline** the titles of:
  - books, magazines, newspapers, government bulletins, and pamphlets
  - musical productions, plays, movies, TV programs
- Do **not** underline or capitalize *a*, *an*, or *the* before a title unless it is part of the title.
- Underline the names of specific ships, trains, aircraft, or space ships.
- Underline unusual foreign words; do not underline common foreign words.

Confirm Your Knowledge

Complete Exercise for Unit 3.8 on page 140.

DEVELOPING YOUR LANGUAGE SKILLS

❍ 3.9 Vocabulary

Definitions

Check your dictionary for the meanings of the following words; then match them up with the definitions given. Write the letter of the definition you choose from Column 2 in the space provided in Column 1.

Column 1	Column 2
_____ bias	a) arrange pages in order
_____ collateral	b) carry, make known
_____ collate	c) a leaning toward one view point
_____ convey	d) cut short
_____ compromise	e) something used in return for a loan
_____ curtail	f) make out, work out a puzzle
_____ chronological	g) in time or date sequence
_____ decipher	h) obtain, come from
_____ depreciate	i) lessen in value
_____ derive	j) settlement of a disagreement by each side's giving up a little
	k) account for

Mini-Test

Complete the following sentences by choosing the most appropriate word from Column 1 under "Definitions."

1. The sequence of events should be recorded in ____________ ordcr.
2. The government has asked us to ___________ our use of electricity to save energy.
3. The illegible handwriting on the paper made it impossible to ___________ the message.
4. The arbitrator was asked to _________ to the union that the administration was ready to effect a ___________ on their demands.
5. It is the clerk's job to ___________ the final draft before it is sent for binding.
6. A ___________ was discovered when the loan officer refused to accept jewelry as ___________ for a loan although he was willing to accept furs or antiques.
7. Cars ___________ so quickly it is almost impossible to sell one at a profit.
8. You will ___________ great satisfaction from volunteer work.

KEY

1. chronological 2. curtail 3. decipher 4. convey, compromise 5. collate 6. bias, collateral 7. depreciate 8. derive.

Be sure you checked your spelling of these words!

Usage

Study the following words carefully so that you are sure which one to use.

coarse/course

coarse—rude, not fine, rough	coarse language, coarse cloth coarse sandpaper
course—way, sequence, plan	A river's course; in the course of things; course of study *Also*: of course

complement/compliment

compl*e*ment—complete (Note the *e*'s)	Drapes to complement the decor.
compl*i*ment— pra*i*se (Note the *i*'s)	She gave Ray a compliment. She complimented him on his work.

could of

never use this—use *could have*	The car could have been repaired.

council/counsel

council—a group of people	the city council, the student council (a city councillor)
counsel (noun)—lawyer, advice	to retain counsel; to seek counsel
counsel (verb)—advise	We counsel street kids. (A counsellor gives advice.)

defer/differ

defer—give in, put off	I defer to your better judgment. May I defer payment until May?
differ—disagree	We differ in our opinions about that.

die/dye

die—a plate for printing; a mould for casting or manufacturing	the die for the flyers a die for small auto parts
dye—to colour; colouring liquid	Dye your shoes green. Use a green dye when dyeing them. (Note spelling of *dyeing*.)

disburse/disperse

disburse—pay out, distribute	Sally will disburse expenses.
disperse—scatter, spread out	The protestors dispersed peacefully.

Mini-Test

Complete the following sentences by choosing the correct word from those shown at the beginning of the sentences.

1. *coarse/course*

   The contractor asked for ___________ gravel to lay along the ___________ of the new road.
2. *complement/compliment*

   Fine accessories will ___________ any outfit and guarantee a ___________ on your good taste.
3. *could of/could have*

   We _______________ completed the work earlier if supplies had been available.
4. *council/counsel*

   Ms. Greene has been elected to the city ___________.

   A counsellor will ___________ you on what courses you should take.

   The ___________ for the defence asked for time to collect more evidence.
5. *defer/differ*

   I would like to ___________ payment of the final instalment as we seem to ___________ in our understanding of the contract.

   We are happy to ___________ to your wishes.
6. *die/dye*

   As soon as the ___________ has been approved for the new part, we shall begin casting.

   The __________ for the new material is too light.
7. *disperse/disburse*

   Be sure to ___________ the money to the participants before they ___________ to go home.

KEY

1. coarse, course 2. complement, compliment 3. could have (never *could of*) 4. council, counsel, counsel 5. defer, differ, defer 6. die, dye 7. disburse, disperse

Spelling

Study the following words very carefully. Write out the words at least ten times each, and be sure you know their meanings!

–ally Words

accidentally	occasionally
basically	incidentally
practically	personally

Final *e* Retained

serviceable	chargeable
noticeable	knowledgeable
manageable	advantageous

Final *e* Dropped

acknowledgment	judgment
argument	

Mini-Test

By using proofreaders' marks or otherwise, correct any spelling errors in the following words. There may be one error, more than one error, or no errors in a line.

1.	manageable	argument	incidently
2.	servicable	knowledgable	personally
3.	judgment	ocasionally	accidentally
4.	practically	chargeable	acknowledgment
5.	advantagous	basically	noticeable

KEY

1. incidently (insert al) 2. servicable (insert e), knowledgable (insert e) 3. ocasionally (insert c) 4. no errors 5. advantagous (insert e)

SUMMARY FOR UNIT 3.9

- Always check your dictionary for the meanings of unfamiliar words.
- Usage
  - a compl*e*ment makes compl*e*te
  - a compl*i*ment pra*i*ses
  - never use *could of*!
- Spelling
  - Remember six *–ally* words
  - Remember three without an *e*
  - a few special ones with an *e* to keep the sound of *c* and *g* soft.

Confirm Your Knowledge

Complete Exercise for Unit 3.9 on page 141.

❍ 3.10 Proofreading

Proofreaders' Marks for Punctuation

The mark for delete (℘) is used for the deletion of punctuation marks as well as for other deletions.

If you can't, come, phone before August 14.

The neighbourhood newspaper needs more contributors'.

To insert most punctuation, use the insert mark and write the punctuation point inside it as in the following examples. If space is limited, write the correct punctuation above the insert mark. Note the correct way to insert an apostrophe.

He did however, agree to submit an estimate of the cost.

Mrs A A Howard will address the delegates.

The question "What is there in it for me" can be easily answered.

Instructions on the use of precision tools calipers, micrometers, and dividers is included in the course.

You do agree with this approach, don t you?

To insert underlining, put the underlining in the correct place and write "u/s" (for "underscore") in the margin.

u/s Have you read Two Solitudes by Hugh MacLennan?

Your article will appear in the June issue of

u/s Newsweek.

Mini-Test

Use the appropriate proofreaders' marks to correct the punctuation in the following passage. Be on the lookout for other errors that need to be corrected, and mark them also.

The possibility of fire terrifies everyone but the possibility of fire in a childrens school is even more terrifying. The article What You Should Do in the Event of Fire should be read and thoroughyl understood. As soon as the fireball rings teachers must stop activities immediately, and collect the children for an orderly exit. The following routine must be used

1. Assemble the children in pairs by the door.
2. Have them walk, not run, to the nearest exit.
3. Keep them together in a group in the playground area.

The teacher must at all times be cool calm and collected the teacher must never show the least sign of panic. Have you any questions If so, ask for the answers now. Tomorrow may be too late.

KEY

The possibility of fire terrifies everyone, but the possibility of fire in a children's school is even more terrifying. The article "What You Should Do in the Event of Fire" should be read and thoroughly understood. As soon as the firebell rings, teachers must stop activities immediately and collect the children for an orderly exit. The following routine must be used:

1. Assemble the children in pairs by the door.
2. Have them walk, not run, to the nearest exit.
3. Keep them together in a group in the playground area.

The teacher must at all times be cool, calm, and collected; the teacher

u/s must never show the least sign of panic. Have you any questions? If so, ask for the answers now. Tomorrow may be too late!

Scoring

If this were an exercise, you would score one point for each correctly used proofreaders' mark with the corresponding correct punctuation. You would deduct one point for any wrongly inserted proofreaders' marks or for the omission of the balancing punctuation where a pair of punctuation marks is necessary. An example of omission of the balancing punctuation would be the omission of closing quotation marks after the word *Fire*. The total possible score for this mini-test is 15.

SUMMARY FOR UNIT 3.10

Proofreaders' marks for punctuation are:

- ℘ delete mark for deletions
- ⋀ ⋀ insert mark with correct punctuation inside or above
- ⋁ inverted insert mark for apostrophes
- u/s ___ underlining in the correct place with "u/s" written in the margin

Confirm Your Knowledge

Complete Exercise for Unit 3.10 on page 143.

PRETEST FOR UNIT 3

Complete all the parts of this test according to the directions for each part. The figures in parentheses are the unit numbers for reference, if necessary, when you have completed the test. Score 1 point for each completely correct answer; no marks are allowed for partially correct punctuation.

Your Goal: To score a total of at least 56 points.

A. General Rules

Are the following statements true or false? If true, circle *T*; if false, circle *F*. Score 1 point for each correct answer.

			Score
1.	Punctuation is used only to make the meaning of the writing absolutely clear to the reader. (3.1)	**T F**	____
2.	Interruptions such as "of course" require only one comma (3.4)	**T F**	____
3.	A semicolon should be used between two sentences that have no connection with each other.	**T F**	____
4.	Use a colon before a list if the words "the following" or "as follows" come in the first part of the sentence. (3.2)	**T F**	____
5.	Never use a comma before a "that" clause. (3.4)	**T F**	____
6.	A comma or a period should always be written inside the quotation marks at the end of the quoted material. (3.1)	**T F**	____
7.	Introductory words coming before the main clause are followed by a comma. (3.4)	**T F**	____
8.	Titles of major works should be in quotation marks; titles of parts of larger works should be underlined. (3.8)	**T F**	____
9.	A comma is not necessary before *and* in a list or series of items. (3.3)	**T F**	____
10.	Two complete sentences joined by *and* or *but* must have a comma before the *and* or *but*. (3.3)	**T F**	____
		Score for Part A	____

B. End Punctuation (3.1)

Insert the correct punctuation at the end of the following sentences.

		Score
1.	She asked, "What is the most popular colour this spring	____
2.	Your flight leaves at 8:30 a.m	____
3.	Will you please return your application before June 30	____
4.	Did he say, "I know a good plumber	____
5.	Ms. Chute wants to know when the drapes will be ready	____
	Score for Part B	____

C. Semicolon (;) and Colon (:) (3.2)

Insert semicolons and colons where necessary in the following sentences. Write *C* beside any sentence that is correct as written.

Score

1. Order your new Apex vacuum cleaner today pay for it in the new year. _____
2. Our photographer will visit our branch stores in Winnipeg, Manitoba Regina, Saskatchewan and Vernon, British Columbia. _____
3. Prizes were awarded to the following contestants Mary Lee, Rick Story, and Patricia Hansen. _____
4. I understand your concern however, you will appreciate we should make a really thorough investigation before we authorize your claim. _____
5. May we have a fresh supply of towels, washcloths, and rubber gloves for the kitchen. _____

Score for Part C _____

D. Commas (3.3, 3.4, 3.5)

Are the commas in the following sentences complete and correct? If so, write *C* at the end of the sentence; if not, write *X* and add or delete commas to make the sentence correctly punctuated.

Score

1. If you need help with the Griffith order let me know. _____ _____
2. He has not completed his final year but he certainly knows his accounting. _____ _____
3. The drug store on Heath Street stocks drugs, candies, soda, tobacco, razors, camera supplies and cosmetics as well as a fine assortment of greeting cards. _____ _____
4. These strong sturdy electric drills have dozens of uses. _____ _____
5. Although your cheque arrived late we have credited your account in full. _____ _____
6. Employees who apply themselves wholeheartedly to their jobs stand a good chance of promotion. _____ _____
7. This is however, the only time I have ever met him. _____ _____
8. He moved to Belleville in March, and found a job within two days. _____ _____
9. Demonstrations will be given in schools, in church halls and at shopping malls. _____ _____
10. You are aware of course that no money is available for paying lunch expenses. _____ _____
11. The electrician who had promised to start work at 8 a.m. did not arrive until 11:30 a.m. _____ _____
12. Ms. Biro, the supervisor of Human Relations, asked for suggestions concerning the keeping of attendance records. _____ _____
13. The notice that is posted by the door sets out the procedures in case of fire. _____ _____
14. Dr. Valenti started work on Tuesday September 1 1991. _____ _____
15. Thank you for replying so promptly Mrs. Mackay. _____ _____

Score for Part D _____

E. Apostrophe (3.6)

Insert apostrophes where necessary in the following sentences. If a sentence is correct as written, write *C* beside it.

Score

1. The plane leaves in two hours time. ______
2. The Murrays have moved to Edmonton. ______
3. Sam doesnt know where to go to find work in his field. ______
4. Our bosses correspondence has not yet been filed. ______
5. The premiers meeting is scheduled for June 15. ______
6. Each member of the group pondered the secretarys reply. ______
7. Mr. Harris contract has been signed. ______
8. Joan and Davids lease will be renewed on March 1. ______
9. The support staffs union will increase the monthly dues paid by its members. ______
10. Pick up your petty cash at the cashiers. ______

Score for Part E ______

F. Parentheses ( ), Brackets [ ], and Dashes—(3.7)

Insert parentheses, brackets, and dashes where necessary in the following sentences.

Score

1. The results of the survey are set out in a table see Appendix A from which you will see how successful the survey has been. ______
2. The illustration of the showerhead assembly Fig. V shows how easily it can be installed. ______
3. The newspaper reported: "The Minister's office said that he was rusting sic comfortably at home after his accident." ______
4. Sun, good food, and exercise these are what you need to promote a feeling of well-being. ______
5. We shall never again I repeat, never again allow our stocks to become so low. ______

Score for Part F ______

G. Quotation Marks and Underlining (3.8)

Insert quotation marks and underlining in the following sentences. If a sentence is correct as written, write *C* beside it. Be careful with the placing of periods and commas!

Score

1. Joanne gave me the advertisement from the magazine Canadian Fashion. ______
2. The article Proofreading for Perfection would be very helpful to you. ______
3. These fabrics, the taylor stated, are exactly what I need for the new uniforms. ______
4. Please reserve four tickets for the show Les Miserables for Saturday, November 21. ______
5. She said that I must improve my work or be discharged. ______

Score for Part G ______

H. Proofreading and Vocabulary (2.10, 2.11)

Using proofreaders' marks, make any necessary corrections in vocabulary, spelling, punctuation, or keyboarding in the following sentences. Score 1 point for using the correct proofreaders' marks and making the correction; no points for partially correct changes. Deduct 1 point for changing a word or punctuation that was correct as written or for missing an error.

Score

Example: The long complicated, highyl technical rport was very difficultto understand. (Score 3 points for correctly marking *highyl, rport,* and *difficultto*; deduct 1 for missing comma after *long*.) 2

Dear Mr. Summers

As secretary of the ratepayer's association for your ward, I hvae been asked to write to you concerning the repaving of Palmer Street.

It appears the contractors are not using the right kind of gravel for the sublayer. The specifications call for course gravel however, a very fine gravel is being used instead. An engineer in our association tells us, that this will result in very poor drainage and subsequent heaving of the top surface after extreme winter weather.

Incidently, you have been most helpful in supporting the private citizen since your appointment to City Counsel. We have all recognized the noticeable improvement in street maintenance and garbage collection—all of which has come about byyour efforts.

We look forward with confidence to your attention to the repaving of Palmer Street. If the the work proceeds using the wrong grade of gravel, worse conditions than before will result. To have to repave the street again within a year would of course, be an unnecessary expenditure for both the taxpayer and the city.

May we have a reply before our next meeting on October 23?

Yours truly

Number of errors found and correctly marked _____

Deduct for errors missed _____

Score for Part H _____

I. Summary (3.2, 3.3, 3.4, 3.8)

Insert or correct punctuation where necessary in the following paragraphs.

The purpose of punctuation is to clarify and simplify the reading of written communications. Unfortunately there is not a strong relationship between pauses and commas or periods. Question marks tell us that an answer is expected but they do not tell us how to read the question aloud. All punctuation marks give the reader a definite message, however, too much punctuation can hide the meaning of the writing

If you are uncertain of the basic rules for punctuation ask your instructor to guide you to the appropriate section in this book. Above all, remember to place a period, a question mark, or an exclamation mark at the end of each complete thought.

Score for Part I _____

Total Score _____

If you achieved your goal of at least 56 points, proceed to Unit 4. If you did not score 56, check with your instructor what parts you need to study. Proceed through Unit 3 doing all the necessary work; then do the posttest for Unit 3.

POSTTEST FOR UNIT 3

Complete all the parts of this test according to the directions for each part. The figures in parentheses are the unit numbers for reference, if necessary, when you have completed the test. Score 1 point for each completely correct answer; no marks are allowed for partially correct punctuation.

Your Goal: To score a total of at least 56 points.

A. General Rules

Are the following statements true or false? If true, circle *T*; if false, circle *F*. Score 1 point for each correct answer.

			Score
1.	Without punctuation, written messages would be very difficult to understand. (3.1)	**T F**	_____
2.	Only one comma is necessary with an interruption such as "in fact" in the middle of a sentence. (3.4)	**T F**	_____
3.	A semicolon should be used between two sentences when the second one begins with "however" or a similar word. (3.2)	**T F**	_____
4.	Use a colon before a list if a complete statement comes before the colon. (3.2)	**T F**	_____
5.	Only one period is necessary at the end of a sentence. (3.1)	**T F**	_____
6.	A question mark is always written inside the quotation marks at the end of quoted material (3.1, 3.8)	**T F**	_____
7.	A sentence beginning with an "if" (dependent) clause must have a comma at the end of the "if" (dependent) clause. (3.4)	**T F**	_____
8.	Quotation marks are used around the actual words someone said. (3.8)	**T F**	_____
9.	Use a comma between adjectives if the word "and" could be inserted. (3.3)	**T F**	_____
10.	The title of a book should be underlined. (3.8)	**T F**	_____
		Score for Part A	_____

B. End Punctuation (3.1)

Insert the correct punctuation at the end of the following sentences.

		Score
1.	He asked, "When are the new cars coming this fall	_____
2.	The ceremony starts are 2:30 p.m	_____
3.	Will you please submit your expenses before April 30	_____
4.	Did she say, "I will begin the reports tomorrow	_____
5.	Ms. Kulik wants to know why her plants are dying	_____
	Score for Part B	_____

C. Semicolon (;) and Colon (:) (3.2)

Insert semicolons and colons where necessary in the following sentences. Write *C* beside any sentence that is correct as written.

Score

1. Let us have your order now we are eager to serve you. _____
2. The elected regional presidents are Baldeo Sairsingh, Ontario Muriel Baines, Alberta Blake Oldham, British Columbia and Jeanne Thibeau, Quebec. _____
3. Awards were presented to the following for their contribution Dick Shorney, Jack Chin, and Louise Barry. _____
4. The cabinets you ordered are out of stock however, another shipment will arrive within the next two weeks. _____
5. Motor manufacturing, petroleum refining, and paper products are three principal Canadian industries. _____

Score for Part C _____

D. Commas (3.3, 3.4, 3.5)

Are the commas in the following sentences complete and correct? If so, write *C* at the end of the sentence; if not, write *X* and add or delete commas to make the sentence correctly punctuated.

Score

1. If you require more time with the McLeod estate let the office know by Monday._____ _____
2. She has successfully completed her first year but she isn't sure if she will continue. _____ _____
3. The hardware store on Front Street stocks nails, screws, paints, clamps, saws, bolts and hammers as well as a good assortment of chisels. _____ _____
4. These strong sturdy power saws have a variety of uses. _____ _____
5. Since your payment arrived late we have disallowed any discount earned. _____ _____
6. Students who do not give wholly of themselves to their studies do not stand a chance of honours. _____ _____
7. Last week in fact, was the first time I had seen a hockey game._____ _____
8. They moved to Brockville in July and had difficulty finding work. _____ _____
9. Puppet shows will be held in parks pools and shopping centres during July and August. _____ _____
10. You know of course that travel in Europe has become very expensive. _____ _____
11. The chauffeur who is prompt and careful will be given the responsibility. _____ _____
12. Mr. Taylor, the personnel manager, requested ideas concerning the interbranch baseball game._____ _____
13. The alarm button that is under the desk is to be used only in case of hold-up. _____ _____
14. James Good retired on Tuesday June 20 1991._____ _____
15. Thank you Ms. Abbatengelo for your support. _____ _____

Score for Part D _____

E. Apostrophe (3.6)

Insert apostrophes where necessary in the following sentences. If a sentence is correct as written, write *C* beside it.

Score

1. Childrens paintings are on display in our foyer. ______
2. When she left, Mary received two months severance pay. ______
3. Its easy to find the firm's location; use this directory. ______
4. There will be a moments delay before the meeting is called to order. ______
5. Chiefs of police from many cities attended the conference. ______
6. She was trying to complete an hours work in thirty minutes. ______
7. The speaker claimed there are differences between womens and mens listening habits. ______
8. My mother-in-laws graduation ceremony took place today. ______
9. The skaters new outfit was purchased on the last day of the sale. ______
10. The Johnsons offer was accepted; ours was rejected. ______

Score for Part E ______

F. Parentheses ( ), Brackets [ ], and Dashes—(3.7)

Insert parentheses, brackets, and dashes where necessary in the following sentences.

Score

1. The first results of the test have been collated see Appendix D, and the findings show how positive are the effects of the drug. ______
2. The diagram of the model airplane assembly Fig. IX illustrates how simply it can be constructed. ______
3. The press announced: "The President is recovering quickly at home after the attempted assignation sic." ______
4. Sugar, flour, eggs, and milk these are what you need to make a cake. ______
5. Never again I repeat, never again will we permit employees to be uninformed about strikes. ______

Score for Part F ______

G. Quotation Marks and Underlining (3.8)

Insert quotation marks and underlining in the following sentences. If a sentence is correct as written, write *C* beside it. Be careful with the placing of periods and commas!

Score

1. Cecile found the article in the digest, Prevention. ______
2. The slogan practice makes perfect refers to everyone and anyone. ______
3. These magazines, the bookseller said, are exactly what I've been looking for regarding the trends in house building. ______
4. Please reserve seven tickets for Guys and Dolls for Monday, February 3. ______
5. My supervisor said my work was being watched closely for promotion or demotion. ______

Score for Part G ______

H. Proofreading and Vocabulary (2.10, 2.11)

Using proofreaders' marks, make any necessary corrections in vocabulary, spelling, punctuation, or keyboarding in the following sentences. Score 1 point for using the correct proofreaders' marks and making the correction; no points for partially correct changes. Deduct 1 point for changing a word or punctuation that was correct as written or for missing an error.

Score

Example: The long complicated, highly technical rport was very difficultto understand. (Score 3 points for correctly marking *highly, rport,* and *difficultto*; deduct 1 for missing comma after *long*.) 2

Dear Mr. Higgins

We have carefully considered you claim for $595.80 for repairs to the car that was damaged in an accident on December 7 of last year. Your policy however lapsed at the end of the 30-day period that started immediately after the due date of your last unpaid premium, October 15. Occasionly we permit late payments but during this grace period, we sent you two notices that you payment was overdue, and we did not hear from you. Your collision coverage lapsed and was not in affect when the accident ocurred therefore we will not be able to reimburse you for the cost of the repairs.

I am sorry this has happened, Mr. Higgins, especially since you have been a long-standing policyholder, but I hope you will understand that we must follow the precise wording of your policy agreement.

We hope that you will continue using your insurance and that in future no problems will arise.

Yours truly

Number of errors found and correctly marked _____

Deduct for errors missed _____

Score for Part H _____

I. Summary (3.2, 3.3, 3.4, 3.8)

Insert or correct punctuation where necessary in the following letter.

Dear Customer

We thought that you might be interested in our spring fashion show, which will display some of our new clothes written about in the article Fashions for Spring in Thursdays newspapers. The show is being held on Tuesday May 2.

This spring the trend is plain colours with accessories in pastel shades. If you bring this card with you you may be a lucky winner of a trip to Paris for two weeks. Be sure to come the door prizes are worth while.

Yours truly

Score for Part I _____

Total Score _____

If you achieved your goal of at least 56 points, proceed to Unit 4. If you did not score 56, check with your instructor what parts you need to review thoroughly; then proceed to Unit 4.

EXERCISE 3.1 PERIOD, QUESTION MARK, AND EXCLAMATION MARK

Insert the correct end punctuation in the following sentences and any other periods, question marks, and exclamation marks that may be necessary. Score one point for each correct end punctuation and one point for each additional punctuation required in the sentence.

Your Goal: To score at least 16 points.

Example: Will you please erect the new sign on Friday? 1

Score

1. Luigi asked whether the extreme cold had affected the fruit trees ______
2. Do you prefer to travel by train or by plane ______
3. Will you please confirm my understanding of the problem ______
4. I am never quite sure what "e g" means and why "pp." stands for pages ______
5. You will stand for re-election, won't you ______
6. "Have you read my previous book" the author asked the enthusiastic fan ______
7. Why have you not sent us the $143 50 you promised last month ______
8. The reporter requested permission to interview the scientist ______
9. Did his telegram state, "Arriving 2:05 a m Saturday ______
10. "Why," you may ask, "should I change my detergent ______
11. Mrs Paolini and Ms Meadows have asked to be excused from the fund-raising drive ______
12. The witness indignantly replied, "How dare you doubt my word ______

Total Score ______

If you achieved your goal of at least 16 points, proceed to Unit 3.2. If you did not score 16, go back and review Unit 3.1 thoroughly; then do Exercise 3.1A and try to achieve your goal this time.

EXERCISE 3.1A PERIOD, QUESTION MARK, AND EXCLAMATION MARK

Insert the correct end punctuation in the following sentences and any other periods, question marks, and exclamation marks that may be necessary. Score one point for each correct end punctuation and one point for each additional punctuation required in the sentence.

Your Goal: To score at least 16 points.

Example: Will you please erect the new sign on Friday. 1

Score

1. He asked whether we knew why the system had broken down ______
2. Did you see the musical *Kiss of the Spiderwoman* ______
3. Will you please come for photographs on May 17 at 11 a m ______
4. Did you know that "p" for "page" and "pp" for "pages" may be used in footnotes to save space ______
5. "How expensive," she asked, "is a trip to Hong Kong ______
6. What a thrill to drive our smooth-running heavy equipment ______
7. We wonder why we have not received your cheque for $167 89 in settlement of our claim ______
8. Dr Smith, when did you become a volunteer for the CNIB ______
9. Children's toys today are quite amazing, aren't they ______
10. "How can you tell the difference" is a question we are often asked ______
11. Have you replied to the customer who wrote, "I have been waiting for six weeks for service ______
12. I see from your resume, Ms Simmons, that you have worked for CHUM in Toronto ______

Total Score ______

If you achieved your goal of at least 16 points, proceed to Unit 3.2. If you did not score 16, ask your instructor for directions before moving on.

Exercise 3.2 Semicolon and Colon

Insert semicolons and colons where necessary in the following sentences. You will also need to insert some commas. Score 1 point for each correct punctuation mark you inserted; deduct 1 point for any semicolons or colons inserted where no punctuation is required.

Your Goal: To score at least 16 points.

Example: Can you work from 5:00 a.m. to 1:00 p m tomorrow? — 2 Score

1. Wear our latest fashions you'll look stunning. ______
2. These are the cities and dates for your appearances Digby, July 10 Halifax, July 12 and Charlottetown, July 16. ______
3. We were delighted to see you we look forward to your next visit. ______
4. Invitations have been sent to the branch managers in Trois Rivières, Québec Fredericton, New Brunswick and Yarmouth, Nova Scotia. ______
5. Mr. Jelinek has appointments all morning however he can see you at 3 p.m. if that is convenient for you. ______
6. If the printing presses run all night, the shop steward says the job will, as far as he can see, be ready on time and shipment will be completed by the end of this week. ______
7. We have agents in Flin Flon, Manitoba Swift Current, Saskatchewan and Medicine Hat, Alberta but we have no agents in Thunder Bay, Ontario. ______
8. The blueprints have finally been approved therefore construction can begin on Monday. ______
9. Some things are better left unsaid for example you should not criticize a child who has tried really hard. ______
10. The following colours are being discontinued gunmetal grey, khaki green, and burgundy. ______
11. The document read in part The trustees shall have sole power to manage the funds of the charity. ______
12. She talks very quickly however she is easily understood. ______

Total Score ______

If you achieved your goal of at least 16 points, proceed to Unit 3.3. If you did not score 16, go back and review Unit 3.2 thoroughly; then do Exercise 3.2A and try to achieve your goal this time.

EXERCISE 3.2A SEMICOLON AND COLON

Insert semicolons and colons where necessary in the following sentences. You will also need to insert some commas. Score 1 point for each correct punctuation mark you inserted; deduct 1 point for any semicolons or colons inserted where no punctuation is required.

Your Goal: To score at least 16 points.

Example: Can you work from 5 00 a.m. to 1 00 p.m. tomorrow? 2 Score

1. It is now the end of May we still have not heard from you. ______
2. Nan enjoys tennis, walking, and entertaining friends Jake likes to watch baseball, play cards, and cook gourmet meals. ______
3. Fall is the time to plant bulbs spring is the time they will fill your garden with blooms. ______
4. On your visit to Paris, be sure to visit the following Notre Dame Cathedral, the Louvre, and the Eiffel Tower. ______
5. Habitation, a practical medieval hotel, sheltered the pioneer travellers and today visitors can still enjoy its hospitality. ______
6. Sarah Luceno, consultant James St. John, stockbroker Harold Malcolm, accountant and Noel Charlavaisc, secretary are on the nominating committee. ______
7. Don't let your tires become too worn otherwise you may find yourself sliding on icy roads. ______
8. These figures have been checked by three people namely Ted, Kwok, and Maral. ______
9. The time capsule contained the following items a newspaper, a compact disc of the top twenty popular songs, videos of the Oscar-winning films, sports memorabilia, and samples of clothing no disc player or video machine was included. ______
10. Here are his excuses for being late his alarm didn't wake him, the dog knocked over his coffee, his car ran out of gas, and a policeman gave him a traffic ticket for screeching his tires! ______
11. The premiums may seem a little high however our coverage is very comprehensive. ______
12. The notice posted in the cafeteria reads Members of the cafeteria staff are no longer responsible for clearing the tables. Your co-operation in helping to keep the cafeteria clean will be appreciated. ______

Total Score ______

If you achieved your goal of at least 16 points, proceed to Unit 3.3. If you did not score 16, ask your instructor for directions before moving on.

EXERCISE 3.3 COMMA

Insert commas where necessary in the following sentences. Score 1 point for each correctly punctuated sentence; no marks for partially correct punctuation. Deduct 1 point for each comma you inserted that was not necessary.

Your Goal: To score at least 8 points.

Example: The company has offices in Toronto, Vancouver, and Halifax. 1

Score

1. The renovations on the house have been started for we hope to offer it for sale within 30 days. ______
2. Some people are raising chickens rabbits and ducks for their own use. ______
3. The police arrived first at the scene of the accident and the firefighters arrived a few seconds later. ______
4. Cash crops in this region include wheat and rye but alfalfa is also grown for feed. ______
5. I explained that our rules applied to everyone but he seemed to think that we were discriminating. ______
6. Proofreading requires careful attention to details of grammar spelling punctuation usage etc. ______
7. Your paper is well written appears to be based on fact and will provide a good base for further study. ______
8. Our shipper mailed the package yesterday and included the invoice. ______
9. The art gallery wanted to exhibit the paintings of Andy Warhol but his executors would not give permission. ______
10. The driveway has not been resurfaced for five years nor has the house been painted in that time. ______

Total Score ______

If you achieved your goal of at least 8 points, proceed to Unit 3.4. If you did not score 8, go back and review Unit 3.3 thoroughly; then do Exercise 3.3A and try to achieve your goal this time.

EXERCISE 3.3A COMMA

Use the same directions as for Exercise 3.3

Your Goal: To score at least 8 points.

	Score
1. Courses in batik basket weaving ceramics pottery etc. are held on Tuesday and Thursday evenings.	_____
2. Mr. Kolar visited Kingston and Belleville on his way back and he signed up two new customers.	_____
3. We advertised in the newspapers we posted signs on telephone posts and we delivered notices to homes.	_____
4. The side door was left open on Thursday night but luckily nothing was stolen.	_____
5. Our advertising budget allows for radio TV and newspaper advertising as well as for handouts at shopping plazas.	_____
6. A career as a journalist is both exciting and demanding.	_____
7. We applied for a liquor licence immediately but we had to wait six months for one.	_____
8. We were assured we could swim all day in a heated pool yet the pool at the hotel was open only in the afternoons.	_____
9. The alternator appears to be working for the current is now coming through.	_____
10. Ms. Mah is a capable engineer but is not experienced enough for the position of chief engineer.	_____
Total Score	_____

If you achieved your goal of at least 8 points, proceed to Unit 3.4. If you did not score 8, ask your instructor for direction before moving on.

EXERCISE 3.4 MORE ABOUT THE COMMA

Insert commas where necessary in the following sentences. Score 1 point for each correctly punctuated sentence; no marks for partially correct punctuation. Deduct 1 point for each comma you inserted that was not necessary.

Your Goal: To score at least 8 points.

Example: The assistant who joined the company only last week is most efficient. (no commas) 1

Score

1. Because Mr. Knight had lost his ticket he had to buy another one before he was allowed to enter the auditorium. _____
2. We can of course hold a reservation for you only until July 15 at the latest. _____
3. When you come to my home you will see above the chesterfield a marvellous painting by Paul Kane. _____
4. The first person who came to my mind was the late Sir Laurence Olivier the famous English actor. _____
5. After accepting the assignment Rosemarie asked for help to complete it on time. _____
6. To be aware of the dangers involved with nuclear energy is to be aware of the need for control. _____
7. I believe it is possible to manufacture a microchip smaller than the dot of an *i*. _____
8. In the ever-expanding field of preventive medicine much hope is placed on educating the public in sensible eating habits. _____
9. Your daily itinerary however can be changed if you want to do something else. _____
10. A car manufactured to run on water would be a marvellous invention. _____

Total Score _____

If you achieved your goal of at least 8 points, proceed to Unit 3.5. If you did not score 8, go back and review Unit 3.4 thoroughly; then do Exercise 3.4A and try to achieve your goal this time.

EXERCISE 3.4A MORE ABOUT THE COMMA

Use the same directions as for Exercise 3.4

Your Goal: To score at least 8 points.

	Score
1. Miss Macdonald will of course include a visit to Prince George on her western schedule.	_____
2. When the suggested cafeteria menus were submitted for approval the board was concerned about nutritional values.	_____
3. Many people believe that winning a lottery will make life easy for them as they believe they will no longer need to work.	_____
4. Wise money management according to economists is the best way to beat inflation.	_____
5. The revised work schedule should I think be better for everyone.	_____
6. Renée is the person to whom you should talk about your suggestion.	_____
7. Madame Sauvé appointed Speaker of the House in 1980 was the first woman to hold that position.	_____
8. If you plan to open a small corner store you must expect to work long hours.	_____
9. Franchises are available for anyone who is interested in handling our products.	_____
10. Having found the ideal location you will agree I am sure that the next step is to find the best builder to build your dream cottage.	_____
Total Score	_____

If you achieved your goal of at least 8 points, proceed to Unit 3.5. If you did not score 8, ask your instructor for direction before moving on.

EXERCISE 3.5 STILL MORE ABOUT THE COMMA

Insert commas where necessary in the following sentences. Score 1 point for each correctly punctuated sentence; no marks for partially correct punctuation. Deduct 1 point for each comma you inserted that was not necessary.

Your Goal: To score at least 8 points.

Example: Will you take this call now, Michelle, or will you call back later? 1

Score

1. If you want a fast-growing shade-giving tree the split-leaf maple is recommended. ______
2. Maclean's Vancouver office is at Suite 600 1111 Melville Street Vancouver British Columbia V6E 3V6. ______
3. Registration for swimming lessons will be held on Monday September 14 from 7:30 p.m. to 9:30 p.m. ______
4. Mr. Huang asked "When can I become a Canadian Citizen?" ______
5. Kay came to Canada in July 1990 and did not return to Scotland for a holiday until August 1992. ______
6. In order to conserve paper towels or sponges should be used for small unexpected clean-up jobs. ______
7. Large fluffy easy-to-wash duvets are available to match our latest line of cotton fitted sheets. ______
8. The inspector asked whether the report of the accident had been submitted to the insurance company. ______
9. The Christmas vacation for that winter Mr. Vilas was from December 24 1991 to January 5 1992. ______
10. There are very very few occasions to write a figure as large as 496 576 834 unless it refers to a serial number a policy number a credit card number or a social insurance number. ______

Total Score ______

If you achieved your goal of at least 8 points, proceed to Unit 3.6. If you did not score 8, go back and review Unit 3.5 thoroughly; then do Exercise 3.5A and try to achieve your goal this time.

EXERCISE 3.5A STILL MORE ABOUT THE COMMA

Use the same directions as for Exercise 3.5

Your Goal: To score at least 8 points.

Score

1. Will you stay with us Miss Palef when you come for the convention in April of next year? ______
2. "How many people" the report asked "will be laid off if the recession continues?" ______
3. The June 1990 issue of *Memo* had a very interesting educational entertaining article on "How to Cope with Advanced Technology." ______
4. The large open fully carpeted livingroom gives the house an atmosphere of elegance. ______
5. It is quite impossible to forecast the future, but it is very very possible to insure against loss of income. ______
6. To many a child singing loudly is an emotional experience that is very enjoyable. ______
7. The director asked how many more scenes are still to be completed before the film is ready for editing. ______
8. Send your order to P.O. Box 144 Summerside Prince Edward Island C1N 4P6 and you will receive your seeds within two weeks. ______
9. The opening ceremonies will be held on Monday June 11 19— at 3 p.m. ______
10. The federal election on Monday February 18 1980 put the Liberals back in power for the fourth time. ______

Total Score ______

If you achieved your goal of at least 8 points, proceed to Unit 3.6. If you did not score 8, ask your instructor for direction before moving on.

EXERCISE 3.6 CONTRACTIONS AND POSSESSIVES

Insert apostrophes and an *s* (if required) where necessary in the following sentences. Score 1 point for each correct insertion; deduct 1 point for any incorrectly used apostrophes.

Your Goal: To score at least 16 points.

Example: The manager's briefcase was stolen, and he's very upset. 2

Score

1. Visit Bart and Flo Snack Bar, the town finest eating place. ____
2. I cant wait to see the Harrises new house. ____
3. The young man application has been sent to the personnel manager office for Ms. Thompson approval. ____
4. His brother-in-law boat has been stolen. ____
5. Kevin estimate for the landscaping is higher than Sam. ____
6. Please arrange a six months trip for Mr. Davies family. ____
7. Our girls dresses and children shoes are very practical. ____
8. Were sorry about the delay, but youll be pleased to hear your order will be shipped in two days time. ____
9. Ms. Norman is annoyed at Vera leaving without saying where she put the customer account. ____
10. Mr. Hodgkins supplies have been put on the front counter. ____

Total Score ____

If you achieved your goal of at least 16 points, proceed to Unit 3.7. If you did not score 16, go back and review Unit 3.6 thoroughly; then do Exercise 3.6A and try to achieve your goal this time. time.

EXERCISE 3.6A CONTRACTIONS AND POSSESSIVES

Use the same directions as for Exercise 3.6

Your Goal: To score at least 16 points.

Score

1. Its too late in the season to enrol, but youre welcome to come and see our facilities. ____
2. Leslie and Edith purses are so alike that theyre forever being taken by the wrong woman! ____
3. Whos next in line for David job when he retires in two months time? ____
4. Starting on September 10, Mr. McGinnis sporting goods store is having a sale on childrens hockey equipment. ____
5. The sun heat is a source of energy which could be used to conserve the world precious oil reserves. ____
6. The Allens have invited you to attend their son opening a new gallery in the city downtown art section. ____
7. Somebody machine was left on high power and blew a fuse; as a result, nobody machine has been working all day. ____
8. The finest wire weve been able to buy is 00 gauge, and were hoping it will be strong enough for the application. ____
9. John replying so abruptly to the supervisor has caused a feeling of tension in the lunch room. ____
10. The crew is currently working on the pool at Mr. Kernahan. ____

Total Score ____

If you achieved your goal of at least 16 points, proceed to Unit 3.7. If you did not score 16, ask your instructor for direction before moving on.

EXERCISE 3.7 PARENTHESES, BRACKETS, ELLIPSIS MARKS, AND DASHES

Punctuate the interruptions shown in italics in the following sentences in the most appropriate way using commas, parentheses, brackets, or dashes. Insert any other dashes that are necessary. Score 1 point for each correctly punctuated sentence; no marks for partially correct punctuation. *Deduct* 1 point for any wrongly inserted punctuation.

Your Goal: To score at least 8 points.

Example: These figures — *can you believe it?* — indicate an increase of 35 percent. 1

Score

1. There is *of course* no reason to refuse the request. ____
2. The bicycle assembly *see booklet for instructions* can be completed in half an hour. ____
3. The bulletin stated: "All competitors must sign in before 9 a.m. in order to be assigned there *sic* starting positions." ____
4. Shady elms, leafy maples, and elegant birches *such trees add beauty to our lots.* ____
5. Although foreign exchange rates are always fluctuating, the dollar has been steady for the last three days. *Business Section, page 5.* ____
6. A substantial amount of money *$35 000* has been set aside for the acquisition of exercise equipment. ____
7. Their strict safety regulations *compulsory use of hard hats, safety glasses, heavy duty boots, and gauntlet gloves* have proved successful in reducing the number of on-the-job injuries. ____
8. Madame Charbonneau began her speech, "I know you expect me to speak in French, but I'm going to speak en anglais!" *Laughter* ____
9. I understand *however* that you have agreed to help us complete the project. ____
10. Almost seven thousand copies *did I tell you this before?* have already been sold. ____

Total Score ____

If you achieved your goal of at least 8 points, proceed to Unit 3.8. If you did not score 8, go back and review Unit 3.7 thoroughly; then do Exercise 3.7A and try to achieve your goal this time.

EXERCISE 3.7A PARENTHESES, BRACKETS, ELLIPSIS MARKS, AND DASHES

Use the same directions as for Exercise 3.7

Your Goal: To score at least 8 points.

Score

1. Mr. Santilli *whom I asked to attend* has replied that he will be delighted to come. ______
2. Statistics for this year *see Table 1 on page 14* show a healthy increase in production. ______
3. Owen's report read: "Toy manufacturers in Switzerland have agreed to expert *sic* samples of our new items by the end of July." ______
4. Miss Ecob *I believe it was Miss Ecob* has suggested that the dressing room for the models should be air-conditioned. ______
5. Wallpaper, water troughs, brushes, paints, sponges, and masking tape *all your requirements for home decorating* are here in our Northtown store. ______
6. There is only one word to describe your new home *magnificent*! ______
7. Routine matters *absences, transfers, trips to the school nurse* can be handled by a counsellor. ______
8. The large number of replies *758 out of 1000 questionnaires sent out* makes the result of the survey very interesting. ______
9. He said *and you may quote me* that he did not want to hear that argument again. ______
10. Do you know *Susan* if the merchandise from Montreal will arrive in time for the sale? ______

Total Score ______

If you achieved your goal of at least 8 points, proceed to Unit 3.8. If you did not score 8, ask your instructor for direction before moving on.

EXERCISE 3.8 QUOTATION MARKS AND UNDERLINING

Insert quotation marks and underlining where necessary in the following sentences. Score 1 point for each correct pair of quotation marks and 1 point for each correct underlining.

Your Goal: To score at least 8 points.

Example: After several hours of discussion, the chairperson said, "Let us now proceed with the next item on the agenda." 1

Score

1. Mr. Green closed his letter with the words May we have the pleasure of serving you again? ____
2. The Gage Canadian Dictionary is a valuable reference. ____
3. Be sure to include the article Computers—What You Should Know About Them in the next month's issue. ____
4. The display artist said, I must have more space. Can you give me two windows? ____
5. Reserve today; make your dream of flying in the Concorde come true. ____
6. Stephen Leacock's essay My Financial Career has been made into a most amusing animated short film. ____
7. A sculpture by Henry Moore called The Archer was purchased by the city of Toronto. ____
8. A special report on the investigation will appear on The National on Wednesday at 10 p.m. ____
9. Most business people read The Financial Post. ____
10. We have marked your account Paid in Full and enclose your receipt. ____

Total Score ____

If you achieved your goal of at least 8 points, proceed to Unit 3.9. If you did not score 8, go back and review Unit 3.8 thoroughly; then do Exercise 3.8A and try to achieve your goal this time.

EXERCISE 3.8A QUOTATION MARKS AND UNDERLINING

Use the same directions as for Exercise 3.8

Your Goal: To score at least 8 points.

Score

1. Authorized car racing in the streets, said the mayor, will never be allowed in this city. ____
2. The chapter headed Investing for the Small Investor contains many helpful suggestions. ____
3. Many customers ask us, How can you keep your prices so low? ____
4. The editorial in last week's Maclean's magazine was very amusing. ____
5. The RCMP ship St. Roch is surprisingly small for the strenuous work it performed. ____
6. Tickets for the show Letters from Wingfield Farm are included in the package. ____
7. The slogan Bring a Friend used by the Red Cross has been very successful. ____
8. The package must be clearly marked Fragile. ____
9. After reading the government's bulletin How to Eat Well and Lose Weight, you will feel motivated to reduce. ____
10. Please renew my subscription to Sports Illustrated for one year. ____

Total Score ____

If you achieved your goal of at least 8 points, proceed to Unit 3.9. If you did not score 8, ask your instructor for direction before moving on.

EXERCISE 3.9 VOCABULARY

Complete the three parts of this exercise according to the directions for each part.

Your Goal: To score at least 18 points.

A. Definitions

Complete the following sentences by choosing the most appropriate words from those given. Score 1 point for each correct answer.

bias	collateral	collate	convey
compromise	decipher	depreciate	derive
curtail	chronological		

Score

1. If you can _______________ the illegible writing, please type the pages; then _______________ them in numerical order for printing. _____
2. We shall _______________ a great deal of satisfaction from knowing that our offer of a _______________ in the dispute is acceptable. _____
3. The letters are clearly date stamped. Please file them in _______________ order with the most recent on top. _____

Score for Part A _____

B. Usage

Use the same directions as for Part A.

coarse	course	complement	compliment
council	counsel	defer	differ
die	dye	disburse	disperse

Score

1. Of _______________ , this material is too _______________ for your design, but we want your opinion of the colour. _____
2. Let me _______________ you an acquiring a full _______________ of trainees. _____
3. Although they _______________ in their ways of handling workers, they will always _______________ to each other if a compromise is needed. _____
4. Unfortunately, we cannot make more parts as the _______________ has cracked. A special _______________ is needed to colour glossy paper. _____
5. Most schools have a very active student _______________ I would like to _______________ you, but I think you would be well advised to seek legal _______________. _____
6. Part of the treasurer's job is to _______________ money when bills have to be paid. Please _______________ the notices for the demonstrations among all the visitors to the exhibition. _____

Score for Part B _____

C. Spelling

By using proofreaders' marks or otherwise, correct any spelling errors in the following words. Write the correct spelling above the word if necessary. Score 1 point for each correctly changed word; deduct 1 point for each word changed that was correct as written.

Score

1.	dyeing	personally	noticable	_____
2.	advantageous	incidentally	servicable	_____
3.	acknowledgment	basicly	knowledgeable	_____
4.	occassionally	manageable	judgment	_____
5.	accidentally	chargable	practically	_____
			Score for Part C	_____
			Total Score	_____

If you achieved your goal of at least 18 points, proceed to Unit 3.10. If you did not score 18, go back and review Unit 3.9 thoroughly before moving on.

EXERCISE 3.10 PROOFREADING

Use the appropriate proofreaders' marks to correct the punctuation in the following passage. Score 1 point for each correctly used proofreaders' mark. *Deduct* 1 point for wrongly corrected punctuation or for the omission of balancing punctuation. There may be other errors which you should also find when you are proofreading. Mark them and score 1 point for each you find.

Your Goal: To score at least 16 points.

Example: The professional photographer of course, demands the best in cameras, film, lighting, and developing materials. (Score 4 points for inserting commas after *course, cameras, film, lighting*; deduct 1 point for missing comma after *photographer.*) 3

The fuel crisis should be of concern to everyone Many people however just will not except the responsibility of of trying to conserve the countrys' resources. It is of course very easy to sit comfortably in a snug well-insulated modern home and say The fuel crisis wont bother me I've done all I can and I can afford to pay the high prices.

The government's recent publication Everyone Can Help should be read carefully. It detials how fuel is misused and gives many hints on how homeowners can conserve in their daily lives.

Businesses are also asked to save as much energy as possble. If everyone co-operates Canadians can be proud of their response to the world's need to conserve energy.

Number of errors found and correctly marked ______

Deduct for errors missed ______

Total Score ______

If you achieved your goal of at least 16 points, proceed to the Posttest for Unit 3. If you did not score 16, you will realize how easy it is to miss mistakes! Review Unit 3.10 thoroughly before moving on.

STYLE

Mechanics of style relates to specific details about writing such as whether a capital letter is used, whether a number is written in words or figures, and whether an abbreviation includes periods. This unit will help you choose the forms generally used in acceptable writing.

CAPITALIZATION

You already know when certain capital letters are required, for example, with your own name. The instances where other capital letters are required are covered by the following rules. When in doubt be sure to check with a dictionary, reference manual, or style guide.

❍ 4.1 Beginnings, Personal Names, Place Names, and Religious and Historical Names

Beginnings

1. Use a capital for the first word of every sentence and direct quotation.

   Franchise operations are becoming more and more popular.

   Rajiv said, "My ticket was for Hawaii, but my luggage went to Fiji!"

2. Use a capital for the first word of an independent clause following a colon if the words preceding the colon are introductory.

   This is the problem: Do we have enough evidence to sue?

Do not use a capital if the word following the colon begins a list.

These are our concerns: not enough money, no skilled labour, and too high taxes.

Proofreaders' Mark

To indicate that a capital letter is required, write three short lines under the letter to be capitalized.

this is an example of what i mean.

Mini-Test

By using the proofreaders' mark for capitalization, show where capitals should be used in the following sentences.

1. here is the situation: we must have a firm commitment by October 31.
2. the foreword started in this way: this report outlines our activities during the past year.
3. a famous quotation of Martin Luther King is "we shall overcome."
4. give details of these items in your estimate: cost of materials, cost of services, wages, and consultant's fees.
5. the bulletin stated: the store will be closed July 15 to July 22.

KEY

1. here...we 2. the...this report 3. a...we 4. give (no other capitals) 5. the bulletin...the

Personal Names

1. Use a capital for the names and initials of persons as well as their titles and degrees when part of the name.

   Mrs. Janine Harding

   Prime Minister Trudeau

   Alan Atkins, Ph.D

   the Reverend Ronald Nickle

   Mayor June Rowlands

   President Wilkinson of

   Kwantlen College

   the Honorable Jean Chretien

Do not use a capital for titles or names of degrees when not part of a person's name.

Mr. Wilkinson has been president of the college for six years.

Nadia earned her fine arts degree at the university in her home town.

The councillor agreed to speak at the meeting.

2. Prefixes in foreign names are capitalized only when no first name appears with the last name. Otherwise, follow the way the person who has the name spells it.

De Klerk F. W. de Klerk
Van Gogh Vincent van Gogh
John De Visser (as in his signature)

3. Use a capital for a title used in place of a full name in direct address.

   Mme. Speaker, the audience eagerly awaits your comments.
   I would like a second opinion, Doctor.

Mini-Test

By using the proofreaders' mark for capitalization, show where capitals should be used in the following sentences or phrases.

1. the election of prime minister thatcher in Great Britain
2. he has completed his master's degree.
3. joan cunnington, m.a.
4. when donald getty was premier of alberta
5. have you asked which professors will be coming?
6. dr. pawloski is the doctor in charge of the case.
7. have you read about de la salle's voyage?

KEY

1. prime minister thatcher 2. he 3. joan cunnington, m.a. 4. when donald getty alberta 5. have (no other capitals) 6. dr. pawloski (no other capitals) 7. have...de la salle's

Place Names

1. Capitalize geographic names.

   the Caribbean
   the St. Lawrence Seaway
   the Fraser River
   Quebec
   Flin Flon, Manitoba
   Mount Logan

2. Some derivatives of place or personal names are not capitalized. Check with your dictionary whenever you are in doubt.

   india ink plaster of paris
   french fries china

But: Bristol board

3. Capitalize names of buildings and other structures, ships, trains, and planes.

   the Empire State Building
   the CN Tower
   the Trans-Canada Highway
   the Polar Bear Express
   the Bluenose
   St. Olaf's Church

4. Capitalize points of the compass when used to identify specific geographic regions or in place names.

   East Kemptville
   the West Coast
   the Eastern Townships
   Northwest Territories
   the South
   the Near East

But: eastern Ontario (with names of provinces)
northern Alberta

Do not capitalize points of the compass when they refer to direction or when they are general adjectives.

west of the Red River
a north wind
his eastern roots

5. Capitalize the words *city, province,* and *state* only when they are used as part of the official names.

   Quebec City
   Pennsylvania State University
   the seal of the Province of New Brunswick

But: Potatoes from the province of Prince Edward Island are world famous.

Mini-Test

By using the proofreaders' mark for capitalization, show where capitals should be used in the following phrases.

1. the canals of venice
2. visit beautiful british columbia
3. the newfoundland scenery
4. climb the rockies
5. frozen french fries
6. the empress hotel
7. the challenger spacecraft
8. our west coast representative
9. work for the province of nova scotia
10. the fishing industry in the maritimes

KEY

1. venice 2. british columbia 3. newfoundland 4. rockies 5. no capitals 6. empress hotel 7. challenger 8. west coast 9. nova scotia 10. maritimes

Religious and Historical Names

1. Use a capital for words referring to a particular religious figure or document.

God the Father	the Pope
the Bible	Buddha
Mohammed	the Koran

But: Books on astrology are her bibles. Computers are often considered gods.

2. Use a capital for names of peoples and races, languages, and religious faiths.

Canadians	Japanese
English	Islam
a Protestant	a Jew
Jewish	Buddhism

Use a capital for names of important documents, historical events, and periods of time. Do not use a capital for the names of centuries.

the Constitution
the British North America Act
the Stone Age
the Gulf War

But: The twenty-first century will be exciting.

Mini-Test

By using the proofreaders' mark for capitalization, show where capitals should be used in the following phrases.

1. an import of belgian crystal
2. the french-canadian population
3. the jewish and christian faiths
4. the income tax act
5. in the eighteenth century
6. a spanish guitar
7. the calgary stampede
8. the arabs in jerusalem
9. swear on the bible to tell the truth
10. the declaration of independence

KEY

1. belgian 2. french-canadian 3. jewish and christian 4. income tax act 5. no capitals 6. spanish 7. calgary stampede 8. arabs in jerusalem 9. bible 10. declaration of independence

SUMMARY FOR UNIT 4.1

- *Always* capitalize:
  - the first word of a sentence and quotation
  - titles coming before and forming part of a name
  - initials standing for degrees
  - prefixes in foreign names if no first name is used—titles used as names in direct address
  - geographical names, names of buildings and other structures
  - names of ships, trains, and planes
  - compass points when part of the specific name
  - words pertaining to a particular religion
  - names of peoples and races, languages, and religious faiths
  - important documents, historical events and periods of time
- *Do not* capitalize:
  - the names of degrees
  - titles coming after a name or used in a general sense
  - place, language, or personal names used for common terms (such as *french fries*)
  - compass points when meaning the general direction or used as a general adjective
  - names of centuries

Confirm Your Knowledge

Complete Exercise for Unit 4.1 on page 170.

4.2 Organizations, Titles, and Other Special Rules

Organizations

1. Capitalize the *full* names of specific governments, organizations, institutions, divisions, and departments.

   Moncton City Council
   the Senate
   the Canadian Government
   Justice Department
   the North York Public Library
   House of Commons
   Lakehead University
   the Faculty of Medicine
   International Nickel Company
   the Board of Directors
   the Business and Commerce Department

Do not capitalize such names when used as adjectives or without the full title.

a senate committee	the administration
the federal government	the city council
the company	the department
the faculty	the board
the parliamentary function	

2. Capitalize the full names of political parties, societies, associations, unions, churches, and similar organizations.

   the New Democratic Party
   Children's Aid Society
   the International Word Processing Association
   Canadian Union of Public Employees
   the Canadian Standards Association

But: the union the association

Mini-Test

By using proofreaders' marks or otherwise, show where capitals are necessary in the following sentences.

1. The board of directors of the ford motor company is meeting this afternoon to discuss union demands.
2. The house of commons has recessed for the summer, but the ministry of the environment is to continue working full time.
3. Ask Ms. Collins if she has the report from the canadian manufacturers' association.
4. Visitors from holland college are expected next week; they want to see our computer centre.
5. Austin Edwards, a prominent figure in the conservative party, has refused to comment on the findings of the committee formed to investigate federal spending.

KEY

1. board of directors...ford motor company 2. house of commons...ministry of the environment 3. canadian manufacturers' association 4. holland college 5. conservative party...(no other capitals as the committee is referred to in general terms, not by its specific name)

Titles

1. Capitalize the first word and other important words in the titles of books, newspapers, magazines, and other publications and of works of art. Do not capitalize *a*, *an*, or *the*, conjunctions, and prepositions unless they are the first word of the title.

   Lord of the Flies
   A Tale of Two Cities
   the *Montreal Gazette*
   The Toronto Star
   National Geographic Magazine
   Kreighoff's *Running the Toll*

2. Only capitalize the second part of a hyphenated word if it would be capitalized on its own or if it is in a title or heading.

   non-Christian communities
   The Life of a Mother-in-Law

But: Mayor-elect Tonks

3. Only capitalize names of parts of a book (table of contents, preface, appendix) if they refer to a specific part within the same book.

   A list of unfamiliar words will be found in Appendix A.

But: The glossary lists all unfamiliar words.

4. Capitalize the names of specific courses listed in a school calendar; do not capitalize the names of subjects used in a general way.

   Introductory Investing
   Philosophy 101

But: I would like to study philosophy.

5. Capitalize titles of catalogues and special promotions, but not if the reference to them is general.
   our Back-to-School Catalogue
   our Tenth Anniversary Fashion Show

But: in your spring catalogue

Other Special Rules

1. Capitalize days of the week, months, and special dates.

Friday	January
Thanksgiving	Ash Wednesday
Ramadan	

2. Only capitalize the names of seasons when used as a person (mainly in poetry) or as part of a title.

   The icy blasts of Winter's breath chilled the travellers.

But: winter holiday fall fashions

Letters

In the opening and closing of letters, only capitalize the first word and any word used in place of a person's name.

Dear Madam	My dear Sir
Yours truly	Yours very truly

Trademarks

Capitalize trademark names.

a can of Pepsi a Maytag washer

Mini-Test

By using proofreaders' marks or otherwise, show where capitals are necessary in the following sentences.

1. Have you read *the adventures of tom sawyer* by Mark Twain?
2. The article in *the vancouver sun* explains why elementary accounting and basic computer programming are such popular courses in the fall semester.
3. Refer to appendix c on page 117 for a schedule of delivery dates.
4. I am returning the adidas track suit that I bought at your st. valentine's day sale.
5. May I call on saturday, october 24, to discuss your homeowner's policy.

KEY

1. the adventures of tom sawyer 2. the vancouver sun...elementary accounting and basic computer programming 3. appendix c 4. adidas...st. valentine's day sale 5. saturday, october 24

SUMMARY FOR UNIT 4.2

- *Always* capitalize the *specific* names of:
  - governments, institutions, organizations, departments, and divisions
  - political parties, societies, unions, associations, churches
  - parts of a book (index, table of contents, bibliography)
  - courses in a school calendar
  - catalogues and special sales
  - holidays, days, and months
  - trademarks
- *Always* capitalize the first word and all
  - important words in:
  - titles of works of art, books, newspapers, and magazines
  - column headings
- *Always* capitalize:
  - the first word only and the word used for the name at the beginning of a letter; the first word only in the closing
- *Do not* capitalize:
  - general references to government and other organizations, departments, divisions, branches, offices
  - *a*, *an*, *the*, conjunctions, or prepositions in the middle of a title
  - general references to parts of a book
  - subjects in general, as opposed to particular courses; languages, however, are always capitalized
  - references to seasons

In short

- *Capitalize* if you are referring to a particular name.
- *Do not capitalize* if you are writing in a general sense.

Confirm Your Knowledge

Complete Exercise for Unit 4.2 on page 172.

Compound Words

4.3 Compound Modifiers, Prefixes, and Numbers

A compound word is made up of two or more words which express a single thought.

bar graph   son-in-law   software

If you are in any doubt about the way a compound word should be written, look up the word in a dictionary or reference manual.

Compound Modifiers

Words used together as a single modifier (adjective or adverb) require special attention. *Temporary compounds* are hyphenated when they appear before the word they modify but are written open (without hyphens) when they come after.

an out-of-town visitor
a visitor from out of town

a double-density disk
The disk is double density.

a full-time job
His job is full time.

a safety-conscious employer
an employer who is safety conscious

a well-known disc jockey
The disc jockey is well known.

Some compound modifiers are always hyphenated.

old-fashioned   left-handed

clear-cut

Note: Adverbs ending in *–ly* are not hyphenated in a compound modifier if the adverb can be omitted.

a greatly superior product
a finely tuned piano
a hurriedly assembled team
a roughly cut stone

But: a friendly-looking person (you could not say a looking person)

Proofreaders' Marks

To show that a hyphen should be used between words, use the insert mark (^) and write the hyphen above it.

clerk typist   self interest
right handed

To show that words should be written together as one word, use close-up marks (⁀‿) to indicate that there should be no space.

text book   proof read

soft ware

Mini-Test

Insert hyphens where necessary in the following groups of words.

1. an out of work philosopher
2. Mr. Larkman is very old fashioned.
3. an up to date statement
4. This fact is well known.
5. the month end report
6. a well known fact
7. Your work is first class.
8. a soft spoken rebuke
9. a cleverly arranged program
10. I must bring my address book up to date.

KEY

1. out-of-work 2. old-fashioned 3. up-to-date 4. no hyphen 5. month-end 6. well-known 7. no hyphen 8. soft-spoken 9. no hyphen 10. no hyphen

Prefixes

Most compound words using prefixes are not hyphenated.

counterbalance	forefront
overdue	microprocessor
multipurpose	subdivision

The following are some of the more common prefixes. Check your dictionary for their meanings.

ante	anti	bi	counter
dis	extra	hyper	in
inter	intra	macro	micro
mini	non	out	over
post	pre	pro	re
retro	sem	sub	super
trans	ultra	un	under

Exceptions

1. Use a hyphen between a prefix and a proper noun

   pre-Confederation pro-Canadian
   mid-February

2. Use a hyphen between the prefix and the main word to separate identical vowels; do not use a hyphen between two different vowels or double consonants.

   pre-eminent co-operate

But: semiannual nonnegotiable

3. Use a hyphen after a prefix if the resulting word could be confused with another word.

   re-cover (cover again)
   recover (improve in health)

4. Use a hyphen with "self" words.

   self-confident self-control
   self-interest

But: selfish, selfless

Mini-Test

By using proofreaders' marks or otherwise, show whether any words in the following groups should be hyphenated or closed.

1. over due account
2. self contained
3. Pre Confederation days
4. re mark the papers
5. trans Canada
6. non aligned
7. semi colon
8. inter office
9. pre empted
10. under stated

KEY

1. over‿due 2. self-contained 3. Pre-Confederation 4. re-mark 5. trans-Canada 6. non‿aligned 7. semi‿colon 8. inter‿office 9. pre-empted 10. under‿stated

Numbers

1. Use a hyphen for compound numbers from twenty-one to ninety-nine when they are spelled out.

   thirty-five
   two hundred twenty-seven (note no need for *and*)

2. Use a hyphen with spelled-out fractions.

   a three-quarters majority
   a majority of three-quarters

3. Use a hyphen for numbers with units of measurement if they come before a noun.

   a 12-character margin
   a 15-floor building
   a four-year-old child

But: a 5 percent tax a building of 15 floors

Further Points to Remember

1. Be sure of the difference between *sometime* (adverb) and *some time* (adjective and noun).

Hint: If you can substitute *a long* for *some*, write two words.

some time ago	(a long time ago)
at some time	(at a long time)
for some time	(for a long time)

sometime later (How later? adverb needed)
Let me try your camera sometime.

Note: Sometimes, meaning "occasionally," is always one word.

Sometimes my camera lets in the light.

2. Be sure of the following words where no hyphens are used.

   nevertheless nowadays
   insofar as today
   tonight tomorrow

Also: thank you (two words; no hyphen)

3. Note the hyphen to replace *to* in some expressions used as adjectives.

   the Winnipeg-Saskatoon train
   the student-teacher ratio

Do not use a hyphen for *to* if there is no noun following.

The train from Winnipeg to Saskatoon will arrive on schedule.
The ratio of student to teacher is too high.

4. If two or more compound adjectives have the same form, the common part may be omitted. The hyphen, however, must be written with the correct spacing as shown in the examples.

   a ten- or twelve-minute delay

   one-, two-, and three-week vacations

Mini-Test

By using proofreaders' marks or otherwise, show whether any words in the following groups should be hyphenated or closed.

1. for some time
2. one or two year contract
3. the Saint John Digby ferry
4. a quorum of thirty three
5. a 90 year lease
6. in as much as
7. Thank you for your help.
8. one half of the replies
9. I have completed three quarters of the work.
10. Some times I feel lazy.

KEY

1. no hyphens 2. one-or two-year 3. Saint John-Digby 4. thirty-three 5. 90-year 6. inasmuchas 7. no hyphen 8. one-half 9. three-quarters 10. Sometimes

Summary for Unit 4.3

- **Compound** words are combinations of two or more words.
  - **Temporary** compounds are hyphenated **before** the noun and open **after** the word modified.
- Some compound modifiers are always hyphenated.
- Adverbs ending in *–ly* are not hyphenated to form a compound.
- Do not hyphenate after a prefix except:
  - if joined to a proper noun
  - to separate identical vowels
  - to distinguish the word from another word
  - in "self" words
- Hyphenate:
  - numbers like twenty-one
  - fractions
  - numbers with units of measurement – before a noun
  - each part in a series of compound adjectives
- Remember:
  - *sometime* is an adverb
  - *some time* is an adjective and a noun (substitute *a long* for *some*)
  - *sometimes* means "occasionally"

Confirm Your Knowledge

Complete Exercise for Unit 4.1 on page 174.

NUMBERS

❍ 4.4 Basic Rules; Addresses, Dates, Times, and Other Uses

Should a number be written in words or figures? The decision is often difficult. The following rules are guidelines for general writing; however, check with a style guide or reference manual for more involved usage.

Basic Rule

Spell out in words numbers used in a general or an approximate sense.

We have already received about three hundred replies.

Over a thousand litres of chemicals were spilled.

Write in figures numbers used in an exact or precise sense and with abbreviations of, or symbols for, units of measurement.

We printed 550 copies of the questionnaire.

The report stated that 1015 L of chemicals had been spilled.

Calculate the interest for 1 year 6 months and 17 days.

General Rules

1. Numbers at the beginning of a sentence must be written in words. If a number is very long, rephrase the sentence so that the number is not at the beginning.

   Thirty-six kilograms is the amount required.

   One thousand two hundred twenty-seven children were vaccinated.

Better: We require 36 kg.

A total of 1227 children were vaccinated.

Note: The word *and* is omitted from large numbers.

2. When two numbers come together, separate them by a comma or write one of them in words and the other in figures.

   By 1990, 110 students had enrolled.

   Split the property into two 100 ha lots.

Large Numbers

1. Exact numbers over ten are usually written in figures.

   They want to add 21 new trucks to their fleet.

   Would you believe only 105 rings were stolen?

2. For ease in reading long numbers, leave a space between groups of three digits.

   a population of 1 792 544 32 453.072 555

Do not leave a space in four-digit figures except in tables. Do not leave a space in house numbers, room numbers, page numbers, or serial, licence, or credit card numbers which should be written in the same way as they appear on the source document.

1250 copies Room 117 $1700

Serial No. 16752-3666

Licence No. V0123-45678-99999

16160 Main Street

But: SIN 123 456 789

Postal Code: M2N 2R2

Note: No hyphens in SIN or postal code numbers

3. Large numbers in millions or billions often combine figures with words.

   a deficit of $1.5 billion

   a bacteria count of 4 million per millilitre

Mini-Test

Are the following numbers written correctly? If so, write *C* on the line provided; if not, write *X*.

1. Bring fifteen writing pads. _____
2. 312 people came to the dance. _____
3. Sign up for 7 4-week sessions. _____
4. $17 450 000 _____
5. a total of 6 million items _____
6. $6,500 _____
7. We sold 312 tickets. _____
8. almost 700 applicants _____
9. 5 500 Yonge Street _____
10. 60 km _____

KEY

1. X 2. X 3. X 4. C 5. C 6. X 7. C 8. X 9. X 10. C

Small Numbers

1. Generally numbers under 11 are written in words. Numbers over 11 that are the only numbers in the material and that can be written as one word may also be written in words.

   The junior day-care group had only five children.

   The senior day-care group had fifteen.

2. Write all figures in a related group in the same way using figures for the smaller numbers.

   The teacher requested 5 desks, 5 chairs, and 25 cushions.

   Trips may be planned for 4, 7, 14, or 28 days.

Ages

A person's age is usually written in words.

She is thirty-five. a six-year-old child

However, for legal purposes when an exact age is required, figures are used.

Her exact age for insurance purposes is 35 years 4 months and 6 days.

Money

Sums of money are written in figures in general writing.

The tickets cost $6 plus tax. (*Note*: Not $6.00 unless used with other amounts that show cents.)

The rent is $900 per month.

In my childhood, a cup of coffee cost 10 cents. (*Not 10¢* or *$0.10*)

The tickets cost $6.90 each including tax.

Mini-Test

Are the following numbers written correctly? If so, write *C* on the line provided; if not, write *X*.

1. He checked over twenty invoices. _____
2. his 30th birthday _____
3. a five dollar tip _____
4. He is 33._____
5. She spent $500.00._____
6. for two, ten, or 15 days. _____
7. The project is only seventeen days old. _____
8. Order 6 cases of pop and 25 packets of chips. _____
9. a pen for 75¢ _____
10. $17 million _____

KEY

1. C 2. X 3. X 4. X 5. X 6. X 7. C 8. C 9. X 10. C

Addresses

1. Use figures for numbered street names above ten. For easy reading double-space or use a dash between the building number and the number of the street.

   23rd Street 23 Street

   224—12th Avenue 224—12 Avenue

But: Sixth Street Fifth Avenue

2. Building numbers are written in figures; however, if a building number appears as a word on the building or on letterhead, then the word should be used. For clarity, the word *one* is generally used instead of the figure 1.

   76 Portage Avenue 5050 Yonge Street

But: One Lakeshore Drive

3. Canadian postal codes are written as follows with no hyphens or other punctuation.

   V6Z lL5 M2N 2Z8 A2D 3Y6

American ZIP codes are written all in figures with no spaces between them.

Bangor, ME 04401 Austin, TX 78702

Dates, Times, and Other Uses

1. Use figures for dates.

   before June 25 (not 25th or 6/25)

   by April 2

Numeric dating is written in year-month-day order.

General: June 25, 1992

Numeric: 92/06/25

2. Use words to give the time of day except with a.m. or p.m.

   by two after two-thirty

   before two o'clock

But: by 2 p.m. after 2:30 p.m.

3. Use words for the names of decades and centuries, but use figures for years.

   the late nineties

   the Roaring Twenties

   the twenty-first century

But: the 1920s 33 A.D.

Mini-Test

Are the following statements true or false? If true, circle *T*; if false, circle *F*.

1. Canadian postal codes must have a hyphen. T F
2. Write 5th Avenue for the famous street in New York. T F
3. The correct way to write a date is May 31st. T F
4. Numeric dating order is day-month-year. T F
5. Always write a numbered street name in words. T F
6. Use figures always with a.m. or p.m. T F
7. Building numbers are written in figures. T F
8. When using o'clock, write the time in words. T F
9. This century should be written as the twentieth century. T F
10. Actual years are always written in figures. T F

KEY

Answers 1 to 5 are false. Be sure you know why!

Answers 6 to 10 are true. Again, be sure you know why!

Special Points to Remember

1. Mixed numbers are written in figures.

   5 1/4 boxes 10 1/2 balls of wool

Fractions are usually written in words; however, if the fraction is awkward in words, it may be written in figures.

   one-quarter of the boxes

   four-fifths of the class

But: 17/20 of the sales

2. In a decimal fraction with no whole number, use a zero before the decimal point.

   0.45 cm of rain

Note: In metric measurements, always use a decimal point to denote fractions.

   a distance of 1.5 km (not 1 1/2 km)

3. Percentages are written in figures without the % symbol (except in tables).

   She admitted that 66 percent of her capital was in bonds.

   The profits next year should be at least 5 percent higher.

4. Ratios, scores, and results of polls are written in figures.

   a patient-nurse ratio of 15 to 1
   The team lost by 48 to 44.
   The response was 8 in favour and 10 opposed.

5. Metric symbols are always used with figures with no period.

   a tower 120 m high
   an order for 53 kg of cement

   The athlete drank 2 L of water. (Note the symbol for litre is a capital *L*.)

6. Use a diagonal stroke (/) for *per.*

   a speed of 80 km/h

   The car's gas consumption is 20 L/100 km on the highway.

If words are used, use the word *per.*

   Calculate the speed in kilometres per hour.

7. Temperature in degrees Celsius is written with no spaces.

   10^0 C

   A temperature of 37^0 C is equivalent to 98.6^0 F.

8. In Canada, metric terms are spelled "-re" rather than "-er." As a result, it is easier to distinguish between "metre," a unit of length, and "meter," a measuring instrument such as a parking meter.

Mini-Test

Are the numbers written correctly in the following groups? If so, write *C* in the space provided; if not, write the correct form in the space.

1. nine percent __________
2. only .75 g of sugar __________
3. a ratio of 6 to 1 __________
4. 2 3/4 hours __________
5. a mass of 15 kilograms __________
6. He put 33 l of gas into the tank. __________
7. Ship 2/3 of the order today. __________
8. a flood covering 35 ha. of farm land __________
9. clocked at 90 km per hour __________
10. a walk of 2 1/2 km __________

KEY

1. 9 percent 2. 0.75 g 3. C 4. C 5. 15 kg 6. 33 L 7. two-thirds 8. 35 ha (no period) 9. 90 km/h 10. 2.5 km

SUMMARY FOR UNIT 4.4

- Use **words** for numbers:
  - at the beginning of a sentence
  - to distinguish between two figures coming together
  - generally for numbers under 11
  - in ages
  - for street names ten and under
  - with o'clock
  - for fractions unless very awkward
  - for decades and centuries
- Use **figures** for numbers:
  - with an abbreviation of, or a symbol for, a unit of measurement
  - for large numbers over ten
  - in sums of money
  - do not use a decimal point with even amounts of money
  - do not use ¢ or $0.20 for cents
  - for street names that are numbers over ten
  - for dates
  - for specific years
  - for mixed numbers, decimals, and percentages
  - for ratios, scores, and results
- Leave spaces in figures of more than four digits for easy reading. Do not use a comma.
- Use the words *million* or *billion* with a figure for very large amounts.
- Serial numbers, etc., must be written as they appear on their source.
- Postal codes have no punctuation.
- Use the words *cents* and *percent* in general writing, not the symbols ¢ and %.
- With metric measurements
  - always use symbols with figures
  - do not use a period after the symbol unless at the end of a sentence.
  - use a decimal fraction only
  - use a diagonal stroke for *per* with symbols.

In short

- Use *words* for general or approximate numbers.
- Use *figures* for exact or precise numbers or for measurements.

Confirm Your Knowledge

Complete Exercise for Unit 4.4 on page 176.

BREVIATIONS

❍ 4.5 General Guidelines; Personal Names, Addresses, Organizations, Dates, and Other Uses

In general writing, try to avoid using abbreviations and contractions. There are, however, certain times when abbreviations are unavoidable. If you are in any doubt about how an abbreviation should be written, check in your dictionary or reference manual. The following guidelines will help you make decisions covering the most common abbreviations.

General Guidelines

1. If there is no particular need to abbreviate a word, write it out!

   The government has renewed the licence. (not *govt.*)

   An invitation was sent to the Lieutenant-Governor. (not *Lt.-Gov.*)

   The show opens on Thursday, September 20. (not *Thurs., Sept. 20*)

2. Certain abbreviations are used regularly and are not followed by a period.

   memo phone ad auto photo

   Bob Sam Tom Sue Meg

3. Periods are disappearing after many abbreviations; however, this practice is not yet universal. Check your dictionary or reference manual for the preferred usage, and be consistent. Common usage at the time of printing has been used in this textbook.

4. Abbreviate only if space is very limited as on printed forms and in tables.

Personal Names

1. The titles *Mr.*, *Mrs.*, *Ms.*, *M.* (*Monsieur*), *Mme.* (*Madame*), *Mlle.* (*Mademoiselle*), *Messrs.* (the plural form of "*Mr.*" pronounced "messers"), and *Dr.* are always abbreviated and followed by a period. (*Note: Miss* is the only title that has no period.) Other titles are abbreviated only when the full name is used.

   Mr. George C. Scott
   Mr. Scott
   Dr. Moira Macintosh
   Dr. Macintosh
   Brig. Gen. Oliver South
   Lt. Gov. Jeanne Arcande
   Rev. Nelson Whyte
   Sen. Jacinthe Morrison
   Prof. John Leakie
   Rt. Hon. Lester B. Pearson

The title must be written out if only the last name is used.

   Brigadier General South
   Lieutenant Governor Arcande
   the Reverend Whyte
   Senator Morrison
   Professor Leakie
   the Right Honorable Mr. Pearson

Note: After the word *the, Reverend* and *Honorable* are always written out.

2. Degrees after names are abbreviated and have a period after each part with no spaces in between.

   B.A. M.Ed. Ph.D. LL.D. D.D. B.Sc.Eng.

Mr., Mrs., Ms., Miss, or *Dr.* are not used with such degrees, but other titles may be used.

   Helga Svend, B.A.
   (*not* Mrs. Helga Svend, B.A.)
   Everett Horton, Ph.D.
   (*not* Dr. Everett Horton, Ph.D.)

But: Dean Richard Tucker, M.Ed, B.Sc.Eng.

Mini-Test

By using proofreaders' marks or otherwise, make any necessary changes in abbreviations in the following sentences. If the sentence is correct as written, write *C* beside it.

1. Please ask Mr Mackie to come for testing on Mon., March 16.
2. Use your phone to place an ad. in our paper.
3. Messrs. Blake and Graydon will arrange matters between them.
4. Both Prof. Heacock and the Rev. Simpson agreed to speak.

5. Dr. Gordon Nore, M.D., has Mrs. Tina Lopez, M.A., for a patient.

KEY

1. Mr. Mackie...Mon. 2. ad 3. C 4. Prof....Rev. 5. Dr....Mrs. (or M.D....M.A.)

Addresses

For specific details, check a reference manual. The following guidelines will help you in most cases.

1. Addresses within a sentence should be written out; however, because some of the provinces have long names, it is acceptable to use the initials of such provinces in sentences.

   He is presently living at 11 Cochrane Street, Corner Brook, Newfoundland.

   Her trip to Charlottetown, P.E.I., is scheduled for the first week in October.

2. Wherever possible, a full address should be displayed so that it can be easily read.

   Mail should be addressed to:
   Mme. Renee Lebow
   07—13th Street, Apt. 7
   Quebec, PQ
   G1L 2K5

3. The postal code must be included in all mailing addresses. It is written as the last line of the address (see sample address above) or, if the address is very long, it may be written on the same line as the province.

   Mr. W. C. McLeod
   Vice President Sales
   The Top Company Limited
   89 Main Street
   Ottawa, ON K1S 1B7

   Miss Ruth Barber
   Marketing Research Department
   Glass and China Co. Ltd.
   1119 Chaplin Street East
   Swift Current, SK S9H 1J9

The following two-letter abbreviations for the provinces and territories are acceptable in mailing addresses, but should not be used in sentences.

Alberta	AB
British Columbia	BC
Manitoba	MB
New Brunswick	NB
Newfoundland	NF
Northwest Territories	NT
Nova Scotia	NS
Ontario	ON
Prince Edward Island	PE
Quebec	P
Saskatchewan	SK
Yukon Territory	YT

4. Other common abbreviations acceptable in addresses are

Apt.	Apartment	Ste.	Suite
Blvd.	Boulevard	Cres.	Crescent

   127 Wellington Street, Ste. 307
   1355 Regina Avenue, Apt. 1012
   7883 Lawton Blvd.

5. American addresses must include the ZIP code number, which is written after the state name.

   Boston, MA 21099
   Chicago, IL 60611
   Phoenix, Arizona 85072

Mini-Test

Are the following addresses written correctly? If so, write *C* in the space provided; if not, write *X*. Write your reason for each *X* answer.

1. Our offices at 756 Bruce Ave., Nanaimo, are open from 8:30 a.m. to 5:30 p.m.

   ____

2. Address the parcel as follows:

   Miss R. Larkin
   575 Vancouver Street, Suite 305
   Victoria, BC ______________

3. The showroom at 700 Crescent Rd. W. has just received the latest models.

   ____

4. Our mailing address in the United States is:

   45 Parkside Drive
   Kansas City, Missouri. ______________

5. Write to 515 Lake Shore Blvd. West, Toronto, ON M5V 1A3 for further information.

KEY

1. X—Avenue should be written out 2. X—postal code is missing 3. X—*Road* and *West* should be written out 4. X—ZIP code is missing 5. C

Organizations

1. Company names should be written in the same way as they appear in the letterhead. Some companies use abbreviations; some do not.

   Fiberglass Canada Ltd.

   Nacon Products Limited

   A. Guinness & Co.

   Shipley Company

   Johns-Manville Canada Inc.

   Greenshields Incorporated

2. If there is no letterhead for reference, write out all the words including *and* unless the name is very long; then the abbreviations *Inc.* for Incorporated and *Corp.* for Corporation may be used.

   Adelman and Company

   Canada Permanent Mortgage Corp.

3. Some companies are well known by their initials with no periods. However, the first time the company name is used, it should be written in full followed by the initials in parentheses.

   Canadian General Electric Co. Ltd. (CGE)

   International Business Machines Ltd. (IBM)

4. Many other groups, such as government agencies, service organizations, and radio stations, are also well known by their initials. They should be spelled out the first time they appear followed by the initials in parentheses, but thereafter the initials without periods may be used. Some common abbreviations follow; be sure you know what they stand for.

   Royal Canadian Mounted Police (RCMP)

CBC	NATO	YWCA	ACTRA
CNIB	UNICEF	OPEC	CRTC

Mini-Test

Are the abbreviations in the following sentences correct? If so, write *C* in the space provided; if not, write *X* and give the reason.

1. The Canadian Union of Public Employees (CUPE) has ratified the vote.

   ____

2. From the information already given, you will see that CIL has made a very worthwhile offer.

   ____

3. I believe Lucia Santilli and Co. is the firm he has hired, but I am not sure of the spelling of the names. ______________
4. Address the letter to Schwab & Co. Limited as that is the way the name appears on the letterhead. ______________
5. Have you the letter from Central Refrigeration and Air Conditioning Corp.? ______________

KEY

1. C 2. C 3. X—*Company* should be written out 4. C 5. C

Dates

Write out the names of months and the days of the week.

July 1 will fall on a Thursday this year.

Classes are held Monday through Friday.

January, February, and March are the best months for ski vacations.

Where space is very limited, the following abbreviations may be used without periods.

Ja F Mr Ap My Je Ju Au S O N D

Su M Tu W Th F Sa

Other Uses

1. Number

The word *number* is always abbreviated to *No.* when immediately followed by a figure. Note the addition of *s* to form the plural and the use of the period.

Model No. 402 Order Nos. 934 and 935

Number is never abbreviated when used without figures.

2. Common Expressions

Certain common expressions are acceptable as abbreviations.

Her new CD stereo system was a bargain. (compact disc)

The cost of TV commercials has risen sharply.

The new ID cards are ready for all personnel. (identification)

Add to these examples as you come across common abbreviations and make sure you know what they mean.

3. **Computer Terms**

   Some computer terms have become very common and can be used as abbreviations. The following are some examples.

   I have just bought a new PC. (personal computer)

   It operates on MS-DOS. (Microsoft Direct Operating System)

   How much RAM and ROM do you need? (Random Access Memory and Read Only Memory)

   The UPC on products makes the cashier's job much faster. (Universal Product Code)

If you work with a computer, you will no doubt be familiar with many more!

Mini-Test

Are the abbreviations in the following sentences correct? If so, write *C* in the space provided; if not, write *X* and give the reason.

1. Miss Romanoff leaves for Europe on Wed., Sept. 10. ____________
2. Head the table of weekdays M Tu W Th F to save space; omit Saturday and Sunday. ____________
3. The forecast for Mar. and Apr. is not encouraging. ____________
4. The PR people are arranging for camera crews to be present. ____________
5. What is the No. of the model replacing Model No. 124? ____________

Key

1. X—Wednesday, September 2. C 3. X—March and April 4. C 5. X—the number of

Summary for Unit 4.5

- Generally, do not abbreviate words in a sentence.
- Company names are written as they appear on the letterhead.
  - If no reference is available, write out all words except *Inc.* and *Corp.* in long names.
  - Use initials with no periods for well-known companies and organizations.
- Abbreviate only if there is insufficient space for the full word.
- Write personal names in full unless used in a familiar sense.
  - Titles such as *Mr.* and *Dr.* are always abbreviated and followed by a period.
  - Abbreviate other titles used with the full name.
  - Titles are not used with degrees unless they are not connected.
- In addresses, it is acceptable to abbreviate:
  - provinces to two letters
  - long provincial names
  - *Apt.* for "Apartment" and *Blvd.* for "Boulevard"
- The Canadian postal code and the American ZIP code **must** be included in all mailing addresses.
- Do not abbreviate:
  - days and months, unless in tables or where space is very limited
  - titles with the last name only
- Use *No.* for number when a figure follows; use the word "number" at all other times.
- Become familiar with the more common computer terms that are abbreviated.
- Check your dictionary or reference manual for correct abbreviations.

Confirm Your Knowledge

Complete Exercise for Unit 4.5 on page 178.

DEVELOPING YOUR LANGUAGE SKILLS

❍ 4.6 Vocabulary

Definitions

Check your dictionary for the meanings of the following words; then match them up with the definitions given. Write the letter of the definition you choose from Column 2 in the space provided in Column 1.

Column 1		Column 2
_____	detrimental	a) to sign on the back
_____	endeavour	b) make a list
_____	endorse	c) wrap around
_____	enumerate	d) harmful, damaging
_____	envelop	e) to put a worth on something
_____	evaluate	f) out in space
_____	exorbitant	g) an exact copy
_____	facsimile	h) load of goods
_____	feasible	i) excessive, very high
_____	freight	j) possible, practicable
_____		k) try, make an effort

Mini-Test

Complete the following sentences by choosing the most appropriate word from Column 1 under "Definitions."

1. The hotel rates were so __________ in New York that I stayed with friends.
2. Both the president and the vice president must __________ cheques before they can be cashed.
3. Supervisors are asked to __________ the performance of each employee every six months.
4. His lawyer will __________ to convince the jury that he is innocent.
5. Pricing goods too high will have a __________ effect on sales.
6. We plan to __________ the total package in clear plastic.
7. Before each general election, the government has to __________ the population.
8. This machine will produce a perfect __________ of any document you want copied.
9. The cost of transporting __________ by road has increased greatly.
10. Because of the drop in sales, it is no longer __________ to stock this item.

KEY

1. exorbitant 2. endorse 3. evaluate 4. endeavour 5. detrimental 6. envelop (*Note:* no final *e*) 7. enumerate 8. facsimile 9. freight 10. feasible

Be sure you checked your spelling of these words!

Usage

Study the following words carefully so that you are fully aware of the differences and can use them correctly.

eminent/imminent

eminent—distinguished	an eminent politician
imminent—about to happen, threatening	an imminent breakthrough A depression is imminent.

fewer/less

fewer—smaller by number (can be counted)	fewer members, fewer babies
less-smaller by quantity (can not be counted)	less friction, less humidity

fix/repair

fix—to fasten securely, settle, set	Fix the clothesline to the post. The unit price has been fixed at $10.
repair—to mend	to repair a torn shirt; to repair the brakes on a car (*not* fix)

formally/formerly

formally—in a dignified way	I was formally introduced to the conductor of the orchestra.
formerly—previously	She was formerly known by the name of Hazlitt.

have

have—do not use *got* with *have*	We have a cat. Have you any pets? *Or:* Do you have any pets? (*not* Have you got any pets?)

Mini-Test

Complete the following sentences by choosing the correct word from those shown at the beginning of the sentences.

1. *eminent/imminent*
   William Osler was an ___________ doctor in Toronto. Faulty wiring is an _________ fire hazard.
2. *fewer/less*
   I am happy to report that _________ apples were bruised in this shipment.
   Try to eat _________ fat in your daily diet.
3. *fix/repair*
   _________ the signs firmly on the posts.
   _________ the signs before using them again.
4. *formally/formerly*
   The invitations require us to dress _________.
   Ontario was ________ known as Upper Canada.

KEY

1. eminent, imminent 2. fewer, less 3. fix, repair 4. formally, formerly

Spelling

Study the following words very carefully paying particular attention to the letters in italics. Write out the words at least ten times each, and be sure you know their meanings!

separ*a*te	benef*i*ted	desp*e*rate
med*i*cine	expl*a*nation	maint*e*nance
defin*i*tely	opp*o*rtunity	simultan*e*ous
assum*p*tion	a*d*justment	mor*t*gage
a*c*quit	contr*o*versy	ex*c*erpt

Mini-Test

By using proofreaders' marks or otherwise, correct any spelling errors in the following words. There may be one error, more than one error, or no errors in a line.

1. benefitted	medicine	acquit
2. excerpt	seperate	simultaenous
3. maintainance	adjustment	morgage
4. oportunity	desperate	deffinitely
5. explantion	controversy	assumtion

KEY

1. benefitted 2. seperate, simultaenous 3. maintainance, morgage 4. oportunity, deffinitely 5. explantion, assumtion

SUMMARY FOR UNIT 4.6

- Vocabulary and definitions are important.
- Study words and be sure of correct **usage.**
  - *Fewer* and *less* are frequently misused—be sure of the difference.
  - Do not use *fix* when you mean repair.
  - Do not use *got* with *have.*
- Study words to be sure of their **spelling.**
  - Remember words that have tricky single letters, particularly vowels.

Confirm Your Knowledge

Complete Exercise for Unit 4.6 on page 180.

4.7 Proofreading

Capital Letters

In Unit 4.1 you learned that three short lines under a letter means that that letter should be a capital.

He lives in winnipeg.

To indicate that a complete word or group of words should be in capital letters, write three lines under them.

Paint Warning in red letters at the top of the notice; paint the words Live Wires in black.

Lower Case (/)

To show that a capital letter should not be used, write an oblique stroke (/) through it. If a whole word or group of words is involved, write lc in the margin. These letters stand for "lower case."

The Chairperson, Mr. Paul Roscoe, opened the meeting promptly at 9 A.M.

In the final copy, these examples would appear as:

The chairperson, Mr. Paul Roscoe, opened the meeting promptly at 9 a.m.

Mini-Test

Use proofreaders' marks to insert or delete capital letters where necessary. The wording of the sign in sentence 3 should be in capitals.

1. Order no. 234 was sent by Expedair on May 11.
2. The woodworkers have signed a Contract effective April 1.
3. Ms. Reisberg wants a desk sign in capital letters reading Office Supervisor.
4. HAVE you heard from London, england, yet?

KEY

1. Order no. 234 2. Contract 3. Office Supervisor
4. HAVE...england

Close-Up (⁀‿)

In Unit 3.4 you learned that the proofreaders' marks (⁀‿) mean that a space should be closed up.

Proof read the copy carefully.

All our materials are fire proof.

Please fax Mr. Jordan a copy o f your memo re garding cost savings.

In the final copy, these examples would appear as:

Proofread the copy carefully.

All our materials are fireproof.

Please fax Mr. Jordan a copy of your memo regarding cost savings.

Mini-Test

Use close-up marks to proofread the following sentences.

1. A speedy key board operator some times leaves s paces in the middle of words.
2. Designers have de cided that fashion should be fun.
3. Mrs. Randy Williams has been appointed chair person.
4. My new lap top computer is very convenient.

KEY

1. key board...some times...s paces 2. de cided
3. chair person 4. lap top

Move

To show that certain words should be moved, circle the part to be moved and add an arrow to show where the material should be inserted.

Mortgage rates are finally starting to come down.

If more than one line is to be moved, use a round bracket at the beginning of the lines in the left margin.

Spray the paint evenly over the surface.

Using a clean, dry cloth, rub gently with one-way strokes.

Thoroughly clean the surface to be painted.

Make sure the surface is dry.

In the final copy, these examples would appear as:

Finally, mortgage rates are starting to come down.

Thoroughly clean the surface to be painted.

Make sure the surface is dry.

Spray the paint evenly over the surface.

Using a clean, dry cloth, rub gently with one-way strokes.

Mini-Test

Improve the following sentences by using proofreaders' marks to move some words.

1. An up-to-date survey in British Columbia of current conditions has been completed by Ottawa.
2. The steelworkers are threatening within two months to go on strike unless their demands are met before then.
3. The project will be finished which was started in February by the end of July.

KEY

1. An up-to-date survey in British Columbia of current conditions has been completed by Ottawa.
2. The steelworkers are threatening within two months to go on strike unless their demands are met before then.
3. The project will be finished which was started in February by the end of July.

SUMMARY FOR UNIT 4.7

- Proofreaders' marks:
  - ≡ Capital letters required
  - – – under one letter or under whole words
  - / Do not write in capitals
  - lc Means "lower case" and is written in the margin.
  - ⁀ Close-up marks—do not leave a space.

Move to point of arrow.

If whole lines are to be moved, use a large round bracket at beginning of lines instead of a circle.

- Remember always to proofread for meaning as well as for grammar, spelling, punctuation, vocabulary, and keyboarding.

Confirm Your Knowledge

Complete Exercise for Unit 4.7 on page 182.

PRETEST FOR UNIT 4

Complete all the parts of this test according to the directions for each part. The figures in parentheses are the unit numbers for reference, if necessary, when you have completed the test. Your Goal: To score a total of at least 48 points.

Your Goal: To score a total of at least 48 points.

A. General Rules

Are the following statetments true or false? If true, circle *T*; if false, circle *F*. Score 1 point for each correct answer.

		Score
1. Numbers used in measurements are always written in figures with the appropriate symbol. (4.4)	**T F**	_____
2. Do not capitalize a title such as *president* or *captain* unless it comes immediately before the name. (4.1)	**T F**	_____
3. The abbreviation for "number" is correctly written as *no.* (4.5)	**T F**	_____
4. Two or more words used together as one adjective before a noun are joined by hyphens. (4.3)	**T F**	_____
5. When initials are used for a company's name, no periods are required (4.5)	**T F**	_____
6. The basic rule for writing numbers is to use figures for exact numbers and words for general numbers. (4.4)	**T F**	_____
7. The names of public and religious holidays should always be written with a capital letter. (4.5)	**T F**	_____
8. The basic rule for abbreviating is "Don't" unless space is very limited. (4.5)	**T F**	_____
9. Postal codes are written as the last line of an address with no punctuation. (4.4)	**T F**	_____
10. The abbreviation for "Apartment" is *Aptmt*. (4.5)	**T F**	_____
	Score for Part A	_____

B. Capitalization (4.1, 4.2)

Use proofreaders' marks (≡) to show where capital letters should be used in the following sentences. If a sentence is correct as written, write *C* beside it. Score 1 point for each correctly capitalized sentence. No points are allowed for partially correct capitalization.

	Score
1. The theatre is on Wellington Street just west of Richmond Street.	_____
2. Paintings by van Gogh will be on display from January 24 to May 31.	_____
3. Sara Beavis, the accountant, checked the figures herself.	_____
4. Margaret Atwood's book the edible woman created quite a stir when it was first published.	_____
5. We travelled through south Dakota on our way south last year.	_____
6. The program has been approved by the city of Brantford with all councillors in agreement.	_____
7. Great advances in electronics have been made during the twentieth century.	_____
8. Please order a new xerox fax machine for the mailing room.	_____
9. Jason has enrolled in a course called computer accounting, but his mathematics is so poor that he is bound to find it difficult.	_____
10. The jewish celebration of hanukkah is in December just before christmas.	_____
Score for Part B	_____

C. Compound Words (4.3)

Insert hyphens or close-up marks (◡)where necessary in the following groups of words. If a group is correct as written, put a checkmark (✓) beside it. Score 1 point for each correct answer.

	Score
1. a French Canadian film	_____
2. twenty three	_____
3. a 25 minute wait	_____
4. a well known consultant	_____
5. an inter office memo	_____
6. The scores are up to date.	_____
7. a privately owned business	_____
8. for some time	_____
9. self contained	_____
10. up to the minute news	_____
Score for Part C	_____

D. Numbers (4.4)

Make any necessary corrections in the use of words or figures in the following sentences. If a sentence is correct as written, write *C* beside it. Score 1 point for each correct answer.

	Score
1. 400 students have written the examination.	_____
2. Pay only $10 now and the balance in three monthly installments of $12.75.	_____
3. The display area is three m by five m.	_____
4. We paid 75c each for these pens.	_____
5. The price of sugar is $0.50 per kg.	_____
6. He spoke for 3/4 of an hour.	_____
7. Exactly 200 people registered for volunteer work.	_____
8. The staff party will begin at four p.m.	_____
9. The rate of inflation in Israel was over one hundred percent.	_____
10. Please reply by January 29th.	_____
Score for Part D	_____

E. Abbreviations (4.5)

Make any necessary corrections in the way abbreviations are used in the following sentences. If a sentence is correct as written, write *C* beside it. Score 1 point for each correct answer.

		Score
1.	Dr. Barry Kincaid, M.D., will report on his research.	_____
2.	Pres. Hoffman has expressed his concern over the closing of the plant for two months.	_____
3.	Our main store will reopen on Thurs., May 16, at 9 a.m.	_____
4.	Has the copy for the new ad. arrived yet?	_____
5.	Ms. Bellamy held a meeting with the branch managers.	_____
6.	He has been absent from work since Jan. 4.	_____
7.	Mary lives on Wilson St. in Saint John, New Brunswick.	_____
8.	The YMCA has excellent physical fitness classes.	_____
9.	On his return from Prince Rupert. Mr. Ying reported on general transportation problems in B.C.	_____
10.	Only 63% of the registrants completed the course.	_____
	Score for Part E	_____

F. Proofreading and Vocabulary (4.6, 4.7)

Proofread the following letter very carefully for all kinds of errors. Score 1 point for each error found and marked correctly; deduct 1 point for each error missed!

Dear Mrs. Hartman

Are you having difficulties just now with the handling of you financial affairs? We at Mortgages Unlimited are a little concerned about your situation as we notice that recently your morgage payments have been falling behind. May we have an opportunity to discuss with you thebest way to help you overcome any problems you may be having? Perhaps a minor ajustment in the method of payment is all that is necessary.

An explaination from you about the reason for the delay would help, of course, in establishing what route we should take. Until we hear further from you, therefore, we shall not proceed with the legal collection of the out standing money you owe us.

alternatively, A certified cheque from you for $231.53 for January's mortgage payment would solve your current problems.

We would still however, like to see whether we can help you avoid future late mortgage payments. The less payments that are late, the better your credit rating will be. Please call us at 762-5555 or come in sometime next week to see what arrangements we can make.

Yours truly

Number of errors found and correctly marked	_____
Deduct for errors missed	_____
Score for Part F	_____
Total Score	_____

If you achieved your goal of at least 48 points, proceed to Unit 5. If you did not score 48, check with your instructor what parts you need to study. Proceed through Unit 4 doing all the necessary work; then do the posttest for Unit 4.

POSTTEST FOR UNIT 4

Complete all the parts of this test according to the directions for each part. The figures in parentheses are the unit numbers for reference, if necessary, when you have completed the test.

Your Goal: To score a total of at least 48 points.

A. General Rules

Are the following statements true or false? If true, circle *T*; if false, circle *F*. Score 1 point for each correct answer.

			Score
1.	The metric symbols must always be followed by a period. (4.4)	**T F**	_____
2.	The abbreviation for the word "number" does not have a capital letter. (4.2)	**T F**	_____
3.	The words "up to date" coming after a noun are not hyphenated. (4.3)	**T F**	_____
4.	Titles are always capitalized even when they appear after a name. (4.1)	**T F**	_____
5.	Amounts of money are always written in figures except in legal documents. (4.4)	**T F**	_____
6.	Abbreviations should be avoided wherever possible in general writing. (4.5)	**T F**	_____
7.	Postal codes must be written with capital letters and no hyphen. (4.5)	**T F**	_____
8.	It is correct to use the initials of well-known companies and organizations if reference has already been made to the full name. (4.5)	**T F**	_____
9.	The word "the" is capitalized in the middle of a book title. (4.2)	**T F**	_____
10.	The abbreviation *Blvd.* for "Boulevard" is an acceptable abbreviation. (4.5)	**T F**	_____
		Score for Part A	_____

B. Capitalization (4.1, 4.2)

Use proofreaders' marks (≡) to show where capital letters should be used in the following sentences. If a sentence is correct as written, write *C* beside it. Score 1 point for each correctly capitalized sentence. No points are allowed for partially correct capitalization.

		Score
1.	The supervisor asked, "who wants to work overtime?"	_____
2.	May I have an appointment with Vida Gamit, the president?	_____
3.	Marion Smith received her master's degree last fall.	_____
4.	Have you read the article "to promote bicycle touring in Canada"?	_____
5.	Bordering lake Ontario are many cottages.	_____
6.	Seventy persons registered for keyboarding 100A.	_____
7.	Travel east on highway 401 to get to yonge Street.	_____
8.	Many builders are members of the construction safety association.	_____
9.	The speaker welcomed the visitors from south America.	_____
10.	Sheila always buys ivory soap.	_____
	Score for Part B	_____

C. Compound Words (4.3)

Insert hyphens or close-up marks (⊂)where necessary in the following groups of words. If a group is correct as written, put a checkmark (✓) beside it. Score 1 point for each correct answer.

Score

1. 32 year old lawyer ______
2. an English speaking announcer ______
3. double checking your order ______
4. re cover from a broken leg ______
5. limited use of emotionally loaded words ______
6. the 100 lot parcel of land ______
7. a well known consultant ______
8. her self confident manner ______
9. door to door service ______
10. up to the second results ______

Score for Part C ______

D. Numbers (4.4)

Make any necessary corrections in the use of words or figures in the following sentences. If a sentence is correct as written, write *C* beside it. Score 1 point for each correct answer.

Score

1. You are entitled to a discount of 3 1/2 percent. ______
2. The cost per litre of premium gasoline is currently 55.5 cents. ______
3. The main store is at Two Niagara Street. ______
4. Your appointment has been changed from three p.m. to four p.m. ______
5. The new tax legislation will increase revenue by $2.6 million. ______
6. We plan to distribute 1000 and fifty copies of the booklet. ______
7. The staff contributed $50.00 for the event. ______
8. The fifty-five television sets were sold within nine days. ______
9. The pattern requires 3 metres of fabric and one metre of trim. ______
10. Send the parcel to my office by February 28th. ______

Score for Part D ______

E. Abbreviations (4.5)

Make any necessary corrections in the way abbreviations are used in the following sentences. If a sentence is correct as written, write *C* beside it. Score 1 point for each correct answer.

Score

1. The names of Ms R. Martinez and Mr J Summers were on the list. _____
2. Dr. Jean Michaels, M.D., was present at the inquest. _____
3. Your order Nos. 5784 will be delivered immediately. _____
4. We bought one kilogram of gold when the price was low. _____
5. Professor Fleming was invited to attend the ceremony. _____
6. Miss Lee Edwards welcomes many visitors to the Canadian Broadcasting Corporation. _____
7. He thanked me for my letter and my cheque of Mar. 30. _____
8. The YMHA is currently offering courses in Yiddish. _____
9. On his return from Charlottetown, Mr. Chen reported on the success of the potato crop in P.E.I. _____
10. The factory will be closed from Mon. to Fri., May 10 to 14. _____

Score for Part E _____

F. Proofreading and Vocabulary (4.6, 4.7)

Proofread the following letter very carefully for all kinds of errors. Score 1 point for each error found and marked correctly; deduct 1 point for each error missed!

Dear Dr. Catherwood

A number of veterinarians have expressed concern about the exorbitant prices pet owners have to pay for medical care for their pets. The doctors are worried that, becuase of the excessive costs, pet owners will not be able to take such good care of their pets. This will, of course mean that many animals will suffer greatly from neglect.

In an affort to overcome this financial burden on pet owners, the Veterinarians association has devised a plan for veterinarian services similar to the government sponsored hospital care programs. The plane is to have members contribute small sums on a regular basis to provide for once-a-year check-ups; for a slightly larger payment, the cost of medecine would also be covered as well as other medical services as they are needed.

Special plans could be arranged to include boarding and grooming; these, of course, would be more expensive. It is felt, however, that there is a great need for all types of cover age.

Do you think that you would be interested in such a plan? A brochure describing in more detail the various types of plans available is enclosed. Please give us a call at 886-4342 for further details.

May we hear from you by Sept. 20 so that we may bring your pets records up to date?

Yours truly

Number of errors found and correctly marked _____

Deduct for errors missed _____

Score for Part F _____

Total Score _____

If you achieved your goal of at least 48 points, proceed to Unit 5. If you did not score 48, check with your instructor what parts you need to review before moving on.

EXERCISE 4.1 CAPITALIZATION: BEGINNINGS, PERSONAL NAMES, PLACE NAMES, AND RELIGIOUS AND HISTORICAL NAMES

By using proofreaders' marks or otherwise, show where capital letters should be used in the following sentences. Score 1 point for each correctly marked capital; deduct 1 point for any incorrectly marked capitals.

Your Goal: To score at least 24 points.

Example: doctor williams is the doctor who recommended a trip to the province of nova scotia.
(Score 4 points for correctly capitalizing *Doctor, Williams, Nova, Scotia.*
Deduct 1 point for capitalizing *the Doctor*) 3

Score

1. The famous flemish painter van dyck lived at the beginning of the seventeenth century. _____
2. The protestants and catholics in northern ireland cannot seem to settle their differences amicably. _____
3. Please congratulate harold on completion of his master's degree at acadia university. _____
4. Mr. R. G. Simpson, president of Moore Corporation, is flying to england on the concorde. _____
5. Is president newnham staying at the fort garry hotel on his trip through the midwestern provinces? _____
6. Ms. Beckerman is learning spanish and french in preparation for her move to south carolina. _____
7. The east coast fishing industry is in a recession at the moment. _____
8. Have you ordered more french fries for the restaurant car on the transcontinental? _____
9. Maria Garcia, b.a., has been appointed travel consultant to the eastern townships. _____
10. The pope's tour of europe was well covered by the press. _____

Total Score _____

If you achieved your goal of at least 24 points, proceed to Unit 4.2. If you did not score 24, go back and review Unit 4.1 thoroughly; then do Exercise 4.1A and try to achieve your goal this time.

EXERCISE 4.1A CAPITALIZATION: BEGINNINGS, PERSONAL NAMES, PLACE NAMES, AND RELIGIOUS AND HISTORICAL NAMES

Use the same directions as for Exercise 4-1.

Your Goal: To score at least 24 points.

Score

1. The canadian author mazo de la roche wrote about life in the nineteenth century. ______
2. The jews and the arabs in the near east are working to settle their differences. ______
3. When will susan complete her bachelor's degree at simon fraser university? ______
4. Mrs. Phyllis m. Carter has been appointed president of National Electric Company. ______
5. The chief of police, Donald Watson, is arranging the security for the conference of first ministers in the royal york hotel. ______
6. Mr. Jones spoke fluent french, italian, and german, a fact which helped him tremendously on his way through europe on the orient express. ______
7. Our west coast representative will have an office in north vancouver. ______
8. Please refill our stock of india ink and manila folders. ______
9. Books on health foods are his bibles. ______
10. Ilona Markowitch, m.d., will explain the diagnosis to the patient. ______

Total Score ______

If you achieved your goal of at least 24 points, proceed to Unit 4.2. If you did not score 24, ask your instructor for direction before moving on.

Exercise 4.2 Capitalization: Organizations, Titles, and Other Special Rules

By using proofreaders' marks or otherwise, show where capital letters should be used in the following sentences. Score 1 point for each correctly marked capital; deduct 1 point for any incorrectly marked capitals.

Your Goal: To score at least 27 points.

Example: In the index to keyboarding for canadian colleges you will find the page number for each letter. (Score 3 points for correctly capitalizing Keyboarding for Canadian Colleges. Deduct 2 points for capitalizing Index and Page.) 1

Score

1. The federal government has decided to rename the unemployment insurance commission. ______
2. The community college in the west end of Toronto is called humber college of applied arts and technology. ______
3. As a member of another union, Mr. Wardle has had conflict in his dealings with the united automobile workers of America, which is a very strong union. ______
4. You should read the *taming of the shrew* before you see the play on stage. ______
5. Please reserve a seat for me on flight 127 on good friday as I want to spend easter with my family. ______
6. We have pepsi, coca cola, and seven-up in the vending machine. ______
7. The ontario labour relations board works hard to ensure safety and has set up a committee to study safety regulations. ______
8. Can I enrol in sociology 201 and psychology 241 in the same semester? ______
9. The conservative party held a fund-raising dinner on november 27. ______
10. Ms. Anderson will show you our latest samples of revlon and yardley makeup. ______

Total Score ______

If you achieved your goal of at least 27 points, proceed to Unit 4.3. If you did not score 27, go back and review Unit 4.2 thoroughly; then do Exercise 4.2A and try to achieve your goal this time.

EXERCISE 4.2A CAPITALIZATION: ORGANIZATIONS, TITLES, AND OTHER SPECIAL RULES

Use the same directions as for Exercise 4-1.

Your Goal: To score at least 27 points.

Score

1. Health and welfare canada is the department responsible for issuing pension plan disability and other welfare cheques. _____
2. Membership in the canadian museums association is open to museums and museum staff across canada. _____
3. We currently offer courses in carpentry, plumbing, and home insulation; auto repairs for the non-mechanic is the title of a course especially suitable for the beginner. _____
4. Farley Mowat's the people of the deer is a fascinating account of life among Canada's native people. _____
5. You should register your raleigh bicycle with the police. _____
6. Convocation at the university of toronto is held in May. _____
7. The winnipeg city council is discussing the budget deficit at tonight's meeting. _____
8. A list of names and addresses is included in appendix c on page 57 of the scarborough arts council directory. _____
9. The names dominion day and canada day were both used when referring to July 1. _____
10. A comparison survey of tide, sunlight, and fab laundry detergent has been completed. _____

Total Score _____

If you achieved your goal of at least 27 points, proceed to Unit 4.3. If you did not score 27, ask your instructor for direction before moving on.

EXERCISE 4.3 COMPOUND MODIFIERS, PREFIXES, AND NUMBERS

By using proofreaders' marks or otherwise, show if any words in the following groups should be hyphenated or closed. Place a checkmark (✓) beside any items that are correct as written. Score 1 point for each correct answer.

Your Goal: To score at least 16 points.

Example:	an out-of-town customer	1
	springlike weather	1
	semicircle ✓	1
		Score

1. a term of 30 days _____
2. two and three week packages _____
3. high priced merchandise _____
4. fifty three _____
5. under stated _____
6. an up to date report _____
7. Please clean the room some time later. _____
8. computer related jobs _____
9. semi detached _____
10. a carefully planned program _____
11. seven eighths _____
12. non essential _____
13. Ian is left handed. _____
14. This item is high priced. _____
15. Thank you. _____
16. micro processor _____
17. pro-Canadian responses _____
18. Bring this report up to date. _____
19. semi invalid _____
20. a well known politician _____

Total Score _____

If you achieved your goal of at least 16 points, proceed to Unit 4.4. If you did not score 16, go back and review Unit 4.3 thoroughly; then do Exercise 4.3A and try to achieve your goal this time.

EXERCISE 4.3A COMPOUND MODIFIERS, PREFIXES, AND NUMBERS

Use the same directions as for Exercise 4.3.

Your Goal: To score at least 16 points.

	Score
1. the end of the month sale	_____
2. non standard	_____
3. seventy eight	_____
4. well chosen words	_____
5. a highly polished surface	_____
6. a sale at the end of the month	_____
7. pre Renaissance	_____
8. semi independent	_____
9. one quarter	_____
10. Some times I'm right!	_____
11. the Vancouver Nanaimo ferry	_____
12. desk top publishing	_____
13. computer generated graphics	_____
14. The problem is thought provoking.	_____
15. self control	_____
16. to re cover the sofa	_____
17. an L shaped room	_____
18. a double density disk	_____
19. inter provincial	_____
20. a five or ten year term	_____
Total Score	_____

If you achieved your goal of at least 16 points, proceed to Unit 4.4. If you did not score 16, ask your instructor for direction before moving on.

EXERCISE 4.4 NUMBERS: BASIC RULE; ADDRESSES, DATES, TIMES, AND OTHER USES

If any numbers in the following sentences are written incorrectly, write the correct form in the space provided. If they are correct as written, write *C*. Score 1 point for each correct answer.

Your Goal: To score at least 16 points.

Example: At the age of 45 he retired. forty-five ______ 1

A total of $28 750 was raised. C ______ 1

Score

1. A five dollar service charge is added for home delivery. ______ ______
2. Only 18% of the entrants completed the marathon. ______ ______
3. Mr. Sanderson has just reached 70 years of age. ______ ______
4. 114 officers received awards of merit. ______ ______
5. Please let us know by November 15th so that the programs can be prepared. ______ ______
6. There has been a three percent drop in accidents this month. ______ ______
7. We need fifteen 10-gauge and twenty 12-gauge railway ties. ______ ______
8. Our packages of stocking stuffers cost only 50¢ each. ______ ______
9. Canada's population was over 24 million by 1980. ______ ______
10. We plan to canvass almost 2000 people for a donation to the Red Cross. ______ ______
11. Awards of merit were given to 114 officers. ______ ______
12. The pattern requires .5 m of velvet ribbon. ______ ______
13. The goods are packaged in boxes of five, 10, or 15 dozen. ______ ______
14. His contribution of $500.00 was very generous. ______ ______
15. The figures should total 9 975 687. ______ ______
16. The freezing point of water is 0° C. ______ ______
17. A lot four ha in area is waiting for you. ______ ______
18. The courts are only 1 1/2 km from our offices. ______ ______
19. He asked for 30 kg of chicken for the barbecue. ______ ______
20. Can you provide a 35 mm projector for the presentation on Thursday? ______ ______

Total Score ______

If you achieved your goal of at least 16 points, proceed to Unit 4.5. If you did not score 16, go back and review Unit 4.4 thoroughly; then do Exercise 4.4A and try to achieve your goal this time.

EXERCISE 4.4A NUMBERS: BASIC RULE; ADDRESSES, DATES, TIMES, AND OTHER USES

Use the same directions as for Exercise 4.4.

Your Goal: To score at least 16 points.

Score

1. A basic charge of twenty-five dollars will be levied for all estimates. _______________ _____
2. Prices must not rise by more than six percent. _______________ _____
3. 30 children have already registered. _______________ _____
4. Bus fares have risen to 80¢ for each trip. _______________ _____
5. Your flight leaves at six-thirty p.m. _______________ _____
6. About 600 people attended the concert. _______________ _____
7. Send an additional 6 small Inuit carvings with our next delivery. _______________ _____
8. The new shopping plaza will cost over $30 million. _______________ _____
9. There are vacancies for 137 campers. _______________ _____
10. We still have fourteen and a half boxes unopened. _______________ _____
11. The speed limit is 60 km per hour. _______________ _____
12. The toaster costs only $24.00. _______________ _____
13. This micrometer will measure thicknesses as small as .002 mm. _______________ _____
14. The exact figure was 71 254 311. _______________ _____
15. Your attendance is required on March 31st to finalize the deal. _______________ _____
16. Room thermostats should be set at 20 C. _______________ _____
17. The specifications call for 300 m hemp rope. _______________ _____
18. The container holds exactly 3 3/4 L. _______________ _____
19. The recipe called for 2 kg of onions. _______________ _____
20. The distance from 24 Sussex Drive to Parliament Hill is 3 kms. _______________ _____

Total Score _____

If you achieved your goal of at least 16 points, proceed to Unit 4.5. If you did not score 16, ask your instructor for direction before moving on.

EXERCISE 4.5 ABBREVIATIONS: GENERAL GUIDELINES; PERSONAL NAMES, ADDRESSES, ORGANIZATIONS, DATES, AND OTHER USES

Are the abbreviations and addresses in the following sentences used correctly? If so, write *C* in the space provided. If not, write *X* and give your reason. Score 1 point for each correct answer.

Your Goal: To score at least 8 points.

Example: Place an ad. in our magazine. X (No period after "ad") 1

Score

1. The war in the Gulf greatly influenced OPEC's pricing of oil. ______ ____
2. Please include our postal code E3V2M9 on our cards. ______ ____
3. Ms. Eliz. Puckering has been appointed chairperson effective Nov. 30. ______ ____
4. Mrs. Abba Sood, M.A., will be the instructor. ______ ____
5. The correct postal abbreviation for British Columbia is Brit. Col. ______ ____
6. We are currently testing Model No. 780 and 781. ______ ____
7. As already mentioned, IBM is expanding rapidly. ______ ____
8. The town will repave Hope Ave. W. next week. ______ ____
9. The school has requested new ID cards for all the students. ______ ____
10. Write to our agent, Miss Chen, at 645 Kalena Avenue, Hilo, Hawaii, for details of our tour packages. ______ ____

Total Score ____

If you achieved your goal of at least 8 points, proceed to Unit 4.6. If you did not score 8, go back and review Unit 4.5 thoroughly; then do Exercise 4.5A and try to achieve your goal this time.

EXERCISE 4.5A ABBREVIATIONS: GENERAL GUIDELINES; PERSONAL NAMES, ADDRESSES, ORGANIZATIONS, DATES, AND OTHER USES

Use the same directions as for Exercise 4.5.

Your Goal: To score at least 8 points.

Score

1. Mr. Jos. Buchmueller is our representative in Borden, Ontario. ______________ _____
2. Dr. Alan McDougall, M.D., is on vacation. ______________ _____
3. Susie's address is 2117 Bayview Avenue, Willowdale, ON M2L 1A2.______________ _____
4. The CBC has agreed to show our documentary film. ______________ _____
5. The two-letter abbreviation for Saskatchewan is SS. ______________ _____
6. The paper plant is Grand Falls, Nfld.,is working to capacity. ______________ _____
7. The Rev. Jones issued a strong appeal for tolerance. ______________ _____
8. The supervisor will be making inspection rounds on Thurs., Aug. 17.______________ _____
9. The serial No. of the car must be shown on the policy. ______________ _____
10. Ask the technician to adjust the PA system before the guest speaker arrives. ______________ _____

Total Score _____

If you achieved your goal of at least 8 points, proceed to Unit 4.6. If you did not score 8, ask your instructor for direction before moving on.

EXERCISE 4.6 VOCABULARY

Complete the three parts of this exercise according to the directions for each part.

Your Goal: To score at least 16 points.

A. Definitions

Complete the following sentences by choosing the most appropriate words from those given. Score 1 point for each correct answer.

detrimental	endeavour	endorse	freight
enumerate	evaluate	exorbitant	facsimile
feasible	envelop		

Score

1. A slight drop in prices is just ______________ because of the very heavy crop yield. ______
2. If you allow someone else to ______________ your credit card, it may be ______________ to your credit rating. ______
3. Please submit a ______________ of your receipts as your expense account is ______________ this month and must be reduced. ______

Score for Part A ______

B. Usage

Use the same directions as for Part A.

eminent	fix	formerly	repair
imminent	less	formally	fewer

Score

1. Mr. Diefenbaker was an ______________ figure in Ottawa for many years. ______
2. Every day there are ______________ instances of vandalism since the new security system became operative. ______
3. As the annual transfer of files is ______________, I suggest you bring your records up to date. ______
4. Please ______________ the price to ______________ the window. ______
5. He ______________ acknowledged the honour in a very short speech. ______
6. Try to use ______________ paper to conserve the trees. ______
7. Mr. Morris was ______________ a lawyer before he became a politician. ______

Score for Part B ______

C. Spelling

By using proofreaders' marks or otherwise, correct any spelling errors in the following words. Write the correct spelling above the word if necessary. Score 1 point for each correctly changed word; deduct 1 point for each word changed that was correct as written.

			Score
1. seperate	mortgage	desperate	______
2. maintenance	explaination	medicine	______
3. controversy	acquit	definately	______
4. ajustment	excerpt	assumption	______
5. simultaneous	benefitted	opportunity	______
		Score for Part C	______
		Total Score	______

If you achieved your goal of at least 16 points, proceed to Unit 4.7. If you did not score 16, go back and review Unit 4.6 thoroughly before moving on.

EXERCISE 4.7 PROOFREADING

Complete each part of this exercise according to the directions given.

Your Goal: To score at least 12 points in total.

Part A

Are the following statements true or false? If true, circle *T*; if false, circle *F*. Score 1 point for each correct answer.

			Score
1.	The letters lc in the margin mean that the material should be written in capital letters.	**T F**	_____
2.	A circle around a word and an arrow means the word should be moved to the point of the arrow.	**T F**	_____
3.	The marks ⌢⌣ mean "close up"; do not leave a space.	**T F**	_____
4.	The meaning of a sentence is very important in proofreading.	**T F**	_____
5.	An oblique stroke (/) through a letter indicates that a capital letter is required.	**T F**	_____
		Score for Part A	_____

Part B

Proofread the following material very carefully for all kinds of errors. Score 1 point for each error found and marked correctly; deduct 1 point for each error missed!

Example: Thank you for you letter of Febuary 10. (Score 1 for correct marking of Febuary; deduct 1 for missing *your* before "letter.") 0

Over the past few years,, it has become evident that more and more people like to seek warmer climates during the cold winter months by going south to Florida and california. I suppose this is only natural, for there is nothing more re laxing than to feel warm and comfortable while you are on the beach or enjoying a restful picnic in a park far from the noise and turmoil of the city.

However, the benefits of the sun can be found in many other ways. The energy provided by the bright sunshine on a cold day can be changed into activity on the ski slops or trails surrounding our Swiss chalet set in mountains of unsurpassed beauty. The feeling of exaltation and exhaustion at the end of a day's ski ing are much more rewarding that the lethargic feeling after lazing around a beach all day!

If skiing one day does not appeal to you, then youcan sample the warmth in our garden indoor pool. Look out through the walls of glass at the cold beauty outside while you enjoy our poolside service.

To Say that our food and accommodation are first class is to say far too little; however, we want you to judge for yourself. Come and visit us for a witner holiday you will never forget.

Number of errors found and correctly marked	_____
Deduct for errors missed	_____
Score for Part B	_____
Total Score	_____

If you achieved your goal of at least 12 points, proceed to the Posttest for Unit 4. If you did not score 12, you will appreciate the need for accurate proofreading! Review Unit 4.7 thoroughly before moving on.

PROBLEMS FACED BY BEGINNING WRITERS

The purpose of all writing is to send information or ideas from one person to another. Sometimes, even though the writer believes the information is clear and can be interpreted in only one way, the reader misunderstands. Inexperienced writers in particular often find their messages distorted by readers. This unit will help you understand some areas that need special attention so that your written communications are clearly understood.

GRAMMATICAL ERRORS

❍ 5.1 Incomplete and Run-on Sentences

Incomplete Sentences

An incomplete sentence (also called a *sentence fragment*) leaves the reader wondering. To be complete, a sentence must contain a subject and a verb. A phrase or a dependent clause cannot stand alone and must always be attached to an independent clause. A sentence must also make sense on its own. (See Unit 1.8.)

Incomplete: The official opening will be on Tuesday. If the weather is good. (The second group of words is a dependent clause, not a sentence.)

Correct: The official opening will be on Tuesday if the weather is good.

Incomplete: In reply to your letter of April 10. Plans for the concert are now well under way. (The first group of words is a phrase and does not make sense on its own.)

Correct: In reply to your letter of April 10, plans for the concert are now well under way.

Incomplete: Politicians always promising but seldom producing. (no complete verb)

Correct: Politicians are always making promises, but seldom are they able to produce results.

In some writing, sentence fragments are acceptable. In general, however, the beginning writer should avoid these constructions.

Conversation: "Why the big smile?" "Just won the jackpot!"

Exclamation: A sellout!

Advertising Copy: Best service in town!

Mini-Test

In the following sentences, underline all fragments or incomplete sentences.

1. Our thermal blankets are especially useful for the year-round camper. Keeping the body warm in winter and cool in summer.
2. Wherever you go in search of the perfect holiday for you and your family. Be sure to stay at our wonderful hotels and motels across the country.
3. Reporters and photographers asking questions and flashing cameras.
4. As soon as you give us a list of what you are looking for in a new house. We will be happy to find the ideal home for you.
5. The economy is improving daily. If you believe the bankers.

KEY

1. Keeping the body warm in winter and cool in summer.
2. Wherever you go in search of the perfect holiday for you and your family.
3. Reporters and photographers asking questions and flashing cameras.
4. As soon as you give us a list of what you are looking for in a new house.
5. If you believe the bankers.

Run-on Sentences

A run-on sentence consists of two independent clauses written together without a period or a conjunction to separate them.

Run-on: The new playground will be officially opened on Tuesday the mayor will perform the ceremony.

Correct: The new playground will be officially opened on Tuesday. The mayor will perform the ceremony.

Instead of a period, either a semicolon or a comma and a conjunction could be used between the independent clauses; or, even better, one part of the sentence could be written as a phrase or dependent clause.

The new playground will be officially opened on Tuesday; the mayor will perform the ceremony.

The new playground will be officially opened on Tuesday, and the mayor will perform the ceremony.

The mayor will perform the ceremony when the new playground is officially opened on Tuesday.

A run-on sentence also results when two independent clauses are joined by only a comma.

Run-on: The new playground is ready, the pool will not be ready from another two weeks.

Correct: The new playground is ready, but the pool will not be ready for another two weeks.

Correct: Although the playground is ready, the pool will not be ready for another two weeks.

Mini-Test

Are the following sentences run-on sentences or correct as written? If run-on, by using proofreaders' marks or otherwise, indicate where one sentence ends and the next begins. If correct, write *C* beside the sentence.

Example: These services are available to you at any time please make use of them.

1. The weather forecast calls for rain, it is seldom wrong.
2. The model you are considering comes in two colour schemes these are
   a) neon green and black with purple dots
   b) neon orange and red with black dots.
3. If we can raise sufficient money from the rummage sale, we shall be able to buy a new furnace for the church.
4. Vaccination for pets against rabies is very important it may save their lives.
5. Mansoor did not buy the security system, the price was higher than he had expected.

KEY

1....rain. It... 2. ...schemes; these are... 3. C 4. ...important. It may... 5. ...system. The price...

Note: There are other ways to correct these sentences by changing the wording.

2.schemes, which are... 4. ...important because it may... 5. ...system as the price...

Summary for Unit 5.1

- An incomplete sentence, sometimes called a **fragment**, leaves the reader without a complete message.
- *Never* leave a dependent clause or a phrase alone as a sentence.
- A *run-on* sentence has two independent clauses run together without a period or a conjunction to separate them.
- Be careful to use a period instead of a comma between two independent clauses; doing so will avoid a run-on sentence.
- The correct forms may be illustrated by diagrams as follows. *Indep. Cl.* stands for independent clause.

  Two separate complete sentences:

  Indep. Cl. . *Indep. Cl.* .

  Two complete sentences joined by a semicolon:

  Indep. Cl. ; *Indep. Cl.* .

  Two complete sentences joined by a comma and a co-ordinate conjunction (and, but, nor, or, for, yet):

  Indep. Cl. , *and* *Indep. Cl.* .

  A dependent clause or phrase and an independent clause making one complete sentence.:

  Dep. Cl. or phrase , *Indep. Cl.* .

- *Remember:* An independent clause must contain a subject and a verb and must be able to stand alone as a sentence.

Confirm Your Knowledge

Complete Exercise for Unit 5.1 on page 209.

❍ 5.2 Dangling, Misplaced, and Confusing Modifiers

Modifiers are words, phrases, or clauses that are used to describe or explain some other word, phrase, or clause in the same sentence. Adjectives and adverbs are the most common modifiers and are usually placed directly before or after the words they describe.

prepasted wallpaper drive *carefully*

However, care is needed in the placement of more complex modifiers. This unit will help you become more confident in your use of modifiers.

Dangling Modifiers

Modifiers are called dangling when they relate to no particular word in a sentence or when they modify the wrong word.

Dangling: While walking in the woods, the birds were singing. (Who was walking?)

Correct: While I was walking in the woods, the birds were singing.

Dangling: To avoid losing customers, prices were lowered. (Who wanted to avoid losing customers?)

Correct: To avoid losing customers, management decided to lower prices.

A simple way to be sure your writing does not dangle at the beginning of a sentence is to avoid beginning a sentence with an "-ing" word.

Dangling: Being confident, the test seemed easy.

Correct: Because he was confident, the test seemed easy.

Mini-Test

Where necessary, make corrections in the following sentences to eliminate any dangling modifiers. If a sentence is correct as written, write *C* beside it.

1. Driving steadily, the kilometres seemed to roll by quickly.
2. When designing playgrounds, the children's safety must come first.
3. Being in a hurry, the traffic seemed heavier than usual.
4. When taking a trip overseas, vaccinations may be required.
5. To ensure a good crowd for opening night, the publicist gave away lots of free tickets.

KEY

Your answers may vary slightly; if you are confident you have corrected any dangling modifiers, accept your answers as correct.

1. Driving steadily, we found the kilometres...
2. When designing playgrounds, the designer must consider the children's safety first.
3. Because I was in a hurry, the traffic...
4. Before you take a trip...
5. C

Misplaced and Confusing Modifiers

Modifiers must be placed in a sentence so that it is absolutely clear which word or words they modify. Usually the best place is either immediately before or immediately after the word to be modified. A misplaced modifier can be confusing, ambiguous, and often very funny.

Misplaced Modifier: Those roses need pruning badly.

Correct: Those roses badly need pruning.

Misplaced Modifier: The lawyer carried a book into the office called "Legal Decisions."

Correct: The lawyer carried a book called "Legal Decisions" into the office.

Ambiguous Modifier: The visitor from Japan spoke at length about Japanese customs after dinner.

Correct: After dinner, the visitor from Japan spoke at length about Japanese customs.

Or: The visitor from Japan spoke at length about customs after dinner in Japan.

Misplaced Modifier: Joni agreed to quickly correct the error.

Correct: Joni agreed to correct the error quickly.

Or: Joni quickly agreed to correct the error.

With *only, hardly, ever,* and *nearly,* care must be taken so that the meaning is absolutely clear.

One Meaning: Only Ms. Martin can sign the cheques. (No one else can sign them)

Another Meaning: Ms. Martin can only sign the cheques. (She cannot do anything else to them.)

Another Meaning: Ms. Martin can sign the cheques only. (She cannot sign anything else.)

Mini-Test

By using proofreaders' marks or otherwise, improve the placement of the modifiers in the following sentences.

1. Our aim is to honestly serve you and earn your goodwill.
2. We have only serviced three cars of that make since we opened.

3. The child brought a picture to give to the teacher of her family.
4. Gabriella enjoyed playing tennis with us very much.
5. The campaign has, in spite of adverse criticism, been a success.

KEY

1. ...to serve you honestly and...
2. We have serviced only three cars ...
3. The child brought a picture of her family to give to the teacher.
4. Gabriella very much enjoyed...
5. In spite of adverse criticism, the campaign has been a success.

SUMMARY FOR UNIT 5.2

- Modifiers describe or explain words, phrases, or clauses.
- Modifiers must have a definite word to describe; if they do not, they dangle.
- Take care with dangling modifiers after *thus*, *thereby*, and *therefore*.
- Avoid dangling modifiers by not beginning a sentence with an "-ing" word such as *being* or *having*.
- Misplaced modifiers can cause ambiguity.
- Try to place modifiers beside the words they describe.
- Take special care with *only*, *nearly*, *hardly*, *ever*, *never*, and *almost*, as meanings change with different placements.

Confirm Your Knowledge

Complete Exercise for Unit 5/2 on page 211.

❍ 5.3 Parallel Structure

Parallel structure occurs when the separate parts in a sentence are written in the same form or grammatical construction.

Not Parallel: The Mountain Ski Lodge offers you efficient lift service, free ski instruction, and you will be thrilled with our exciting runs conveniently located near two major highways.

Parallel: The Mountain Ski Lodge offers you efficient lift service, free ski instruction, and exciting runs conveniently located near two major highways.

Parallel structure can be shown in diagram form as follows. Each of the short lines must be in the same form and must combine with the first and last lines correctly.

Diagram

The Mountain Ski Lodge offers you	________________
efficient lift service,	____________ ,
free ski instruction,	____________ , and
exciting runs	____________
conveniently located near two major highways.	________________

Take care with *a* or *an* in parallel constructions. A diagram will help if you keep the *a* or *an* on the short lines.

Not Parallel: For a vacation to remember, you might enjoy a helicopter ride, snowmobiling through the woods, or an exhilarating dip in the hot springs.

Parallel:	Diagram
For a vacation to remember, you might enjoy	____________
a helicopter ride,	____________,
a snowmobile ride through the woods, or	____________, or
an exhilarating dip in the hot springs.	____________.

Not Parallel: Purposes of stage lighting:

1. To see the actors
2. Creating atmosphere
3. For isolating stage areas

Parallel: Purposes of stage lighting:

1. To see the actors
2. To create atmosphere
3. To isolate stage areas

Take care when only two parts are involved.

Not Parallel: His object is to further confuse the issue, thereby embarrassing the chairperson.

Parallel: His object is to further confuse the issue and thereby to embarrass the chairperson.

Mini-Test

By using proofreaders' marks or otherwise, correct the errors in parallelism in the following sentences.

1. The principal is well known for his strictness, having a passion for rules, and always ready to help students with problems.
2. Three reasons to quit smoking: 1) You will feel better 2) Clothes won't smell of smoke 3) Save money.
3. If you want to redecorate and money is no problem, hire a professional designer.
4. She knows what will amuse her husband and what he doesn't find funny.
5. We have sent you annual reports regularly, and you have received four quarterly reports on your investments.

Key

Your answers may vary slightly; if the constructions are parallel and the meanings are clear, accept your answers as correct.

1. ...his strictness, his passion for rules, and his readiness to help...
2. ...better 2) You will find your clothes don't smell of smoke 3) You will save money.
3. ...redecorate and if money is...
4. ...husband and what will not (amuse him). 5. We have sent you regular annual reports and four quarterly reports on your investments.

More Parallel Constructions

In the following situations, the use of diagrams helps in creating parallel constructions.

Also

Also joins or adds items that are similar. The *also* expression should be parallel to the one coming before it.

Not Parallel: Ilona is ordering the flowers. She has also arranged the transportation.

Parallel: Ilona is ordering the flowers. She is also arranging the transportation.

Not only...but (also)

The words following *not only* and *but (also)* must be in parallel construction.

Not Parallel: Not only will regular maintenance improve the efficiency of your furnace, but the savings will be substantial.

Parallel:	Diagram
Regular maintenance will	____________
not only improve the efficiency of your furnace,	not only ________,
but also provide substantial savings	but also ________.

Either...or

Be particularly careful with *either...or, neither...nor* constructions.

Not Parallel: The finish on our counter tops will be damaged neither by hot pans nor if you drop a lighted match on them.

Parallel: The finish on our counter tops will neither be damaged by hot pans nor marked by a lighted match dropped on them.

Or: The finish on our counter tops will be damaged neither by hot pans nor by lighted matches dropped on them.

Again a diagram helps:

____

neither ______

nor ______.

Nonparallel Ideas

Be careful not to include in parallel constructions ideas or thoughts that are not similar.

Not Parallel: You will need one of our long-lasting flashlights for your cottage, for your car, and for the security it provides.

Parallel: For the security it provides, you will need one of our long-lasting flashlights for your cottage and for your car.

Mini-Test

By using proofreaders' marks or otherwise, correct the errors in parallel construction in the following sentences.

1. Your carpet tiles are being sent today. Also we have sent a large can of adhesive which should be sufficient for the area you are covering.
2. Not only do we guarantee all our labour, but you will also receive the manufacturer's warranty which covers all parts.
3. Conclude your report either with a summary of the main points or you can make recommendations on a course of action.
4. The fall fabrics now in stock are excellent for shirts, jackets, suits, and easy handling.
5. Our company benefits not only provide for your health care but also generous holidays and pensions.

KEY

Your answers may vary slightly; if the constructions are parallel and the meanings are clear, accept your answers as correct.

1....Also we are sending... 2. ...but also the manufacturer gives a warranty... 3. ...or with recommendations... 4. ...stock are easy to handle and are excellent for shirts, jackets, and suits. 5. ...but also allow for generous...

Summary for Unit 5.3

- **Parallel construction** means that parts of a sentence in a series or sequence of related thoughts are written in the same way.
- Diagrams help in checking parallel constructions.
- Take care with *a* or *an*, *also*, *not only...but also*, *either...or*, *neither...nor*.
- Do not include an unrelated item in a parallel construction.

Confirm Your Knowledge

Complete Exercise for Unit 5.3 on page 213.

CLARITY AND COHERENCE

Sometimes a piece of writing, though grammatically correct, may still be misunderstood. Good writers are very careful to choose appropriate words and arrange them carefully so that the meaning is absolutely clear.

Inexperienced writers can improve their skills by criticizing their writing through the eyes of the reader. This unit will help you recognize where difficulties often occur and help you guard against them.

5.4 Conjunctions and Inconsistencies

Conjunctions

In Unit 1.3, you learned about the different kinds of conjunctions. In writing, be careful to choose the conjunction most appropriate to show the relationship between the parts it is connecting.

The use of a conjunction can help to clarify the meaning.

Ambiguous: Mr. Doyle transferred three installers from the construction site; the siding will not be installed until next week. (Did Mr. Doyle transfer the installers because the siding is not being installed until next week, or is the siding not being installed until next week because Mr. Doyle transferred three installers?)

Better: Since Mr. Doyle has transferred three installers from the construction site, the siding cannot be installed until next week.

Or: Mr. Doyle transferred three installers from the construction site because the siding is not being installed until next week.

And

And is the grammatical plus sign; it joins parts together. However, *and* is often used incorrectly or loosely. It should only be used to join parts of equal strength and form.

Correct use of and: The letter carrier filled out the form for the registered letter and asked the addressee to sign for it.

Incorrect: We have no record of your telephone order, and we will be sure to send you your supplies today.

Better: Although we have no record of your telephone order, we will be sure to send you your supplies today.

Loose: Thank you for your kindness and sympathy and let me know if there is anything I can do for you.

Better: Thank you for your kindness and sympathy. Please let me know if there is anything I can do for you.

Mini-Test

And is used incorrectly or loosely in the following sentences. Revise each sentence to eliminate the conjunction *and* or to make sure it is used correctly. Use a variety of constructions in your answers.

1. Older people are more adventurous today, and travel agents are designing tours particularly for them.
2. Please send us tickets for the show on May 31, and do you want us to return the tickets we are cancelling for the show on May 30?
3. The gallery has just received a series of new prints, and they will be on display in the main rotunda.
4. Safer and stronger cars were designed, and safer and smoother roads were built; and all drivers benefited.
5. Politicians want to cut back on services, and the public wants more services for its tax dollars.

KEY

Your answers may very considerably. Check the use of *and,* and if you are satisfied your sentences are correct, accept them.

1. Because older people are more adventurous today, travel agents are designing tours particularly for them.

2. Please send us tickets for the show on May 31. Do you want us to return the tickets we are cancelling for the show on May 30? OR: Please...May 31. What do you want us to do with the tickets we are cancelling...?
3. The gallery has just received a series of new prints which will be on display in the main rotunda.
4. As safer and stronger cars were designed, safer and smoother roads were built; all drivers benefited.
5. While politicians want to cut back on services, the public wants more services for its tax dollars. OR: Politicians want...services, but the public keeps wanting more services...

Inconsistencies

Be careful to keep your writing consistent. Do not hop around from using one person or number to another, from present to past tense, or from active to passive voice. Be sure you can identify the inconsistencies in the following examples.

In Person: *One* can master most things if *you* are really determined.

Better: *You* can master most things if *you* are really determined.

In number: Hunt and Peck *is* opening a new service for *their* out-of-town customers.

Better: Hunt and Peck *is* opening a new service for *its* out-of-town customers.

Or: Hunt and Peck *are* opening a new service for *their* out-of-town customers.

In Tense: The director *keeps* the dancers until 6 p.m. and *expected* them to rehearse again at 8 p.m.

Better: The director *kept* the dancers until 6 p.m. and *expected* them to rehearse again at 8 p.m.

In voice: The coach *selects* all players for a particular game and *is given* the responsibility of making sure they have transportation to the game.

Better: The coach *selects* all players for a particular game and *is* responsible for making sure they have transportation to the game.

Mini-Test

Revise the following sentences to eliminate the inconsistencies. Use a variety of constructions in your answers.

1. The children all helped in the design of the posters, and they will be hung on the classroom walls.
2. You can improve your credit rating if they will only pay their bills on time.
3. The Art Gallery of Ontario is the largest in Ontario, but they had to close for several months because of lack of money.
4. The auditor checks the accounts twice and found a number of discrepancies.
5. Rudi prepared the vegetables for the chef's soup, and the soup is made by Rudi when the chef is away.

KEY

1....posters, which the children will hang on the classroom walls. 2. ...if you will only pay your bills on time. 3. ...of Ontario, the largest in Ontario, had to close for... 4. The auditor checked the accounts... 5. Rudi prepares the vegetables and makes the soup when the chef is away.

Summary for Unit 5.4

- Be sure to use the appropriate conjunction to make your meaning clear.
- *And* should only be used to connect parts of equal strength and form.
- Do not change your point of view unnecessarily.
- Keep tenses the same.
- Keep voices the same.
- Keep person and number of pronouns the same.

Confirm Your Knowledge

Complete Exercise for Unit 5.4 on page 215.

WRITING STYLE

In fashion, style is the way you express yourself in dress; in writing, style is the way you express your thoughts on paper. You already know the importance of correct grammar and the need for making sure your message is understood. This unit covers some further points to consider to help you improve your writing style.

❍ 5.5 Sentence Composition, Choppiness, and Passive Voice

Sentence Composition

A piece of writing may consist of one or more sentences to convey a particular message. As long as each part relates to the same thing, one sentence may be enough. Beginning writers should avoid very long sentences that are hard to understand. You can make your writing clear by building your sentences in a simple but interesting style. The following examples show how to build sentences in a variety of ways. (See Unit 1.3 for a review of conjunctions.)

1. Use co-ordinate conjunctions to join two independent clauses that are of equal importance.

   Rod Beattie won the best male actor award, and Nicola Cavendish won the best female actor award.
2. Make one clause dependent.

   When Rod Beattie won the best male actor award, the audience gave him a standing ovation.
3. Use a bridging word such as *therefore, consequently, for example, however, instead,* between two complete sentences.

   Rod Beattie won the best male actor award, and Nicola Cavendish won the best female actor award; however, neither won an award for directing.

   The fire marshall decided that the fire was not accidental; instead, he was convinced it was a case of arson.

   Football players and hockey players both have heavy training schedules. For example, they all start their days with strenuous exercises.

   I would love to visit Greece while I'm in Europe; however, I don't think I will have time.

   They have failed to submit their tender on time; consequently, we shall use another supplier.

Mini-Test

Rewrite the following sentences to improve their style. Use a variety of constructions.

1. She wears glasses for driving. She has poor long-distance vision.

   ____

   ____
2. You take notes in shorthand. In this way you can make sure you don't miss any important points.

   ____

   ____
3. Harry Goodyear has a collection of stones. They are of all kinds of minerals. He made his collection over a period of years.

   ____

   ____
4. Productivity in a factory is relatively easy to measure. The measurement of "productivity" in a classroom is much more difficult.

   ____

   ____
5. This play is full of action, and it was written by William Shakespeare.

   ____

   ____

KEY

Your sentences may be quite different from the suggested answers given here. If you have used a variety of constructions and are happy with the results, accept your sentences as correct. After all, you are writing in your style!

1. She wears glasses for driving because she has poor long-distance vision.
2. By taking notes in shorthand, you can make sure you don't miss any important points.
3. Over the years, Harry Goodyear has made a collection of all kinds of mineral stones. 4. Productivity in a factory is relatively easy to measure, but the measurement of "productivity" in a classroom is much more difficult.

OR: While productivity in a factory is relatively easy to measure, the measurement of "productivity" in a classroom is much more difficult.

5. This play by William Shakespeare is full of action.

Choppy Style

A choppy style of writing describes a style that uses many short sentences that do not connect the ideas. Choppiness gives a roughness to the writing that can be irritating to the reader. The following sentences are an exaggerated example of choppiness.

> Our adjusters examined the chair you returned. It was badly damaged. They found it had been dropped from a height. This caused the damage. We want you to have a comfortable chair. We cannot, however, accept the responsibility for this type of damage. We suggest you get in touch with the transit company. They delivered your chair. You can submit a claim to them. The damage probably occurred when the chair was being loaded onto the truck. It may have occurred when it was being unloaded.

This passage can be revised in many ways to make it smooth and easy to understand. One way is given here.

> On examination, our adjusters find that the damage to the chair you returned was caused by its having been dropped from a height. You will appreciate that we cannnot accept responsibility for this kind of damage. We do suggest, however, that you submit a claim to the transit company that delivered your chair as the damage probably occurred during the loading of your chair onto or off their truck.

Sometimes writing is choppy because it does not contain all the necessary information. By adding the details, you make the writing not only smooth but also more effective.

Choppy: Be sure to come to the meeting. Your vote is important.

Better: Be sure to come to the meeting on Wednesday, May 3, at 7 p.m. to discuss the cancelling of junior kindergarten classes. Your views and vote are very important.

Mini-Test

Combine the following choppy sentences to produce clear, smoothly flowing sentences. Do not change the meaning, but leave out any information that is repetitive. You may need more than one sentence for each group, and you may change the wording.

1. Health clubs are opening all over town. The Macho Mice Health Club offers programs at all levels. You can easily afford the membership. It is centrally located. It can be reached by public transit.
2. Tony's Barber Shop is looking for a barber. He or she should be ready to work long hours. A partnership in the business is being offered. Tony needs an assistant right away.

KEY

Your answers will vary, but if you feel your sentences are clear, varied in length, and not choppy, accept them as correct.

1. The Macho Mice Health Club offers programs at all levels. Centrally located and easily reached by public transit, the club's membership fee is affordable. (*Note:* The original first sentence is not really relevant to the rest of the message.)
2. Tony's Barber Shop is offering a partnership in the business to a barber who is willing to work long hours and who is ready to start right away.

Passive Voice

In Unit 1.4, you learned that verbs in the active voice pass the action on to an object. With verbs in the passive voice, the subject receives the action.

Active: Steven mailed the letter.

Passive: The letter was mailed by Steven.

Generally, verbs are active; however, passive verbs may be used in the following situations.

1. To be tactful:

   An error was made in your account. (You don't want to say who made the error.)

2. To involve the reader:

   Your X-rays have been examined by the specialist. (You are more important than the specialist.)

3. To give information that cannot be given any other way:

   The project will be abandoned if no new funds are found.

Take care not to overuse the passive voice. The active voice is much stronger and usually much more easily understood. Note the difference in the strengths of the following sentences.

Weak Passive:	Name tags were attached to the children before they boarded the bus.
Active:	Ms. Solomon attached name tags to the children before they boarded the bus.
Weak Passive:	A walk along the shores of our lake will be remembered by you when you return home.
Active:	When you return home, you will remember your walks along the shores of our lake.

Mini-Test

Are the passive verbs necessary in the following sentences? If so, write *C* beside the sentence; if not, rewrite the sentences using active verbs or strong passive verbs.

1. More errors were discovered by the auditor today.
2. You have been advised by your counsellor to pay the fine.
3. Your luggage has been traced to Dorval.
4. Your furniture will be delivered on July 3.
5. These fabrics are designed in Montreal by Suzanne Sheers Inc.

KEY

1.The auditor discovered more errors today. 2. Your counsellor has advised you to pay the fine. 3. C 4. C 5. Suzanne Sheers Inc. design these fabrics in Montreal.

SUMMARY FOR UNIT 5.5

- Avoid very long involved sentences.
- Vary the length and composition of your sentences.
- Avoid too many short, choppy sentences.
- Use the passive voice:
  - to be tactful
  - to involve the reader
  - to give information that cannot be given any other way
- Avoid overuse of passive verbs.

Confirm Your Knowledge

Complete Exercise for Unit 5.5 on page 217.

❍ 5.6 Problem Words

The following words are often used incorrectly but are accepted in informal speech. In writing, however, they must be used correctly. This unit will help you to learn their correct usage.

So *and* Such

1. Do not use *so* for *so that.*

   Informal: We moved the room divider so we could communicate more easily.

   Better. We moved the room divider so that we could communicate more easily.

2. Correctly used, *so* and *such* should be followed by ...*that.*

   The weather was *so* bad *that* we cancelled the picnic.

   He has *such* a gentle nature *that* he is perfect for the job.

Is where *and* Is when

In defining words, do not use *is where* and *is when.*

Wrong: A riot *is when* a violent public disturbance occurs.

Better: A riot is a violent public disturbance.

Wrong: A parable *is where* a short story is told to illustrate a truth or moral lesson.

Better: A parable is a short story told to illustrate a truth or moral lesson.

Note: If you use the same form after *is* as before it, you will have the proper construction for a definition. In other words, a definition must have parallel structure.

Noun: A Laplander is an inhabitant of Lapland.

Adjective: To be fortunate is to have good luck.

Verb: To decompose is to decay or rot.

As if/Like

Remember that *as if* and *as though* are conjunctions introducing a clause. *Like* is a preposition which must be followed by an object.

It looks as though (*or* as if) interest rates will stay low for some time. (Conjunction)

It looks like a mushroom. (Preposition)

It seems as if I am repeating myself by stressing this point. (Conjunction)

It seems like a good idea. (Preposition)

She looks as though she might faint.

She looks like her sister.

The picnic will be held indoors if it looks as if it might rain.

The picnic will be held indoors if it looks like rain.

Plus

Plus is a preposition, not a conjunction, and must be followed by an object.

Incorrect: We had a long meeting *plus* we had a lengthy lunch.

Correct: We had a long meeting plus a lengthy lunch.

Correct: We had a long meeting and we had a lengthy lunch.

The reason is...

Use *that* after the reason is, not *because*.

Incorrect: The reason for the low prices is because we are currently overstocked.

Correct: The reason for the low prices is that we are currently overstocked.

Incorrect: Our reasons for closing this branch are because sales and revenues have dropped drastically.

Correct: Our reasons for closing this branch are that sales and revenues have dropped drastically.

Mini-Test

Make any necessary corrections in the following sentences. If a sentence is correct as written, write *C* beside it.

1. It looks like the meeting will have to be postponed.

2. The reason the meeting has been postponed is because Ms. Jacobi is ill.
3. A time and motion study is when management decides to analyse the efficiency of an operation.
4. Sam's work has been so satisfactory that Mr. Sapone has recommended an increase in his salary.
5. To be economical is to be thrifty and economic conditions are where the amount of wealth is concerned.

KEY

1....looks as if... 2. ...postponed is that Ms. Jacobi... 3. A time and motion study is an analysis by management of the efficiency of an operation. 4. C 5. ...economic conditions are conditions relating to wealth.

Where/That

Do not use *where* in place of *that.*

Wrong: I understand where these classes are being moved to Yorkdale.

Correct: I understand that these classes are being moved to Yorkdale.

Wrong: We were told where changes in the curriculum are being considered.

Correct: We were told that changes in the curriculum are being considered.

Which

Because *which* is a relative pronoun, it must have a clear antecedent when used as a conjunction. A phrase or clause cannot be used as an antecedent.

Ambiguous: Give our foods to your baby, which should be kept in the refrigerator.

Clear: Give our foods, which should be kept in the refrigerator, to your baby.

Vague: We can show you many homes in your price range, which is the benefit of our experience.

Clear: Because we are experienced, we can show you many homes in your price range.

Which usually introduces a nonrestrictive or nonessential clause, which is set off by commas. *That* introduces a restrictive or essential clause. Note the difference in meaning and in punctuation in the following sentences.

The car, which belonged to Michael McGarry, was stolen from the parking lot.

The car that belonged to Michael McGarry was stolen from the parking lot.

Sometimes a shorter sentence omitting *which* is better.

Michael McGarry's car was stolen from the parking lot.

Mini-Test

Make any necessary corrections in the following sentences. If a sentence is correct as written, write *C* beside it.

1. We have just heard where your company was awarded the hydro contract.
2. The rain has been heavy and unbroken, which has played havoc with the scheduling of the golf tournament.
3. Have they completed painting the fence round the garden, which they said they would do last spring?

KEY

1....heard that your... 2. The heavy, unbroken rain has played... 3. garden, which work they...

Summary for Unit 5.6

- Do not use *so* for *so that.*
- Use *so* and *such* correctly always followed by *that.*
- In definitions, do not use *is when* or *is where*; use the same form before and after the word *is.*
- Use *like* and *plus* only as prepositions followed by a noun or pronoun, never by a clause.
- Use *the reason is that,* not *is because.*
- Do not use *where* incorrectly instead of *that.*
- *Which* must have a clear antecedent; a phrase or a clause cannot be used as an antecedent.
- A *which* clause is nonrestrictive and is set off by commas.
- Write shorter sentences to eliminate the use of *which* wherever possible.

Confirm Your Knowledge

Complete Exercise for Unit 5.6 on page 218.

Developing Your Language Skills

❍ 5.7 Vocabulary

Definitions

The words in this unit at first glance will all seem familiar; however, each of these words has a special meaning when used in business. Check your dictionary to find these particular meanings; then match up the words with the definitions given. Write the letter of the definition you choose from Column 2 in the space provided in Column 1.

Column 1	Column 2
____ exercise	a) rise in value
____ realize	b) offer to build or supply
____ concern	c) have, use
____ tender	d) change into money
____ appreciate	e) material to be set in type
____ copy	f) a business
____ minutes	g) consider, discuss
____ execute	h) put into effect, carry out
____ deliberate	i) without meaning
____ quotation	j) offical record of a meeting
	k) a stated price

Mini-Test

Complete the following sentences by choosing the most appropriate word from Column 1 under "Definitions."

1. The firm will ___________ the agreement faithfully.
2. May we have your ___________ for the construction materials so that we can compare it with other offers?
3. By selling your stock now, you will ___________ $20 000.
4. Please ___________ restraint when repeating the incident to the newspapers.
5. Although Cathy's Crafts had difficulties last year, it is now a going ___________ employing nine people.
6. The stock market ___________ was up a little today.
7. The jury had to ___________ for four hours before coming to a decision.
8. The ___________ of the last meeting were read.
9. Harbourside homes are guaranteed to ___________ over the years.
10. Is the ___________ ready to go with the photos for the fall advertisements?

Key

1.execute 2. tender 3. realize 4. exercise 5. concern 6. quotation 7. deliberate 8. minutes 9. appreciate 10. copy

Usage

Study the following words carefully so that you are fully aware of the differences and can use them correctly.

in regard to (not *regards*)	
	In regard to your order...
irregardless/regardless	
	irregardless—no such word!
regardless—without taking into account	Regardless of the results of the poll...
later/latter	
later—after a particular time	I will see you later.
latter—the second one of two items	Which do you like better of the two? I prefer the latter.
learn/teach	
learn—to gain knowledge	I plan to learn Arabic.
teach—to give knowledge	He agreed to teach me Arabic.
eligible /legible/illegible	
eligible—fit, desirable	an eligible bachelor
legible—easily read	Her writing was quite legible.
illegible—not able to be read	The writing on the prescription was illegible.
likely/liable	
likely—expresses probability	They are likely to pay the bill
liable—responsible	as they are liable for the amount owing.

Mini-Test

Complete the following sentences by choosing the correct word from those shown at the beginning of the sentences.

1. *in regard to/regardless*

   ___________ your request for an extended vacation, we regret this cannot be arranged _________ of the amount of overtime you have worked.

2. *later/latter*

   Please consider Betty's proposal along with Winston's although I prefer the ___________.

   Please let me have your decision ___________ this week.

3. *learn/teach*

   Ms. Savory will ___________ you how to operate the equipment.

   Ms. Hayman will ___________ from her experiences at the international exhibition.

4. *eligible/legible/illegible*

   The ___________ handwriting on the document made it

   impossible to know whether or not he was ___________ for the position.

   Be sure the figures are ___________ so that no errors will be made.

5. *likely/liable*

   You are ___________ to incur heavy expenses if you are involved in an accident and are ___________ for the damages.

KEY

1. In regard to, regardless 2. latter, later 3. teach, learn 4. illegible, eligible, legible 5. likely, liable

Spelling

Words from French

Many French words are now commonly used in English. Study the spelling and meaning of the French words and the "tricky" ones in the following list. Write out the words at least ten times each.

French Words

restaurant	liaison	lien
in lieu of	connoisseur	resume
reservoir	chauffeur	

Tricky Words

rhythm	develop	ninth
forty	wholly	eighth
thoroughly		

Mini-Test

By using proofreaders' marks or otherwise, correct any spelling errors in the following words. There may be one error, more than one error, or no errors in a line.

1. liasion	resume	reservoir
2. connoisseur	throughly	restaurant
3. develop	rythm	lien
4. chauffeur	wholly	nineth
5. in lieu of	eighth	fourty

KEY

1. liasion 2. throughly 3. rythm 4. nineth 5. fourty

SUMMARY FOR UNIT 5.7

- Some common words have other meanings in business.
- Never use *in regards to* or *irregardless*!
- Be sure of any confusing words.
- Pay particular attention to the spelling of words from another language and "tricky" words.

Confirm Your Knowledge

Complete Exercise for Unit 5.7 on page 220.

❍ 5.8 Proofreading

Review of Proofreaders' Marks

Insert	Capital letters required
Delete	Insert period
Transpose	Insert comma
Space	Close up; leave no space
Reinstate; leave as before	Move to point of arrow.
No capitals; lower case	Move to left.
Underline	Line up with other lines.

Mini-Test

Proofread the following passage which contains numerous errors! Use as many of the proofreaders' marks as you can.

> Have you ever considered a job a s a medical Secretary? We offer a special course called medical Secretarial Practice and we we believe it offers the best training available in the city. Because our students work on own and proceed at their own pace, theyenjoy learning the new language of medicine without pressure The book My Career as a Medical Secertary might help you ot make up your mind, a copy of which is attached.

Before you check your work with the key, have you used every symbol except the reinstate symbol? Now change the word "their" in the phrase "at their own pace" to "there" for practice in using the reinstate procedure.

KEY

Have you ever considered a job a s a medical secretary? We offer a special course called medical Secretarial Practice and we we believe it offers the best training available in the city. Because our students work on own and proceed at their own pace, theyenjoy learning the new language of medicine without pressure. The book My Career as a Medical Sectrary might help you of make up your mind, a copy of which is attached.

Correcting or Entering from Proofread Material

Preparing the final copy from proofread material demands great care and skill in interpretation of the proofreaders' marks. Before starting, read the material carefully and mark in coloured pen or pencil any part that you think might cause you trouble. For example, you may be expected to insert a paragraph from another page, and a coloured mark would help you to find the insert quickly at the time of entering.

Practise re-entering from material you have proofread yourself; you could start by keying in the paragraph you corrected in the last mini-test.

Mini-Test

Key in or write in final form the following paragraph that has already been proofread.

Holland for many years has been considered the country that produces the best cheeses. Dutch cheeses are excellent and full of exciting flavours. However, they are experiencing competition today from the Canadian cheesemakers. At the last international conference of cheese producers held in Switzerland, Canadian cheddar and Edam cheeses one first prizes in there categories. Other Canadian cheeses also were given high praise and many world famous hotels are now using Canadian cheeses in preference to those from Holland.

KEY

For many years, Holland has been considered the country that produces the best cheeses. Dutch cheeses are excellent and full of exciting flavours. They are, however, experiencing competition today from the Canadian cheesemakers. At the last International Conference of Cheese Producers held in Switzerland, Canadian Cheddar and Edam cheeses won first prizes in their categories. Other Canadian cheeses were also given high praise, and many world-famous hotels are now buying Canadian cheeses in preference to those from Holland.

SUMMARY FOR UNIT 5.8

- Review of Proofreaders' Marks
  - ^ Insert
  - Delete
  - Transpose
  - # Space
  - stet Reinstate
  - lc Delete capitals; lower case
  - u/s Underline
  - Capital letters required
  - Insert period
  - Insert comma
  - Close up
  - Move to point of arrow.
  - Move to left.
  - Line up with other lines.
- Key carefully from proofread material.
- Read before entering.
- Mark in colour anything that might be missed or cause difficulty.

Confirm Your Knowledge

Complete Exercise (for Unit 5.8) on page 222.

Pretest for Unit 5

Complete all the parts of this test according to the directions for each part. The figures in parentheses are the unit numbers for reference,if necessary, when you have completed the test.

Your Goal: To score a total of at least 40 points.

A. General Rules

Are the following statements true or false? If true, circle *T*; if false, circle *F*. Score 1 point for each correct answer.

			Score
1.	A fragment is an incomplete sentence which does not give the reader a complete message. (5.1)	**T F**	_____
2.	The position of a modifier (a describing word, phrase, or clause) does not affect the meaning of a sentence. (5.2)	**T F**	_____
3.	The word "which" should always have a clear, one-word reference. (5.6)	**T F**	_____
4.	Choosing conjunctions carefully will help you to make your writing clear. (5.4)	**T F**	_____
5.	A diagram helps in checking for parallel structure. (5.3)	**T F**	_____
6.	The word *and* should only be used to join parts of a sentence of equal value and in the same form. (5.4)	**T F**	_____
7.	It is not important to be consistent with tenses or pronouns. (5.4)	**T F**	_____
8.	The longer your sentence, the easier it will be to understand. (5.5)	**T F**	_____
9.	In writing definitions, do not use *is when* or *is where*. (5.6)	**T F**	_____
10.	Run-on sentences in which two sentences are separated by a comma instead of a period are quite acceptable. (5.1)	**T F**	_____
		Score for Part A	_____

B. Incomplete and Run-on Sentences (5.1)

Make any necessary changes to correct the following sentences. You may add or delete words, but do not change the meaning. Score 1 point for each correct sentence.

		Score
1.	Referring to the advertisement in Monday's issue of *The Globe and Mail.* Please consider me as a candidate for the position of market research analyst.	_____
2.	The glass required for car windshields must be shatterproof, your specifications seem to meet this requirement.	_____
3.	The items listed on page 27 of our Fall Catalogue relating to our power tools the home repairer should have on hand for emergencies.	_____
4.	If you are interested in purchasing insurance that will guarantee you an adequate income when you retire. Call Mr. Williams at 827-1532 to arrange an appointment to discuss our retirement income plan.	_____
5.	Mr. Seagram has completed his initial research. he will start his tests on Monday.	_____
	Score for Part B	_____

C. Dangling, Misplaced, and Confusing Modifiers (5.2)

Make any necessary changes to correct the following sentences. You may add or delete words to make the meaning absolutely clear. Score 1 point for each correct answer.

Score

1. Thank you for your order for cake decorating supplies dated February 1. ______
2. Having written three times for information, the brochures finally arrived today from the travel agent. ______
3. Tom said that Mr. Horton had told him that he was being given the Woolley account. ______
4. While working on the pipeline, the extreme cold caused many pipe fitters to suffer frostbite. ______
5. At the meeting, Mr. Wrong decided to suddenly leave. ______

Score for Part C ______

D. Parallel Structure (5.3)

Correct any sentences that have errors in construction. If a sentence is correct as written, write *C* beside it. Score 1 point for each correct answer.

Score

1. Use our safety mats to prevent falls, to provide insulation, and for protecting floor surfaces. ______
2. Your order has been sent today. Also we are enclosing our latest catalogue with it. ______
3. You may pay either by sending a cheque or by charging the amount to your VISA account. ______
4. Not only have our meters proved to be reliable but you will have no difficulty reading them. ______
5. Both the patience of the teacher and having the backing of the parents helped the child gain confidence. ______

Score for Part D ______

E. Clarity and Coherence (5.4)

Revise the following sentences to make them clear and easy to understand. Be careful with the use of conjunctions. Score 1 point for each correct answer.

Score

1. Please send me a list of your agents in Vancouver, and do you have any agents in Victoria? ______
2. We now have the franchise for Berto products, and they will be promoted in our sidewalk sale next month. ______
3. Mrs. Ralfe spoke for about thirty minutes and then leaves for the airport to catch her flight to New York. ______
4. One can learn welding on the job, and you can earn money at the same time. ______
5. The instructions are quite clear and concise and easy to understand and you will find that you have no difficulty assembling the sprinkler. ______

Score for Part E ______

F. Writing Style (5.5)

Improve the following sentences by using a variety of structures and making sure that the verbs are used in the most direct way. Score 1 point for each correct answer.

Score

1. You will receive a call from Miss Schwyola to arrange for a demonstration. _____
2. The routing of orders is confusing. It needs to be made more clear. New employees do not understand it. _____
3. The new paper for the posters has been received. It is being tried out. If it is satisfactory, we shall use it for the next printing of posters. _____
4. The checking of the figures by Vernon brought to light an error in the computer software. _____
5. All overtime has been cancelled by the manager. _____

Score for Part F _____

G. Problem Words (5.6)

Revise or rewrite the following sentences to eliminate errors. Score 1 point for each correct sentence.

Score

1. He worked until 11:30 p.m. so he could finish the report and go on holiday with a clean slate. _____
2. It looks like the recession is finally over. _____
3. The reason for the delay in commencing construction is because the heavy equipment has not cleared the site yet. _____
4. An anthology is when a number of pieces of writing are collected into one book. _____
5. The supplies for the new project have been received, which means that work on it can be started immediately. _____

Score for Part G _____

H. Vocabulary (5.7)

From the list of words given, choose the most appropriate word to complete the following sentences. Score 1 point for each correct answer.

concern	exercise	tender	copy
minutes	appreciate	realize	execute
deliberate	quotation		

Score

1. Be sure to _________ great care when working with explosives. _____
2. The writing of advertising _________ is a specialized form of writing. _____
3. The _________ of the previous meeting were read and approved. _____
4. Gold continues to _________ although other metals are going down in value. _____
5. If you want to _________ a good return on your capital, you must invest wisely. _____

Score for Part H _____

I. Proofreading

Proofread the following paragraphs very carefully for all kinds of errors. Score 1 point for each error found and marked correctly; deduct 1 point for each error missed!

Although the need for good handwriting skills is not so important thes days because so much is handled by computers, one area that required excellent penmanship was bookkeeping. The bookkeeper had to record entires in ledgers clearly and neatly so the information could be easily read by someone else.

Many employers required applicants for jobs as bookkeepers to send in a handwritten letter with their application forms so that the quality of their handwriting could be taken in to consideration. If you were in any doubt about the quality of your handwriting you were advised to take a special course to make sure that your writing was completely legible and would not let you down when you applied for a bookkeeper's job.

Number of errors found and correctly marked _____

Deduct for errors missed _____

Score for Part I _____

Total Score _____

If you achieved your goal of at least 40 points, proceed to Unit 6. If you did not score 40, check with your instructor what parts you need to study. Proceed through Unit 5 doing all the necessary work; then do the posttest for Unit 5.

POSTTEST FOR UNIT 5

Complete all the parts of this test according to the directions for each part. The figures in parentheses are the unit numbers for reference,if necessary, when you have completed the test.

Your Goal: To score a total of at least 40 points.

A. General Rules

Are the following statements true or false? If true, circle *T*; if false, circle *F*. Score 1 point for each correct answer.

			Score
1.	Sentence fragments are acceptable. (5.1)	**T F**	_____
2.	A modifier (a describing word, phrase, or clause) should be placed close to the word it modifies. (5.2)	**T F**	_____
3.	The words *like* and *plus* can be used as conjunctions to join parts of a sentence. (5.6)	**T F**	_____
4.	The careful choice of words will help you avoid having your writing misunderstood. (5.4)	**T F**	_____
5.	Outlining the sentence in diagram form will help you to check for parallel structure in a long sentence. (5.3)	**T F**	_____
6.	The word *and* should not be used to join parts of a sentence of unequal value or in the different form. (5.4)	**T F**	_____
7.	It is acceptable to change from active to passive voice in the same sentence. (5.4)	**T F**	_____
8.	Short, choppy sentences do not give writing a smoothly flowing style.	**T F**	_____
9.	It is correct to write "The reason is because..." when giving an explanation. (5.6)	**T F**	_____
10.	Run-on sentences where two sentences are separated by a comma instead of a period are not acceptable. (5.1)	**T F**	_____
		Score for Part A	_____

B. Incomplete and Run-on Sentences (5.1)

Make any necessary changes to correct the following sentences. You may add or delete words, but do not change the meaning. Score 1 point for each correct sentence.

		Score
1.	Referring to your report dated May 16. Have you received the figures for the cost of developing the pilot project as outlined on page 17?	_____
2.	The fabric we need for the manufacture of safety clothing must be very durable, we are interested in your suggestions.	_____
3.	The specifications detailed on the draft plan submitted by the contractors for municipal housing in the city centre.	_____
4.	When you have decided where you would like to travel for your spring vacation. Call Mr. Watts at 226-8765 to arrange a trip that will be memorable in every way.	_____
5.	Mr. Gaulin has requested an early retirement, he will have completed 30 years of service on June 30.	_____
	Score for Part B	_____

C. Dangling, Misplaced, and Confusing Modifiers (5.2)

Make any necessary changes to correct the following sentences. You may add or delete words to make the meaning absolutely clear. Score 1 point for each correct answer.

Score

1. We appreciate your request for floral arrangements dated October 22. _____
2. Having telephoned last Monday, the stationery we require has still not arrived. _____
3. Mr. Bartolo told Mr. Duff that he had to take his vacation in early September. _____
4. While checking the steam valves, the switches on the controls were found to be overheating. _____
5. Ms. Black has agreed immediately to start the investigation. _____

Score for Part C _____

D. Parallel Structure (5.3)

Correct any sentences that have errors in construction. If a sentence is correct as written, write *C* beside it. Score 1 point for each correct answer.

Score

1. Arrange to visit our school, take part in some of the programs, and your child can be enrolled at the same time. _____
2. Your evergreens have been sent today. Also we are sending a sample of our seeds for your garden. _____
3. Payment may be either by cheque or you can charge your purchases to your credit card account. _____
4. Not only are our drivers totally reliable, but you will pleased to know our trucks are radio dispatched. _____
5. Both the cleanliness of the washrooms and having really comfortable locker rooms appealed to the athletes. _____

Score for Part D _____

E. Clarity and Coherence (5.4)

Revise the following sentences to make them clear and easy to understand. Be careful with the use of conjunctions. Score 1 point for each correct answer.

Score

1. Please let me know the dates you will be in Winnipeg, and when do you plan to visit Brandon? _____
2. We have just received approval for the plans for the conference which came from our office in Edmonton. _____
3. Miss Houston arranged for a demonstration of the new fax machine, and then she leaves before it is over. _____
4. One has to be selective in choosing a day-care centre, and you should check with the health authorities. _____
5. The recipes are step-by-step with clear pictures and you will easily be able to follow all the directions. _____

Score for Part E _____

F. Writing Style (5.5)

Improve the following sentences by using a variety of structures and making sure that the verbs are used in the most direct way. Score 1 point for each correct answer.

Score

1. You will receive a call from Dr. Henderson's nurse to arrange for an appointment. _____
2. The winners are being interviewed on the radio. They should be made to feel at ease and comfortable. It is the responsibility of the interviewer to do this. _____
3. The new schedule for May is ready. It will be posted on the notice board on Friday. If you have any questions, see me before then. It cannot be changed after posting. _____
4. The report of the discrepancy by Ruth enabled the final tax return to be completed on time. _____
5. All draperies are being cleaned by the custodial staff. _____

Score for Part F _____

G. Problem Words (5.6)

Revise or rewrite the following sentences to eliminate errors. Score 1 point for each correct sentence.

Score

1. She phoned the police so she could report the theft. _____
2. He seemed like he was really pleased with the compliment. _____
3. The reason for the change in procedures is because the old machinery has been replaced by modern equipment. _____
4. An embargo is where a restriction is put on trading between two countries. _____
5. The fuel for the new motors is specially prepared, which will raise the price considerably. _____

Score for Part G _____

H. Vocabulary (5.7)

From the list of words given, choose the most appropriate word to complete the following sentences. Score 1 point for each correct answer.

concern	exercise	tender	copy
minutes	appreciate	realize	execute
deliberate	quotation		

Score

1. How much did you _________ from the sale of your franchise? _____
2. ___________ each step in the procedure very carefully to ensure a satisfactory result. _____
3. The secretary produced the _________ and circulated them to all who attended the meeting. _____
4. Real estate will usually _________ greatly if the general economy is good. _____
5. The executive committee had to ___________ for four hours before they could come to a decision. _____

Score for Part H _____

I. Proofreading

Proofread the following paragraphs very carefully for all kinds of errors. Score 1 point for each error found and marked correctly; deduct 1 point for each error missed!

The furnishings in our luxurious motel rooms are of top quality. The mattresses have coil springs guaranteed to provide you with a perfect nights sleep. The draperies are fully lined, which prevents early morning light from disturbing the vacationer who wants to sleep late. The carpets are of a soft wool to soothe your feet after a hard day's drive. The colour television set in each room is capable of giving you your choice of 27 channels with perfect pictures. Pay TV is also available in each room. The small fridge in each room is fully stocked with snacks and light drinks for your refreshment at any time. Coffee or tea can be made right in your room for that quick pick-up.

You will see from the enclosed brochure the beautiful ground surrounding our motel. The swiming pool is heated for those cool evenings in spring and fall. The tennis courts are floodlit, and the gift shop willbe sure to supply you with many souvenirs of your trip as well as any grooming essentials you may have forgotten.

May we have the pleasure of reserving a room for you soon?

Number of errors found and correctly marked _____

Deduct for errors missed _____

Score for Part I _____

Total Score _____

If you achieved your goal of at least 40 points, proceed to Unit 6. If you did not score 40, check with your instructor what parts you need to review before moving on.

EXERCISE 5.1 INCOMPLETE AND RUN-ON SENTENCES

By using proofreaders' marks or otherwise, make any necessary changes to correct the following sentences. If any sentence is correct as written, do not make any change and write *C* beside it. Score 1 point for each correct answer.

Your Goal: To score at least 8 points.

Example: In response to your letter, your complaint is being investigated. 1

Score

1. The renovations are almost complete you should be able to move in on Saturday. ______
2. I do not anticipate my application's being rejected. As many scientists have already received grants. ______
3. Unfortunately, we are no longer able to service a 1932 model, however, we can recommend an independent technician who can. ______
4. Checkers failing to report shortages and thereby causing inventory discrepancies. ______
5. The school records are listed by the student's last name there is no list arranged by grade average. ______
6. All staff relocations are arranged through our Toronto office. Whether the move is local or long distance. ______
7. Managers failing to notice staff conflicts and thereby allowing tension to increase. ______
8. Referring to page 61 of your fall catalogue. Please send me two aluminum toboggans No. 92-6032X. ______
9. Most of the summer staff at the research station were students, and some of them had experience in entomology. ______
10. The scenery in New Brunswick is breathtaking don't miss the beauty of the St. John River and the grandeur of Fundy National Park. ______

Total Score ______

If you achieved your goal of at least 8 points, proceed to Unit 5.2. If you did not score 8, go back and review Unit 5.1 thoroughly; then do Exercise 5.1A and try to achieve your goal this time.

EXERCISE 5.1A INCOMPLETE AND RUN-ON SENTENCES

Use the same directions as for Exercise 5.1.

Your Goal: To score at least 8 points.

	Score
1. As you were kind enough to return my call, I would like to place a second order.	_____
2. Let me stress one fact I am sure you all realize that the future of this venture rests on the results of this promotion.	_____
3. The electricians, having negotiated for almost six months and still not closer to a settlement.	_____
4. The carpet manufacturer recommends daily vacuuming. Especially in high traffic areas.	_____
5. We had large audiences when the show first opened attendance is less now, however.	_____
6. With reference to your request which I received this morning. I could attend an interview on May 3.	_____
7. If you would like help in selecting a course, ask for an appointment with a counsellor.	_____
8. The information you request will be faxed to your office on Monday. Unless you would prefer us to mail it.	_____
9. The cottage has a large kitchen, a screened porch overlooks the lake.	_____
10. Mr. Seager will miss the opening speech, he will be in time for the awards ceremony.	_____
Total Score	

If you achieved your goal of at least 8 points, proceed to Unit 5.2. If you did not score 8, ask your instructor for direction before moving on.

EXERCISE 5.2 DANGLING, MISPLACED, AND CONFUSING MODIFIERS

By using proofreaders' marks or otherwise, correct any errors in modifiers in the following sentences. There are a number of ways in which the sentences may be changed. Make sure the meaning of the corrected sentence is perfectly clear. If any sentence is correct as written, do not make any change and write *C* beside it. Score 1 point for each acceptable answer.

Your Goal: To score at least 8 points.

Example: While I was visiting the hospital, the fire alarm rang. 1

Score

1. After applying to the arts council six times, a grant was finally received. ______
2. Your order for a stepladder dated July 6 will be shipped to you immediately. ______
3. Your letter to our board of directors lists your concerns about our financial situation which we understand. ______
4. Being afraid of the dark, many children prefer to have night lights. ______
5. When rigging flying scenery, your rope must always be in good condition. ______
6. I heard while in Montreal you were moved to St. John's. ______
7. She nearly knew everything about repairing modems. ______
8. Ms. Quarly, having completed her inventory review, began filling in the analysis form. ______
9. Mrs. Sampson has agreed to finally promote our line of cosmetics. ______
10. Severely dented, the customer brought in the damaged bicycle. ______

Total Score ______

If you achieved your goal of at least 8 points, proceed to Unit 5.3. If you did not score 8, go back and review Unit 5.2 thoroughly; then do Exercise 5.2A and try to achieve your goal this time.

EXERCISE 5.2A DANGLING, MISPLACED, AND CONFUSING MODIFIERS

Use the same directions as for Exercise 5.2.

Your Goal: To score at least 8 points.

		Score
1.	By staying after hours, Jill completed the assignment first.	_____
2.	Geoffrey learned small engine repair to better be able to run a small marina.	_____
3.	The standard bail was reported paid by the judge.	_____
4.	You have a unique chance to purchase these cut flowers for 25 cents that will last two weeks.	_____
5.	Amy has nearly developed all of the photographs.	_____
6.	Aiming to reduce pollution, bicycles should be used more than cars.	_____
7.	Our only concern was for the safety during the demonstration of the spectators.	_____
8.	Mr. Georges has agreed to finally coach our basketball team.	_____
9.	To be sure not to miss the first pitch, the 5 p.m. train should be taken.	_____
10.	Travelling leisurely, the 200 km to Fredericton can be covered in a little over two hours.	_____
	Total Score	_____

If you achieved your goal of at least 8 points, proceed to Unit 5.3. If you did not score 8, ask your instructor for direction before moving on.

EXERCISE 5.3 PARALLEL STRUCTURE

By using proofreaders' marks or otherwise, make any corrections in the following sentences. There are a number of ways in which the sentences may be changed. Make sure the meaning of the corrected sentence is perfectly clear. Score 1 point for each acceptable answer.

Your Goal: To score at least 8 points.

Example: Remember to bring a swimsuit and ~~you should have~~ sunscreen, ~~too~~. ______

Score

1. May we suggest four ways that you can enjoy our park's facilities: biking, hiking, swim, in the caves. ______
2. A letter must be written carefully, it must be produced accurately, and you must be sure to proofread it. ______
3. I not only like a lot of ketchup on my fries but some salt is good, too. ______
4. The length of a performance is calculated by measuring the length of each scene to get the total length and then you subtract the length of the intermissions. ______
5. She instructed me to arrive early and that I should disarm the security system when I arrived. ______
6. We suggest you either increase the memory in your computer or you should reduce the number of programs running. ______
7. Both the talent of the artist and if the paintings are good should be reviewed. ______
8. The reduction in ticket sales is, although not as bad as expected, having an effect on the players' morale. ______
9. If Sally is available and should John and Martin be willing, the four of us could car pool this fall. ______
10. Fruit should be picked just before it is ripe and you should store it in a paper bag to ripen it fully. ______

Total Score ______

If you achieved your goal of at least 8 points, proceed to Unit 5.4. If you did not score 8, go back and review Unit 5.3 thoroughly; then do Exercise 5.3A and try to achieve your goal this time.

EXERCISE 5.3A PARALLEL STRUCTURE

Use the same directions as for Exercise 5.3.

Your Goal: To score at least 8 points.

		Score
1.	The contract has neither a date for completion nor does it have a clause concerning insurance.	_____
2.	Your report should include recommendations on how to save fuel, cut down on the use of paper, and also include ideas for better delivery service.	_____
3.	There are two types of politicians: those who succeed by their talent and effort and there are those who are lucky or they get their jobs through knowing the right people.	_____
4.	The restaurant's kitchen has neither air conditioning nor does it have a fan in the ceiling.	_____
5.	The program should suggest how good nutrition can be achieved, how recipes can be adapted, and what to do to keep within a budget.	_____
6.	Pablo is eager, articulate, and has the desire to become an excellent journalist for the paper that hires him.	_____
7.	Yvonne wants to renovate the customer service area and have new lighting installed.	_____
8.	We hope that you will enjoy your new trailer and hope for a pleasant vacation.	_____
9.	We have a large stock of lumber and immediate delivery is guaranteed.	_____
10.	Not only does swimming provide good exercise but it is also a lot of fun.	_____
	Total Score	_____

If you achieved your goal of at least 8 points, proceed to Unit 5.4. If you did not score 8, ask your instructor for direction before moving on.

EXERCISE 5.4 CONJUNCTIONS AND INCONSISTENCIES

Rewrite the following sentences to improve the use of conjunctions, to make sure and is used correctly, and to eliminate any inconsistencies in point of view. Rewrite each sentence once only although you should try to use variety in your constructions. Score 1 point for each sentence correctly revised.

Your Goal: To score at least 8 points.

Score

1. These books were received on Friday, and you should distribute them to your dealers immediately. _____
2. The electric utility does not make connections on the weekend, and the freezer room is warm; and there is nothing I can do about it. _____
3. I am enjoying my new dishwasher. Its magical cleaning ability is making me lazy. _____
4. We have your invoice of November 12, and payment will be sent at the end of the month. _____
5. My aunt thinks I should become a dancer; therefore I am taking tap lessons. _____
6. Collision, our newest game, is very demanding, and skill is also required for our other games. _____
7. Try our low-calorie butter, and we know it will be suitable for your baking needs. _____
8. One has to be careful when making investments, and you must use only a registered broker. _____
9. We had no record of your new address, and your order was sent to your old address last week. _____
10. The conductor keeps the musicians until 7 p.m. and wanted them to be ready to perform at 8 p.m. _____

Total Score _____

If you achieved your goal of at least 8 points, proceed to Unit 5.5. If you did not score 8, go back and review Unit 5.4 thoroughly; then do Exercise 5.4A and try to achieve your goal this time.

EXERCISE 5.4A CONJUNCTIONS AND INCONSISTENCIES

Use the same directions as for Exercise 5.4.

Your Goal: To score at least 8 points.

Score

1. These requests were received on Monday, and you should answer them by Thursday. _____
2. The curtain rod in the shower fell down and cracked the tub and it was only held up by pressure. _____
3. Ms. Blythe asked the staff to assist in the recycling program. They agreed to make every effort to help. _____
4. Our neighbour has decided to plant potatoes; insects have eaten all his tomato plants. _____
5. You can take wonderful photographs with the Scenic camera, and one can have prints or slides from the negatives. _____
6. The child searched everywhere; they could not find the lost toys. _____
7. We arrived at the station and found that the ticket line was very long. We missed the train. _____
8. The medicine was prescribed by Dr. Yassaf and he also told me to stay in bed for two days. _____
9. The sun suddenly came out from behind the clouds, and then everyone began to discard sweaters. _____
10. Pomona Mills is hosting a provincial tennis tournament, and our club should host a similar one. _____

Total Score _____

If you achieved your goal of at least 8 points, proceed to Unit 5.5. If you did not score 8, ask your instructor for direction before moving on.

EXERCISE 5.5 SENTENCE COMPOSITION, CHOPPINESS, AND PASSIVE VOICE

Rewrite the following sentences to improve their composition and create a smooth writing style. Correct any wrong use of the passive voice. Score 1 point for each sentence correctly revised.

Your Goal: To score at least 4 points.

Score

1. Replacement parts for your electric lawnmower can be supplied by any Cut-It-Smooth registered dealer. ______
2. We slow-cure our hams in special ovens. Turning them regularly for even curing. This keeps in all the natural flavour. ______
3. You want to repave the driveway. The first step is to remove the old asphalt. The second step is to add more crushed stone before applying the new coating of asphalt. The asphalt should be at least 10 cm thick. ______
4. You will be visited by our representative on July 3 to have the contract completed. ______
5. This book is very rare. Please be careful with it. I need one copy of each page that I have indicated. I have indicated 30 pages. Use both sides of the paper. ______

Total Score ______

If you achieved your goal of at least 4 points, proceed to Unit 5.6. If you did not score 4, go back and review Unit 5.5 thoroughly; then do Exercise 5.5A and try to achieve your goal this time.

EXERCISE 5.5A SENTENCE COMPOSITION, CHOPPINESS, AND PASSIVE VOICE

Use the same directions as for Exercise 5.5

Your Goal: To score at least 4 points.

Score

1. Travel arrangements for your trip to Europe can be made through any authorized travel agent. ______
2. Some politicians like to make long speeches. They are not considered to be good politicians necessarily. Their actions tell their constituents more about them. ______
3. Lulu cut her hand with an axe. She was chopping wood. Luckily the cut was not serious, but she did go to the hospital for stitches. ______
4. I like detective stories. I especially like them when there is no murder involved. Also I like them to have two mysteries to solve in the same story. ______
5. The announcement was made by Mr. Saunders that a profit was made by the company for the third successive year. ______

Total Score ______

If you achieved your goal of at least 4 points, proceed to Unit 5.6. If you did not score 4, ask your instructor for direction before moving on.

EXERCISE 5.6 PROBLEM WORDS

Make any necessary corrections in the following sentences. If a sentence is correct as written, write *C* beside it. Use variety in your answers. Score 1 point for each acceptable answer.

Your Goal: To score at least 8 points.

		Score
1.	A monopoly is where one company has the exclusive control of a product or service.	_____
2.	We have been informed where prices have been increased without our approval.	_____
3.	The house sits well back from the road, which needs painting.	_____
4.	Your eavestroughs should be replaced so rain water will be carried away efficiently.	_____
5.	It looks like we shall be able to stay within our budget this year.	_____
6.	The recession is still on, so we cannot hire any students this summer.	_____
7.	The reason our laundry detergent is safe for the environment is because it does not contain phosphates.	_____
8.	Many of the replies are handwritten which makes them hard to read.	_____
9.	Has Ms. Lennan completed the work schedule for next month like she said she would do last week?	_____
10.	She has just heard where the kitchen staff are planning a surprise party for the supervisor.	_____
	Total Score	_____

If you achieved your goal of at least 8 points, proceed to Unit 5.7. If you did not score 8, go back and review Unit 5.6 thoroughly; then do Exercise 5.6A and try to achieve your goal this time.

EXERCISE 5.6A PROBLEM WORDS

Use the same directions as for Exercise 5.6.

Your Goal: To score at least 8 points.

Score

1. To foreclose is when a person takes back property because payments on it have not been kept up. ______
2. Mr. Richardson heard where the city council has rezoned the area where he is living. ______
3. The copier, which produces the best results for the money, is the one we should buy. ______
4. The reason our ice cream facility was inspected is because a customer found a hair in one of our packages. ______
5. The merchandise has been sent by road transport instead of by rail express which is why you have not received it yet. ______
6. It seems like Robert really wants the job because he sent in his application so promptly. ______
7. The reason for her headaches is because she refuses to wear the glasses that her doctor prescribed. ______
8. Much of the produce has been spoiled by bad packaging so we shall need to bring in fresh supplies. ______
9. Have the executors probated the will yet which they assured us they would do by April 15? ______
10. Jake learned yesterday where he is being transferred to South Africa next month. ______

Total Score ______

If you achieved your goal of at least 8 points, proceed to Unit 5.7. If you did not score 8, ask your instructor for direction before moving on.

EXERCISE 5.7 VOCABULARY

Complete the three parts of this exercise according to the directions for each part.

Your Goal: To score at least 16 points.

A. Definitions

Complete the following sentences by choosing the most appropriate words from those given. Score 1 point for each correct answer.

exercise	realize	tender	concern
minutes	deliberate	quotation	copy
execute	appreciate		

Score

1. The value of the land continues to __________ daily. _____
2. How much did you __________ from the sale of your business? _____
3. __________ extreme caution when dealing with chemicals. _____
4. The executive committee will __________ that point at tomorrow's meeting. _____
3. Is the __________ for the catalogue ready for the printer yet? _____

Score for Part A _____

B. Usage

Use the same directions as for Part A.

later	eligible	learn	latter
likely	legible	teach	liable
illegible			

Score

1. Of the two tenders, the __________ is more acceptable. _____
2. May we __________ you how to use our latest drill? _____
3. I have compared last week's figures with those of the previous week, and the __________ were higher. _____
4. If it is __________to rain, do not spray your lawn. _____
5. How many employees are __________ for a month's vacation? _____
6. You can __________ how to use it in only three lessons. _____
7. We are not __________ for delivery expenses. _____
8. If your handwriting is __________, you will not be considered for a position as a bookkeeper as __________ handwriting is essential for that job. _____

Score for Part B _____

C. Spelling

By using proofreaders' marks or otherwise, correct any spelling errors in the following words. Score 1 point for each correctly changed word; deduct 1 point for each word changed that was correct as written.

				Score
1.	throughly	restaurant	develop	_____
2.	ninth	resevoir	chauffeur	_____
3.	connoisseur	rhythm	eigth	_____
4.	wholely	lien	in lieu of	_____
5.	résumé	liason	forty	_____

Score for Part C _____

Total Score _____

If you achieved your goal of at least 16 points, proceed to Unit 5.8. If you did not score 16, go back and review Unit 5.7 thoroughly before moving on.

EXERCISE 5.8 PROOFREADING

Complete each part of this exercise according to the directions given.

Your Goal: To score at least 12 points in total.

Part A

Are the following statements true or false? If true, circle *T*; if false, circle *F*. Score 1 point for each correct answer.

			Score
1. A colour pencil helps to mark parts that may be missed in rekeying proofread material.	**T**	**F**	_____
2. You should always proofread for meaning and accuracy of information such as dates and totals.	**T**	**F**	_____
3. Entering from proofread material requires great care.	**T**	**F**	_____
4. The word "stet" and a dotted line mean the original words are correct.	**T**	**F**	_____
5. To indicate that capital letters are needed, write three short lines beneath the letters.	**T**	**F**	_____
Score for Part A			_____

Part B

Proofread the following material very carefully for all kinds of errors. Score 1 point for each error found and marked correctly; deduct 1 point for each error missed!

Dear Mrs. Leslie

Thank you for your letter of Nov. 23 concerning the painting of flats for our next production. Your interest in our theatrical group is very encouraging.

We are presently negotiating for the use of the hall at the back of the library for the painting of the flats with the City. We always have problems with the storage and painting of the large pieces of stage equipment. Particularly so in this instance as we do not have the use of the theatres main stage until the day before the show is scheduled to open! It is therefore impossible to paint scenry right in the theatre. We shall have to find other quarters for the preparation of the backdrops and bring them to the theatre for placement just in time for the opening.

Referring to your offer. You would be most welcome on Teusday, December 10, at 10:30 a.m. We are setting aside that date for an all-out effort to get all painting completed, and the scenery ready for moving on the Wednesday, the day for the final dress rehearsal.

Yours sincerely

Number of errors found and correctly marked	_____
Deduct for errors missed	_____
Score for Part B	_____
Total Score	_____

If you achieved your goal of at least 12 points, proceed to the Posttest for Unit 5. If you did not score 12, you will appreciate the need for accurate proofreading! Review Unit 5.8 thoroughly before moving on.

BUSINESS COMMUNICATION

Business communication uses the same language, except for technical terms, that literate people use in everyday speech. The goal of written business communication is to have the reader understand immediately the purpose of the message and act or respond in accordance with that message.

To achieve these goals, write clearly and concisely and be aware of the influences of logic and psychology in making the reader respond. When the response to your communication is the one you wanted, then the purpose of your communication has been achieved.

This unit will focus on particular points to help you to strengthen the language you use in your written communications.

THE LANGUAGE OF COMMUNICATION

❍ 6.1 Specific Terms, Concrete Material, Precise Words, and Appropriate Words

Specific Terms

Specific words identify a definite thing; general words identify a wide range of things. *Reference manual* is specific; *book* is general. *Pitman Office Handbook* is even more specific than *reference manual.* Specific terms give the reader a clear message, whereas general terms leave the reader wondering exactly what is meant.

General:	There will be exams and tests throughout the course.
Specific	There will be a test every two weeks and mid-term and end-of-term exams.
General:	I'll get back to you next week.
Specific:	You'll have my reply by Friday, May 10.
General Words:	go, make, some, soon
Specific Words:	run, fly, drive, construct, bake, twelve, Friday

Mini-Test

Revise the following sentences substituting specific words for any general terms used. Add any information necessary to make your sentences clear.

1. I have sold some tickets for the show that opens soon.

   ____

   ____

2. Our Top Flight safety harness is a little more expensive than our Fly Secure style.

   ____

   ____

3. He spoke to us last week about our ailments.

   ____

   ____

4. Please let us know your decision soon so that we can do a survey.

   ____

   ____

5. Send the merchandise there and a quantity of packing cases, also.

   ____

   ____

Key

Your answers may be quite different, but as long as you have used specific terms, accept your sentences as correct.

1. I have sold 43 tickets for *Evita*, which opens on March 12.
2. Our Top Flight safety harness costs $325, a little more than our Fly Secure style, which costs $279.
3. On Wednesday, July 15, Dr. Renaldi spoke to us about arthritis and osteoporosis.
4. Please let us know your decision before June 15 so that we can complete our survey.
5. Send the merchandise to 10 Main Street along with 15 packing cases.

Concrete Material

Concrete words give the reader exact information because they refer to actual definite things. Abstract words, on the other hand, often leave the reader wondering because they are vague and need further explanation. Illustrations, descriptions, details, and explanations are examples of concrete material. References to ideas and generalities are abstract.

Abstract: Sport is good exercise.

Concrete: A hard game of singles at tennis will raise your heart rate and stimulate your muscles.

Abstract: Your tennis racquet has to meet many demands.

Concrete: Your tennis racquet must be strong, flexible, strung to the right tension for you, and the right weight for you.

Mini-Test

Revise the following sentences substituting concrete words for any abstract terms used. Add any information necessary to make your sentences clear.

1. He enjoyed visiting Florida.

____

____

2. The talk was about space travel in the twenty-first century.

____

____

3. We stock anything you need to beautify your home.

____

____

4. Use paint to prevent rust on your car.

____

____

5. Fruit trees and other trees should be sprayed in the spring.

____

____

KEY

Your answers may be quite different, but as long as you have used concrete terms, accept your sentences as correct.

1. On his visit to Clearwater in Florida, he enjoyed swimming in the warm seawater.
2. The talk explained the need for manned space stations before extended space travel would be feasible.
3. We stock fresh flowers from California and the West Indies as well as ceramic vases to beautify your home.
4. Paint your car with Rustgone enamel to prevent rust.
5. Fruit trees and other deciduous trees should be sprayed in the spring to prevent insect damage.

Precise Words

English is full of synonyms, words that mean the same or almost the same. For example, synonyms for *walk* are *amble*, *shuffle*, and *stride*. Each of these words gives a more precise picture of the action than the word walk. By using precise words, the writer can give the reader more exact information and make the message much easier to understand. A good thesaurus will help you find synonyms. Be careful, however, not to make your writing sound unnatural.

	Synonyms
good	excellent, beneficial, valuable, useful
do	make, perform, achieve, manage, complete
very	exceedingly, highly, unusually, remarkably
give	donate, assign, allow, supply, grant, provide

Mini-Test

Using a thesaurus or a dictionary, find more precise words for the words in italics in the following sentences.

1. Vaclav has proved himself to be *very* competent, and we suggest that he be *given* a more challenging project.

 ____

 ____

2. The *fine* water in our lakes provides *great* fishing year round.

 ____

 ____

3. The Rogers Company wants to *use* a new welder to make the *funny-shaped* joints in the new pipes.

 ____

 ____

KEY

1. very—extremely, outstanding; given—assigned 2. fine—pure, clear; great—excellent, abundant 3. use—employ, hire; funny—intricate, unusual, odd

Appropriate Words

Appropriate words are words that are well known and will be easily understood by the reader. Long and unfamiliar words create a very affected style that can be annoying as well as confusing to the reader. The acronym KISS, which stands for *Keep It Short and Simple*, will help you to remember to use well-known words.

Affected: To effect the execution of the project required the collaboration of everyone.

Simplified: To complete the job needed everyone's co-operation

Technical Terms

Technical terms and jargon that relate to particular industries, trades, or professions should be used only in writing to people within these specialized areas. General writing should not include technical terms or jargon.

Technical: Proportional and compressed fonts squeeze more characters onto each line.

Simplified Various sizes of print may reduce the length of each line.

Trite Expressions

Trite expressions are phrases that have been greatly overused and are often unnecessary or meaningless. Because you may still see them in many pieces of writing does not mean that you should use them. Try to avoid trite expressions by using a simple or more original expression. Sometimes just omitting part of the expression is all that is necessary.

Trite	Better
due to the fact that	because, since, as
under date of	dated
at this point in time	now
attached hereto	attached
advise us	let us know
each and every	each
in conclusion	finally
wish to thank you	thank you
acknowledge receipt of	have received, thank you for
in the amount of $50	for $50
under separate cover	(be specific e.g. by parcel post)
kindly send (Never use *kindly* unless you mean the opposite of *unkindly*.)	please send

Mini-Test

Rewrite the following sentences taking out all trite expressions and using familiar words that are easily understood.

1. Overindulgence in alcoholic beverages causes people to become inebriated.

 ____

 ____

2. The disposal of ferrous and non-ferrous waste from our industrial complexes is a major problem.

 ____

 ____

3. Please be advised that your cheque in the amount of $500 should be mailed at this point in time.

____

____

KEY

1. Too much alcohol makes people drunk. 2. The disposal of scrap iron and other waste from our factories is a major problem. 3. Please send your cheque for $500 now.

SUMMARY FOR UNIT 6.1

- Use **specific** rather than general words.
- Use **concrete** rather than abstract words.
- Use **precise** words to convey exact meanings.
- Be aware of synonyms.
- Use **appropriate** words that are familiar.
- Remember KISS—*Keep It Short and Simple.*
- Avoid using trite expressions or jargon in general writing.

Confirm Your Knowledge

Complete Exercise for Unit 6.1 on page 239.

❍ 6.2 The Seven Cs

In most writing, the author is trying to appeal to or influence the reader in some way. The writer may want to receive a specific response, to create a feeling of goodwill, or to soften a refusal. In all instances, the writer should consider how to appeal to the interests of the reader.

Generally, readers are interested in what will benefit them. Put yourself in the reader's shoes and think how you would feel if you were to receive your communication.

Your communication will probably succeed in its purpose if, when writing, you pay attention to the Seven Cs. The Seven Cs that will help you to accomplish your purpose are clarity, coherence, completeness, conciseness, correctness, courtesy, and consideration.

Clarity

Clarity is the result of clear thinking. In order to help you think clearly about your writing, remember the following guidelines:

1. Understand clearly the reason for your writing and the hoped-for result.
2. Make a plan so that your writing flows logically.
3. Understand your readers and think how they are likely to react.
4. Read your writing aloud to make sure it is clear.

Unclear: Rho told Mark his vacation plans had been approved. (Whose vacation plans?)

Clear: When Rho heard his vacation plans had been approved, he told Mark.

Or: Mark was delighted that his vacation plans had been approved and thanked Rho.

Coherence

Coherence is achieved when there is a logical connection in the order in which ideas or information is written and sentences flow smoothly from one to the next. To help you achieve coherent writing review Unit 5 and:

1. be sure all structures are parallel,
2. check for misplaced or dangling modifiers, and
3. use appropriate conjunctions.

Completeness

To be complete, a message must have all the information to be thoroughly understood so that the reader can respond in the way you want.

Incomplete: I'll be staying at the Fort Garry Hotel. Please meet me there on Wednesday about an hour before my plane leaves.

Complete: I'll be staying at the Fort Garry Hotel. Please meet me there in the foyer on Wednesday, June 11, at 3 p.m. This will give us about an hour before I have to catch my plane.

Mini-Test

Revise the following sentences to make them clear, coherent, and complete. Use your imagination to supply missing information.

1. Richard wrote to Franco telling him that he had been fired.

____

____

2. Please send flowers to Mr. and Mrs. Howard Johnston on their anniversary.

____

____

3. Mr. Rose's client read the account of the accident in the newspaper which made him very angry.

____

____

4. Take care in assembling the unit as the wiring must be correct and you should secure it by welding.

____

____

5. While washing your car should not be in hot sunshine.

____

____

KEY

Your answers may be quite different. As long as your sentences are perfectly clear, coherent, and complete and will present no misunderstanding to the reader, accept them as correct.

1. When he was fired, Richard wrote to Franco with the news.

Or: As Richard had to fire Franco, he wrote him a letter.

2. Please send one dozen long-stemmed roses to Mr. and Mrs. Howard Johnston, 110 Holcolm Avenue, Willowdale, Ontario, on their 25th wedding anniversary. Please include a suitable card signed "With much love, Sam and Sue."
3. When Mr. Rose's...newspaper, he was very angry.
4. ...correct and secured by welding.
5. While being washed, your car should not be in hot sunshine.

Conciseness

To be concise, a message must be written using appropriate words, all of which are necessary. The acronym KISS (see Unit 6.1) applies here.

Rambling: The firm has decided to help improve relations between the management and the union to allow shop stewards an hour between 12 noon and 1 p.m. on Fridays to meet with the personnel manager and other department heads over lunch, which the company will provide, in the small conference room.

Concise: To help improve relations, the company invites shop stewards to have lunch on Fridays with the personnel manager and other department heads. Sandwiches and coffee will be provided in the small conference room from noon till 1 p.m.

Correctness

To be correct, a message must be accurate in the information given and have no errors in usage, grammar, spelling, or punctuation.

Incorrect: The store will be closed from Christmas Day, December 24, until the New Year, January 2.

Correct: The store will closed for the holidays on December 24 at 5 p.m. and reopen on January 2 at 9 a.m.

Courtesy

To be courteous, the message must be sincere, honest, and considerate of the reader.

Impolite: If you really think we can wait any longer for your payment, you don't understand financing!

Better: You will appreciate that payment is needed immediately so that your credit rating can be maintained.

Insincere: You are the only person being offered this fine opportunity.

Sincere: This fine opportunity is being offered to only a few of our regular customers.

Or: We are offering you this special opportunity as you have been a valued customer for many years.

Consideration

Closely tied to courtesy is consideration which means thinking about the effect your writing will have on your reader. It means presenting your message with the reader's feelings and point of view in mind rather than your own, and being positive—that is, stressing what *can* be done instead of what *cannot* be done.

Inconsiderate: You told me in June that you would select me to represent your firm.

Considerate: When I spoke to you in June, I understood that I would be selected to represent your firm.

Negative: I cannot possibly review your report now.

Positive: Your report will be reviewed immediately on completion of my present project on May 31.

Mini-Test

Revise the following sentences to make them concise, correct, courteous, and considerate. Use your imagination.

1. The Nominating Committee has contacted six members who are both eligible and enthusiastic to serve on the Executive Committee.

   ____

   ____

   ____

2. The materials cost $75.80 and the labour will cost $132, making a total for the repair of $206.80.

   ____

   ____

3. If maintainance on equipment is needed urgently, kindly advise Mr. Stoker at extension 351.

   ____

   ____

4. You will be glad to know that at last the reservation you requested has been made and confirmed on Flight 342 to Calgary at 4:50 p.m. on October 23.

   ____

   ____

5. Your failure to add oil to the engine has caused the annoying noise that you have been hearing.

   ____

   ____

6. Report your decision by May 10.

____

____

KEY

Your answers may be quite different. As long as they are concise, correct, courteous, and considerate, accept them as correct.

1. ...has contacted six eligible, enthusiastic members to serve...
2. ...a total for the repair of $207.80.
3. ...maintainance...kindly advise Mr. Stoker...
4. Your reservation has been confirmed on Flight 342 to...
5. The noise in your engine can be eliminated with the use of a good lubricating oil.
6. Would you please let me have your decision by May 10.

SUMMARY FOR UNIT 6.2

- Keep in mind the *Seven Cs:* clarity, coherence, completeness, conciseness, correctness, courtesy, and consideration.
- In other words, your writing should be:

clear – easily understood
coherent – in logical order, one thing following the other
complete – no information missing
concise – short and to the point
correct – no errors of any kind
courteous – polite, sincere, friendly, with feeling for the reader
considerate – positive, aware and respectful of the reader's point of view

Confirm Your Knowledge

Complete Exercise for Unit 6.2 on page 240

DEVELOPING YOUR LANGUAGE SKILLS

❍ 6.3 Vocabulary

Definitions

Check your dictionary for the meanings of the following words; then match up the words with the definitions given. Write the letter of the definition you choose from Column 2 in the space provided in Column 1.

Column 1	Column 2
____ stipulate	a) to go before
____ remuneration	b) pay back for money spent
____ subsidize	c) person who receives something
____ reimburse	d) wages, pay for services
____ patronize	e) to collate papers
____ recipient	f) uppermost, superior
____ precede	g) visit or give business to regularly
____ prerogative	h) right, special privilege
____ presumption	i) help with gift of money
____ predominant	j) something taken for granted
	k) state specifically

Mini-Test

Complete the following sentences by choosing the most appropriate word from Column 1 under "Definitions."

1. The __________ of the award will be asked to make a short speech.
2. The government has agreed to __________ the dairy farmers in an effort to help them meet rising costs.

3. If you will ___________ our store, we can guarantee you excellent service.
4. May we exercise our ___________ to ask for more time?
5. The signing of the contract before the year end is ___________ in the negotiations at the moment.
6. A short prayer will ___________ the meal.
7. The insurance company will ___________ you for all expenses.
8. Because we did not submit our tender on time, the ___________ is that we shall not get the contract.
9. The conditions ___________ that the goods must be sealed in an airtight package.
10. The rate of ___________ for the new position has not been set yet.

KEY

1. recipient 2. subsidize 3. patronize 4. prerogative 5. predominant 6. precede 7. reimburse 8. presumption 9. stipulate 10. remuneration

Usage

Study the following words carefully so that you are fully aware of the differences and can use them correctly.

loan/lend

loan—used as a noun only	negotiate a loan at the bank
lend—used as a verb only	I want the bank to lend me $5000.

lose/loose

lose—misplace, be defeated	lose your keys; lose a race
loose—not firm, not tight	a loose board; loose clothing

passed/past

passed—past tense of past	We passed the new building today.
past—ended, beyond	Our troubles are past. past due account

personal/personnel

personal—individual, private	personal letter; a personal remark
personnel—referring to a group of persons, especially employees	the personnel manager New personnel should report to Mr. Bruce.

Hint: "Personnel" deals with more than one person; the word has more than one *n*.

perspective/prospective

perspective—view of the relationships of facts	Keep things in their right perspective.
prospective—probable in the future	a prospective customer

Mini-Test

Complete the following sentences by choosing the correct word from those shown at the beginning of the sentences.

1. *loan/lend*

   Can you ___________ me $100 as my ___________ from the bank has not come through yet?
2. *lose/loose*

   We may _________ the sale if our delivery schedule is too _________.
3. *passed/past*

   The final date for the payment for your _________ due account has now _________.

   In the _________, we have always _________ such matters over to the production manager.
4. *personal/personnel*

   Don't let ___________ problems interfere with your work.

   The ___________ manager is responsible for the hiring of all new ___________.
5. *perspective/prospective*

   As you look for a job, remember that ___________ employers are looking for good ___________ in the people they want to hire.

KEY

1. lend, loan 2. lose, loose 3. past, passed; past, passed
4. personal, personnel, personnel 5. prospective, perspective

Spelling

Most words ending in *–ble* end in *–able.* However, a few end in *–ible.* Study these words and memorize them; then any word not in this group probably ends in *–able.* Be sure you know the meanings of all these words.

–ible Words

permissible	divisible	eligible
convertible	possible	compatible
responsible	legible	accessible
sensible	feasible	susceptible
visible	flexible	admissible

Mini-Test

Because you know that all these words end in *–ible,* check them carefully for other errors. Correct any words that are misspelled.

1. divisible	admisible	legible
2. flexible	feesible	responsible
3. elligible	accessible	susceptible
4. sensible	permisible	possible
5. conpatible	visible	convertible

KEY

1. admisible 2. feesible 3. elligible 4. permisible 5. conpatible

---

SUMMARY FOR UNIT 6.3

- Always check a dictionary for the meaning of an unfamiliar word.
- **Personnel**—more than one person—has more than one *n*.
- Remember *–ible* words—the others probably end in *–able.*

Confirm Your Knowledge

Complete Exercise for Unit 6.3 on page 241

❍ 6.4 Proofreading

Remember the importance of the method and technique you use for proofreading. A pencil following the line and letters you are reading will help you to pay attention to the detail and content. Concentration is another key factor in helping you to proofread accurately.

New Paragraph ¶

To indicate that a new paragraph is required, use the ¶ mark. Remember that a paragraph should deal with one and only one idea and should be no longer than six or eight lines.

> Thank you for the invitation to attend the opening of your exhibition on Friday, June 27. Unfortunately, I have to be in Ottawa on that date and therefore cannot accept ¶ Congratulations on the well-deserved recognition you are now receiving. I wish you continued success in the future.

In the final copy, this example would appear as follows:

> Thank you for the invitation to attend the opening of your exhibition on Friday, June 27. Unfortunately, I have to be in Ottawa on that date and therefore cannot accept.
>
> Congratulations on the well-deserved recognition you are now receiving. I wish you continued success in the future.

Double-Spacedds and Single-Spacess

To show that material should be changed to double- or single-spacing, write ds or ss in the margin beside the lines to be changed.

> The advertising for the next three months has been approved, and the wording to accompany the photographs is attached to each photo. The following paragraph should appear at the top of the layout.
>
> > Bullodin invites you to test its products
> > ss and see for yourself at no cost their true-
> > worth to your company. Read on!
>
> ds Display this paragraph as you think best to give a good balance to the whole ad.

The final copy would appear as:

> The advertising for the next three months has been approved, and the wording to accompany the photographs is attached to each photo. The following paragraph should appear at the top of the layout.
>
> > Bullodin invites you to test its products and see for yourself at no cost their true worth to your company. Read on!
>
> Display this paragraph as you think best to give a good balance to the whole ad.

Mini-Test

Indicate by using the correct proofreaders' marks where new paragraphs should be started in the following letter. Also proofread the letter for all types of errors. Apart from marking paragraphing, there are twelve errors to be found!

> Referring to your let ter October 14 applying for a job as r cashier. Your résumé shows that in the passed you have had some part-time experience as a cashier and that you are continuing your education at night school. You express an interested in marketing as a career.
>
> Our company likes tohire people who have firm career goals. We also offer many training programs to help our employees reach thpse goals and we have found our training of marketing personel to be specially effective. We have no penings for cashiers at the moment, but you are elligible for a position now open as a sales clerk. Can you come for a interview at 10:30 a.m. on Monday, June 23, to discuss a possible career with us? Please call 223-5757 to confirm your appointment.

KEY

As you should by now be very proficient in proofreading, you have no doubt picked up all twelve errors. If not, reread very carefully till you find them. Remember to check punctuation as one error is a missing comma. Your paragraph suggestions may be slightly different depending on how you corrected the first sentence; however, a new paragraph is definitely required after "effective" and preferably after "clerk."

Summary for Unit 6.4

- Remember the importance of method and technique.
- A pencil will help you pay attention to detail and content.
- Concentration is a key factor in proofreading.
- More proofreaders' marks:

  ¶ New paragraph

  ds Double space ss Single space
- Always proofread for all kinds of errors.

Confirm Your Knowledge

Complete Exercise for Unit 6.4 on page 243

PRETEST FOR UNIT 6

Complete all the parts of this test according to the directions for each part. The figures in parentheses are the unit numbers for reference,if necessary, when you have completed the test.

Your Goal: To score a total of at least 36 points.

A. General Rules

Are the following statements true or false? If true, circle *T*; if false, circle *F*. Score 1 point for each correct answer.

			Score
1.	The language of written communication is the same as the language used everyday by well-spoken people.(6.1)	**T F**	______
2.	A general word such as *soon* gives the reader enough information. (6.1)	**T F**	______
3.	The rule "Keep It Short and Simple" is a good rule to follow in written communication. (6.1)	**T F**	______
4.	"Kindly advise us" is much better than "Please let us know." (6.1)	**T F**	______
5.	A letter should be written with consideration for the reader, not for the writer. (6.2)	**T F**	______
6.	Overused, trite expressions such as "Please find enclosed" are a sign of good writing. (6.1)	**T F**	______
7.	It is a good idea to state what can be done, not what can not be done. (6.2)	**T F**	______
8.	A writer should choose words carefully to give the exact meaning to the reader. (6.1)	**T F**	______
9.	There are only five "Cs" to consider in writing a business communication. (6.2)	**T F**	______
10.	It is not necessary to check whether dates and totals are correct. (6.2)	**T F**	______
		Score for Part A	______

B. Specific Terms, Concrete Material, Precise Words, and Appropriate Words (6.1)

Improve the following sentences using more specific, concrete, precise, and appropriate words. Score 1 point for each correct sentence.

		Score
1.	Please let me know as soon as possible whether or not you can come on July 7.	______
2.	If you use our paper towels, you can save money.	______
3.	He wrote a good account of the accident.	______
4.	Send us some leaflets and a few posters about the show.	______
5.	Enclosed please find our invoice in the amount of $270.	______
6.	Kindly let us have your reply by December 21.	______
7.	Please advise us when Ms. Baun is being transferred to the Brazil office.	______
8.	We cannot send your table at this point in time.	______
9.	In the event that the roads are closed because of bad weather we shall endeavour to reach you by phone.	______
	Score for Part B	______

C. The Seven Cs (6.2)

Improve the following sentences checking that they are clear, coherent, complete, correct, concise, courteous, and considerate. Score 1 point for each correct answer.

Score

1. The meeting will be held on Thursday in the Conference Room. Please be on time. _____
2. While reading your report, the telephone repeatedly interrupted me. _____
3. Send roses to Mrs. Plunkett on St. Valentine's Day, which is February 15. _____
4. Mr. Marchese wants to see Mr. Richards about his vacation schedules. _____
5. Your order won't be shipped for two weeks. _____
6. Please do not send payments in after ten days if you want a discount. _____

Score for Part C _____

D. Vocabulary (6.3)

Check the following sentences carefully for errors in word usage or spelling. Make any necessary corrections. If a sentence is correct as written, write *C* beside it. Score 1 point for each correct answer.

Score

1. Would you please loan us a copy of your operating manual. _____
2. Prospective employees should report to the Personnel Department for an application form. _____
3. Never loose sight of your career goals. _____
4. Olympic athletes always strive to beat their personal best scores. _____
5. Your suggestion has been past to the vice president for his consideration. _____

Score for Part D _____

E. Proofreading

Proofread the following letter very carefully for all kinds of errors. Score 1 point for each error found and marked correctly; deduct 1 point for each error missed!

Dear Dr. Abraham

"Memberhsip in an athletic club should be a top priority for office workers." This strong statement was made at a conference on preventive medicine recently held in Montreal by a well known doctor. His comment were supported by his colleagues on the panel, one of whom went so far as to say that it was the responsibility of each employer to make sure that employees did in fact exercise!

Perhaps you dont want to go so far as to insist that your employees exercise, but you are no doubt concerned about their absenteeism. Statistics have shown that the employee who exercises regularly and is interested in sports and atheletics is rarely absent from work. The reports go even further to say that the truly fit employee is a much more productive employee.

With all these facts before you would you seriously consider our "Exercise in the Office" program for your staff. Details are fully explained in the attached brochure, but here I would like to summarize them for you.

1. A trained athletic adviser will come to your office to see how an exercise program could be implemented.
   2. A general session for all employees would be arranged.
3. Two minutes a day would be set aside for exercises right at the work station.
4. Once a week a class for everyone interested would be aranged at a suitable location, either on your premises or in our gym.
5. Medical check-ups can also be arranged for those wishing to take a more rigorous program.

You will be amazed at hte feeling of well-being that our program produces in everyone. Stress is greatly relieved and absenteeism drops notably.

Ms. Anderson will call you next week to set a time for a appointment to discuss our program more thoroughly.

Yours truly

Number of errors found and correctly marked _____

Deduct for errors missed _____

Score for Part E _____

Total Score _____

If you achieved your goal of at least 36 points, proceed to Unit 7. If you did not score 36, check with your instructor what parts you need to study. Proceed through Unit 6 doing all the necessary work; then do the posttest for Unit 6.

POSTTEST FOR UNIT 6

Complete all the parts of this test according to the directions for each part. The figures in parentheses are the unit numbers for reference, if necessary, when you have completed the test.

Your Goal: To score a total of at least 36 points.

A. General Rules

Are the following statements true or false? If true, circle *T*; if false, circle *F*. Score 1 point for each correct answer.

			Score
1.	The language of written communication is quite different from everyday English. (6.1)	**T F**	_____
2.	The words *recently* and *some* do not give the reader exact information. (6.1)	**T F**	_____
3.	A good rule to follow in writing is "Keep It Short and Simple." (6.1)	**T F**	_____
4.	Technical terms should be used only in messages to people familiar with those terms. (6.1)	**T F**	_____
5.	The writer should always consider the reader's point of view. (6.2)	**T F**	_____
6.	Phrases such as "Enclosed herewith" should be used often to impress the reader. (6.1)	**T F**	_____
7.	It is a good idea to emphasize what cannot be done rather than what can be done. (6.2)	**T F**	_____
8.	To be sure that your message is clear, you should know exactly what action is required by you or the reader. (6.2)	**T F**	_____
9.	All correspondence should be thoroughly checked for accuracy in all details.(6.2)	**T F**	_____
10.	Exaggerated statements will impress your reader. (6.2)	**T F**	_____
		Score for Part A	_____

B. Specific Terms, Concrete Material, Precise Words, and Appropriate Words (6.1)

Improve the following sentences using more specific, concrete, precise, and appropriate words. Score 1 point for each correct sentence.

		Score
1.	May we have your reply at your earliest convenience so that programs can be prepared.	_____
2.	Please let us have a quantity of felt markers.	_____
3.	Our rope is not very expensive.	_____
4.	The company has given quite a lot to charity.	_____
5.	One of our evaluators will come to give you an estimate on the fire damage.	_____
6.	We lost the contract due to the fact that our bid was late.	_____
7.	Thank you for your payment in the amount of $135.	_____
8.	Kindly forward your reply by return mail.	_____
9.	In regard to your letter of June 12, we will be pleased to be of assistance.	_____
	Score for Part B	_____

C. The Seven Cs (6.2)

Improve the following sentences checking that they are clear, coherent, complete, correct, concise, courteous, and considerate. Score 1 point for each correct answer.

Score

1. The conference is scheduled for May. Do you think you will be attending? _____
2. When checking invoices, a red pen should be used. _____
3. Unfortunately, we don't have parts, and so your vacuum cannot be repaired until the end of the month. _____
4. The paint costs $17.50 and the brushes cost $7.50, a total of $24.50. _____
5. Vida spoke to Lynda about her suggestion for parking arrangements. _____
6. Telephone by noon Friday. _____

Score for Part C _____

D. Vocabulary (6.3)

Check the following sentences carefully for errors in word usage or spelling. Make any necessary corrections. If a sentence is correct as written, write *C* beside it. Score 1 point for each correct answer.

Score

1. We notice with surprise that your account is passed due. _____
2. The personel manager will interview all applicants for the job in computer accounting. _____
3. Banks will not loan money to bad risks. _____
4. The writing on the notice must be legible. _____
5. Why did we loose the right to submit an estimate? _____

Score for Part D _____

E. Proofreading

Proofread the following letter very carefully for all kinds of errors. Score 1 point for each error found and marked correctly; deduct 1 point for each error missed!

> Dear Miss Wang
>
> Thank you for your letter of Febuary 14 regarding the development scheduled for the corner of King and Wellington. Unfortunately, I am not in a position to answer all your questions, but I shall do certainly what I can to alleviate your concerns.
>
> First of all, let me state the future correspondence should be addressed to Mr. Hugh Baker, Chairperson, Planning and Zoning Committee, at City Hall. His Committee meets every Thursday, and the meeting on the first Thursday of every month is open to the public. You would be most welcome to attent such a meeting.
>
> Present plans for the development at King and Wellington include the construction of 20 2-bedroom townhouses and a six-storey apartment building containing 120 apartments. There are no stores or other commercial buildings planned for the developement at this time, although it is possible that at some future date the adjacent land might be used for that purpose.

It has not been decided yet whether the aprtment building will be an "adults only" building or whether families will be allowed. The apartments will be quite small, with one or two bedrooms, and the facilities offered will include a laundry room and underground parking. Plans for recreational facilities are still being discussed.

Your concern, Miss Wang, regarding the flow of traffic in the area is of great importance to use as well. Mr. Baker has detials of how he sees these problems being resolved, and I suggest you call him for further information. The involvement of the citizens in this development will be of great importance when the recreational facilities are being finalized. If you ask Mr. Baker at which meeting this will be discussed, you should try to attend so that you can take part in the planing.

The development at this point in time does not include the vacant land further west on King Street which is currently zoned for commercial use. Submissions are being requested from developers for their suggestions, and planning for that section will begin in six months. Again, Mr. Baker is the person who can give you the exact date.

I look forward to meeting you at some of the meetings for the development of this area

Yours truly

Number of errors found and correctly marked _____

Deduct for errors missed _____

Score for Part E _____

Total Score _____

If you achieved your goal of at least 36 points, proceed to Unit 7. If you did not score 36, check with your instructor before moving on.

EXERCISE 6.1 SPECIFIC TERMS, CONCRETE MATERIAL, PRECISE WORDS, APPROPRIATE WORDS

Make any necessary changes in the following sentences to make the wording specific, concrete, precise, and appropriate. Use your imagination to add any information required. Score 1 point for each acceptable answer.

Your Goal: To score at least 8 points.

Example: Can you attend the ^manager's^ meeting ~~next week?~~ *Friday at 2 p.m.?* 1

Score

1. She has completed a few courses and wants to continue to earn a degree. ____
2. Our rest home is near a major hospital and can be reached by rail. ____
3. I hope that these changes meet with your approval. ____
4. Your proposal under date of January 15 has been received. ____
5. You can complete this training session as quickly as you please and be prepared for the licensing exam sooner. ____
6. It is very nice of you to offer your help. ____
7. Our cruises visit many interesting places. ____
8. Enclosed please find a cheque in the amount of $24. ____
9. Kindly advise us where to send your free samples. ____
10. I have your request and in reply would like to say that we are happy to oblige you. ____

Total Score ____

If you achieved your goal of at least 8 points, proceed to Unit 6.2. If you did not score 8, go back and review Unit 6.1 thoroughly; then do Exercise 6.1A and try to achieve your goal this time.

EXERCISE 6.1A SPECIFIC TERMS, CONCRETE MATERIAL, PRECISE WORDS, APPROPRIATE WORDS

Use the same directions as for Exercise 6.1.

Your Goal: To score at least 8 points.

Score

1. We must have your reply as soon as possible. ____
2. Please send us some blouses for our fall sale. ____
3. If all the work is done by 4 p.m., the office will close early. ____
4. Attached hereto is the servers' schedule for July. ____
5. In the event that our quotation is too late, please return all our documents. ____
6. Allow me to repeat that we appreciate your help. ____
7. Our store is located not far from the bus terminal. ____
8. Please meet me on Thursday. ____
9. At your convenience, kindly complete the enclosed survey. ____
10. At this point in time, I want to say that we are happy to reopen your claim. ____

Total Score ____

If you achieved your goal of at least 8 points, proceed to Unit 6.2. If you did not score 8, ask your instructor for direction before moving on.

EXERCISE 6.2 THE SEVEN CS

Rewrite the following sentences in accordance with the Seven *C*s. Score 1 point for each sentence that is clear, coherent, complete, concise, correct, courteous, and considerate.

Your Goal: To score at least 5 points.

When Martin completed his job, he told Simon.

Example: ~~Martin told Simon that his job was complete.~~ 1

Score

1. Have your work finished by 4 p.m. every day. ______
2. As chair of the board of directors, I have many demands on my time and am unable to accept your kind invitation to visit your new facilities. ______
3. The photographs were late; we had to redesign the layout. ______
4. The amount you owe us should be sent soon. ______
5. Four factors to consider are price, availability, and quality. ______
6. Her associate is one who is highly respected as a lawyer. ______

Total Score ______

If you achieved your goal of at least 5 points, proceed to Unit 6.3. If you did not score 5, go back and review Unit 6.2 thoroughly; then do Exercise 6.2A and try to achieve your goal this time.

EXERCISE 6.2A THE SEVEN CS

Use the same directions as for Exercise 6.2.

Your Goal: To score at least 5 points.

Score

1. Using inferior roofing tiles to save costs as some builders do is not the case in any houses that we build. ______
2. In checking the plumbing, an unconnected pipe was discovered from the dishwasher waste pipe to the drainpipe. ______
3. Enclosed herewith is our cheque in the amount of $350. ______
4. Since you have failed to return the questionnaire we sent you, we cannot design a special costume for the parade. ______
5. If raw milk upsets your child, boil it. ______
6. We have already tested so many recipes that I very much doubt that your entry will even be considered. ______

Total Score ______

If you achieved your goal of at least 5 points, proceed to Unit 6.3. If you did not score 5, ask your instructor for direction before moving on.

Exercise 6.3 Vocabulary

Complete the three parts of this exercise according to the directions for each part.

Your Goal: To score at least 14 points.

A. Definitions

Complete the following sentences by choosing the most appropriate words from those given. Score 1 point for each correct answer.

stipulate	remuneration	subsidize	reimburse
patronize	precede	prerogative	predominant
recipient	presumption		

Score

1. If the government were to ___________ the transportation of oil, taxes would probably have to be raised. _____
2. The police department has the ___________ to enforce the laws even though those laws may be out of date. _____
3. You should ___________ on your application the hours you are available for work. _____
4. The ___________ for each step on the wage scale is set by the union. _____
5. We shall ___________ you for out-of-pocket expenses. _____

Score for Part A _____

B. Usage

Use the same directions as for Part A.

loan	loose	passed	personnel
lend	past	perspective	lose
personal	prospective		

Score

1. We have been asked to ___________ one of our bulldozers to Ramjit's Contracting Company. _____
2. The maintenance of the equipment is the responsibility of the custodial ___________. _____
3. We have ___________ your complaint to our service department for their attention. _____
4. Please visit Mr. Simpson immediately as he is a ___________ client and we would like to serve him. _____
5. We may ___________ sales if we cut back on advertising. _____
6. Over the _________ ten years, our kitchens have always ___________ all government inspections. _____
7. The ___________ wires behind the terminal are a fire hazard. _____

Score for Part B _____

C. Spelling

By using proofreaders' marks or otherwise, correct any spelling errors in the following words. Score 1 point for each correctly changed word; deduct 1 point for each word changed that was correct as written.

				Score
1.	accesible	responsible	possible	_____
2.	convertible	compatible	feesible	_____
3.	susceptible	vissible	sensible	_____
4.	divisible	elegible	admissible	_____
5.	flexible	permisible	legible	_____
			Score for Part C	_____
			Total Score	_____

If you achieved your goal of at least 14 points, proceed to Unit 6.4. If you did not score 14, go back and review Unit 6.3 thoroughly before moving on.

EXERCISE 6.4 PROOFREADING

Complete each part of this exercise according to the directions given.

Your Goal: To score at least 12 points in total.

Part A

Are the following statements true or false? If true, circle *T*; if false, circle *F*. Score 1 point for each correct answer.

		Score
1. Concentration is a key factor in accurate proofreading.	**T F**	_____
2. The symbol ¶ is used for a new paragraph.	**T F**	_____
3. The letters ds written in the margin mean that the material should be single spaced.	**T F**	_____
4. The method or technique you use is not important in helping you find errors.	**T F**	_____
5. It is not necessary to proofread for grammar or spelling errors in material you have written yourself.	**T F**	_____
	Score for Part A	_____

Part B

Proofread the following letter very carefully using proofreaders' marks to make corrections where necessary. Be sure to check for errors in paragraphing as well as other kinds of errors. There should be three new paragraphs. Score 1 point for each error found and marked correctly; deduct 1 point for each error missed!

Dear Mr. D'Alfonso

Thank you for your letter requesting information about microwave ovens and microwave cooking. You will see from the enclosed brochures that we handle quite an extensive line of microwave oven, any one of which might suit your requirements, however, in order to help you make a decision, we are outlining below the characteristics that you should consider when buying a microwave oven.

First of all, how many are there in your family? This will help you decide on the size of unit you need. Our brochures have beside each model the reccommended family size. It is not economical to buy to large an oven, nor is it practical to buy one that will not adequately meet your family's needs. Secondly, what kind of cooking do you intend using the oven for? Are you primarily interested in casserole cooking, baking, or roasting? Considering these points will help you decide whether or not you need a browning attachment. Thirdly, doyou require automatic timers that will start the oven when you are out and shut the oven off when the cooking is completed?

You will see from these questions and from the brochures that the choice of microwave oven is a very personal matter. For this reason, I suggest that you discuss your needs Ms. Petriw, who will be telephoning you to make an appointment The best plan would be for you to come to our showroom for a practical demonstration. We also arrange for our customers to have three free lessons in microwave cooking whenever they purchase a microwave from us. Ms. Petriw will be pleased to give you more details.

We look forward to serving you, Mr. D'Alfonso.

Yours truly

Number of errors found and correctly marked	_____
Deduct for errors missed	_____
Score for Part B	_____
Total Score	_____

If you achieved your goal of at least 12 points, proceed to the Posttest for Unit 6. If you did not score 12, you will appreciate the need for accurate proofreading! Review Unit 6.4 thoroughly before moving on.

LETTERS, MEMOS, AND REPORTS

A business communication is always written for a purpose. Once that purpose has been clearly defined, then the type of communication best suited to fulfill that purpose must be chosen. For example, if the purpose is to get a supply of stock for your store from a regular supplier, then you would either send in an order form or write an order letter. If the purpose is to ask someone's advice on how to clean rugs, then you would use a request letter. In general, however, all business letters have the same form.

INTRODUCTION

❍ 7.1 Parts, Handwritten Letters, Envelopes

Parts

Letters usually consist of eight principal parts:

1. letterhead 2. dateline 3. inside address 4. salutation 5. text or body of the letter 6. complimentary closing 7. signature 8. reference initials

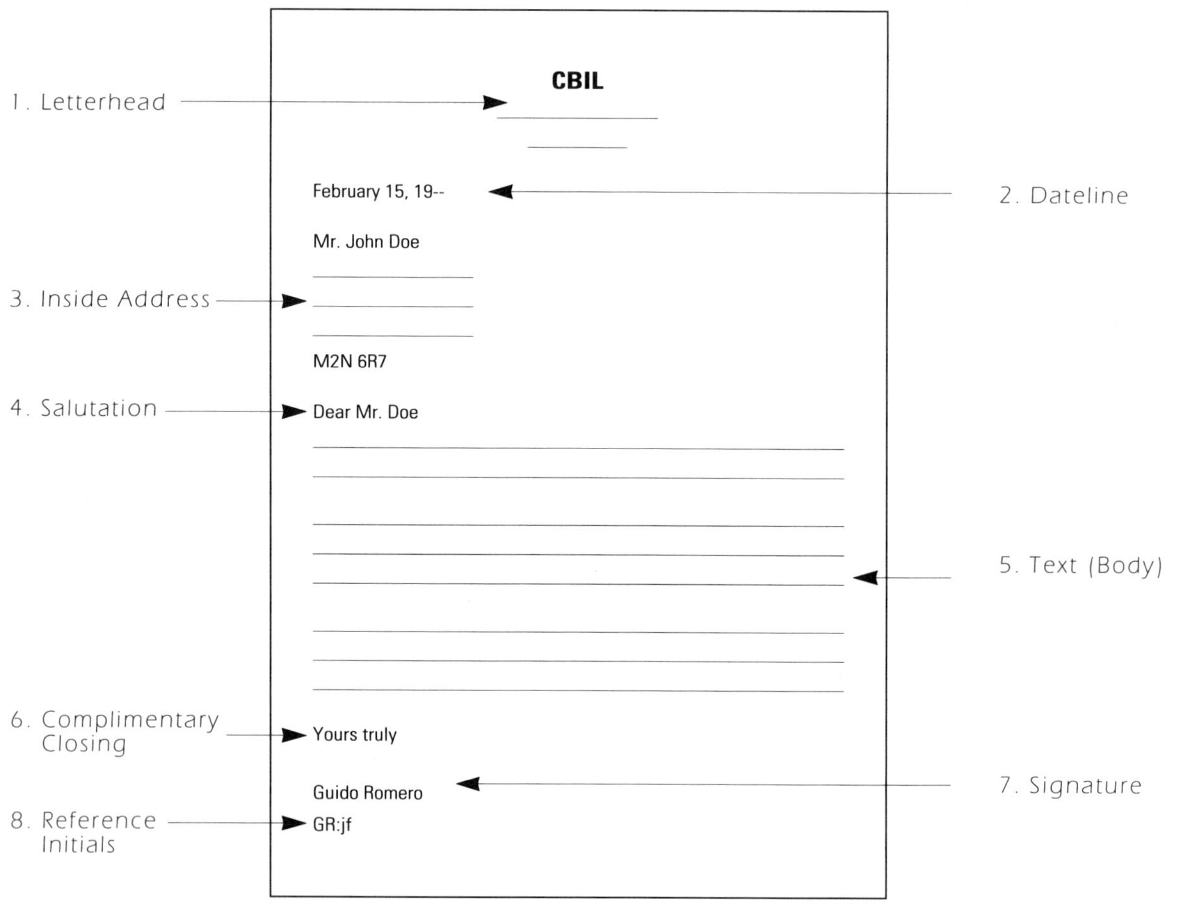

The appearance of a letter is very important, and certain guidelines have been established to help you. Consult a reference manual or keyboarding text, such as *Keyboarding for Canadian Colleges*, for specific details on how to place the different parts of a letter on a page.

Text or Body

The text or body of the letter is the part containing the information. If possible, the text should have two or three paragraphs. Letters are usually single-spaced with one blank line between paragraphs. If a letter is very short, however, it may be double-spaced. Remember in all double-spaced material paragraphs must be indented five or ten spaces.

Handwritten Letters

In business, a letter is seldom, if ever, handwritten. However, personal business letters sent from home are sometimes handwritten. Care must be taken to ensure that a handwritten letter is legible and that it is as pleasing in appearance and format as a keyboarded letter.

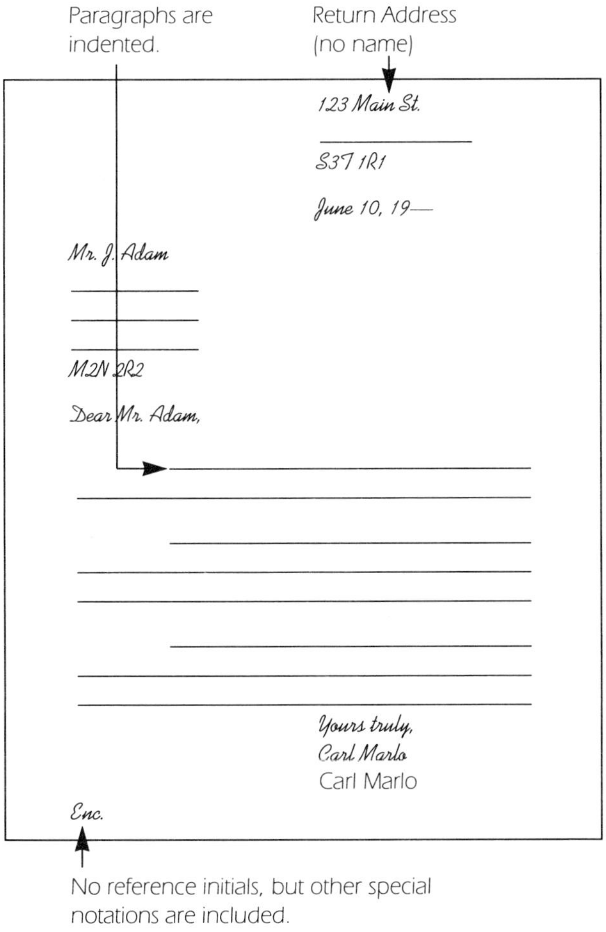

Paragraphs are indented.

Return Address (no name)

123 Main St.

S3T 1R1

June 10, 19—

Mr. J. Adam

M2N 2R2

Dear Mr. Adam,

Yours truly,
Carl Marlo
Carl Marlo

Enc.

No reference initials, but other special notations are included.

The parts of a handwritten letter are the same as those of a keyboarded letter with the following exceptions.

1. There is usually no letterhead and the return address must therefore be written in. Note that no name is included in the return address.
2. No reference initials are needed.
3. A printed signature should appear underneath the written signature.

Handwritten material is usually single-spaced and always indented for ease in identifying paragraphs.

Mini-Test

Are the following statements true or false? Circle *T* if true; circle *F* if false.

1. If keyboarded material is double-spaced, the paragraphs must be indented. F F
2. The text of a letter should have at least two, preferably three paragraphs. T F
3. It is not important where the different parts of a letter are placed. T F
4. Handwritten material must always have indented paragraphs. T F
5. Business letters are usually handwritten. T F

KEY

1. T 2. T 3. F 4. T 5. F

Envelopes

The various parts of an envelope are shown according to current postal regulations.

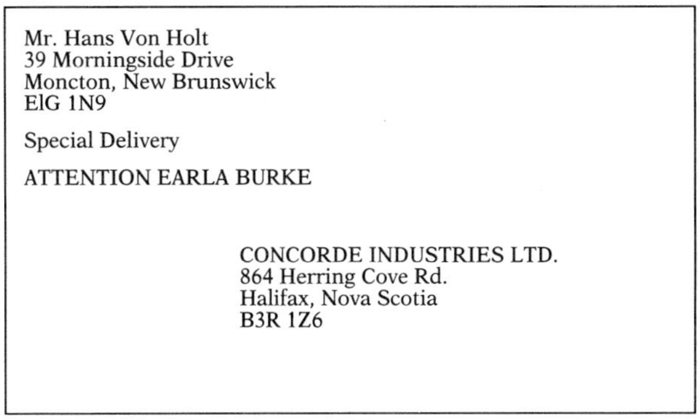

Mr. Hans Von Holt
39 Morningside Drive
Moncton, New Brunswick
ElG 1N9

Special Delivery

ATTENTION EARLA BURKE

CONCORDE INDUSTRIES LTD.
864 Herring Cove Rd.
Halifax, Nova Scotia
B3R 1Z6

Note the following points:

1 The return address information must be shown in the upper left-hand corner.
2. A special mailing notation, such as SPECIAL DELIVERY, is shown in solid capitals at the left-hand side under the return address.
3. An attention line or a personal and confidential notation is also shown at the left-hand side under the return address.
4. Addresses are always single-spaced with the city and province on the same line. The postal code must be included in all addresses and is the last line of the address. Begin writing the address halfway down the envelope and slightly to the left of centre.
5. For American addresses, the city, state, and ZIP Code are all on the same line.
   World Science Corporation
   1090 Shary Circle, Suite 200
   Concord, CA 94518
   U.S.A.

Mini-Test

Are the following statements true or false? Circle *T* if true; circle *F* if false.

1. A return address should always be shown on an envelope. F F
2. A keyboarded address on an evelope should be double-spaced. F F
3. The postal code appears by itself as the last line in an address. F F
4. The American ZIP Code is written on the same line as the city and state. F F
5. Personal and confidential notations are not shown on an envelope. F F

KEY

1.T 2. F 3. T 4. T 5. F

SUMMARY FOR UNIT 7.1

- A letter has eight parts:
  1. the letterhead, containing the company name and address
  2. the dateline
  3. the inside address
  4. the salutation
  5. the text or body containing the message
  6. the complimentary closing
  7. the signature, handwritten and keyboarded or printed
  8. reference initials
- Refer to a reference manual or keyboarding text for details of placement and usage of the different parts of a letter.
- Envelopes must be prepared according to postal regulations.
  - The **postal code** is the last line of the address.
- Handwritten letters and envelopes follow the same rules as keyboarded letters and must be clearly legible.
- Paragraphs in double-spaced or handwritten material must be indented.

Confirm Your Knowledge

There is no exercise for this unit as it is for reference only. Move on to Unit 7.2 whenever you are ready.

7.2 Plans and Paragraphs

Good writing is the result of good planning. Before you write anything, you must have a clear understanding of the goal of your message and plan how you are going to achieve that goal. You must determine exactly what you want to say and how you are going to say it. Preparing plans and understanding the function of paragraphs will help you to produce a successful written communication.

Plans

In Unit 6, the language of communication was discussed. Once you know who will be receiving your letter, then you know the most appropriate type of language to use (whether technical or general).

Before you write anything, though, collect all the materials you require to give you the information you will need for your letter (for example, the incoming letter, the correspondence file, price lists, catalogues, appointment calendar).

Step 1

Write down the purpose of the letter in as few words as possible.

To make hotel reservations in Regina—Oct. 22-24
Ack. order—shipment being made today
Refuse request for free samples—can send if willing to pay

Step 2

Write down in rough point form what you have to say. Don't try to write sentences or worry about how you are going to word your letter at this time. For example, in replying to a letter asking for free samples, your draft plan might look like this.

Purpose: Refuse request for free samples—can send if willing to pay.

Plan: Ack. letter
Charge for samples—handling, etc.
Samples good and effective in increasing sales
Can send immediately
Explained on p. 2 of catalogue copy enclosed
Still want them? How many?

Step 3

Rearrange your plan to produce the most logical, effective message. To help you decide on the best arrangement, keep in mind the acronym *AIDA* which stands for:

A – Get the reader's *attention*

I – Get the reader's *interest* or provide some *information.*

D – Develop a *desire* in the reader or give more *details.*

A – State *action* required either by the reader or writer.

Rewrite your plan clearly in order, putting beside the points *A*, *I*, *D*, or *A* so that you can see how you have identified the parts of your letter.

Purpose: Refuse request for free samples—can send if willing to pay.

Plan: A–Ack. letter
I–Samples good & effective in increasing sales
D–Can send immediately
D–Refer to p. 2 of catalogue (copy enclosed)—charge for handling—$2.50 for each set of five samples
A–Let us know how many sets of samples you would like.

Importance of Plans

Plans in point form are very valuable aids in composing all kinds of writing. They provide a visual reference for you to check that you have included everything. Moreover, they allow you to change your mind and add or delete items before you start to write. Plans are also valuable at times when you might be interrupted and have to come back to your writing at a later time; your previous thoughts are right there to enable you to go ahead from where you were interrupted.

Even very experienced writers will make notes before they write anything. The plan is the framework on which successful writing is built.

Mini-Test

Make a plan in point form for each of the following letters. Remember to state the purpose of the letter first; then rearrange the points you listed into the most effective sequence writing *AIDA* beside them as appropriate.

1. Arrange a meeting with a real estate agent to discuss moving your offices to larger premises. Provide enough details to enable your reader to come to the meeting.

Purpose

Plan

2. Reply to a letter you received inviting you to attend a conference on June 13 in Halifax. You will be in Winnipeg on that date, but you wish them every success. You would like to receive copies of any materials handed out at the conference Add any other information you feel is necessary.

Purpose

Plan

KEY

Your answers may be quite different from the following. However, if you have stated a purpose, listed information in point form, made changes, and rearranged the points according to ***AIDA***, your plans will be acceptable.

1. Purpose: To meet with real estate agent about moving offices
   - A —Want to move to large premises
   - I —Meet Thurs., April 6, your office, 10 a.m.?
   - D—Interested in new building corner of King and Mackenzie
   - A —Must know if meeting OK by April 1
2. Purpose: To refuse invitation to attend conference in Halifax
   - A —Thanks for invitation—Halifax, June 13
   - I —In Winnipeg then
   - D—Would like copies of materials handed out
   - A —Wish you success. Would like to attend next year's conference.

Note: Be sure to keep your plans as you will need them for the mini-tests in Unit 7.3.

Paragraphs

Paragraphs group together points relating to the same idea. By using *AIDA* in your plan, you have already identified those items that go together and those that stand alone.

Good paragraphing helps the reader to understand the message quickly and accurately as relevant details are grouped together. The following points will help you decide where to paragraph.

1. Be sure each paragraph deals with one and only one idea.
2. Include enough details to make that idea clear and effective.

3. Arrange your paragraphs in logical order so that the message flows easily from one idea to the next.
4. Keep your paragraphs short for easy reading, usually six or seven lines. Avoid a series of two- or three-line paragraphs as this style looks choppy and unco-ordinated.

A careful plan or outline before you begin writing will help you arrange your paragraphs effectively.

Paragraphs in Business Letters

Generally, a business letter will have three or more paragraphs: an opening paragraph, one or more paragraphs giving information and details, and a closing paragraph.

Opening Paragraphs

The opening paragraph is very important. It should be short to introduce the subject and tell why the letter is being written. The purpose of the opening paragraph is to attract attention and make the reader want to read on to find out more about the subject.

The following opening paragraphs illustrate the advantage of concise, direct writing.

> You can save money by shopping at Suburbia's Super Mall.
>
> Did you know that our service department is open 24 hours a day?
>
> Please send us the following supplies.
>
> Your advertisement in today's *Sun* for...
>
> Mr. Santilli of Wasche & Wype recommended...

The most direct opening is "Thank you for..." and can be used in many letters. Remember, though, that you do not thank "in advance"; you thank only for what you have actually received.

Middle Paragraphs

Middle paragraphs, the meat of the letter, give the information and details that develop interest and desire. Each paragraph should contain only one main idea and be no more than six or seven lines long. Depending on the subject of the letter, there may be two or three or even more middle paragraphs.

> Your Rotary X-126 blender has been carefully checked and is now in perfect working order. A loose small bearing had caused the motor to seize. You will have no further trouble now.
>
> The enclosed personal data sheet outlines in detail my qualifications. In particular, you will see that I gained top honours in accounting and plan to continue my studies in that area at night school.
>
> The gala festival of plays will have dramas by well-known Canadian playwrights as well as a few of the standard classics that are always so well loved. Full details will be announced shortly when you will receive notice on how and where to get your tickets.

Closing Paragraphs

The closing paragraph is possibly more important than the opening paragraph as its purpose is to convince the reader to take particular action or to inform the reader what action is being taken and what the next step is.

The following closing paragraphs illustrate different kinds of action.

> Call Acme Fuel Company today. Our number is 663-0712.
>
> Mail your order today for quick delivery.
>
> Drop in to see us the next time you are in...
>
> Please sign the enclosed documents and return them immediately.
>
> We shall start work on the new design as soon as we have approval from the Ministry.
>
> You will hear from us as soon as we hear from Mr. Snowdon.

If you are initiating the correspondence, a good closing paragraph is often a question. The reader can then reply very easily.

> May I have an appointment on...?
>
> May we have your answer by July 1?
>
> When can you deliver the layouts for approval?

Mini-Test

Are the following statements true or false? Circle *T* if true; circle *F* if false.

1. An opening paragraph should be short and tell why the letter is being written. T F
2. It does not matter how many ideas are contained in one paragraph. T F
3. A business letter usually has only one paragraph. T F
4. The closing paragraph states what action is required or being taken. T F
5. A question is often a good closing paragraph. T F

KEY

1. T 2. F 3. F 4. T 5. T

SUMMARY FOR UNIT 7.2

- Planning is very important in writing.
- There are three steps in making a plan:
  1. Identify the purpose of the writing.
  2. Write down the points to be included.
  3. Check and rearrange the plan.
- Remember *AIDA*.
  - *A* Attention (in opening paragraph)
  - *I* Information or Interest
  - *D* Details or Desire
  - *A* Action—by reader or writer (in closing paragraph)
- Paragraphs
  - contain only one idea.
  - are arranged in logical order.
  - should be short, not more than six or seven lines.
  - usually number three or more in a business letter.
  - that open or close a business letter are very important.
- Many letters can open with "Thank you for..."
- A question makes a good closing paragraph.

Confirm Your Knowledge

Complete Exercise for Unit 7.2 on page 298.

7.3 Writing the Letter

All business communications have the same purpose—to get the reader to react in the way you want. How you get that reaction depends a great deal upon the tone of the letter, as discussed in Unit 6, but it also depends on the organization of the letter. This unit will help you produce a well-organized letter that will get the result you want.

In Unit 7.2, you learned about letter plans. The three steps in preparing a plan are:

1. Write down the purpose of the letter.
2. Write down all the points you need to include.
3. Check and rearrange with *AIDA* in mind.

Once you have prepared your plan, draft and revise your final letter using the following routine:

1. Prepare a rough draft. Write as though you were speaking to your reader.
2. Revise your draft letter. Check:

_____	paragraphing	_____	seven Cs
_____	that all points are included	_____	point of view
		_____	*AIDA*

3. Rewrite the letter on letterhead.
4. Proofread for errors in grammar, spelling, punctuation, and format.

From the sample plan used in Unit 7.2, proceed as follows to prepare the final letter.

Rough Draft

Dear Mr. Heldt,

Thank you for your letter of June 6 asking for free samples.

Our samples are very complete and agents have found them most useful in increasing sales. We can send some to you immediately.

However, if you refer to page 2 of our summer catalogue, a copy of which is enclosed, you will see that there is a charge of $2.50 for each set of five samples. This is to offset handling and special packaging costs. The value of the samples far outweighs this small charge.

Please let us know how many sets of samples you would like, and we shall send them out to you the day we receive your letter.

Revised Draft

Dear Mr. Heldt,

Thank you for your letter of June 6 asking for free samples.

Our samples ~~are very complete and~~ Agents have found ~~them~~ most useful in increasing sales. We can send some to you immediately.

However, on ~~if you refer to~~ page 2 of our summer catalogue, a copy of which is enclosed, you will see that there is a charge of $2.50 for each set of five samples. which ~~This~~ is to offset handling and special packaging costs. The value of the samples far outweighs this small charge.

If you ~~Please~~ let us know how many sets of samples you would like, ~~and~~ we shall send them out to you the day we receive your instructions ~~letter~~.

The end result of the letter to Mr. Heldt, keyed, proofread, and ready for mailing would look like this:

CANADIAN BUSINESS INDUSTRIES LIMITED
Serving business in every field — manufacturers, distributors, wholesalers, retailers, and consultants

REGIONAL OFFICES
1107–210 Willett St.
Halifax, NS
B3M 3C6

4230 West Hill Ave.
Montreal, PQ
H4B 2S7

517 Wellington St. W.
Toronto, ON
M5V 1G1

610A 70th Ave. S.E.
Calgary, AB
T2H 2J6

Main Post Office
Box 2010
Vancouver, BC
V6B 3P8

Halifax
June 10, 19--

Mr. Karl Heldt
200 Lincoln Road
Grand Falls, NF
A2A 1P8

Thank you for your letter of June 6 asking for free samples.

Agents have found our samples most useful in increasing sales. We can send some to you immediately.

However, on page 2 of our summer catalogue, a copy of which is enclosed, you will see that there is a charge of $2.50 for each set of five samples. The value of the samples far outweighs this small charge, which is to offset handling and special packaging costs.

If you let us know how many sets of samples you would like, we shall send them out to you the day we receive your instructions.

Yours truly,
James Stevens
James Stevens

JS:KV
Encl.

Mini-Test

Prepare draft letters only from the two plans prepared in the mini-test in Unit 7.2. Make any changes you feel are necessary, but do not try to produce final letters. Both letters should have at least three paragraphs. Keep your revised draft letters.

KEY

If you have followed your plans and checked your drafts according to the five items in step 2 of the routine, accept your rough drafts. The final letter you produce later will be carefully evaluated.

Addresses for Practice Letters

In order to provide you with realistic practice, your letters should be written on letterhead. For the purposes of the exercises in this unit, assume you are working for Canadian Business Industries Limited, known as CBIL. This is a large organization with regional offices in Halifax, Montreal, Toronto, Calgary, and Vancouver and branch offices and agents across Canada. Letterhead showing the company's addresses in Halifax, Montreal, Toronto, and Vancouver is used by everyone in the company. (Photocopy the sample on page 253 to give you a supply.)

If you are writing from one of the regional offices, you do not need to use a return address as it is already printed on the letterhead. You only need to show the name of the city.

Toronto May 10, 19--	Vancouver November 3, 19--

If however, you are writing from a branch office or if you are an agent working out of your home, use the address of your school or your home as the return address.

3700 Willingdon Avenue Burnaby, BC V5G 3H2 September 17, 19--	485 Rustbank Court Bathurst,NB E2A 2K4 January 22, 19--

Mini-Test

Are the following statements true or false? If they are true, circle *T*; if not, circle *F*.

1. The first step in preparing the final letter from a plan is to write a draft letter.
2. Step 2 includes checking for point of view and the "Seven Cs" as well as for paragraphing.
3. Use of letterhead provides realistic practice.
4. For the exercises in this book, assume you are working for Canadian Business Industries Limited.
5. If you are working on your own, use your home address as the return address.

KEY

All the statements are true.

SUMMARY FOR UNIT 7.3

- The purpose of all business letters is to get the reader to react in the way you want.
- The final letter is:
  - written in **draft first** from a plan
  - **revised** for paragraphing, the Seven Cs, point of view, and *AIDA*
  - **rewritten** on letterhead
  - **proofread** carefully
- Write as you would speak.
- Use Canadian Business Industries Limited letterhead.
  - Use regional office address, your school address, or your home address for the return address.

Confirm Your Knowledge

Before you complete Exercise for Unit 7.3 on page 300, study the following evaluation chart shown here.

Evaluation Chart	Your Score	Checker's Score
Well-prepared plan		
Good opening paragraph		
Considerate		
Clear in meaning		
Complete in detail		
Ideas expressed concisely		
Positive, not negative		
Attractively set up		
No trite expressions		
Good closing paragraph		
Total		
Deduction for errors missed or for untidy final letter		
Final Total		

The exercise for Unit 7.3 asks you to prepare final letters from the plans made in Part B of the previous exercise. If no plans are available, make some.

Check your final letters carefully according to the evaluation chart and *always* have your work checked by someone else after you have scored yourself.

Marking Guidelines

One point is *earned* for the correct application of each item in the evaluation chart; *two* points are *deducted* for each error in grammar, punctuation, and spelling, and for badly corrected errors and generally untidy letters! Total your own evaluation of your letter; then have it evaluated by someone else. It is very difficult to check your own work objectively, and your checker will much more easily evaluate your letter through the eyes of the person receiving the letter.

This is the marking guideline that will be used for evaluating all letters you will write. Your goal is to score at least 9 points; you will probably score many 10s because if you check your work carefully against this chart, there is no need for you to lose any points.

CANADIAN BUSINESS INDUSTRIES LIMITED

Serving business in every field – manufacturers, distributors, wholesalers, retailers, and consultants

REGIONAL OFFICES

1107–210 Willett St.
Halifax, NS
B3M 3C6

4230 West Hill Ave.
Montreal, PQ
H4B 2S7

517 Wellington St. W.
Toronto, ON
M5V 1G1

610A 70th Ave. S.E.
Calgary, AB
T2H 2J6

Main Post Office
Box 2010
Vancouver, BC
V6B 3P8

TYPES OF LETTERS

❍ 7.4 Request Letters

Letters Making Requests

Letters of request may be simple or complex depending on the nature of the request. Whichever kind is needed requires careful planning and tactful presentation.

Whatever the request may be, try to find at least one point that will make your reader want to grant your request. You may be a potential customer or you may be able to do a favour for your reader in some way. If the reader feels that he or she will benefit from granting the request, you are very likely to receive a favourable answer.

Preparation

1. Collect all the materials you need.
2. Clearly define the purpose of your letter.
3. Prepare a plan. (See Unit 7.2.)
4. Prepare a rough draft. (See Unit 7.3.)
5. Check the draft against the evaluation chart.
6. Write the final letter from your rough draft and re-evaluate it carefully.

Recommended Writing Suggestions

- Know precisely what you are requesting.
- Make your request a reasonable one. Don't write "Please tell me all you know about the catering business." Instead, ask specific questions.
- Include all necessary information. If you want an itinerary planned, give the proposed dates of your trip, means of transportation, length of time available, places you want to visit, and type of accommodation.
- Explain why you want an answer.
- Ask for answers; don't demand them.
- Assure your reader information will be kept confidential.
- Include a stamped envelope with the return address.
- Say when you need the information; be reasonable.

Sample Letter Making a Request

You have been asked to write to various companies asking for copies of their letters to be included in a new training manual, *Successful Letter-Writing.* This manual will be used to help transcribers become proficient at producing realistic letters. You also need permission to use their letters. Study the following steps in composing the letter.

1. *Plan*

Purpose: To get sample letters for manual
To get permission to use them

A 1. Preparing new manual
2. Need for up-to-date materials
I 3. Want a variety of actual letters
D 4. To be used in variety of ways
– different speeds
– pauses & speed-ups
– changes, corrections, additions, deletions
5. To be transcribed exactly as actual letters from business
A 6. Want 12 letters
7. Need written permission

2. *Rough Draft*

We are preparing a new manual, Successful Letter-Writing so that the letters used for training office employees are up to date.

We should like to include a variety of actual letters that have been used by well-known business organizations, and your cooperation in this matter will be greatly appreciated.

Teachers will use these letters in many different ways — at uneven rates of dictation, with frequent stops and starts, with additions, deletions, corrections, and interruptions. The letters that are finally transcribed will be exactly the same as those submitted by the firms whose help we are seeking.

Will you please send us 12 letters by members of your company? We also must have your written permission to use them in a manual.

3. *Revised Draft*

We are preparing a new manual, Successful Letter-Writing, ~~so that the~~ letters are used for training office employees, to be sure that up-to-date ~~are up to date.~~

We ~~should like~~ want to include a variety of actual letters that have been used by well-known business*es* organizations, and your cooperation ~~in this matter~~ will be greatly appreciated.

~~Teachers~~ Instructors will use these letters in many ~~different~~ ways — at uneven rates of dictation; with frequent ~~stops~~ pauses and ~~starts~~ speed-ups; with additions, deletions, corrections, and interruptions. The letters ~~that are~~ finally transcribed will be exactly the same as those submitted by the firms whose help we are seeking.

Will you please send us ~~12~~ twelve letters by members of your ~~company~~ firm? We also ~~must have~~ need your written permission to use them in a manual.

4. *Final Letter*

CANADIAN BUSINESS INDUSTRIES LIMITED

Serving business in every field – manufacturers, distributors, wholesalers, retailers, and consultants

REGIONAL OFFICES

1107–210 Willett St.
Halifax, NS
B3M 3C6

4230 West Hill Ave.
Montreal, PQ
H4B 2S7

517 Wellington St. W.
Toronto, ON
M5V 1G1

610A 70th Ave. S.E.
Calgary, AB
T2H 2J6

Main Post Office
Box 2010
Vancouver, BC
V6B 3P8

Toronto,Ontario
September 2, 19--

Mr. Simon Peters
Educational Director
Canadian Brass Company
201 Metcalfe Street
Ottawa, Ontario
K2P 1P6

Dear Mr. Peters:

To be sure that up-to-date letters are used for training office employees, we are preparing a new manual, Successful Letter-Writing.

We want to include a variety of actual letters that have been used by well-known businesses, and your co-operation would be greatly appreciated.

Instructors will use these letters in many ways – at uneven rates of dictation; with frequent pauses and speed-ups; with additions, corrections, deletions, and interruptions. The letters finally transcribed will be exactly the same as those submitted by the firms whose help we are seeking.

Will you please send us twelve letters written by members of your firm? We also need your written permission to use them in our manual.

Sincerely yours,

Richard Samuels

Richard Samuels
Vice President — Training

mga

Evaluation Chart	Your Score	Checker's Score
Well-prepared plan		
Good opening paragraph		
Considerate		
Clear in meaning		
Complete in detail		
Ideas expressed concisely		
Positive, not negative		
Attractively set up		
No trite expressions		
Good closing paragraph		
Total		
Deductions for errors missed or for untidy final letter		
Final Total		

Mini-Test

Prepare a plan, a rough draft, and the final letter for the following situation. Remember *AIDA* and check your final letter against the evaluation chart. Be sure to have the *purpose* of the letter clearly stated in your plan.

As program convenor of the social committee of your office or organization, write a letter to a local lawyer whom you would like to have speak to your group. Your budget does not allow for payment to speakers, but you would be glad to provide transportation and other expenses. Tell the reader the subject you have in mind; the size and type of audience; the time, place, and occasion and the amount of time available. Use your imagination to provide details.

Purpose

___

Plan

___

Evaluation Chart	Your Score	Checker's Score
Well-prepared plan		
Good opening paragraph		
Considerate		
Clear in meaning		
Complete in detail		
Ideas expressed concisely		
Positive, not negative		
Attractively set up		
No trite expressions		
Good closing paragraph		
Total		
Deduction for errors missed or for untidy final letter		

KEY

Your work may be quite different, but as long as you have carefully evaluated your final letter and scored ten points on someone else's evaluation, accept your letter as correct.

Purpose: To invite Mr. Donald McCarthy, of Blake, McCarthy, and Russell, to speak at Sept. mtg. of social club.

Plan:

A 1. Would like you as speaker at Sept. meeting

I 2. Well-known & respected for your work on reform of family law and children's rights

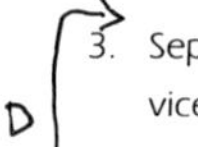

3. Sept. 20 – Thurs – 7:30 p.m., 1 hour + 30 min. questions, or vice-versa – coffee and cake

4. No fee, expenses paid

5. Speak on progress in establishing children's rights

A 6. Let us know by Sept. 6 – programs & notices

Final Letter

Dear Mr. McCarthy:

Our Social Club would very much like to have you as guest speaker at our September meeting. Your reputation for the excellent work you have done to speed the reform of family law and to protect children's rights makes us very eager to hear your comments on the progress being made in these areas.

The meeting is scheduled for 7:30 p.m. on September 20 in the Canadiana Room of the Royal Hotel. May we suggest you talk for about one hour and have a 30-minute question period, or vice versa if you prefer. Light refreshments of coffee and cakes will be served at 9 p.m.

Our club will be pleased to pay any expenses you incur, but our budget does not have funds to pay you a fee. We shall be happy to arrange transportation and accommodation.

So that programs and notices can be prepared to enable our members to plan to attend, will you please let us know your decision by September 6.

Yours very truly,

Letters Granting Requests

When you grant a request, you have a wonderful opportunity to build goodwill for your company. Many companies have form letters to acknowledge routine requests for brochures, catalogues, etc.; however, for special requests, a carefully written reply will create a more personal feeling of goodwill.

Procedure

1. Collect all the materials.
2. Clearly define the purpose.
3. Prepare a plan.
4. Prepare a draft.
5. Revise draft.
6. Produce the final letter on letterhead.
7. Proofread and evaluate.

Note: This is the procedure to be followed for all letters. From now on it will be assumed you know the steps as they will not be repeated again.

Recommended Writing Suggestions

- Express a genuine interest in the request.
- Tell your reader *immediately* that you are able to grant it.
- Reply in a clear and easily understandable form.
- Answer questions in the same order.
- Include additional information that may be helpful.
- Supply any supplementary material that might be useful.
- Express an interest in your correspondent's project. Wish him or her success and suggest that you would like to hear more about the project.
- Be sincere in your closing paragraph.
- Answer all letters promptly. Should there be any delay, apologize and briefly explain the reason for it.

Sample Letter Granting a Request

The following letter is a reply to the letter written by Mr. Samuels on page 255 sending a copy of the manual published by his company and letters the company uses for training programs.

CANADIAN BRASS COMPANY
201 Metcalfe Street, Ottawa, Ontario K2P 1P6

September 9, 19--

Robert Samuels
Vice-President – Training
Canadian Business Industries Ltd.
517 Wellington Street West
Toronto, Ontario
M5V 1G1

Dear Mr. Samuels:

I was greatly interested in your letter of September 2 in which you tell of your plans for your new manual, Successful Letter-Writing.

A manual that we recently published to assist our own staff in the correct manner of writing CANADIAN BRASS COMPANY letters is enclosed.

On pages 34 through 43 are sample letters typical of those written in our office. I have also included copies of other letters that have been used in our own training seminars.

You have my permission to publish these letters.

If I can help in any other way, I would like to do so. All you have to do, Mr. Samuels, is to let me know.

When your manual has been printed, may I have a copy?

Very truly yours,

Simon Peters

Simon Peters
Educational Director

JC:pt
enc.

Mini-Test

Prepare a plan, a rough draft, and a final letter for the following situation. Remember *AIDA* and check your final letter against the evaluation chart. Have someone else check your work as usual.

You have received a request from Natasha Cominenci, a student at a college near you, for a copy of your company's style manual for correspondence for her to use in a business course she is currently taking. You are glad to help her as your manual gives details of company style and explains company policies for various kinds of letters. Include in your reply any points about good letter writing that you feel are really important. Because these manuals are quite expensive to produce, tell Ms. Cominenci that you are unable to send her any more copies and that she should share hers with her classmates if they are interested.

Purpose

Plan

Evaluation Chart	Your Score	Checker's Score
Well-prepared plan		
Good opening paragraph		
Considerate		
Clear in meaning		
Complete in detail		
Ideas expressed concisely		
Positive, not negative		
Attractively set-up		
No trite expressions		
Good closing paragraph		
Total		
Deduction for errors missed or for untidy final letter		
Final Total		

KEY

The following letter is one way in which this letter could be written. Check your letter carefully, and if you score 10 points on someone else's evaluation, accept your letter.

Dear Ms. Cominenci

I am delighted to send you a copy of our Correspondence Manual. You will find in it an outline of the style used by our company and our policies about various kinds of correspondence.

Letters are the voice of the company. Sincerity and a courteous, clearly expressed interest in the reader give your reader a very positive feeling.

At the moment, Ms.Cominenci, our supply is rather low. If others in your class are interested in one, would you please share your copy with them.

I wish you success in your course, and if we can be of any further assistance to you, please let us know.

Yours very truly,

Note: Future mini-tests for letters will not have keys. If you follow the procedure regularly and have your letter evaluated by someone else, you will become quite competent. However, if you have difficulty at all, ask your instructor for help before going on to another unit.

Letters Denying Requests

Letters denying requests are a little more difficult to write because, although you cannot grant the request, you do want to keep the goodwill of the reader.

Recommended Writing Suggestions

- Open with a warm and sincere first sentence so that the reader will want to read on.
- Find a point of agreement and prepare your reader for your refusal.
- Be tactful and considerate.
- Avoid trite, negative phrases such as *We are sorry, We cannot, We regret.* Such phrases tend to overemphasize the refusal.
- Stress what *can* be done; offer alternative suggestions.
- Close on a positive note.

Sample Letter Denying Request

CANADIAN BUSINESS INDUSTRIES LIMITED
Serving business in every field – manufacturers, distributors, wholesalers, retailers, and consultants

REGIONAL OFFICES
1107–210 Willett St.
Halifax, NS
B3M 3C6

4230 West Hill Ave.
Montreal, PQ
H4B 2S7

517 Wellington St. W.
Toronto, ON
M5V 1G1

610A 70th Ave. S.E.
Calgary, AB
T2H 2J6

Main Post Office
Box 2010
Vancouver, BC.
V6B 3P8

Montreal, Quebec
October 2, 19--

Miss Freida Holt
7 rue Gagnon
Levis, PQ
G6V 6L7

Dear Miss Holt:

Thank you for thinking of us in connection with your report on glass production.

I should very much like to be able to give you complete information; however, we are distributors only of some of the finest glass available. The three enclosed brochures describe in detail the lines we handle.

We are also enclosing the names and addresses of manufacturers of different types of glass. If you were to write to them, you would no doubt receive all the information you require.

I wish you success in preparing your report. May I have a copy of it when it is finished?

Sincerely yours,

Rudi Heintzman

Rudi Heintzman

eg
Enclosures (4)

Mini-Test

a) There are four paragraphs in the sample letter denying a request. Number these 1 to 4 and answer the following questions. You may need more than one number to answer a question.

1. Which paragraphs want action from the reader?
2. Which paragraphs create a good feeling before the denial?
3. Which paragraphs tell the reader what help can be given?
4. Which paragraph gets the reader's attention?
5. Which paragraphs overemphasize the negative and apologize too much?

KEY

1. 3, 4 2. 1, beginning of 2 3. 2,3 4. 1 5. none of them

b) Following the usual procedures, write a letter to Ruth McDonald, advertising manager for Johnston College Yearbook, 830 Chester Place, Prince Albert, Saskatchewan S6V 6Y8. You received a letter from her asking for an advertisement for the yearbook. However, the advertising department operates on a strict budget that makes even small extra expenditures impossible. Write a friendly letter denying this request but remember to keep goodwill. Have your work evaluated in the usual way.

Purpose

Plan

Evaluation Chart	Your Score	Checker's Score
Well-prepared plan		
Good opening paragraph		
Considerate		
Clear in meaning		
Complete in detail		
Ideas expressed concisely		
Positive, not negative		
Attractively set up		
No trite expressions		
Good closing paragraph		
Total		
Deduction for errors missed or for untidy final letter		
Final Total		

Summary for Unit 7.4

- Follow this **routine** for preparing all letters:
  - Collect all the materials.
  - Clearly define the purpose.
  - Prepare a plan.
  - Prepare a draft.
  - Revise the draft.
  - Produce the final letter on letterhead.
  - Proofread and evaluate.
- When writing request letters:
  - Know exactly what you want.
  - Ask specific questions.
  - Include all details.
  - Explain why.
  - Ask; don't demand.
- When granting requests:
  - Tell your reader immediately.
  - Answer questions in order asked.
  - Add more information that might be helpful.
  - Answer promptly.
  - Build goodwill by expressing interest and desire to hear more from reader.
- When denying requests:
  - Start on friendly sincere note of agreement.
  - Don't rush to deny.
  - Give your reader helpful advice.
  - Don't overemphasize the negative aspects.
  - Emphasize what can be done.
  - End on positive note.

Confirm Your Knowledge

Complete Exercisefor Unit 7.4 on page 301.

❍ 7.5 Order Letters

Most companies, including mail order houses, supply purchase order forms for ordering goods or services. Order letters, therefore, are generally written by individuals who do not have blank order forms. Following the same procedures as outlined in Unit 7.4, write personal order letters using your home address.

Recommended Writing Suggestions

- Use your first sentence to say exactly what it is you are ordering.
  Please send me six packets of...
- Make sure you give accurate, specific, and complete details.
- List the items you are ordering in a table if the required information is at all complex. (See sample letter.) Abbreviations may be used in tables.
- Give specific shipping instructions, and say when you need your order.
- Say how you will pay for the order, avoiding trite expressions.
  Poor: Enclosed herewith is..
  Better: A money order for $90 is enclosed.
- Use your last sentence for any special important instructions.

Sample Order Letter

63 Canada Crescent
Brandon, Manitoba
R7B 2Z7
July 16, 19--

The Mayfair Importers Inc
607 Stanley Avenue
Selkirk, Manitoba
R1A 0R6

Gentlemen

Please send me the following storage units by Purolator Courier Service before August 1.

Quantity	Catalogue Number		Total Price	Total
3	637P36	Wellmade Roughneck Totes	3.99	11.97
3	637P37	Wellmade Treasure Chests	14.99	44.97
3	63W41	Wellmade Keepers Window Bins	7.79	23.37
		Total		80.31
		10% Sales Tax		8.03
		7% GST		5.62
				93.96

My cheque for $93.96 is enclosed.

Would you please let me know immediately you receive any new items of Wellmade as I am very interested in their products.

Yours very truly

Arthur Beamish

Arthur Beamish

Enclosure

Four checks for order letters:

1. details complete
2. when needed
3. how to ship
4. how to pay

Mini-Test

Following the usual routine, prepare an order letter for the following situation. Remember the four special checks for an order letter. Evaluate your final letter against the chart and have someone else evaluate it. Use plain paper and your own address.

Confirm your telephone order to Sandhurst Shoes in your area for two pairs, Size 8, Ladies' walking shoes, brown, one pair in Style 455K and the other pair in Style 736B. These shoes were advertised in the local paper at $59.99 a pair. You need extra-wide fitting which the ad said was available. These shoes are to be delivered to your home and charged to your account No. 7577877. As you are going on vacation at the end of next month, you would like to receive the shoes by the 15th of the month so that you have a chance to break them in before you leave.

Purpose

____

____

Plan

____

____

____

____

____

Evaluation Chart	Your Score	Checker's Score
Well-prepared plan		
Good opening paragraph		
Considerate		
Clear in meaning		
Complete in detail		
Ideas expressed concisely		
Positive, not negative		
Attractively set up		
No trite expressions		
Good closing paragraph		
Total		
Deduction for errors missed or for untidy final letter		

Letters Acknowledging Orders

Many companies acknowledge orders with the invoice or by a printed postcard or form letter. Letters are occasionally sent to acknowledge an especially large order, an order from a new customer, or an order from an old customer who has not ordered for a long time.

Recommended Writing Suggestions

- Use the first sentence to thank the customer for the order.
- Refer to date, order number, and items ordered.
- Tell the customer how and when the order will be delivered. Be sure your delivery date is realistic so that you can fulfill your promise.
- Use the last sentence to reassure your customer that you appreciate the order and that you would like to be of further service.

Sample Letter Acknowledging Order

MAYFAIR IMPORTERS INC.
607 Stanly Avenue
Selkirk, Manitoba R1A 0R6

July 20, 19--

Mr. Arthur Beamish
63 Canada Crescent
Brandon, Manitoba
R7B 2Z7

Dear Mr. Beamish:

Thank you for your order dated July 16 for Wellmade storage units. These will be shipped to arrive before August 1 as requested.

You can always rely on Wellmade products to meet your requirements, and we shall be happy to tell you of any new items we are able to supply as soon as they become available.

You may also be interested in some of our other storage units which our customers have found very satisfactory. I am thinking particularly of the latest interlocking, heavy-duty plastic, household recycling bins that enable the homeowner to separate items for recycling more easily. They come in sets of three at $17.95 per set or may be sold separately at $6.50 each. The colours available are white, blue, or grey, and are listed on page 35 of our catalogue, a copy of which is enclosed.

If we can help you choose other storage items for your customers, or if we can be of service in any other way, please let us know. We shall be happy to serve you.

Yours very truly,

Sandra Halvorson

Sandra Halvorson
General Sales Manager

Mini-Test

Follow the usual procedures in writing the following letter.

As sales promotion manager of CBIL, write to Marion Ziv, Activities Director, Playfair Indoor

Racquets Club, located near you, thanking her for the order of 75 trophies for tennis tournament events to be held two months from now. Delivery can be promised by the end of next month. Ask if any special inscriptions will be needed after the tournament is finished.

Purpose

Plan

Evaluation Chart	Your Score	Checker's Score
Well-prepared plan		
Good opening paragraph		
Considerate		
Clear in meaning		
Complete in detail		
Ideas expressed concisely		
Positive, not negative		
Attractively set up		
No trite expressions		
Good closing paragraph		
Total		
Deduction for errors missed or for untidy final letter		

SUMMARY FOR UNIT 7.5

- Most firms use forms to place orders.
- If a letter is used, check that:
  - all details are correct and complete date needed is stated
  - shipping instructions are given
  - method of payment is included
- An order acknowledgment letter may be sent:
  - if the order is very large
  - if the order came from a new customer
  - if the order came from an old customer who had not ordered for a long time

Confirm Your Knowledge

Complete Exercise for Unit 7.5 on page 303.

7.6 Credit and Collection Letters

Credit Letters

In most companies credit letters are written by the credit manager, who has the job of encouraging customers to buy on credit to increase sales yet must discourage credit buying if bad debts are likely to result. The credit manager must also keep the loyalty of the customer and promote goodwill. Credit correspondence is very important.

Much of the correspondence of a credit department is handled by the use of carefully prepared forms. Printed forms are used for applications for credit, for requests for information from references, and for answers to these requests. Some companies, however, prefer to write individual letters rather than use forms.

Recommended Writing Suggestions

- Thank the customer for the order or interest.
- Explain tactfully why you need information about credit standing.
- Ask specifically what information you need.
- Reassure your customer that obtaining this information is a usual procedure for new accounts and that all such information will be kept confidential.
- Maintain goodwill during the processing of the account.
- Promise prompt and careful attention to any application.
- Do not promise immediate credit because of the possibility of a refusal.
- Explain why an immediate reply will be advantageous to your customer.

Sample Letter Asking for Credit Information

Calgary, AB
November 15, 19--

Walkman Construction Ltd.
851 Coach Side Crescent N.W.
Calgary, AB
T3H 1A6

Gentlemen

Thank you for your order dated November 10 for insulation. We appreciate the opportunity to supply your needs.

We would very much like to ship your order immediately, but before we can do so, may we have some more information about your company? A copy of your latest financial statement would greatly help us in coming to a decision regarding granting credit.

Would you also please let us have the names and addresses of three companies who currently supply some of your needs on credit. This information will, of course, be kept confidential.

As soon as we have this information, your request for credit will be reconsidered.

Yours truly

L. M. Norwood

L.M. Norwood
Credit Manager

Mini-Test

Prepare a plan, a rough draft, and a final letter for the following situation. Remember *AIDA*, and check your final letter against the evaluation chart. Have someone else evaluate your work using the marking guidelines outlined in Unit 7.3.

Mr. F. G. Guignon, the local representative for CBIL, has forwarded an order from Specialty Ribbons Company, 146 Main Street, Winnipeg, Manitoba R3C 1A4, for merchandise totalling $600. CBIL has no credit information on this company, and the buyer who placed the order with Mr. Guignon was unwilling to give him any references. You cannot send any merchandise until you have confirmed the customer's credit standing. Write a tactful letter to the sales manager of Specialty Ribbons Company asking for the necessary information so that the order can be filled promptly.

Purpose

___

___

___

Plan

___

___

___

___

___

___

___

___

___

___

___

___

___

Evaluation Chart	Your Score	Checker's Score
Well-prepared plan		
Good opening paragraph		
Considerate		
Clear in meaning		
Complete in detail		
Ideas expressed concisely		
Positive, not negative		
Attractively set up		
No trite expressions		
Good closing paragraph		
Total		
Deduction for errors missed or for untidy final letter		
Final Total		

Granting Credit

Once again, form letters are often used to confirm that credit has been granted specifying the limit of the credit. However, in order to establish goodwill, a more personal letter may be written to accompany the standard form letter.

Recommended Writing Suggestions

- Tell the reader immediately that credit has been granted.
- Tell what action is being taken—order shipped, credit card enclosed.
- Explain the credit terms thoroughly, clearly stating the credit limit and explaining how to use the credit card.
- Explain the advantages of keeping the account cleared.
- Point out any special features of your service, e.g. cash discounts.
- Close with a positive suggestion that the customer use the account.

Sample Letter Granting Credit

Vancouver, BC
November 15, 19--

Ms. Yoko Merrill
355 Lawson Avenue
North Vancouver, BC
V7S 1H6

Dear Ms. Merrill

Here is your new personal charge card for use at any of our retail stores. Will you please sign the card on the back to validate it.

So that you can get the maximum benefit from your new card, please note the following points.

1. Give your card to the cashier whenever you want to charge merchandise.
2. Give your card number to the order clerk when ordering goods by phone.
3. Let us know immediately if the card is lost or stolen or if you change your name or address.

You will receive a statement at the end of each month which is payable within ten days. In order to keep your credit rating in good standing, we suggest you try to clear your account each month as interest can accumulate rapidly!

You are welcome to use our personal shopping services and other special services detailed in the enclosed brochure.

Thank your for choosing us for your shopping. We are happy to serve you.

Yours truly

Rose Fidelino

Rose Fidelino
Credit Manager

Enc.

Mini-Test

Prepare a plan, a rough draft, and a final letter for the following situation. Remember *AIDA*, and check your final letter against the evaluation chart. Have someone else evaluate your work using the marking guidelines outlined in Unit 7.3.

Dr. James Mason has applied to Canadian Business Industries Limited for a charge account. The information on his application form and the references he supplied are very satisfactory. Write a letter to Dr. Mason confirming that you have opened an account for him, adding any further information you think would be appropriate. Use a local address for Dr. Mason.

Purpose

Plan

Evaluation Chart	Your Score	Checker's Score
Well-prepared plan		
Good opening paragraph		
Considerate		
Clear in meaning		
Complete in detail		
Ideas expressed concisely		
Positive, not negative		
Attractively set up		
No trite expressions		
Good closing paragraph		
Total		
Deductions for errors missed or for untidy final letter		
Final Total		

Refusing Credit

In a letter refusing credit, you must be very considerate and tactful to avoid too much disappointment and maintain the customer's goodwill. You should emphasize that it is in the best interests of both the customer and the company to deny credit just now; however, make suggestions to help the customer improve his or her credit standing so that the application can be reviewed at a later date.

Recommended Writing Suggestions

- Thank the customer for the order or interest.
- Comment favourably on the customer's business or application.
- Give a reasonable explanation for not granting credit just now.
- Give helpful suggestions—order in smaller quantities, pay cash, or order on a COD basis, postpone buying until items on sale.
- Be willing to review credit position in the future.
- Say that you hope your company still has the customer's goodwill and confidence.

Sample Letter Refusing Credit

Calgary, AB
November 22, 19--

Walkman Construction Ltd.
851 Coach Side Crescent N.W.
Calgary, AB
T3H 1A6

Gentlemen

Thank you for your letter of November 19 and for the financial statement that you have enclosed.

You have made great progress in three years. Your statement shows that you are operating profitably and that you are earning a good return for your investment.

Your latest figures, however, show that you are still having difficulty with ready working capital. We feel it would be putting an extra strain on you if we were to grant full credit just now.

Our company policy with new accounts is to begin with a small amount of credit and gradually increase it as your payments warrant. Your order was for more than $2000. May we suggest that you send us a cheque for $1000 to cover part of your order, which we will then ship immediately. Full payment will be due on receipt of the merchandise.

This arrangement will help you to spread your payments and enable us to establish your future credit requirements.

Please let us have your initial payment of $1000 as soon as possible so that we can process your order.

Yours truly

L.M. Norwood

L.M. Norwood
Credit Manager

Mini-Test

Prepare a plan, a rough draft, and a final letter for the following situation. Remember *AIDA*, and check your final letter against the evaluation chart. Have someone else evaluate your work using the marking guidelines outlined in Unit 7.3.

CBIL has received an order for back-to-school items from Great Gizmos store at 1039 Barclay Street, Vancouver, B.C. V6E 1G5, totalling $256.54. The balance of the Great Gizmos account is $823, not due until the end of the month, and the credit limit allowed this store is $1000. Write a letter from the credit manager asking for a cheque for $79.54 or more on the old balance so that you may send their back-to-school supplies and stay within the $1000 credit limit.

Purpose

____

____

____

Plan

____

____

____

____

Evaluation Chart	Your Score	Checker's Score
Well-prepared plan		
Good opening paragraph		
Considerate		
Complete in detail		
Ideas expressed concisely		
Positive, not negative		
Attractively set up		
No trite expressions		
Good closing paragraph		
Total		
Deductions for errors missed or for untidy final letter		
Final Total		

Collection Letters

Collection letters are letters sent to customers who are behind in settling their accounts. There are three kinds of collection letters:

1. A first letter, a reminder, sent to customers who usually pay on time but are now overdue.
2. A second letter, a follow-up, sent to customers who have not yet paid in spite of receiving a reminder.
3. A third letter, a pay-now-or-else letter, sent to customers who have still not paid.

Reminder Letters

- Remind the customer gently that the account is overdue.
- State the exact amount owing.
- Reassure the customer that there is probably a good reason for the delay.
- Enclose an addressed return envelope.

Follow-up Letters

- Remind the customer that the account is still overdue.
- State the exact amount owing.
- Mention concern at not having received payment.
- Suggest the customer might like to discuss the problem with you.
- Appeal to the customer's sense of fairness.
- Enclose an addressed return envelope and suggest the customer use it to mail a cheque today.

Pay-Now-or-Else Letters

- Remind the customer of how long the account is overdue.
- State the exact amount owing.
- Mention that the customer's credit standing is in jeopardy.
- Explain that accounts that are long overdue may be turned over to a collection agency.
- Remind the customer that if the account is paid immediately, the customer's credit rating will not be affected.

Sample First Reminder Letter

CANADIAN BUSINESS INDUSTRIES LIMITED
Serving business in every field – manufacturers, distributors, wholesalers, retailers, and consultants

REGIONAL OFFICES

1107–210 Willett St.
Halifax, NS
B3M 3C6

4230 West Hill Ave.
Montreal, PQ
H4B 2S7

517 Wellington St. W.
Toronto, ON
M5V 1G1

610A 70th Ave. S.E.
Calgary, AB
T2H 2J6

Main Post Office
Box 2010
Vancouver, BC
V6B 3P8

Halifax, N.S.
June 12, 19--

Mr. Sam Mistretta
5 Deacon Lane
St. Stephen, N.B.
E3L 3A9

Dear Mr. Mistretta:

Summer is a time for relaxation and recreation. We hope you are making the most of these glorious days.

Perhaps you have been away or there may be some other reason, but have you forgotten your account with us is overdue by $270.80? This amount has been overdue since May 15.

A stamped envelope is enclosed for you to send us a cheque or to let us know when we may expect payment.

Very truly yours,

Calvin Averti
Credit Manager

dk

Sample Second Reminder or Follow-Up Letter

CANADIAN BUSINESS INDUSTRIES LIMITED
Serving business in every field – manufacturers, distributors, wholesalers, retailers, and consultants

REGIONAL OFFICES

1107–210 Willett St.
Halifax, NS
B3M 3C6

4230 West Hill Ave.
Montreal, PQ
H4B 2S7

517 Wellington St. W.
Toronto, ON
M5V 1G1

610A 70th Ave. S.E.
Calgary, AB
T2H 2J6

Main Post Office
Box 2010
Vancouver, BC
V6B 3P8

Halifax, N.S.
July 15, 19--

Mr. Sam Mistretta
5 Deacon Lane
St. Stephen, N.B.
E3L 3A9

Dear Mr. Mistretta:

Money matters and summer days sometimes don't go together. However, we are surprised to find that we have not heard from you about the $270.80 that has been outstanding on your account since May 15.

Is there anything we can do to help you meet this payment? Your payments have always been very regular in the past, and we know you appreciate that a good credit rating is an excellent asset.

Won't you please either send us your cheque for $270.80 today — a stamped envelope is enclosed — or let us know by return mail why payment is being delayed.

Yours very truly,

Calvin Averti
Credit Manager

dk

Sample Pay-Now-or-Else Letter

CANADIAN BUSINESS INDUSTRIES LIMITED
Serving business in every field – manufacturers, distributors, wholesalers, retailers, and consultants

REGIONAL OFFICES

1107–210 Willett St.
Halifax, NS
B3M 3C6

4230 West Hill Ave.
Montreal, PQ
H4B 2S7

517 Wellington St. W.
Toronto, ON
M5V 1G1

610A 70th Ave. S.E.
Calgary, AB
T2H 2J6

Main Post Office
Box 2010
Vancouver, BC
V6B 3P8

Halifax, N.S.
August 14, 19--

Mr. Sam Mistretta
5 Deacon Lane
St. Stephen, NB
E3L 3A9

Dear Mr. Mistretta:

A person's credit rating is a most valuable possession. For this reason, we wonder why you have consistently disregarded your outstanding balance of $270.80 and our letters reminding you about it. Perhaps you do not realize that your account is now three months overdue.

Ordinarily, such a long overdue account is referred to our legal department. But your previous good record prompts us to call your attention, once again, to the facts before we consider drastic steps. It is now up to you.

We are sure that you now understand the seriousness of this situation and that you will want to send us a cheque for $270.80 immediately.

Very truly yours,

Calvin Averti
Credit Manager

dk

Because collecting money can sometimes be an awkward or embarrassing situation, some collection letters may be better expressed in a humorous way.

June 15, 19--

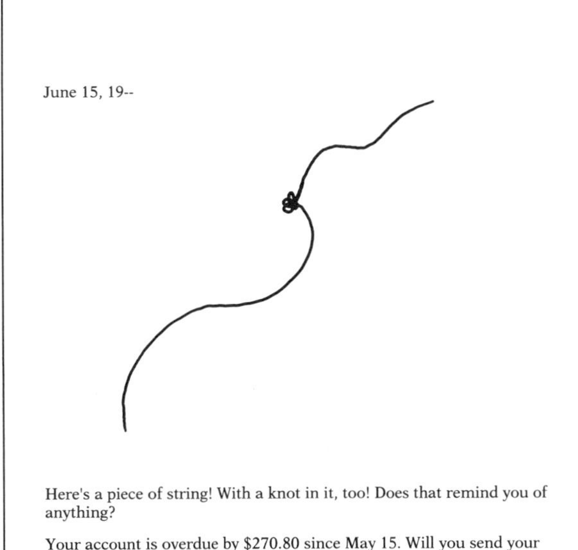

Here's a piece of string! With a knot in it, too! Does that remind you of anything?

Your account is overdue by $270.80 since May 15. Will you send your cheque today in the envelope enclosed.

Then we can untie the knot!

Mini-Test

Prepare a plan, a rough draft, and a final letter for the three collection letters to cover the following situation. Check your final letters against the evaluation chart. Have someone else evaluate your work using the marking guidelines outlined in Unit 7.3.

Write a series of collection letters to Mrs. Vera Traynor, of 203 Notre Dame Street, Summerside, PE C1N 1R7, who has not paid the last statement we sent her showing a balance of $115.45 owing. Date your letters approximately three weeks apart. The first reminder could be in a humorous tone, but the second and third collection letters are not usually humorous.

Purpose

Plan

Evaluation Chart	Your Score	Checker's Score
Well-prepared plan		
Good opening paragraph		
Considerate		
Clear in meaning		
Complete in detail		
Ideas expressed concisely		
Positive, not negative		
Attractively set up		
No trite expressions		
Good closing paragraph		
Total		
Deductions for errors missed or for untidy final letter		
Final Total		

Purpose

Plan

Evaluation Chart	Your Score	Checker's Score
Well-prepared plan		
Good opening paragraph		
Considerate		
Clear in meaning		
Complete in detail		
Ideas expressed concisely		
Positive, not negative		
Attractively set up		
No trite expressions		
Good closing paragraph		
Total		
Deductions for errors missed or for untidy final letter		
Final Total		

Purpose

Plan

Evaluation Chart	Your Score	Checker's Score
Well-prepared plan		
Good opening paragraph		
Considerate		
Clear in meaning		
Complete in detail		
Ideas expressed concisely		
Positive, not negative		
Attractively set up		
No trite expressions		
Good closing paragraph		
Total		
Deductions for errors missed or for untidy final letter		
Final Total		

SUMMARY FOR UNIT 7.6

Credit letters

- *Asking* for credit information requires tact.
  - Explain why you need the information.
  - Do *not* promise immediate credit.
- When *granting* credit, let the customer know immediately.
  - Explain the use of your services.
  - Explain the value of keeping accounts up to date.
- When *refusing* credit, do so gently.
  - Give a reason and make suggestions.
  - Leave the door open for future negotiations.
  - *Always* remember to keep the customer's goodwill.

Collection Letters

- Make the first letter a gentle reminder.
- In the second letter, suggest a discussion of how to pay.
- Make the third letter an ultimatum or pay-now-or-else letter.
- All letters must clearly state the amount owing.
- Remind the customer of the value of a good credit rating.
- Always suggest immediate payment–enclose envelope
- Try a little humour, but don't overdo it!
- Remember *AIDA* and the Seven Cs.
- Use the evaluation chart to check each letter.

Confirm Your Knowledge

Complete Exercise for Unit 7.6 on page 305.

❍ 7.7 Claim and Adjustment Letters

Modern technology has made the process of doing business much more efficient. However, in spite of the most sophisticated computers, errors do occur. These errors are unfortunate and can cause inconvenience, but most people are reasonable and realize that they are unintentional. In dealing with a customer's claim. you have a great opportunity to retain the goodwill of the customer.

Claim Letters

If you think an error has been made or if you want to make a claim, consider the following points in your letter asking for an adjustment.

Recommended Writing Suggestions

- Do not write when you are angry; wait until you have cooled down.
- Give all the details of the transaction involved, including order or invoice numbers and date.
- State in detail exactly what is wrong.
- State what you think would be a reasonable adjustment.
- Express appreciation of the action you hope will be taken.

Sample Claim Letter

August 28, 19--

Citizen's Gas Company
500 Consumers Road
Willowdale, Ontario
M2J 1P8

Gentlemen

Re: Invoice 03684 — 7 Relmar Gardens

I have just received here at my summer home the July bill for $25.28 for gas service to 7 Relmar Gardens, Toronto, my permanent home. An error has been made in this bill as my home has been vacant since June 6 when the gas service was disconnected by one of your servicemen.

The May account was paid in full on June 10 by my cheque for $23.86 covering the period from May 1 to June 1.

Please look into this matter, make the adjustment, and send me a corrected statement as soon as possible to my St. Andrew's address.

Sincerely yours,

Carol Rook

Carol Rook
5 Brandy Cove Road
St. Andrew's, NB
E0G 2X0

Mini-Test

Prepare a plan, a rough draft, and a final letter for the following situation. Remember *AIDA*, and check your final letter against the evaluation chart. Have someone else evaluate your work using the marking guidelines outlined in Unit 7.3.

On September 3, Specialty Movers picked up your set of drums to move them from your home in Winnipeg to Brandon, Manitoba. When they arrived, one of the drums had a tear in it. You have a signature to say that the drums were in perfect condition when they left Winnipeg. You want to know whether you should have the drum repaired locally or whether Specialty Movers will arrange for the repairs. The matter is urgent as you need your drums for a gig at the end of the month.

Purpose

____

____

Plan

____

____

____

____

____

Evaluation Chart	Your Score	Checker's Score
Well-prepared plan		
Good opening paragraph		
Considerate		
Clear in meaning		
Complete in detail		
Ideas expressed concisely		
Positive, not negative		
Attractively set up		
No trite expressions		
Good closing paragraph		
Total		
Deductions for errors missed or for untidy final letter		
Final Total		

Adjustment Letters

Adjustment letters cover three types of claims:

1. The customer is right; the company has made an error.
2. The customer is partially right and the company is partially right.
3. The customer is wrong; the company has made no error.

The following suggestions, with modifications, can be used for all three types of complaints.

Recommended Writing Suggestions

- Keep in mind that you want to keep the customer's goodwill and business.
- Reply promptly, restating the claimant's problem.
- If you are granting the claim, say so immediately.
- Be positive in all statements. Place the emphasis on what you can do, avoiding, if possible, any reference to what you can not do.
- If you cannot grant the claim, explain courteously and specifically why you cannot do so.
- Thank the customer for bringing the problem to your attention; reassure the customer that the problem is being rectified, if it is.
- Don't be afraid to apologize if you are at fault, but be aware of overdoing it and sounding insincere.

Sample Adjustment Letter Where the Customer is Right

Citizen's Gas Company
500 Consumers Road • Willowdale, Ontario M2J 1P8

September 2, 19--

Ms. Carol Rook
5 Brandy Cove Road
St. Andrew's, NB
E0G 2X0

Dear Ms. Rook:

Invoice 03684 — 7 Relmar Gardens

Thank you for your letter of August 28 about the bill you received for $25.28.

Yes, Ms. Rook, you are right. An error has been made, and a corrected statement is enclosed. You will see that there is only a small balance of $2.75 outstanding, which you can pay at your convenience when you return to Relmar Gardens next month.

In today's automated world with sophisticated computers to do much of the work, there are few occasions when human errors do occur. This, however, is one of those times, and your records have now been corrected and brought up to date.

When you are ready to have your gas supply reconnected at 7 Relmar Gardens, our service representative will be there as soon as you let us know.

Yours very truly,
CITIZEN'S GAS COMPANY
Frank Vestfals
Frank Vestfals
Manager, Accounts Department

FV:ked

Sample Adjustment Letter Where the Customer is Partially Right

CANADIAN BUSINESS INDUSTRIES LIMITED
Serving business in every field – manufacturers, distributors, wholesalers, retailers, and consultants

REGIONAL OFFICES
1107–210 Willett St.
Halifax, NS
B3M 3C6
4230 West Hill Ave.
Montreal, PQ
H4B 2S7
517 Wellington St. W.
Toronto, ON
M5V 1G1
610A 70th Ave. S.E.
Calgary, AB
T2H 2J6
Main Post Office
Box 2010
Vancouver, BC
V6B 3P8

Montreal, Quebec
April 23, 19--

Ms. Jacqui Renault
4 rue Frontenac
Hull, Quebec
J8X 1Y6

Dear Ms. Renault:

Thank you for your letter of April 17 explaining the concerns you have about the liquid paper you received on invoice No. 246B.

We have checked the bottle you returned and agree that it is not suitable for use as is. However, this liquid paper was sold at a special price to get rid of old stock, and all sales were final. We cannot, therefore, exchange the whole shipment.

You are not the only customer who has brought this to our attention, Ms. Renault, and we feel that perhaps we can help by sending you six bottles of thinner at no charge so that you can use the supply of liquid paper you bought. Just add a few drops of the thinner to each bottle and shake thoroughly.

You'll be pleased to know our new line of paper in cream and light beige is now available. Some samples are enclosed, and prices are printed on the samples. Let us know if you would like a supply. Delivery is within one week.

Yours very truly,
Colette Duras
Colette Duras
Manager, Customer Service

ked

Sample Adjustment Letter Refusing the Claim

Halifax, NS
February 12, 19--

Mrs. Ruth Christie
7 Miles Lane
Glace Bay, NS
B1A 1P1

Dear Mrs. Christie:

Thank you for returning the damaged rug-hooking frame for our inspection.

You are right. The holes for the roller screws are too large. Consequently, the rollers will not stay firm enough to withstand the weight of a rug. However, on examination, it is obvious these holes have been enlarged after leaving our factory as they are not even, have been made in a slanting direction, and are too deep. We regret, therefore, that we cannot give you a refund for this frame.

May we suggest that we repair the frame for you and return it to you for a small charge of $27.50 plus taxes. You could have the frame back within a week of our receiving a cheque to cover this work. You will then be able to continue working on your rug easily and in comfort.

Let us know your decision so that we can go ahead with the repairs.

Yours truly,
Lila Schmidt
Lila Schmidt
Manager
Customer Service

Mini-Test

Prepare a plan, a rough draft, and a final letter for the following situation. Remember *AIDA,* and check your final letter against the evaluation chart. Have someone else evaluate your work using the marking guidelines outlined in Unit 7.3.

You have received a letter dated last Wednesday from Charles Leduc saying that he won't be able to continue the computer technician course CBIL holds on Tuesdays and Thursdays from 7 to 10 p.m. He is claiming a refund of his fee of $140. Write to Mr. Leduc, who lives near you, explaining that as he attended more than four nights, no refund is applicable; however, the same course is offered on Mondays and Wednesdays, and if he would like to switch to these nights, the fee could be transferred.

Purpose

Plan

Evaluation Chart	Your Score	Checker's Score
Well-prepared plan		
Good opening paragraph		
Considerate		
Clear in meaning		
Complete in detail		
Ideas expressed concisely		
Positive, not negative		
Attractively set up		
No trite expressions		
Good closing paragraph		
Total		
Deductions for errors missed or for untidy final letter		
Final Total		

SUMMARY FOR UNIT 7.7

- Do not write a claim letter when you are angry.
- State exactly what is wrong, including all details.
- Say what you think would be a suitable adjustment.
- There are three types of adjustment letters:
  - customer right
  - customer partially right
  - customer wrong
- Reply quickly; be positive, emphasizing what you *can* do.
- Apologize for any error, but don't overdo it!
- Reassure the customer and always keep goodwill.

Confirm Your Knowledge

Complete Exercise for Unit 7.7 on page 307.

❍ 7.8 Sales Letters

The purpose of all sales letters is to get the reader to purchase the merchandise or use the service offered. Writing effective sales letters is a specialized skill, and analysing sales letters you receive will help you acquire this skill.

Before you begin writing a sales letter, study the following points.

1. Know the product or service and its background.
   What is it for?
   How does it work?
   What are its good qualities?
   What raw materials are used?
   Is it recyclable?
   How often is the service offered?
2. Know the customer.
   What are the customer's interests?
   Where does the customer live—house or apartment?
   How can you adjust your message to the customer's individuality?
3. Choose the selling appeal.
   What is the reason for buying?

Goods	*Services*
– economical	– prompt service
– one-time offer	– skilled workers
– highest quality	– modern equipment
– recyclable	– shopping done for you
– time-saving	– more time to relax

4. Remember *AIDA*
   Create *desire* by stressing the benefits.
5. Make your letter eye-catching.
   Use coloured stationery.
   Use different sizes of paper.
   Use a variety of display techniques.
6. Final check.
   Make sure your letter is complete.
   Help your reader to act in the way you want.

Sample of a Sales Letter Selling a Service

LUCIENS LAKESIDE LODGE
P.O. Box 410, Quebec City, PQ
G1R 4R3

November 29, 19--

Dr. Marcel Garneau
59 Eustane Street
Summerside, PEI
C1N 2V9

Dear Dr. Garneau:

Whenever business or vacation brings you to Quebec City. LUCIEN'S LAKESIDE LODGE is there with a warm welcome.

Our accommodation is modern and comformtable, with each room facing the lake. Our dining room is one of the best in Quebec and is open for room service 24 hours. Our staff are all eager to make your stay a pleasing experience.

As an introductory offer, we are enclosing a first-time guest discount card which will entitle you to preferred choice of rooms at 15 percent discount and a similar discount in our dining room.

Because Lucien's Lakeside Lodge is a complete resort, yet located within easy access of Quebec City's business district, you will find staying here for business trips allows you that well-earned rest and relaxation to keep you alert. You can even book one of our conference rooms so that you don't have to travel at all!

Please read the enclosed brochure carefully and let us help you enjoy your stay in Quebec City by staying at Lucien's Lakeside Lodge.

Sincerely yours,

Marie Bourassa

Marie Bourassa
Manager

Sample of a Sales Letter for General Distribution Promoting a Product

COOL BREEZE AIR-CONDITIONING

Dear Homeowner:

Working people today enjoy the comfort of AIR-CONDITIONING in their work places, but...

DO THEY HAVE THAT COMFORT AT HOME?

Our low cost, portable air-conditioners make it possible for everyone to be cool and comfortable during the sizzling hot days of summer. Let others swelter! Your home deserves the pleasure of controlled temperature surroundings.

FEELING IS BELIEVING!

Come to our showroom at 236 Hawthorne Blvd. any day between 9:30 a.m. and 10 p.m., and we shall be pleased to let you experience the refreshing breath of fresh, cool air that our air-conditioners can bring to your home.

Visit our COOL BREEZE showrooms today, and your home could be a cool oasis tomorrow.

Cordially yours,

F.R. Stowes

F.R. Stowes
President, COOL BREEZE AIR-CONDITIONING

P.S. If you can't come to us, we will come to you! Just call 226-7854, and a sales representative will make an appointment to come and give you a demonstration in your own home.

Mini-Test

Prepare a plan, a rough draft, and a final letter for the following situation. Remember *AIDA*, and check your final letter against the evaluation chart. Have someone else evaluate your work using the marking guidelines outlined in Unit 7.3.

Write a letter for the promotion of a new soft drink. Use your imagination for its taste and appeal. The mailing will be to current purchasers of our other soft drinks who will have the opportunity to market it exclusively before it is put on the open market.

Purpose

Plan

Evaluation Chart	Your Score	Checker's Score
Well-prepared plan		
Good opening paragraph		
Considerate		
Clear in meaning		
Complete in detail		
Ideas expressed concisely		
Positive, not negative		
Attractively set up		
No trite expressions		
Good closing paragraph		
Total		
Deductions for errors missed or for untidy final letter		
Final Total		

SUMMARY FOR UNIT 7.8

- A sales letter must make the reader want to buy the goods or services offered.
- An analysis of sales letters you receive will help you recognize a good sales letter.
- Consider the following points:
  - Know the product or service thoroughly.
  - Know the customer
  - Choose the selling appeal.
  - Remember *AIDA*, particularly *D*—desire!
  - Make your letter eye-catching.
  - Help the reader act the way you want.

Confirm Your Knowledge

Complete Exercise for Unit 7.8 on page 309.

7.9 Goodwill and Public Relations Letters

In fact, all letters sent out by a business are essentially goodwill letters. They want the reader to have a favourable impression of the company. Some letters, however, are written specifically to create goodwill, such as letters of congratulations, sympathy, or thanks for exceptional service.

Some suggestions as to when goodwill letters are appropriate and examples of such letters follow.

Occasions when goodwill letters are appropriate

1. **Acknowledgment** of large or first-time orders, suggestions, criticisms, and praises.
2. **Appreciation** for long service, long association, ideas and suggestions, recommending the company to a new customer.
3. **Congratulations** for promotions, special anniversaries, new appointments.
4. **Encouragement** on loss of contract, failed exam.
5. **Holiday greetings** at Christmas, Hannukah, New Year.
6. **Invitations** to openings, special demonstrations, lectures.
7. **Sympathy** for death, illness, fire.
8. **Welcome** to new employee or newcomer to town.

Sample Letter of Gratitude

Calgary, AB
May 27, 19--

Ms. Mila Vasilek
806 Outlook Avenue
Moose Jaw, SK
S6H 5T9

Dear Ms. Vasilek:

It seems that human nature is all too ready to complain or find fault. It was therefore a very great pleasure for us to receive your letter praising our product.

Your humorous account of your efforts to rescue your watch from a snowdrift made us laugh, and your surprise at finding the watch still going in mid-April when the snow had cleared made us smile. We are very proud of our products and have every confidence in them, but it is very nice to know that a customer has had an exceptional experience to prove their worth.

Thank you, Ms. Vasilek, for writing such a wonderful letter. You made us feel very good.

Yours sincerely,

Georgina Christie

Georgina Christie
Production Manager

Sample Letter of Thanks for Commending an Employee

Toronto, ON
March 10, 19--

Mr. Gordon Baker
43 Sheppard Avenue East
Willowdale, ON
M2N 2Z8

Dear Mr. Baker:

Thank you very much for your letter of March 3 commending one of our reception personnel for assisting you when you became ill and accompanying you to the hospital two weeks ago. We are glad to hear that you are fully recovered now.

We are always happy to hear when a member of our staff has shown initiative and consideration for our customrs. Sylvia Price, the receptionist involved, has been shown your letter and a note has been placed in her personnel file noting her special concern for your welfare.

Thank you for taking the time to let us know about this incident.

Yours sincerely,

Fiona Mackay

Fiona Mackay
Personnel Manager

Sample Letter of Sympathy

Calgary, AB
June 17, 19--

Mrs. Tanya Moisevitch
757 Campbell Street
Regina, SK
S4T 5N9

Dear Mrs. Moisevitch:

Word has just reached us of the death of your husband Boris, and we want to send you our sincere sympathy.

Boris was a client of ours for many years and it was always a pleasure doing business with him. He built a business that has an excellent reputation; we like to feel that we had some part in helping him establish that business.

As a person, Boris was well respected by all those who had dealings with him. We shall miss him.

Please remember, Mrs. Moisevitch, that we are here to help you over this difficult time if you need any assistance in business matters.

Yours truly,

Susan Wong

Susan Wong
Personnel Manager

Recommended Writing Suggestions

- Always be sincere—phony expressions are easily spotted.
- Keep your letters simple and direct.
- Remember to think how you would feel on receiving such a lctter.
- Offer assistance whenever appropriate.
- Be prompt in writing "thank-you" letters.
- Let courtesy and common sense be your guide in goodwill and public relations letters.
- Remember that a goodwill letter is not a sales letter.

Mini-Test

Prepare a plan, a rough draft, and a final letter for the following situation. Remember *AIDA*, and check your final letter against the evaluation chart. Have someone else evaluate your work using the marking guidelines outlined in Unit 7.3.

Write a letter to your local TV or radio station to thank them for promoting your company in connection with an upcoming community baseball tournament. CBIL agreed to pay for the accommodation for visiting teams so that as many teams as possible could enter, as not all teams could find sponsors. You did not expect a TV or radio station to acknowledge your offer, but you very much appreciate the free advertising.

Purpose

Plan

Evaluation Chart	Your Score	Checker's Score
Well-prepared plan		
Good opening paragraph		
Considerate		
Clear in meaning		
Complete in detail		
Ideas expressed concisely		
Positive, not negative		
Attractively set up		
No trite expressions		
Good closing paragraph		
Total		
Deductions for errors missed or for untidy final letter		
Final Total		

Summary for Unit 7.9

- Goodwill is inherent in all business letters.
- Acknowledgments, congratulations, invitations, sympathy, and welcome are some types of goodwill and public relations letters.
- A goodwill letter is not a sales letter.
- Be sincere at all times.
- Be simple and direct.
- Offer appropriate assistance.
- Keep the reader's feelings uppermost in your mind.

Confirm Your Knowledge

Complete Exercise for Unit 7.9 on page 311.

7.10 Job Applications and Résumés

Job Applications

The language, style, and appearance of a letter of application deserve special attention. The purpose of the letter is to get you an interview, and your chances will be improved if you write a letter that will single you out as the best candidate for the job.

Letters of application may be in answer to an advertisement or in the hope that a position is available. In either case, remembering the following points will help you write a strong letter.

Recommended Writing Suggestions

1. Make sure your letter is attractive to create a good first impression—no smudges or badly corrected errors.
2. Make sure your letter is original, not copied from a textbook, and written with a specific job in mind. If you want to use the same letter to apply for the same job at another company, use your computer to vary the wording and to rearrange the content, if appropriate.
3. Use clear language that is grammatically correct.
4. Use a positive first sentence that suggests you are the one for the job. Refer to the advertisement or the position you want.
5. Draw attention to any special qualifications you may have that make you suitable for the job.
6. Ask for an interview, giving your telephone number and, if appropriate, the best time to reach you.

Sample Letters of Application

441 College Avenue
Brandon, Manitoba
R7A 1E8
January 20, 19--

MR. Yves Ranier, Manager
Human Resources Department
East/West Enterprise Ltd.
3419 McDonald Avenue
Brandon, Manitoba
R7B 0B5

Dear Mr. Rainer:

I believe I have the skills and personal qualities called for in your advertisement for a word processing operator in last night's Free Press. Please consider this letter as my application for the job.

As you will see from the enclosed résumé, I have successfully completed the two-year Word Processing Secretarial Program at Sheridan Park Community College. This program included extensive training in English language skills, the use of word processing and transcribing equipment, accounting, business management, and business procedures. In addition, since 19-- my part-time position at Shaffer Real Estate has given me experience in handling the telephone effectively, organizing sales meetings, managing records, and drafting correspondence. The job has also taught me to deal successfully with members of the public and to establish good relationships with fellow workers.

It is my hope that experience as a word processing operator will add to my qualifications and prepare me for my goal of a management position in your company.

I will welcome the opportunity of discussing my application with you and would appreciate an interview at any time convenient to you. My home telephone number is 489-2672.

Yours very truly,
Pietra Spenseri
Pietra Spenseri

220 Laurier Ave.
North Bay, ON
P1B 1T7

April 16, 19--

Ms. Garbara Gaudet
Yukon-Writer
500 Lewes Blvd.
Whitehorse, YT
Y1A 2C6

Dear Ms. Gaudet:

I found your advertisement in the *Yukon-Writer* so exciting that I had to apply right away. As a writer, the chance to practise my craft, help untangle the legal system for the public, and see the Yukon combine to form the perfect job.

I am enclosing a résumé which describes my education and work experience.

What the résumé cannot tell you is that I am friendly, outgoing, and work very well with people. I can also key approximately 40 wpm, largely as a result of the amount of writing I enjoy doing. I like travelling and meeting new people. I am quite fluent in both written and spoken French.

Whilst distance makes an interview difficult, I am available at any time should you wish to speak with me further. I appreciate your consideration of my application, and I hope you will find me ideal for this position.

Yours sincerely,
Kenneth Sinclair
Kenneth Sinclair

Mini-Test

Prepare a plan, a rough draft, and a final letter for the following situation. Check your final letter against the evaluation chart. Have someone else evaluate your work using the marking guidelines outlined in Unit 7.3.

Pick an advertisement from a local paper for a job in which you are interested, or choose a local company for whom you would like to work. Write a letter applying for that job or a position with the company you have chosen.

Purpose

___

___

Plan

___

___

___

___

___

___

___

___

___

___

___

___

___

___

Evaluation Chart	Your Score	Checker's Score
Well-prepared plan		
Good opening paragraph		
Considerate		
Clear in meaning		
Complete in detail		
Ideas expressed concisely		
Positive, not negative		
Attractively set up		
No trite expressions		
Good closing paragraph		
Total		
Deductions for errors missed or for untidy final letter		
Final Total		

Personal Data Sheets

Personal data sheets, or résumés, give particulars about your education and work experience. They also include information about any other skills or qualifications you may have that are pertinent to the job for which you are applying. Personal data sheets should be prepared with a particular job in mind and should be designed to emphasize your suitability for that job.

There are many styles of personal data sheets. Examine the two given here and check your library, a reference manual, or a keyboarding text for other examples. Note how each style is broken down into clear units for easy reference.

Recommended Writing Suggestions

1. Make sure your personal data sheet is clear, clean, and attractively set up.
2. Try to keep it to one page if possible.
3. Include only those points of education and work experience that are appropriate for that particular job. Nobody is interested in where you went to nursery school.
4. Under work experience, give a brief outline of your responsibilities on each job.

5. Be sure to include any special qualifications you may have, for example, a foreign language, community work.
6. Check, check again, and recheck to make absolutely sure there are no errors of any kind!

Samples of Personal Data Sheets

RÉSUMÉ

Pietra Spenseri
441 College Avenue
Brandon, Manitoba
R7A 1E8

Business: (204) 489-2672
Residence: (204) 763-1867

EDUCATION

Sheridan Park Community College
1460 Portage Avenue, Winnipeg, Manitoba R3G OV6

Secretarial (Word Processing) Diploma, 19--
(Program included courses in business management, accounting, and economics)

Brandonbridge High School
71 Franklin Street, Brandon, Manitoba R7A 5P2

Secondary School Graduation Diploma, 19--
Grade 12 average - 81%
(Courses in word processing, accounting, law, and marketing)

Special Achievements
Keyboarding Speed Certificate 70 wpm
Second prize in County Accounting Contest
Business Studies Endorsement
Co-operative Education Certificate (Word Processing)

Extracurricular Activities
High school volleyball team for three years
President of Students' Council in Grade 12
Participated in school fashion show and drama club presentations

BUSINESS EXPERIENCE

November, 19-- present
Part-time (after college and during holiday periods) assistant at Shaffer Real Estate,
29 Pacific Ave., Brandon, Manitoba R7A OH3

Handled correspondence and customer enquiries, filing, telephone and reception.
Mr. W. Shaffer, Owner (731-1694)

June, 19-- - August, 19--
Part-time (summer) Person Friday at Valencia Foods,
25 Dennis Street, Brandon, Manitoba R7A 5C7

Prepared invoices and some correspondence, helped with inventory and bank deposits.
Mrs. V. Stanton, Office Manager (851-2843)

VOLUNTEER EXPERIENCE
Candy striper for two years at Brandon General Hospital.
Brown Owl for the local Brownie pack.

INTERESTS
Writing, photography, racquet sports, computers

CAREER GOALS
To acquire administrative skills leading to a role in management

REFERENCES
Available on request

RÉSUMÉ

PAULINE PATTISON

10 Knightsbridge Way
Markham, Ontario
L3P 3W5
(416) 294-9019

POSITION DESIRED

An administrative position incorporating word processing skills, use of initiative, and the opportunity to function as part of a team and perform a variety of office procedures.

EDUCATION

19-- - 19--
SENECA COLLEGE OF APPLIED ARTS AND TECHNOLOGY (Sheppard Campus).

Diploma: Office Administrative Assistant

Skills:
Word Processing Operator (AES Plus)
Machine Transcription
Bookkeeping - up to and including post-closing trial balance
Familiar with High-End Desktop Publishing Systems.

19-- - 19--
BRENTWOOD TEACHER TRAINING COLLEGE, Brentwood, England

Diploma: Cambridge Certificate of Education, 1974
(Comparable to Faculty of Education for high school)

EMPLOYMENT

19-- - 19--
Music Teacher
MARKHAM NURSERY SCHOOL, Markham, Ontario
Duties:
- taught all arithmetic classes as well as music and dance

PAULINE PATTISON

Page 2

Jan. 19-- - July 19--
General Secretary
GENERAL ACCIDENT ASSURANCE COMPANY
(368-4733)

- initially hired to help out in an overload situation in preparing a manual for publication. Asked back by the same department on two separate occasions to assist with account reconciliation when files were computerized. Worked alone and on my own initiative and found this environment very satisfying.

19-- - 19--
Elementary School Teacher
CUTHBERT MAYNE JUNIOR SCHOOL, Cranleigh, England
Duties:
- included all subjects taught for grades 2 and 3

19-- - 19--
History and English Teacher
FOREST GIRLS' SCHOOL, Horsham, England
Duties:
- class teacher and year supervisor responsible for the care and welfare of 200 girls

19-- - 19--
English Teacher
HAZELWICK COMPREHENSIVE SCHOOL,
Crawley, England
Duties:
- responsible for 11-19 year age group
- on the committee responsible for external examination marking and standardization

19-- - 19--
Teacher of English and History
DUNRAVEN COMPREHENSIVE SCHOOL, London, England
Duties:
- also class teacher responsible for 11-15 year age group

INTERESTS/HOBBIES
Reading, crafts, music, history, and home decorating

Remember that your personal data sheet will need constant updating. As you gain more experience, you may wish to focus on skills rather than chronology.

Be prepared to give references if asked, but it is not necessary to include references on your personal data sheet. Make sure you have three references available from people who have given you permission to use them as references.

Steps in Preparing a Personal Data Sheet

1. Collect all your information. If you have been out of school for some time, you may need to search your memory for dates. The same goes for dates relating to work experience.
2. Do not leave any gaps in time! If you had a number of short-term, part-time jobs, you can put them all together. For example:

   19--–-- Various temporary part-time jobs in the Post Office, as a truck driver, as a sales clerk, to gain experience.

   Or

   19--–-- At home full time with young children.
3. If you have not had a full-time job before, detail any volunteer work or activities you have participated in (church, community, political) to let the prospective employers know your abilities. You'll be surprised at what you have done! Helping in day-care centres, reading to shut-ins, door-to-door collecting for charity are all important activities.
4. Once you have a complete list of everything you have done, and of your skills or abilities, select those items that are of real importance to the job you are seeking. For example, if you are applying for a job in advertising, you might want to emphasize your creativity and flexibility; whereas if you are applying for a job with a law firm, you might want to emphasize your reliability and sense of confidentiality.
5. Make your résumé attractive by using ruled lines to set off special points. Display is very important. The examples of some imaginative résumés shown here should help you design your own personal data sheet so that it will receive attention.
6. There must be *no errors* in a personal data sheet!

Mini-Test

Prepare your own personal data sheet. Collect all the information necessary and arrange it in rough draft; then try two or three different ways of displaying the information. Try to use only one page, but do not sacrifice appearance by crowding; use two pages or more if necessary. Check your own work carefully and ask your instructor for suggestions on how to improve your personal data sheet. Keep this as you will need it for Exercise 7.10 on page 313,

SUMMARY FOR UNIT 7.10

- Applications for jobs are very important letters.

  They must be:
  - attractive
  - original
  - correct in every way
  - pertinent
- Ask for a interview – you can give more details then.
- A personal data sheet or résumé consists of:
  - a heading
  - details of education
  - details of work experience
  - summary of special skills or abilities
  - other activities or interests
  - references – attached or available on request
- Do not leave any gaps – account for all your time.
- Change the emphasis depending on the job applied for.
- Make sure your data sheet is attractive and correct in every way.

Confirm Your Knowledge

Complete Exercise for Unit 7.10 on page 313.

7.11 Memos and Notices

Memos

Correspondence within a company is often informal and written on special interoffice memorandum forms. These forms usually have a printed heading that contains the company name and four subheadings: *To, From, Date,* and *Subject*. If no printed form is available, the four subheadings are all that is required.

Memos are generally shorter than letters because the attention paragraph is often the subject line. Although memos are written informally, the "Seven Cs" and other principles of letter writing must be considered.

Memos are written to supply or request information that concerns only the staff of that business. They may be used in the following situations:

1. To request or supply information.
2. To announce staff changes, plant or office reorganization, or changes in company policy.
3. To write a short, informal report.

Memos quite often begin "This is to inform you..." or "I am happy to announce..."

Remember that memos must always be signed or initialled.

Sample Memos

The following samples are set up in styles generally acceptable. Many companies have their own style manual which clearly outlines the way in which memos are to be displayed. If you are not sure, refer to previous memos in the company files for guidance or consult a keyboarding text or reference manual for exact details.

CANADIAN BUSINESS INDUSTRIES LIMITED

Interoffice Memorandum

To: Mr. R.G. Wang
Montreal Regional Office
Date: October 23, 19--

From: Joanne Wilson
Moncton, NB

Subject: Visit to Montreal – November 15

This is to let you know that I plan to visit Montreal on November 15, 19--, and would like to spend some time with you to discuss plans for next summer.

Would you please let me know by October 31 whether this is a convenient date for you and also what time would suit you best for our meeting.

J.W.

ag

CANADIAN BUSINESS INDUSTRIES LIMITED

Inter-Departmental Correspondence

To: Ms. Joanne Wilson
Moncton, NB
Date: October 26, 19--

From: R.G. Wang
Montreal Regional Office

Subject: Your visit – November 15, 19--

I confirm that November 15 will be suitable for meeting with you to discuss next summer's plans.

I have set aside two hours for our discussion from 10 a.m. to 12 noon. I have also reserved a table for lunch in the dining room so that if necessary we can continue our discussion over lunch.

Your timing is excellent: Since we have just received outlines from Toronto of their plans for next year, we should have plenty to talk about. I shall send you some of the materials we received so that you will have a chance to study them before your visit.

R.G.W.

SR

Notices

Notices are similar to memos in that they concern only the staff, not anyone outside the company. They may be written in memo form, but more often they are designed in an original way to attract attention. The wording of a notice must be complete and correct in all details including spelling.

Notices are used to announce company picnics, the opening of new premises, the appointment of new staff, and similar occasions.

Sample of a Notice

GRAND OPENING

Come and join us for the official opening of the brand new Mapleview Tennis Association clubhouse.

Date: Saturday, May 30

Time: 11 a.m.

Place: 485 Lever Street

Refreshments • Free Draws • Door Prizes • Balloons

Bring the whole family!

Mini-Test

Are the following statements true or false? Circle *T* if true; circle *F* if false.

1. Memos are written among people within the same organization. T F
2. Memos follow the usual principles of letter writing. T F
3. Notices are used for special announcements to attract attention. T F
4. It is not necessary to sign or initial a memo. T F
5. Apart from the company name, there are only three pieces of information to be included in the heading of a memo: *To, From,* and *Date.* T F

KEY

1.T 2.T 3.T 4.F 5.F

Mini-Test

Make a plan, rough draft, and the final memo, using appropriate headings, for the following situation. The chart for evaluating a memo is slightly different; check your own work before you have it evaluated by someone else.

You asked your supervisor this morning if you could have two days off next month to attend your sister's wedding in California. Your supervisor asked you to put your request in writing. Write a memo to your supervisor (instructor) giving all the necessary details so that plans can be made for your absence.

Purpose

___

___

Plan

___

___

___

___

___

___

___

___

Evaluation Chart	Your Score	Checker's Score
Well-prepared plan		
Clear		
Complete		
Concise		
Correct		
Attractively set up		
Total		
Deduction for errors missed		
Final Total		

SUMMARY FOR UNIT 7.11

- Memos are the most common form of business correspondence
- Memos are usually written informally but still must conform to the "seven Cs" and other principles of good letter writing.
- Memos are usually written on preprinted forms with space in the heading for *To, From, Date,* and *Subject*; memos written on plain paper must also contain these headings.
- Notices may be designed artistically to attract attention to special occasions

Confirm Your Knowledge

Complete Exercise for Unit 7.11 on page 315.

❍ 7.12 Reports

Reports are written communications containing the results of surveys, details of sales trips, financial information, facts concerning ongoing projects, and many other types of information.

Informal reports are usually short and written in memo form. Formal reports are usually quite long and are organized in a formal style for presentation.

Informal Reports

Many informal reports such as expense reports are written on special forms. If no form is available, a simple memo is used to make the report. Write objectively, using *I* or *we*, presenting the information clearly and concisely in point form wherever possible. Be sure to check your report for grammatical errors.

A review of Unit 7.11 covering Memos will help you to write informal reports.

Formal Reports

Because a formal report may be very complex and contain the results of extensive research, its organization is very important. A formal report not only gives the facts, but may draw conclusions and make recommendations.

The Parts of a Formal Report.

1. A cover
2. A title page (with title of the report, the author, and the date)
3. Table of Contents
4. Lists of illustrations and tables (if included)
5. Summary
6. Body of the report broken down into sections
7. Any appendices
8. Any bibliography
9. Index (if required)

Refer to a report-writing text or an office systems and procedures text such as *The Canadian Office: Systems & Procedures* for the exact details of format and content of the different parts.

Sample Title Page for a Report

Kyoshi, Parent Inc.

MARKET AND BANKING TRENDS

THEIR EFFECT ON FIVE-YEAR PROJECTIONS

Submitted to

Faith McDowell
Executive Vice-President, Finance
October 27, 19--

Prepared by

Emma Lorenz
Corporate Research Officer
Research & Planning Department

Sample Table of Contents for a Report

TABLE OF CONTENTS

Recommended Writing Suggestions

- Collect all the relevant data; check all data thoroughly before starting to write.
- Make a detailed outline to organize the material. This will be the basis of the Table of Contents.
- Include an introduction and a conclusion.
- Break down each section into sub-sections, if appropriate, using paragraphs for easier reading. (See Unit 7.2 for paragraphing.)
- Report facts only, not personal opinions.
- Define any special terminology and use graphs if necessary to make your report more easily understood.
- Include footnotes and bibliography where necessary.
- Be sure your report is correct in grammar, spelling, and punctuation.

Mini-Test

Are the following statements true or false? If true, circle *T*; if false, circle *F*.

1. A report is a way of giving information in written form. T F
2. Informal reports are short, often written on special forms or interoffice memos. T F
3. Your own opinions are as important as the facts in report writing. T F
4. Before you begin writing a formal report, you must arrange your material carefully and make a detailed outline. T F
5. Headings, subheadings, and tables are not often used in formal reports. T F

KEY

1. T 2. T 3. F 4. T 5. F

SUMMARY FOR UNIT 7.12

- Reports are written to make sure that information is recorded and easily available.
- Informal reports include:
  - expense accounts
  - daily or weekly records of sales calls
  - replies to requests for information from within the organization
  - progress reports
  - inventory reports
- Formal reports follow a special format, details of which you will find in an office manual or advanced keyboarding text.
- The steps in preparing formal reports are:
  - Collect and arrange information.
  - Make a detailed outline, including an introduction and a summary.
  - Use headings, subheadings, and graphs.
  - Use facts only, not opinions.
  - Remember to include a conclusion and recommendations.
  - Check carefully for clarity, completeness, and accuracy.
  - Keep your report as short as possible!

Confirm Your Knowledge

Complete Exercise for Unit 7.12 on page 316.

Supplementary Letters for Unit 7.4

Request Letters

1. Write to Terrific Ticket Printing to request quotes for printing the tickets for your upcoming theatre season. Your theatre seats 400 people and you need tickets for four different shows, each to run for five nights and one matinee. Matinee tickets will be lower in price. Ask the printing company to suggest a design that fits within your budget of approximately $100.
2. Write to a local travel agent asking for information concerning the best way to arrange for a sales conference in Toronto. You are inviting all the sales personnel from your regional offices across Canada. You do have a limited budget, but you would like to have some indication of the differences in cost between air and rail or bus travel. The conference is to be from 9 a.m. Monday, September 15, to 12 noon Friday, September 20.
3. Write to the Director of Personnel of a large company for information on the type of training the company offers its employees who want to enter the field of personnel work.
4. Write to a local college or university asking for an interview with a placement officer. You would like to outline the employment opportunities with CBIL for graduates.

Replies to Requests

1. CBIL has just advertised a new kind of tape that will adhere to all surfaces; however, it won't be ready for the market for approximately six months. You have been inundated with requests for prices, delivery dates, particulars of guarantees, etc. Prepare a letter suitable for all inquiries explaining the situation and advising that you will write again as soon as details are established.
2. CBIL manufactures minicomputers, and you have received a request from a student for any materials you have that will help him in his project on the computer industry in your province. Reply, telling him that you are presently out of stock of literature but will send something later on.

Supplementary Letters for Unit 7.5

Order Letters

1. Write to the Community News Agency at an address in your area ordering ten copies of a weekly paper *The Mirror* and two copies of *Trends in Business*, a bi-monthly magazine. These are to be delivered to your office and you will pay for three months in advance if they will send you an invoice. Delivery is to start with the first issues of next month.
2. Your boss is retiring and your colleagues have asked you to order a silver tray, catalogue No. 1150, from a local jeweler. You want the tray to be inscribed "On Your Retirement – from your friends at CBIL." The tray costs $315.00 to which tax has to be added. Enclose a cheque with your order. Remember to state when you will need the tray.
3. Write to a local stationer ordering a supply of at least four different items, such as paper clips, needed for your desk. Be sure to be specific in your details; you can check descriptions from supplies you already have, from advertisements in magazines or newspapers, or from a stationery catalogue. Remember payment, delivery, and date details.

Acknowledgment of Order Letters

1. You have just received an order from Califone Industries Limited, 1305 Odlum Drive, Vancouver, BC V5L 3M1, for 3 marble pen and pencil desk sets, priced at $54.95 each. You are currently out of stock of these sets, but you can supply 3 black and brass sets at $45.95 each if there is an immediate need for the sets. The marble ones will be available in four weeks' time.
2. Write to the local hospital thanking them for the order for scotch tape. You appreciate the size of the order and look forward to supplying more of their office needs in the future.

Supplementary Letters for Unit 7.6

Credit Letters

1. A well-known businesswoman in your city has sent an order to CBIL for $2000 worth of supplies. You have not had business with this person before, but her credit references are excellent. Write to the person concerned thanking her for her order and explaining your credit arrangements. Be sure to mention a credit limit.
2. Write a letter suitable for sending to all customers who have not bought anything from you for over a year. You would be sending this letter only to customers whose credit rating had been satisfactory and from whom you would like to hear again.
3. Mr. Marcel Simard, of 6351 Chester Avenue, Montreal, Quebec H4V 1J6, has ordered a new electric typewriter with a memory feature. He would like delivery by the end of the month. However, Mr. Simard has not yet paid his account amounting to $547.95, which has been overdue for two months. Explain to Mr. Simard that you cannot grant him any more credit until he pays off his outstanding bill.

Collection Letters

1. Pedro Sampras, a long-time customer of CBIL who usually pays his bills promptly, has fallen behind with his current account. He now owes $765.43 which is 60 days overdue. One reminder was sent two weeks ago, but he has not replied. It is so unusual for Mr. Sampras to be late in paying that the credit manager has decided to write a letter asking for an explanation. If the customer needs some help in meeting this bill, let him ask for it, but be careful not to make any promises. Stress the need for keeping his credit standing intact, but also stress the need for payment.
3. Design a collection letter that will attract attention in an amusing way to be sent to customers who usually pay on time but who currently owe a small balance. Be original in your wording, making sure you mention the amount that is owing
3. As publicity director for a small theatre company, write a letter to collect for unpaid program advertisements. Emphasize how successful the production was and how many people saw the show and read the program. As you are a non-profit organization, be sure to thank the advertiser for the support given to your company.

Supplementary Letters for Unit 7.7

Claim Letters

1. CBIL today received a shipment of 6000 light bulbs from Look Brite Manufacturing Co., 11 Princess Street, Amherst, NS B4H 1W5. Unfortunately, at least half of the bulbs were broken because of poor packaging. Write a letter to Look Brite asking for a refund of $600 to cover the breakages. You do not want a replacement as you needed the bulbs immediately and had to buy them locally.
2. Write a claim to a local transport company for damage done to one of CBIL's loading docks. The driver backed into a lighted sign causing $175 worth of damage.

Adjustment Letters

1. Ms. Rozanne Jarvis bought insulating tape from CBIL and has returned it claiming that it will not adhere to any surface. On examination it is evident the tape has been immersed in water for some time. Explain to Ms. Jarvis that water will destroy the glue on the back of the tape, but that once the tape has been firmly attached it will effectively keep water out. We are not accepting liability for this claim as the tape is shipped in watertight containers and clearly marked "Keep Dry."
2. Cedars Brae Restaurant near you recently asked for 32 brown uniforms for its waitresses and inadvertently CBIL sent green uniforms. As the order clearly stated brown, we are sending the correct uniforms by special courier today. Write a letter explaining what happened.

Supplementary Letters for Unit 7.8

Sales Letters

1. You have designed a gadget for helping people with arthritis in their hands to do up buttons. Your gadget has been very well received in seniors' homes and centres and is widely marketed in the large cities. You would now like to see it available in smaller cities across the country. Write a letter to the directors of Chambers of Commerce in various places describing your gadget, how it works, and the price and asking them to send you a list of prospective retailers in their areas.
2. Write a letter to Mrs. Louise Jefferson, who has bought duplicating equipment from CBIL in the past. You know she would be interested in the latest model just on the market. Describe the equipment to her (look in business magazines for details) and ask her if you may come to give a demonstration.
3. CBIL has purchased a recreational club in your neighbourhood suitable for all ages. A number of activities and a variety of facilities are available at all times of the day and evenings seven days a week. Membership fees are very reasonable. Write a letter that will encourage people to join the club and take part in the activities.

Supplementary Letters for Unit 7.9

Goodwill and Public Relations Letters

1. Write a letter of sympathy to Mr. Jacques Villeneuve, maître d' of La Ronde, a French restaurant next door to your office. The restaurant had a fire last night and will have to be closed for two weeks for repair. You often go there for lunch with others from the office. Assure Mr. Villeneuve you look forward to his reopening. Is there any way in which you might help?
2. You were stranded in The Pas with no transportation and had an urgent appointment in Winnipeg. Mr. Sharp, the owner of a small private plane, arranged for you to be flown to Winnipeg in plenty of time. Write a letter to Mr. Sharp, P.O. Box 150, The Pas, MN R9A 1K3, giving your appreciation for the consideration he gave you.
3. Maria Rossi, the branch manager in Halifax, was director of the local United Appeal drive, which exceeded its goal by a wide margin. Write a letter of congratulations to Ms. Rossi.

Supplementary Memos for Unit 7.11

1. Write a memo to the Regina or Winnipeg Office asking for their help in supplying you with transistor batteries. Your supplier has let you down and you desperately need batteries of all sizes for the holiday season. Can the Regina or Winnipeg Office let you know where you should go for your requirements? Specifics of your requirements are enclosed on a separate sheet.
2. Assume that you are overstocked on 2 m extension cords with three-prong plugs. Write a memo to all the branches in your area asking if they would like to help you reduce your inventory. You are willing to trade or to sell them at 30 percent discount (that is, $1.50 per cord).
3. Write a memo to all members of your staff advising them that as of Monday next free parking on the company's lot will be discontinued. Charges for parking will be $1.50 per day, but with a company sticker the charge will be only 50 cents. Stickers may be obtained from the personnel office at no charge. There are only a limited number of parking spaces, and these will be allocated on a first come, first served basis.
4. Write a memo to your supervisor (instructor) making a suggestion for improving a particular routine in the company.

DEVELOPING YOUR LANGUAGE SKILLS

❍ 7.13 Vocabulary

Definitions

Check your dictionary for the meanings of the following words; then match them up with the definitions given. Write the letter of the definition you choose from Column 2 in the space provided in Column 1.

Column 1	Column 2
___ perforate	a) appropriate, to the point
___ persuade	b) probability of happening
___ pertinent	c) punch with holes
___ perusal	d) begin, start
___ tentative	e) add to, complete
___ potential	f) try to influence, convince
___ supplement	g) plan of travel
___ itinerary	h) prepare from nothing, make do
___ initiate	i) experimental, as a tryout
___ improvise	j) a reading or scanning

Mini-Test

Complete the following sentences by choosing the most appropriate word from Column 1 under "Definitions."

1. Keep your remarks _______________ to the point of discussion.
2. Would you please _______________ the forms along the dotted line for easy tearing off.
3. I shall try to _______________ him that you have earned a raise.
4. Mr. Graves would like a copy of your _______________ for your trip to Europe.
5. A fast _______________ of the will shows the estate to be worth almost $3 million.
6. We plan to _______________ proceedings ourselves as no one else seems willing to take the first step.
7. Although talks are not over yet, the two sides have reached a _______________ agreement.
8. On a rainy day, you can _______________ an umbrella from a newspaper.
9. Tablets are used by many people today to _______________ their daily intake of vitamins.
10. There is a good _______________ for attracting large numbers of visitors if we use radio and television advertising.

KEY

1. pertinent 2. perforate 3. persuade 4. itinerary 5. perusal 6. initiate 7. tentative 8. improvise 9. supplement 10. potential

Usage

Study the following words carefully so that you are fully aware of the differences and can use them correctly.

principal/principle

principal–the animal (person-noun)	the principal of a school
–the amount (money-noun)	the principal and interest
–the m*a*in thing (as an *a*djective)	the principal reason

Hint: Remember all the *a*s!

principle–rule, standard of conduct	a principle of mathematics; a person of high principles

respectfully/respectively

respectfully – with respect	Welcome prospective customers respectfully.
respectively – in order	Ms. Zavitz and Mr. Bittel asked for coffee and tea respectively. Ms. Zavitz asked for coffee; Mr. Bittel, tea.)

rite/right/write

rite–a ceremony	marriage rites
right –privilege	the right to remain silent
–correct	the right answer
–opposite of left	on the right side
write –communicate by writing	Please write to Mr. Howard.

stationary/stationery

stationary – fixed in place	A p*a*rked c*a*r is station*a*ry
stationery – writing supplies	The station*e*r sells stationery

weather/whether

weather – atmospheric conditions	The weather is good today.
whether – choice of two	I cannot decide whether to work or play tennis.

Mini-Test

Complete the following sentences by choosing the correct word from those shown at the beginning of the sentences.

1. *principle/principal*

   The law is based on the _______________ that work expands to fill the time available.

   What is the _______________ obligation of agents to their _______________ ?

   My _______________ difficulty is in calculating the interest payable on the _______________ still owing. The school _______________ is a person of strong moral _______________ .

2. *respectively/respectfully*

   May we _______________ remind you that your first and second installments are due on June 1 and June 15 _______________ .

3. *rite/right/write*

   Please _______________ a short description of the particular burial _______________ you will speak about.

   If you are _______________ , we shall exercise our _______________ to ask for a retrial.

4. *stationary/stationery*

   The _______________ supplies are in the cupboard. The market is stable at the moment and prices are _______________ .

5. *weather/whether*

   _______________ you like it or not, the _______________ will not stop the garden party being held on Saturday.

KEY

1. principle; principal, principal; principal; principal, Principal, principle 2. respectfully, respectively 3. write, rite; right, right 4. stationery; stationary 5. Whether, weather

Spelling

The final spelling list contains long-time favourites for spelling quizzes and evaluation tests. Study these words very carefully paying particular attention to the letters in italics. Write them out ten times each and be sure again that you know the meaning of each word.

Favourites for Spelling Tests

privil*ege*	techn*ique*	*sei*ze
mis*cell*aneous	proc*ed*ure	ga*u*ge
mischiev*ous*	gover*n*ment	di*ss*atisfied
para*ll*el	ben*e*ficial	acknowl*edg*ment
super*sede*	cons*c*ient*io*us	*critic*ism

Mini-Test

Correct any errors in the following words.

1. mischievious	procedure	conscientious
2. supersede	goverment	gauge
3. seize	priviledge	technique
4. benificial	parallel	criticism
5. disatisfied	miscellaneous	acknowledgment

KEY

1.mischievous – This error usually results from mispronunciation. Take care! 2.government – The suffix "-ment" is just added to the root word. 3. priviledge – Be really sure of this one. 4. benificial – from bene meaning "good: 5. disatisfied – The prefix "dis-" is just added to the root word.

SUMMARY FOR UNIT 7.13

- Your dictionary is indispensable – keep using it!
- Be sure of *principal* and *principle.*
- You will use a lot of *stationary whether* you move along or remain *stationary* in your career.
- Good spelling is vitally important; all the words you have been studying in these units must be thoroughly known.

Confirm Your Knowledge

Complete Exercise for Unit 7.13 on page 317.

❍ 7.14 Proofreading

Spotting Errors

Proofreading requires paying attention to detail, examining the material letter for letter, and making sure it makes sense. Even with very careful reading, however, you may miss an error. This unit will point out areas where errors often are undetected.

Line Ends

Check particularly line beginnings and line ends for errors of omission or duplication. Always, of course, check for keying errors!

> Customs officials at the Canadian-U.S border at
> at Niagara Falls confiscated all of the luggage
> for Mr. Ames even though he had made out a
> declaration form correctly.

Lines Omitted

Reading carefully for content will usually locate an omitted line. However, occasionally the content will make sense even though a large section has been left out. Checking the material line by line, word by word, is the only way to be absolutely sure nothing has been left out.

> Customs officials at the Canadian-U.S. border at
> Mr. Ames even though he had made out a dec-
> laration from correctly.

Errors in Headings

Column headings, side headings, page headings, addresses and dates on letters, and footnotes should be especially carefully checked as errors are often overlooked in these parts.

Quatity Description Unt Cost Total Cost

CANADAN RESOURCES Page10

Mrs. Ruby Bridges Febuary 18, 19

10 Brent Boulevard

Halifax, NB

B2N 5E3

Yours truly,

Manger

Errors in Content

Accuracy of content must always be checked. Simple dates, sums of money, totals, or other easily checked facts can be confirmed by the proofreader; however, technical material or complicated tables, lists, statistical material, legal or scientific documents should always be checked by two or more people working as a team. It cannot be overemphasized how easy it is to overlook errors in one's own work. Always have someone else check anything you are not absolutely sure about!

Clusters of Errors

You will find that quite often errors are clustered together. Whenever you find an error, therefore, be even more careful in checking the next few words. Errors often occur at the very beginning or at the very end of a long passage of keying.

Mini-Test

Are the following statements true or false? If true, circle *T*; if false, circle *F*.

1. Totals, dates, and sums of money should always be checked carefully. T F
2. Lines omitted are usually easily found, but sometimes the content will make sense even though a part has been left out. T F
3. Legal and highly technical material should be checked by two people. T F
4. Errors often occur in clusters or at the beginning or end of lines. T F
5. It is very easy to find errors in your own work. T F

KEY

1.T 2.T 3.T 4.T 5.F

Review of Proofreading Routines

1. Expect errors and you will find them. *Concentrate!*
2. Check first for content and meaning:
   - –accuracy of data
   - –grammar
   - –correct use of words
   - –no lines or words omitted
3. Check second for keying errors:
   - –spelling and punctuation
   - –transpositions
   - –wrong spacing
   - –general set-up
4. Check again:
   - –spelling
   - –punctuation

Review of Proofreading Methods

- Use a ruler and a pencil to guide you as you read.
- Use the eraser end of a pencil or some other non-metallic object to help you proofread a screen.
- Check copied material line by line with the original, using the left hand on the original and right hand on the copy.
- Have someone else check the copy while you read aloud from the original giving all the punctuation.
- *Always* have figures in statistical work checked with someone else. Totals *must* also be checked.
- Read tables *across the* page, not down the columns.

Mini-Test

Proofread the following letter very carefully using proofreaders' marks to make corrections where necessary. Be sure to check for all kinds of errors.

Dear Miss Creek:

Thank you for your inquiry on February 12 about the number of fast-food outlets in this area.I hope the following information wil be of some assistance to you,

Type of Food Served	No of locations
Hamburgers	15
Submarine Sandwiches	9
Pizza	12
Chinees food	7
Deep Fried Chicken	8
Fish and Chips	11
Total fast-food outlets	61

If you would like any further help with your project I would be delightd to help you. Just give me a call at 75-58833.

Yours sincerly,

KEY

There are 10 errors. Did you notice that the second paragraph was not indented? If you cannot find all the errors, you will appreciate the need for very careful proofreading.

SUMMARY FOR UNIT 7.14

- Check these special areas for errors:
  - line beginnings and line ends
  - headings – column headings, side heading, page headings
    - names and addresses, dates
    - footnotes
  - clusters – errors usually occur close together
  - beginnings and ends of long documents
- Take special care in checking content.
  - Check dates and times.
  - Check sums of money, prices, and total costs.
  - Check *all* figures very carefully – with a partner or in a team.
- Review proofreading routines.
- Review proofreading methods.

Confirm Your Knowledge

Complete Exercise for Unit 7.14 on page 318.

PRETEST FOR UNIT 7

Complete all the parts of this test according to the directions for each part. The figures in parentheses are the unit number for reference, if necessary, when you have completed the test.

Your Goal: To score a total of at least 40 points.

A. General Rules

Are the following statements true or false? If true, circle *T*; if false, circle *F*. Score 1 point for each correct answer.

			Score
1.	The purpose of all business letters is to get the reader to react in the way you want. (7.3)	**T F**	_____
2.	The first step in planning a letter is to define the purpose of the letter clearly. (7.2)	**T F**	_____
3.	The preparation of a plan in point form is not important in preparing to write a letter. (7.2)	**T F**	_____
4.	A paragraph should contain only one idea and be fairly short. (7.2)	**T F**	_____
5.	The opening paragraph is very important as it attracts the reader's attention. (7.2)	**T F**	_____
6.	Letters of application should not include a request for an interview.(7.10)	**T F**	_____
7.	Each letter should be checked for a positive point of view as well as the Seven Cs. (7.3)	**T F**	_____
8.	The closing paragraph describes the action to be taken by the reader or the writer. (7.2)	**T F**	_____
9.	The only details necessary when you are ordering goods are complete details of what you want. (7.5)	**T F**	_____
10.	It is not necessary to state the amount the customer owes in a collection letter because the customer knows. (7.6)	**T F**	_____
		Score for Part A	_____

B. Letters and Memos

Prepare a plan, a rough draft, and a final letter or memo for *two* of the following situations. Check your final letter or memo against the evaluation chart. Have someone else check your work deducting two points for any kind of error that you missed!

Your Goal: To score at least 8 point for each letter or memo

1. Your office would like to persuade some of the merchants of a nearby shopping plaza to donate prizes for a lucky draw at the next conference you are hosting for branch managers and sales representatives from right across Canada. You would like to receive approximately 50 prizes altogether. The conference will be from March 10 to March 14, and an afternoon has been set aside for shopping. Write a request letter to one of the merchants giving all the necessary details.
2. You have just received a supply of fiberglass insulating materials from a regular supplier in your area. Unfortunately, the shipment was badly damaged and some of the material will not be usable. Write a fax to the suppliers asking them to pick up the damaged merchandise and to replace it. You need this material urgently. Be sure to include all the details necessary to be sure the supplier knows to what you are referring.
3. Write a memo to your regional manager requesting a demonstration of the latest equipment advertised in a circular you have received from the regional office. This equipment will not be available for sale until the new year, but you would like to be fully aware of what it can do before you go out and sell it. Suggest a time and place that would be convenient to you and provide any other details you consider relevant.

Letter

Evaluation Chart	Your Score	Checker's Score
Well-prepared plan		
Good opening paragraph		
Considerate		
Clear in meaning		
Complete in detail		
Ideas expressed concisely		
Positive, not negative		
Attractively set up		
No trite expressions		
Good closing paragraph		
Total		
Deductions for errors missed or for untidy final letter		
Final Total		

Memo

Evaluation Chart	Your Score	Checker's Score
Clear		
Complete		
Concise		
Correct		
Attractively set up		
Total		
Deduct for errors missed or for untidy memo		
Final Total		

Score for Part B _____

C. Vocabulary (7.13)

Check the following sentences carefully for errors in word usage or spelling. Make any necessary corrections. If a sentence is correct as written, write *C* beside it. Score 1 point for each correct sentence.

Score

1. Place orders for stationery at the supplies desk. _____
2. I shall write to you confirming the new procedure. _____
3. His critisism of the government's plan is well founded. _____
4. May I respectively remind you that we have not received your signed agreement yet. _____
5. What technicque should we develop for checking stress? _____
6. Ms. Ramsay would like to know wether the samples will be ready by May 10. _____
7. The principal of digital electronics is not difficult to understand. _____
8. We are looking for a conscientious worker to be responsible for the incoming and outgoing mail. _____
9. Mr. Chen's bulletin dated June 6 supersedes the one he issued on May 29. _____
10. We take pride in never having a disatisfied customer. _____

Score for Part C _____

D. Proofreading (7.14)

Proofread the following letters very carefully using proofreaders' marks to make corrections where necessary. Be sure to check for all kinds of errors. Score 1 point for each error marked correctly; deduct 1 point for each error missed!

Dear Sir:

I am interested in finding out more about the courses you have advertised on electronics in Saturday's issue of *the News*. I understand you are offering courses in all phases of electronics, from CB radio to digital.

I have been a ham radio operator for 6 years and want to turn this hobby into a profitable career. I have just recently retire from permanent employment and now have time available for full-time study. If at all possible however, I would prefer to take a correspondence course. I realize that much of the work demands practical application, but I have access to an electronics laboratory where I could do experiments under the supervision of a very reliable electronics engineer.

This may seem strange to you, but I assure you that I am serious in my undetraking. All I want from your school is an outline of study and texts, exercises, experiments, and tests to support that outline. I am not able to attend classes for other reasons, much as I would like to.

Please give my request your consideration; I hope that we can work something out.

Yours truly,

Order Depardment

Please send by Courier the following blouses to reach me by April 30 for my summer sale:

Quantity and Size	Catalogue No.	Colour	Unit Cost	Total Cos
6 size 10	10555	Peach	$25.00	$125.00
6 size 12	12556	Mint	25.00	125.00
6 size 14	14555	Peach	25.00	135.00
6 size 16	16556	Mint	25.00	125.00
				$400.00

Please charge to my account No. 3377-4444.

Yours truly,

Number of errors found and correctly marked _____

Deduct for errors missed _____

Score for Part D _____

Total Score _____

If you achieved your goal of at least 40 points, you have completed the work in this textbook. Congratulations! If you did not score at least 40 points, review Unit 7 thoroughly; then do the Posttest for Unit 7 and try to achieve your goal this time.

POSTTEST FOR UNIT 7

Complete all the parts of this test according to the directions for each part. The figures in parentheses are the unit numbers for reference, if necessary, when you have completed the test.

Your Goal: To score a total of at least 40 points.

A. General Rules

Are the following statements true or false? If true, circle *T*; if false, circle *F*. Score 1 point for each correct answer.

			Score
1.	A return address must be included in a handwritten letter. (7.1)	**T F**	_____
2.	Before you try to write any letter, you should collect all the necessary information. (7.2)	**T F**	_____
3.	It is a good idea to write a rough draft from a plan before writing a final letter. (7.2)	**T F**	_____
4.	Although paragraphs should be short, you should avoid a succession of two-line paragraphs. (7.2)	**T F**	_____
5.	It is not necessary to consider the person who will be receiving the letter. (7.3)	**T F**	_____
6.	Letters asking for information should be written in general terms with no specific questions. (7.4)	**T F**	_____
7.	In denying a request, you should say so in the first paragraph and not waste time offering help. (7.4)	**T F**	_____
8.	A question often makes a good closing paragraph. (7.2)	**T F**	_____
9.	It is not necessary to say how you are going to pay in an order letter. (7.5)	**T F**	_____
10.	Application letters should include a request for an interview. (7.10)	**T F**	_____
		Score for Part	_____

B. Letters and Memos

Prepare a plan, a rough draft, and a final letter or memo for *two* of the following situations. Check your final letter or memo against the evaluation chart. Have someone else check your work deducting *two* points for any kind of error that you missed!

Your Goal: To score at least 8 points for each letter or memo.

1. You have been asked to write to the editor of a local paper requesting permission to reprint an article entitled "How to Use Your Money Wisely" which appeared in last Wednesday's paper. Your company wants to include this article in its monthly magazine for employees, and you would be willing to pay a reasonable fee. Include any other details you think are appropriate.
2. Three months ago, you were charged for six calls you did not make to cities in the United States. Write a letter to the local telephone company complaining that your telephone bill has still not been corrected although you have called about the error on three occasions. Be specific in identifying the calls, the dates of your complaints, and the action you expect the company to take or that you will take if the error is not corrected.
3. Write a memo to your supervisor outlining a suggestion you have for improving your work area. If you are suggesting adding furniture or equipment, be sure to include a rough estimate of the cost. Include as many details as you can pointing out the advantages of such changes.

Letter

Evaluation Chart	Your Score	Checker's Score
Well-prepared plan		
Good opening paragraph		
Considerate		
Clear in meaning		
Complete in detail		
Ideas expressed concisely		
Positive, not negative		
Attractively set up		
No trite expressions		
Good closing paragraph		
Total		
Deductions for errors missed or for untidy final letter		
Final Total		

Memo

Evaluation Chart	Your Score	Checker's Score
Clear		
Complete		
Concise		
Correct		
Attractively set up		
Total		
Deduct for errors missed or for untidy memo		
Final Total		

Score for Part B ______

C. Vocabulary (7.13)

Check the following sentences carefully for errors in word usage or spelling. Make any necessary corrections. If a sentence is correct as written, write *C* beside it. Score 1 point for each correct sentence.

Score

1. A rubber mat under the machine will keep it stationery. ______
2. List small expenditures under "Miscellaneous" in the ledger. ______
3. The principle reason for the delay was the rail strike. ______
4. The host respectfully referred to his guest as a well-known politician. ______
5. Tax returns must be submitted to the goverment by April 30. ______
6. Space flights that are returning to land require perfect wether conditions for reentry ______
7. The principal and interest on your loan have now been reduced by $1500. ______
8. What gage of wire is required for that job? ______
9. The customs officers will seize any illegal goods being smuggled across the border. ______
10. Please write down the proceedures in detail. ______

Score for Part C ______

D. Proofreading

Proofread the following letters very carefully using proofreaders' marks to make corrections where necessary. Be sure to check for all kinds of errors. Score 1 point for each error marked correctly; deduct 1 point for each error missed!

Dear Ms. Blakeney:

Thankyou very much indeed for the most interesting presentation you made at our recent convention. It is thrilling to hear from someone so involved with current advances in technology how these advances will affect our lives.

It is not so long ago that people were awed by the thought of space travel, yet such an idea is certainly not outside the bounds of possibility today. One a smaller scale, electronic developments in industry and commerce are taken for granted already. Such technology is becoming available for the private user in the home, and the future holds endless opportunities for those willing to learn and adapt to this new era.

We live in exiting times Ms. Blakeney, and We really appreciate your bringing us a little further up-to-date.

Yours truly,

Dear Mr. Leakie:

I am returning to you the following shirts that were recieved in a damaged condition:

Quantity	Descriptiom	Type of Damage
3	Arrow 15-33	Buttons missing
2	Cardin 16-35	Sleeve seams open

Please replace these with exactly the same shirts in perfect condition.

Would you please also let me have some more order forms as I am ready to make up my order for the christmas season.

Yours truly,

Number of errors found and correctly marked _____

Deduct for errors missed _____

Score for Part D _____

Total Score _____

If you achieved your goal of a least 40 points, you have completed the work in this textbook. Congratulations! If you did not score at least 40, ask your instructor for direction.

EXERCISE 7.2 PLANS AND PARAGRAPHS

Part A

Are the following statements true or false? If true, circle *T*; if false, circle *F*. Score 1 point for each correct answer.

Your Goal: To score at least 8 points.

	Statement		Score
1.	The first step in planning a letter is to write down the purpose of the letter.	**T F**	_____
2.	It is not necessary to attract the reader's attention in the first paragraph.	**T F**	_____
3.	A paragraph should contain only one idea.	**T F**	_____
4.	The "D" in the acronym *AIDA* stands for "desire" or "details."	**T F**	_____
5.	A plan should contain full, complete grammatical sentences.	**T F**	_____
6.	A paragraph should not be longer than six or seven lines.	**T F**	_____
7.	The action required is usually stated in the middle paragraph.	**T F**	_____
8.	A business letter usually has three or more paragraphs.	**T F**	_____
9.	A good opening paragraph where appropriate is "Thank you for..."	**T F**	_____
10.	A question should never be used as a final paragraph.	**T F**	_____
		Score for Part A	_____

If you achieved your goal of at least 8 points, proceed to Part B of this exercise. If you did not score 8, review Unit 7.2 thoroughly before moving on.

Part B

1. Make a plan in point form for each of the following letters.
2. Check your plans against the evaluation chart for each.
3. Enter your scores. (Score 1 point for each item and total both plans for final mark.)
4. Have your work checked to confirm your scores since it is very difficult to evaluate your own work objectively.

Your Goal: To score a total of at least 9 points when your plans are checked by someone else.

Plan 1

Reply to a letter from a local community organization asking you to donate prizes for a fall fair. Explain that you will have no items available in time for the fair but that another time you would be happy to help if given more notice. Wish the organizers success.

Evaluation Chart	Plan 1 Your Score	Plan 1 Checker's Score
Purpose clearly stated		
Items listed in point form		
Items arranged logically		
First item attracts attention		
Last item specifies action		
Final Total		

Plan 2

Write to a local college requesting a calendar of night school courses. You are interested in becoming a lecturer for your company and would like to take some public speaking courses. Add any other information you feel should be included.

Evaluation Chart	Plan 2 Your Score	Plan 2 Checker's Score
Purpose clearly stated		
Items listed in point form		
Items arranged logically		
First item attracts attention		
Last item specifies action		
Final Total		

After your plans have been checked and marked, show them to your instructor, who will confirm the score. If you scored at least 9 points, proceed to Unit 7.3. If you did not score 9, your instructor will give you more practice at preparing plans before you move on.

Note: Be sure to keep these plans since they are needed for the exercise in Unit 7.3.

EXERCISE 7.3 WRITING THE LETTER

From the plans prepared in Part B of Exercise 97, prepare final letters on letterhead. If you do not have these plans, the situations are repeated so that you can prepare plans before writing the final letters. Check your work carefully against the evaluation chart and enter your total; have your work checked by someone else who will check your total, deduct points for errors missed or untidiness, and enter the final total score for your letters.

Your Goal: To score at least 8 points for each letter.

Letter 1

Reply to a letter from the local community organization asking you to donate prizes for a fall fair. Explain that you will have no items available in time for the fair but that another time you would be happy to help if given more notice. Wish the organizers success.

Evaluation Chart	Your Score	Checker's Score
Well-prepared plan		
Good opening paragraph		
Considerate		
Clear in meaning		
Complete in detail		
Ideas expressed concisely		
Positive, not negative		
Attractively set up		
No trite expressions		
Good closing paragraph		
Total		
Deductions for errors missed or for untidy final letter		
Final Total		

Letter 2

Write to a local college requesting a calendar of night school courses. You are interested in becoming a lecturer for your company and would like to take some public speaking courses. Add any other information you feel should be included.

Evaluation Chart	Your Score	Checker's Score
Well-prepared plan		
Good opening paragraph		
Considerate		
Clear in meaning		
Complete in detail		
Ideas expressed concisely		
Positive, not negative		
Attractively set up		
No trite expressions		
Good closing paragraph		
Total		
Deductions for errors missed or for untidy final letter		
Final Total		

If you scored at least 8 points in each letter on someone else's evaluation, proceed to Unit 7.4. If you did not score 8 in either letter, review Unit 7.3 thoroughly before moving on.

EXERCISE 7.4 REQUEST LETTERS

Part A

Are the following statements true or false? If they are true, circle *T*; if false, circle *F*. Score 1 point for each correct answer.

Your Goal: To score at least 8 points in total for Parts A and B.

		Score
1. You must know exactly what you want when writing a request letter.	**T F**	_____
2. Don't ask direct questions.	**T F**	_____
3. Refuse a request in the first sentence.	**T F**	_____
4. Emphasize what you can do, not what you cannot do.	**T F**	_____
5. Answer letters promptly to build goodwill.	**T F**	_____
	Score for Part A	_____

Part B

Write, in correct order, the *five steps* which make up the *procedure* for writing all letters. Score 1 point for each correct step. The wording may vary slightly, but the meaning must be clear.

1. ______________________________ _____
2. ______________________________ _____
3. ______________________________ _____
4. ______________________________ _____
5. ______________________________ _____

Score for Part B _____

Score for Parts A and B _____

Part C

Following the usual procedures, prepare a plan, a rough draft, and the final letter for the following situations. Remember *AIDA* and check your letters against the evaluation charts. Have someone else evaluate your letters using the marking guidelines outlined in Unit 7.3.

Your Goal: To score at least 9 points for each letter.

Letter 1

Write to the editor of your favourite magazine asking for permission to reprint in your company newsletter an article that you thought particularly interesting. Give the title of the article and the issue of the magazine in which it appeared. As human resources director for your company, you feel that this article will be of great interest to the employees. Use your imagination to supply details.

Letter 2

As a well-known disc jockey at your local radio station, you have been asked to speak to a group of communications students at your local school or college on the good and bad points of working as a disc jockey. You would very much like to help out, but unfortunately you have a previous engagement for the night in question and therefore cannot accept. Suggest your willingness to address the group at some other time.

Purpose

Plan

Evaluation Chart	Your Score	Checker's Score
Well-prepared plan		
Good opening paragraph		
Considerate		
Clear in meaning		
Complete in detail		
Ideas expressed concisely		
Positive, not negative		
Attractively set up		
No trite expressions		
Good closing paragraph		
Total		
Deductions for errors missed or for untidy final letter		
Final Total		

Purpose

Plan

Evaluation Chart	Your Score	Checker's Score
Well-prepared plan		
Good opening paragraph		
Considerate		
Clear in meaning		
Complete in detail		
Ideas expressed concisely		
Positive, not negative		
Attractively set up		
No trite expressions		
Good closing paragraph		
Total		
Deductions for errors missed or for untidy final letter		
Final Total		

If you achieved your goal of at least 9 points for each letter on someone else's evaluation and at least 8 points in total for Parts A and B, proceed to Unit 7.5. If you did not score 8 points for each letter or 10 for Parts A and B, review Unit 7.4 thoroughly; then check with your instructor which of the supplementary letters on page 285 you should do before moving on.

EXERCISE 7.5 ORDER LETTERS

Part A

Complete the questions below and score 1 point for each correct item.

Your Goal: To score at least 5 points.

Score

1. What are the four points to check in an order letter?

_____ _____
_____ _____
_____ _____
_____ _____

2. Give two instances when an acknowledgment of an order letter might be sent.

_____ _____
_____ _____

Score for Part A _____

Part B

Following the procedures outlined in Unit 7.4, prepare a plan, a rough draft, and a final letter for each of the following situations. Remember the checks for an order letter. Check your final letter against the evaluation chart. Have someone else evaluate your work using the marking guidelines outlined in Unit 7.3.

Your Goal: To score at least 8 points on each letter.

Letter 1

Your boss has asked you to order two copies of *Colombo's Canadian Quotations*, published by Hurtig Publishers, and distributed by McClelland & Stewart, 481 University Avenue, Toronto, Ontario M5G 2E9, as gifts for two employees who are leaving at the end of next month. Write a letter ordering these books from a local bookstore and asking them to let you know the price immediately. You will pay for the books C.O.D.

Purpose

_____
_____

Plan

_____
_____
_____
_____
_____

Letter 2

You have just received a very large order for office furniture from IBM in your area. This is the first time you have dealt with this company and you are excited about having it as a customer. Write a letter of acknowledgment adding any other information you think is relevant.

Purpose

_____
_____

Plan

_____
_____
_____
_____
_____

Evaluation Chart	Your Score	Checker's Score
Well-prepared plan		
Good opening paragraph		
Considerate		
Clear in meaning		
Complete in detail		
Ideas expressed concisely		
Positive, not negative		
Attractively set up		
No trite expressions		
Good closing paragraph		
Total		
Deductions for errors missed or for untidy final letter		
Final Total		

Evaluation Chart	Your Score	Checker's Score
Well-prepared plan		
Good opening paragraph		
Considerate		
Clear in meaning		
Complete in detail		
Ideas expressed concisely		
Positive, not negative		
Attractively set up		
No trite expressions		
Good closing paragraph		
Total		
Deductions for errors missed or for untidy final letter		
Final Total		

If you achieved your goal of at least 8 points for each of your letters and at least 5 points for Part A, proceed to Unit 7.6. If you did not score 8 for each letter of 5 or Part A, review Unit 7.5 thoroughly; then check with your instructor which of the supplementary letters on page 285 you should do before moving on.

EXERCISE 7.6 CREDIT AND COLLECTION LETTERS

Part A

Are the following statements true or false? If they are true, circle *T*; if false, circle *F*. Score 1 point for each correct answer.

Your Goal To score at least 7 points.

			Score
1.	Most companies have printed forms of credit applications.	**T F**	____
2.	Be sure to promise credit even though you do not have all the information.	**T F**	____
3.	When granting credit, explain the credit terms and state the credit limit.	**T F**	____
4.	When refusing credit, do so without making any helpful suggestions.	**T F**	____
5.	Remind a customer of the value of a good credit rating.	**T F**	____
6.	The first letter to a customer about an unpaid bill explains that the account is being handed over to an agency for collection.	**T F**	____
7.	Never mention the amount owing when writing to a customer whose account is overdue.	**T F**	____
8.	Enclose an envelope to make it easier for a customer to send a cheque.	**T F**	____
		Score for Part A	____

Part B

Following the procedures outlined in Unit 7.4, prepare a plan, a rough draft, and a final letter for the following situation. Check your final letter against the evaluation chart. Have someone else evaluate your work using the marking guidelines outlined in Unit 7.3.

Your Goal: To score at least 8 points.

Mr. Robert Bass, the owner of a local office machines service business, has applied to CBIL for credit. He has placed an order for $1200 worth of supplies. You have his financial statements and note that he already owes his other creditors a considerable amount. His business seems to be stable, but you do not think he should get more credit until he has cleared up some of his outstanding accounts. Write him a letter explaining all this and suggesting alternative means of payment for him.

Purpose

____

____

Plan

____

____

____

____

____

____

____

____

____

Evaluation Chart	Your Score	Checker's Score
Well-prepared plan		
Good opening paragraph		
Considerate		
Clear in meaning		
Complete in detail		
Ideas expressed concisely		
Positive, not negative		
Attractively set up		
No trite expressions		
Good closing paragraph		
Total		
Deductions for errors missed or for untidy final letter		
Final Total		

If you achieved your goal of at least 8 points for your letter and scored at least 7 points for Part A, proceed to Unit 7.7. If you did not score 8 for your letter or 7 for Part A, review Unit 7.6 thoroughly; then check with your instructor which of the supplementary letters on page 286 you should do before moving on.

EXERCISE 7.7 CLAIM AND ADJUSTMENT LETTERS

Part A

Are the following statements true or false? If they are true, circle *T*; if false, circle *F*. Score 1 point for each correct answer.

Your Goal: To score at least 4 points.

			Score
1.	Claim letters should state clearly and exactly what the problem is	T F	_____
2.	It is not necessary to mention invoice, order, or account numbers in claim letters.	T F	_____
3.	There are three kinds of adjustment letters.	T F	_____
4.	Stress what cannot be done and mention only briefly what can be done.	T F	_____
5.	Reassure the customer wherever possible.	T F	_____
		Score for Part A	_____

Part B

Following the procedures outlined in Unit 7.4, prepare a plan, a rough draft, and a final letter for each of the following situations. Check your final letter against the evaluation chart. Have someone else evaluate your work using the marking guidelines outlined in Unit 7.3.

Your Goal: To score at least 8 points on each letter.

Letter 1

The last shipment of transistor batteries from a hardware distributor in your area was received in a damaged condition. The packages were ripped and some of the batteries were dented. CBIL can use some of the batteries, but we do not feel we should have to pay the full amount of the order. About half the batteries were damaged, and we feel a credit for half the amount of the invoice would be a fair adjustment. The invoice, numbered A-1007 and dated last Tuesday, amounts to $858.00 Write a letter to the hardware distributor explaining the situation and asking for a credit note.

Purpose

_____

_____

Plan

_____

_____

_____

_____

_____

Letter 2

CBIL has received a letter from Ms. Ruth Leberman complaining that her CD player is not working. She wants it replaced under warranty. Explain that the warranty covers only workmanship and faulty parts. It appears that the player has been dropped from a height as it is badly cracked. Suggest that if she would like you to repair the player, there will be a charge of at least $63.50 for labour in addition to the cost of any parts that may be required. The warranty does not cover accidental damage. Add any other information you think might help keep this customer's goodwill.

Purpose

_____

_____

Plan

_____

_____

_____

_____

_____

Evaluation Chart	Your Score	Checker's Score
Well-prepared plan		
Good opening paragraph		
Considerate		
Clear in meaning		
Complete in detail		
Ideas expressed concisely		
Positive, not negative		
Attractively set up		
No trite expressions		
Good closing paragraph		
Total		
Deductions for errors missed or for untidy final letter		
Final Total		

Evaluation Chart	Your Score	Checker's Score
Well-prepared plan		
Good opening paragraph		
Considerate		
Clear in meaning		
Complete in detail		
Ideas expressed concisely		
Positive, not negative		
Attractively set up		
No trite expressions		
Good closing paragraph		
Total		
Deductions for errors missed or for untidy final letter		
Final Total		

If you achieved your goal of at least 8 points for each of your letters and scored at least 4 points for Part A, proceed to Unit 7.8. If you did not score 8 for each letter or 4 for Part A, review Unit 7.7 thoroughly; then check with your instructor which supplementary letters on page 286 you should do before moving on.

EXERCISE 7.8 SALES LETTERS

Part A

Are the following statements true or false? If true, circle *T*; if false, circle *F*. Score 1 point for each correct answer.

Your Goal: To score at least 4 points.

			Score
1.	The only purpose of a sales letter is to tell people about new products.	T F	_____
2.	It is not necessary to consider the customer in writing a sales letter.	T F	_____
3.	Creating desire in the reader is a good point.	T F	_____
4.	A sales letter should have eye appeal.	T F	_____
5.	All sales letters are exactly the same whether you are selling goods or a service.	T F	_____
		Score for Part A	_____

Part B

Following the procedures outlined in Unit 7.4, prepare a plan, a rough draft, and a final letter for each of the following situations. Check your final letter against the evaluation chart. Have someone else evaluate your work using the marking guidelines outlined in Unit 7.3.

Your Goal: To score at least 8 points on each letter.

Letter 1

Write a letter urging a subscriber to renew a lapsed subscription to one of the business magazines circulated by CBIL. Choose the name of a magazine you read and study several issues of the magazine for suggestions.

Purpose

____

____

Plan

____

____

____

____

____

____

____

____

____

Letter 2

Write a sales letter to be circulated to store owners in your area describing a new security alarm system CBIL is distributing. Use your imagination to give the system a name and to supply all the information necessary.

Purpose

____

____

Plan

____

____

____

____

____

____

____

____

____

Evaluation Chart	Your Score	Checker's Score
Well-prepared plan		
Good opening paragraph		
Considerate		
Clear in meaning		
Complete in detail		
Ideas expressed concisely		
Positive, not negative		
Attractively set up		
No trite expressions		
Good closing paragraph		
Total		
Deductions for errors missed or for untidy final letter		
Final Total		

Evaluation Chart	Your Score	Checker's Score
Well-prepared plan		
Good opening paragraph		
Considerate		
Clear in meaning		
Complete in detail		
Ideas expressed concisely		
Positive, not negative		
Attractively set up		
No trite expressions		
Good closing paragraph		
Total		
Deductions for errors missed or for untidy final letter		
Final Total		

If you achieved your goal of at least 8 points for each of your letters and scored at least 4 points for Part A, proceed to Unit 7.9. If you did not score 8 for each letter or 4 for Part A, review Unit 7.8 thoroughly; then check with your instructor which supplementary letters on page 287 you should do before moving on.

EXERCISE 7.9 GOODWILL AND PUBLIC RELATIONS LETTERS

Part A

Are the following statements true or false? If true, circle *T*; if false, circle *F*. Score 1 point for each correct answer.

Your Goal: To score at least 4 points.

		Score
1. Letters of congratulations are examples of goodwill letters.	**T F**	_____
2. Sincerity is not important in public relations letters.	**T F**	_____
3. Customers sometimes write goodwill letters to a company.	**T F**	_____
4. The reader's feelings are very important.	**T F**	_____
5. An offer of assistance is not a goodwill gesture.	**T F**	_____
	Score for Part A	_____

Part B

Following the procedures outlined in Unit 7.4, prepare a plan, a rough draft, and a final letter for each of the following situations. Check your final letter against the evaluation chart. Have someone else evaluate your work using the marking guidelines outlined in Unit 7.3.

Your Goal: To score at least 8 points on each letter.

Letter 1

Ms. Sophie Fassette, a client of CBIL, has just been appointed president of Phoenix Engineering, a company in your area. You saw the appointment in today's paper. Write a letter of congratulations for Mr. Johnston, manager of your CBIL office, to sign.

Purpose

_____

_____

Plan

_____

_____

_____

_____

Letter 2

Write a letter to Mr. Williams, owner of Williams Welding Ltd., 7 Fraser Avenue, Sydney NS B1V 2B8. Your office of CBIL was the only one able to supply Mr. Williams with special protective eye shields for his welders when he had a need for them in a hurry. Thank Mr. Williams for the opportunity to help him out of a difficulty and inform him of the offices we have across Canada for serving industry. Invite him to visit us at any time if he is in our area and to call on us for help with his other needs.

Purpose

_____

_____

Plan

_____

_____

_____

_____

Evaluation Chart	Your Score	Checker's Score
Well-prepared plan		
Good opening paragraph		
Considerate		
Clear in meaning		
Complete in detail		
Ideas expressed concisely		
Positive, not negative		
Attractively set up		
No trite expressions		
Good closing paragraph		
Total		
Deductions for errors missed or for untidy final letter		
Final Total		

Evaluation Chart	Your Score	Checker's Score
Well-prepared plan		
Good opening paragraph		
Considerate		
Clear in meaning		
Complete in detail		
Ideas expressed concisely		
Positive, not negative		
Attractively set up		
No trite expressions		
Good closing paragraph		
Total		
Deductions for errors missed or for untidy final letter		
Final Total		

If you achieved your goal of at least 8 points for each of your letters and scored at least 4 points for Part A, move on to Unit 7.10. If you did not score 8 for each letter or 4 for Part A, review Unit 7.9 thoroughly; then check with your instructor which supplementary letters on page 287 you should do before moving on.

EXERCISE 7.10 JOB APPLICATIONS AND RÉSUMÉS

Part A

Are the following statements true or false? If true, circel *T*; if false, circle *F*. Score 1 point for each correct answer.

Your Goal: To score at least 8 points.

			Score
1.	A personal data sheet is sometimes called a résumé.	**T F**	_____
2.	A letter of application should let the reader know what kind of person you are.	**T F**	_____
3.	You should ask for an interview when writing about a job.	**T F**	_____
4.	Be sure to ask permission before using someone as a reference.	**T F**	_____
5.	Making your résumé as attractive as possible will make it more likely to receive attention.	**T F**	_____
6.	A letter of application or a personal data sheet must be correct in all details.	**T F**	_____
7.	List work experience and education in reverse chronological order, that is, start with the most recent and work backwards	**T F**	_____
8.	Include any volunteer or other activities that might help an employer assess your capabilities.	**T F**	_____
9.	Account for all your time during school or since leaving school.	**T F**	_____
10.	Be specific in identifying the job you want.	**T F**	_____
		Score for Part A	_____

Part B

Choose a job from your local newspaper or from a selection your instructor will give you, and write a letter of application for that job. Write a plan, a rough draft, and a final letter in the usual way using blank paper and your own address as the return address. Check your letter and have someone else evaluate it in the usual way.

Your Goal: To score at least 4 points.

Purpose

_____

_____

Plan

_____

_____

_____

_____

_____

_____

_____

Evaluation Chart	Your Score	Checker's Score
Well-prepared plan		
Good opening paragraph		
Considerate		
Clear in meaning		
Complete in detail		
Ideas expressed concisely		
Positive, not negative		
Attractively set up		
No trite expressions		
Good closing paragraph		
Total		
Deductions for errors missed or for untidy final letter		
Final Total		

Part C

Prepare another personal data sheet similar to the one you prepared in the *Mini-Test* in Unit 7.10 but displaying the information in another way. Refer to your previous data sheet for details. Give yourself up to 10 points for a well-prepared résumé; if you like, ask someone else to check it, deducting 1 point for *any* error of any kind that is found!

Your Goal: To score at least 8 points.

If you achieved your goal of at least 8 points for your résumé, at least 8 points for Part A, and at least 4 points for Part B, proceed to Unit 7.11. If you did not achieve your goals, review Unit 7.10 thoroughly; then check with your instructor how you can improve your work before moving on.

Exercise 7.11 Memos and Notices

Following the procedures outlined in Unit 7.4, prepare a plan, a rough draft, and a final memo for the following situation. Check your final memo against the evaluation chart. Have someone else evaluate your work using the marking guidelines outlined in Unit 7.3.

Your Goal: To score at least 4 points for each memo.

Memo 1

As personnel director for your company, write a memo to all department heads asking them to survey their staff about the need for a daycare facility in your building. Ask them to list the ages of children who could use the service. Also ask for any suggestions they might have about the necessary hours of operation and any other relevant details.

Memo 2

Design an announcement to be posted on all notice boards giving details of the forthcoming company picnic. Be sure you include all details of date, time, place, and transportation arrangements, etc., that you think appropriate. Try to design your announcement to encourage attendance at the picnic.

Purpose

____

____

Plan

____

____

____

____

____

____

____

____

Evaluation Chart	Your Score	Checker's Score
Clear		
Complete		
Concise		
Correct		
Attractively set up		
Total		
Deductions for errors missed		
Final Total		

If you achieved your goal of at least 8 points, proceed to Unit 7.12. If you did not score 8, go back and review Unit 7.11 thoroughly; then check with your instructor which supplementary memos on page 287 you should do before moving on.

Exercise 7.12 Reports

Following the steps outlined in Unit 7.12, prepare reports for the following situations. Check your reports against the evaluation charts and have someone else also evaluate them.

Your Goal: To score at least 4 points for each report.

Report 1

The operations manager has requested suggestions on how the company can cut back on parking spaces. Prepare a short formal report for the operations manager on the results of a survey you have conducted regarding the ways in which people could be encouraged to use public transport or car pools rather than individual cars. Divide your report into sections dealing with how people are currently travelling to work and how they might do so. Conclude with some positive recommendations suggesting ways in which the company might help.

Evaluation Chart	Your Score	Checker's Score
Clear		
Complete		
Concise		
Correct		
Attractively set up		
Total		
Deductions for errors missed		
Final Total		

Report 2

Write a short formal report for the Student Council on part-time work available for students. This report could cover summer work and/or shift work that could be fitted in between classes. Any entrepreneurial work you are familiar with could also be included. Remember, though, that students must still have time to study!

Evaluation Chart	Your Score	Checker's Score
Clear		
Complete		
Concise		
Correct		
Attractively set up		
Total		
Deductions for errors missed		
Final Total		

If you achieved your goal of at least 4 points for each of your reports, proceed to Unit 7.13. If you did not score at least 4 for each report, go back and review Unit 7.12 thoroughly; then ask your instructor for directions before moving on.

EXERCISE 7.13 VOCABULARY

Complete the three parts of this exercise according to the directions for each part.

Your Goal: To score at least 12 points in total.

A. Definitions

Complete the following sentences by choosing the most appropriate word from the list given. Score 1 point for each correct answer.

perforate	persuade	supplement	improvise	pertinent
tentative	potential	initiate	itinerary	perusal

Score

1. A good background in mathematics will increase your ______________ as a trainee for program analyst. _____
2. We now have all the facts ______________ to the case. _____
3. Report to Ms. Ramsay when you arrive; she will ______________ you into the routines of the office. _____
4. A quick ______________ of the statement showed that it seemed to be complete. _____
5. We have ordered an extra hot sealing machine to ______________ the one that we currently have. _____

Score for Part A _____

B. Usage

Use the same directions as for Part A.

principal	right	stationery	whether	principle
write	respectively	weather	rite	stationary
respectfully				

Score

1. You are ______________ in your calculation of the interest on a ______________ of $2500. _____
2. He ______________ reasurred me that even an older person could easily learn computer operation. _____
3. Please tell the adjuster ______________ the car was moving or ______________ when it was hit by the truck. _____

Score for Part B _____

C. Spelling

Correct any spelling errors in the following words. Score 1 point for each correct answer.

				Score
1.	proceedure	mischievous	criticism	_____
2.	privilege	misellaneous	technique	_____
3.	disatisfied	acknowledgment	beneficial	_____
4.	guage	conscientious	seize	_____
5.	supersede	government	paralell	_____

Score for Part C _____

Total Score _____

If you achieved your goal of at least 12 points, proceed to Unit 7.4. If you did not score 12, go back and review Unit 7.13 thoroughly before proceeding to Unit 7.14.

_____

EXERCISE 7.14 PROOFREADING

Complete each part of this exercise according to the directions given.

Your Goal: To score at least 12 points in total.

Part A

Are the following statements true or false? If true, circle *T*; if false, circle *F*. Score 1 point for each correct answer.

			Score
1.	Quite often errors occur in clusters or groups.	**T F**	_____
2.	Statistical material, legal documents, and scientific material should be checked with a partner or as a team.	**T F**	_____
3.	It is very easy to proofread your own work and be confident you have found all the errors	**T F**	_____
4.	Content must be checked for accuracy in totals, dates, prices, and all other facts.	**T F**	_____
5.	It is not necessary to check headings or footnotes when proofreading.	**T F**	_____
		Score for Part A	_____

Part B

Proofread the following letters very carefully using proofreaders' marks to make corrections where necessary. Be sure to check for all kinds of errors. Score 1 point for each error marked correctly; *deduct* 1 point for each error missed!

Letter 1

Dear Mr. Boyce:

Thank you for your cheque for $854.56 in settlement of your March rent.

May we remind you that you still owe us $354.56 for February as we agreed to allow you to pay only $500 that month as you were having a little difficulty meeting your obligations. You stated that you would be able to pay the balance along with your March payment.

Unless a cheque is received by march 15 for $354.56, interest will be charged on the amount owing starting from that date. The rate of interest is 17%.

Your payment of $845.56 has been credited to your March account, and we look forward to receiving your cheque for the balance of February's rent by return mail.

Yours very turly,

Letter 2

Dear Mr. Hanson:

You will be pleased to know that we are at lost able to offer you service from our Danforth station. The repairs after the fire have been completed, and our doors are opening to the public again on Saturday, June 12, at 9 a.m..On the afternoon of Friday, June 12, we are inviting our special customers for a celebration at our renovated premises. Cockatils and hors d'oeuvres will be served from 2 to 5 a.m., and we would be very pleased if you would come to our little party. We look forward to seeing you on June 12.

Sincerely,

Number of errors found and correctly marked _____

Deduct for errors missed _____

Score for Part B _____

Total Score _____

If you achieved your goal of at least 12 points, proceed to the posttest for Unit 7. If you did not score 12, you will appreciate the need for accurate proofreading! Review the proofreading units thoroughly before moving on.